THE ENGLISH HOSPICE
IN ROME

IGNEM VENI MITTERE IN TERRAM

THE VENERABILE SEXCENTENARY ISSUE

THE ENGLISH HOSPICE IN ROME

THE VENERABILE

SEXCENTENARY ISSUE

MAY 1962

VOLUME XXI

PRINTED AT
CATHOLIC RECORDS PRESS
EXETER

JOANNI XXIII PONT. MAX.

FELICITER REGNANTI

DEVOTO ANIMO

DICAMUS

Photo Giordani

PREFACE

When Cardinal Gasquet published his *History of the Venerable English College, Rome*, in 1920, he did not claim that it furnished a complete history of the institution. It was rather his concept of the main features of the history, gathered, as he said, from 'a rapid survey of the material existing in the archives of the *Venerabile* and elsewhere'. His immediate purpose had been to prepare a record for the celebration in 1918 of the first centenary of the reopening of the College after the French occupation at the close of the eighteenth century. The First World War made such celebrations impossible and his work was eventually published in 1920—I quote the Cardinal again —'in the hope that, until something better is given to the public by one who can devote more time to the work than I have been able to do, these pages may serve to awaken or keep alive the memory of the history of what I believe to be one of the most interesting—if, indeed, not the most interesting —of the English institutions on the continent of Europe'.

A complete history of the College still remains to be written but we hope that this situation will be remedied in the not too distant future. Since Cardinal Gasquet's time, much research work has been done in the College archives and much valuable information has been brought to light. This information has been published from time to time in articles in THE VENERABILE and other journals. Since this present volume is intended for the commemoration of the sixth centenary of the foundation of the old Hospice, it naturally deals for the most part with the years before the College came into existence. The matter it contains will be of great value to the future historian of the College, but it has also a much wider scope : it makes a valuable contribution to the long and fascinating story of England and Rome.

Our very sincere thanks are therefore due to all those who have laboured so hard to make this publication possible. The greater part of the work was done by the students themselves, but we are indebted also to others outside the College. A formal acknowledgement of their help is to be found elsewhere in this volume. To all, we extend our congratulations on the success of their efforts.

G. W. TICKLE,
Rector.

CONTENTS

ACKNOWLEDGEMENTS

The compilers of this History would like to express their gratitude to the Very Reverend Godfrey Anstruther O.P., and to Professor G. B. Parks of New York, for their scholarly contributions ; to Dottore Aleci of the Vatican Library for assisting researches in the Vatican Archives ; to the Reverend Stephen Forte O.P., for transcribing various documents ; to Mr Oscar Eclund of the Swedish Institute in Rome for furnishing information concerning the old Swedish Hospice ; to the Trustees of the British Museum and Mr F. T. Baker M.A., F.S.A., Director of the Lincoln City and County Museum, for permission to reproduce photographs of the Hospice seal ; to the Director of the Archivio di Stato, Rome, for permission to print the will of John Shepherd ; and to the Reverend H. E. G. Rope M.A., whose patient work over the years has proved of inestimable value.

CONTINUITY, 1362-1962

On 27th January 1926 *The Times* carried a leader entitled 'The Venerabile', a subject, it said, very dear to us all. The occasion was a proposal of the Roman City planners to demolish part of the College building to make room for a covered market. *The Times'* protest, along with many others, had the desired effect of inducing the authorities to change their minds.[1] The Venerabile has survived, and this oldest English institution abroad celebrated its sixth centenary on 27th January this year.

It has been said of this part of Rome that 'it is for ever England'.[2] Wiseman, on his arrival at the College in 1818, wrote : 'One felt at once at home . . . it was English ground, a part of the fatherland, a restored inheritance'.[3] As early as 1497 King Henry VII had written 'to the worshipful Stewards of Our Hospice of St Thomas the Martyr at Rome'.[4] And the start of it all was the initiative of a group of Englishmen, most of them merchants, who bought a house on 27th January 1362 for the convenience and use 'of the poor, sick, needy and distressed people coming from England to the City'.[5]

---

[1] The *Giornale D'Italia* was inclined to minimise the affair. On 30.1.1926 it wrote : *Trattandosi di cosa che interessa gl'inglesi, potrebbe definirsi col titolo di una commedia shakespeariana :* Much ado about nothing, *molto strepito per nulla.* It commented that anyone who had any experience of *piani regolatori* which had been declared *definitivi* since 1870 would not be alarmed. Moreover, it was proposed to demolish only part of the College, not the entire building !

[2] THE VENERABILE, XII, 8 (Nov. 1944) ; XVIII, 66 (May 1957).

[3] W. Ward, *Life and Times of Cardinal Wiseman*, I, 15.

[4] *Lib.* 17, f. 20 : 10.3.1497.

[5] *Memb.* 27.1.1362.

Englishmen in Rome were no newcomers. From the time of Benedict Biscop (mid-seventh century), the religious and cultural influence of Rome drew pilgrims and churchmen to the Eternal City. Caedwalla, king of the West Saxons, came :

Sospes enim veniens supremo ex orbe Britanni,
Per varias gentes, per freta, perque vias,
Urbem Romuleam vidit, templumque verendum
Aspexit Petri, mystica dona gerens.[6]

He was followed by Ine, who wished 'to spend some of the time of his earthly pilgrimage in the vicinity of the holy places, hoping thereby to merit a warmer welcome from the saints in heaven. At this period, many English people followed this custom, both noble and simple, layfolk and clergy, men and women alike.'[7]

The story of the Schola Saxonum, a foundation which was the outcome of this incessant travel, is not for these pages.[8] Although the district in which it was situated is to this day called the *Borgo in Sassia*, the national character of the institution ceased in the year 1201. Whether the Schola was a forerunner rather than an ancestor of the present College is open to dispute. That the possibility of the latter cannot be denied *a priori* is shown in the chapter on the foundation of the Hospice.[9] It is certain that after the loss of the Schola English pilgrims to the city lacked a national home.

The promise of the thirteenth century, the Rome of the Cosmati and Romanesque, bore disappointing fruit. After the outrage of Anagni the papacy had migrated to Avignon. The Empire had crumbled ; France and England were at each other's throats ; the Turk was advancing westwards ; and Rome, the Rome confined by Hadrian's wall, was two-thirds a desert, lorded over by barons. Not for Rome the *arti* of Florence (though even these came to be dominated by a new patriciate) ; not for Rome the trade guilds of Cologne and Strasbourg. In Rome barons fought :

barons private profit,
Jealousy raging possession of the fiend.

Colonna and Orsini, neither strong enough to curb the other and thus ensure at least an absence of war, struggled to gain

---

[6] Bede, *Hist. Angl.* V, cap 7.
[7] Ibid., V, cap. 7 : Penguin translation, p. 275.
[8] The best account is that by Dr W. J. Moore, *The Saxon Pilgrims to Rome and the Schola Saxonum*, Fribourg 1937.
[9] Cf. infra, p. 15.

the mastery over an impoverished city. The Black Death appeared and perhaps decimated the already dwindling populace. Cola di Rienzo came, and dazzled, and conquered; but his fall was as swift as his rise, and Rome became once more the prey and battleground of the patricians. At last Innocent VI sent Rienzo and his legate, the Spanish Cardinal Gilles Albornoz, to restore order. Rienzo's insolence was again his downfall, this time final, and it was the energetic cardinal who restored legitimate government in Rome between the years 1353 and 1363.

This was the immediate background to the establishment of the English Hospice—and of Hospices for the Germans and Portuguese, the Spaniards and the Swedes. For if Rome was politically and artistically sterile in the fourteenth century, she gave birth in that same century to those institutions which were to link her more closely to her northern and western neighbours. The pope might be in Avignon; but had he not declared the Jubilee of 1350? Rome might be but a shadow of her former glory—and a forlorn shadow at that. But then, was it not to be expected that the crises of Europe should find their repercussions on the *caput mundi*? Above all, was she not still *Roma omnium patria*, sheltering the shrines of the Apostles? So the pilgrims came. Perhaps no more than a few hundred made the journey from England in the Jubilee year of 1350.[10] It is not certain how many they found of their fellow country-men in Rome. The next decade, however, definitely saw the growth of an English colony there, consisting mainly, if not wholly, of merchants: rosary-sellers,[11] a goldsmith, perhaps some of those foreigners always to be found in important cities. They were probably joined by others of a different trade. During this decade the export of wool from England, hitherto that country's main trade link with Europe, was forbidden; instead cloth was manufactured at home and sent abroad—a booming industry—and with the cloth came merchants. By 1358 some, at least, of the English in Rome had formed a confraternity;[12] and four years later one of their number sold his house to the confraternity to become a hospice for their own countrymen. With the pope away from Rome, it was the laity's task to provide for the needy. Nor were the English alone in this.

[10] G. B. Parks, *The English Traveler to Italy*, Rome 1954, I, 356–7.
[11] A more correct description would be 'beads-sellers', as the rosary did not then have the same form as it has today.
[12] *Lib.* 232, f. 34 v.

The Hospice of *S. Maria de Anima, hospitale nationis Alamanniae,* was begun by a German married couple. Women from Sweden, Portugal and Spain started hospices for their fellow countrymen. Such was the reflection on Rome of the growing nationalism of the countries of Europe.

One need not seek mercenary motives in the foundation of the English Hospice : it has been justly ascribed 'in almost equal proportions to national pride, national piety, and national distaste for being fleeced by foreigners'.[13] The story of the foundation follows this introduction, and the actual deeds may be read in the appendices. This account of the foundation, a definitive treatment of an often-told but also often-confused tale, may now be added to those of Dr Croke as an authoritative work.

The chapter on the development of the Hospice uses hitherto unexplored sources.[14] The story is pieced together from various parchments in the College archives and from the accounts of travellers and historians. In sum, the picture is one of steady growth, apparently uninfluenced by the 'broils within or dangers from without' which continued to disturb the city until well into the fifteenth century. Alongside St Thomas's Hospice there grew the Hospice of St Edmund. The account in this History is the fullest treatise yet to appear concerning this establishment.[15] It corrects many errors and dispels many half-truths hitherto connected with that Hospice. The lack of material has made a complete picture impossible and one can only wish that more might be discovered to supplement the tantalizing evidence so far yielded.

Even after the return of the pope to Rome the Great Schism put an end to hopes of restoring the city. Not until the pontificate of Martin V was any progress made. Under him and his successor, Eugene IV, Rome was gradually restored and rebuilt. The Hospice of St Thomas must have shared in this restoration, and mention is made of the Hospice church in a Bull of Eugene IV dated 1446. It was by then the spiritual centre of the English in Rome, for the Bull states that large numbers of the Roman Court and of the English nation 'are wont to assist at divine worship and the like' there. Margery

---

[13] THE VENERABILE, XII, 7 (Nov. 1944).
[14] Cf. infra, p. 43.
[15] Cf. infra, p. 82. The fullest account so far was that in Cardinal Gasquet's *History of the Venerable English College, Rome,* pp. 31–37.

Kempe had visited the Hospice in 1416. John Capgrave
mentions it in 1450. In 1445 there were a 'large number' of
books in the Hospice library. Perhaps William Grey enriched
it while he was in Rome, although his library of 200 volumes
went to his old college, Balliol.[16] Later donors were Caxton,
probably the printer, and, to anticipate, Reginald Pole, Nicholas
Sanders, Alan Cope and William Allen.

Meanwhile, the connection of the Hospice with the English
Crown was growing stronger. Thomas Polton, Henry V's envoy
and bishop of Chichester, had been a member of St Edmund's
confraternity in the 1420's and, most probably, of that of St
Thomas as well. Andrew Holes and William Grey, also king's
envoys, were members later in the century. Subsequently
many royal envoys became members of the Hospice under the
Yorkist kings and some of them served as its officials. The
firma Angliae, an arrangement whereby money was collected
in England and sent every year to the Hospice, was by now in
operation. It was common for Englishmen studying at Italian
universities to come to Rome and be received into the confraternity; a number of them held office in the Hospice as well.
Most of these students were lawyers, but both in the middle
and at the end of the fifteenth century some of the most famous
of English humanists became members. Thomas Linacre was
custos of the Hospice in 1491; William Lily had joined the
Hospice confraternity with him on the same day (4th November
1490). William Warham had been admitted in the previous
May; John Giglis was elected a member in 1491, followed two
years later by Christopher Bainbridge and John Colet. The
circle that charmed Erasmus was almost complete. Soon afterwards, Richard Charnock and William Latimer were admitted.

A later chapter[17] traces the growth of royal interest in the
Hospice, an interest which reached its peak in the reign of
Henry VII, who twice wrote to the Hospice and took it under
his control. He was anxious for the Hospice to make more
provision for students, and to give hospitality to his ambassadors.
In his reign the accounts were sent home to England for inspection by the king, and a royal warship brought out the
year's instalment of the *firma Angliae* in 1502. This began a
connection with the Royal Navy which is very much alive
today. In letters between King Henry and the Hospice, the

[16] Parks, op. cit., I, 431.
[17] Cf. infra, p. 145.

latter is unequivocally described as the King's Hospice, a description borne out by the presence of the royal arms on the Hospice seal and by the king's appointment of the custos.

The connections of the Hospice with the English Church were equally strong. Many of its members attained high positions, among them William Warham, Archbishop of Canterbury; Christopher Bainbridge, Cardinal Archbishop of York; John Clerk, Bishop of Bath and Wells; Hugh Inge, Archbishop of Dublin; and many more. Among laymen who were members may be mentioned Edward IV's brother-in-law, Anthony Woodville, Earl Rivers, who came with the Earl of Ormonde in 1475. An increasing number of pilgrims came; we have the names of 489 who came between the years 1504 and 1507.[18] Thomas Cromwell came in 1514. At times during the Jubilee Years the Hospice reached its capacity of a hundred guests. The bustle of life at the Hospice, especially at the close of the fifteenth century and the beginning of the sixteenth, is vividly captured in the chapter entitled 'Pilgrims and the Hospice'.[19]

After Henry VII's death, it was left to the king's ambassadors to take a personal interest in the Hospice, for neither Henry VIII nor Wolsey was concerned with it. Bainbridge, Sylvester Giglis, Bishop of Worcester, and John Clerk all intervened in the affairs of the Hospice during this period. But the sack of Rome in 1527 by the mutinous army of Charles V and Henry's breach with the papacy combined to deal it a disastrous blow. The sack meant the loss of its plate and damage to its property; the breach with Rome meant an almost complete stop to the flow of pilgrims, then at its height. Professor Parks[20] treats of the repercussions of the Reformation on the Hospice during this period and the years immediately following. It has been thought advisable to allow some overlapping of material between his chapter and the preceding one because of the different aspects considered by the two. The last royal custos, John Borobrigg, appointed in 1532, remained in office until 1538, during which time he worked in the interests of the Crown. Pope Paul III authorized his replacement by Cardinal Reginald Pole, the first of the English Catholic exiles for religion. Associated with Pole were other English exiles, among them Thomas Goldwell, later bishop of St Asaph. When Pole was

[18] Appendix 13, p. 125.
[19] Cf. infra, p. 99.
[20] Cf. infra, p. 193.

almost elected pope in the conclave of 1549–50 the Hospice was guarded by soldiers to prevent its looting by the Roman mob, while Bishop Peto of Salisbury moved to the Bridgettine Hospice next door.[21]

Queen Mary's reign promised a revival of the connection of the Hospice with the English Crown. Mary sent a large embassy to Rome in 1555, and her resident ambassador, Sir Edward Carne, later became custos of the Hospice. He chose to die in Rome rather than return to England when Elizabeth became queen.

With the accession of Elizabeth I the Hospice became the residence of English exiles, so that by the year 1576 less than ten per cent of its income was spent on providing for pilgrims ; the board and salaries of the inmates took the main part. The Hospice of these years is well compared with an Oxford senior common room, and its story is ably recounted by Dr Kenny.[22] At the instigation of William Allen and Owen Lewis, former fellows respectively of Oriel and New College, Pope Gregory XIII issued the Bull of Foundation of the English College, dated 1st May 1579. In this Bull, Gregory lays down that 'if the said College should at any time come to be dissolved for any reason whatsoever, We declare that the buildings, church, and all other goods of the said Hospice shall be as if the Bulls and rescripts founding the said College had never been issued ; and in such an event all the said goods revert again *in toto* to the Hospice'. Not until the Bull was promulgated did the College officially succeed the Hospice. The inscription in the *Liber Ruber* puts it as follows : 'In the year of our Lord 1580, on the 23rd day of the month of December, to the praise and glory of the Most Holy Trinity and of St Thomas the Martyr, was despatched the Bull of Foundation of this College : the Bull did not reach us until the aforesaid day, though it had been granted by the Supreme Pontiff Gregory XIII in the April of the preceding year.[23] This Bull, among many other privileges

[21] For the voting in the conclave cf. *Lib. Rub.*, ff. C–D., published in THE VENERABILE, I, 231–4 (Oct. 1923) ; for the soldiers and Peto, cf. *Lib.* 33, ff. 80–80 v.

[22] Cf. infra, p. 218.

[23] Perhaps this entry contributed to the confusion surrounding the date of the Bull of Foundation. Tierney, Gasquet and others give it as 23rd April 1579. This date was the day on which Sherwin and his fellow students took the missionary oath and was the occasion for the famous '*potius hodie quam cras*' episode : cf. *Liber Ruber* f. 4 r ; C.R.S., 37, 8. Moreover the Bull of Foundation bears at the end the date '*Anno Millesimo quingentesimo Septuagesimo nono Kal Maii*'. At first reading this '*nono*' could easily be taken with '*Kal Maii*', thus giving 23rd April. It should, of course, be taken with '*Septuagesimo*', so giving the correct date : 1st May 1579.

and favours both spiritual and temporal, unites all the goods of the English Hospice to the College ; we therefore took possession of them on the 29th day of December, which is sacred to St Thomas the Martyr. Also, although the Bull makes no explicit mention of this, the Pope declared *viva voce* that this college is bound to receive and entertain English pilgrims according to the statutes of the said hospice.'[24] A more detailed account of these statutes is given in the Pilgrim Book : 'In the year of our Lord 1580, on the 29th day of the month of December which day is sacred to St Thomas the Martyr, this English College took corporal possession of the English Hospice and its goods by virtue of a Bull of our most Holy Lord Gregory XIII, but with this obligation, of receiving and entertaining according to the statutes of the said hospice any Englishmen visiting the City out of devotion. These statutes demand that poor guests be entertained for eight days, gentlefolk and rich people for three days.'[25]

Constant hospitality was shown to Englishmen of different creeds. The entries in the Pilgrim Book reveal a large number of visitors of all classes. The first name in the book is that of Sir Thomas Arundel. 'On this same day (29th December 1580), the illustrious D. Thomas Arundel, an Englishman of the diocese of . . .'[26] was this day admitted as the first guest and remained with us for three days.' Sir Thomas was later to distinguish himself at the battle of Gran, and became the first Baron Arundel of Wardour in 1605. Many of the old Catholic families appear : Pole, Paston, Fortescue, Yelverton, Walpole, Bedingfield and others. On 12th October 1636 William Harvey, described as 'Medicus Regis Angliae', dined in the refectory. Two years later John Milton, fresh from his Etrurian shades of Vallombrosa, is entered. Another poet, Richard Crashaw, arrived on 28th November 1646. 'A pilgrim', he stayed for fifteen days and was a frequent visitor afterwards. During this period the custom was continued of inviting all the English residents in Rome to dinner on the feast of St Thomas of Canterbury, patron of College and Hospice. John Evelyn refers to the occasion in his Diary for the 29th December 1644 : 'We were invited to the English Jesuits to dinner, being their great

[24] *Lib.* 303 (i.e. *Liber Ruber*), pars 2a, f. 12.
[25] *Lib.* 282, f. 3 r. The translations quoted above from the Bull of Foundation, the *Liber Ruber* and the Pilgrim Book may be read in the original in Appendix 29, p. 271. The Bull of Foundation appears in Tierney's Dodd, II, App. LVII.
[26] The name of the diocese is not inserted.

feast of Saint Thomas of Canterbury. We dined in their Common Refectory and afterwards saw an Italian Comedy acted by their alumni before the Cardinals.' On that day the entry in the Pilgrim Book states that 'about fifty dined in the College beside the celebrant bishop'. That the English College continued to be the centre of national life in Rome, even after the change of religion in the homeland, is shown by the above and by numerous other entries. It was sought out by English travellers and residents alike.

At first sight it may seem strange that an account of Owen Lewis appears in a history of the Hospice. Yet Owen Lewis, more than any other man, effected the transition from Hospice to College ; and although he was respected and trusted by Allen and Persons, his name has been stained by subsequent historians. It is therefore appropriate that this History should conclude with an apologia of this great man. He may have lacked discretion in his dealings with the students. He certainly found it difficult to treat with them as men, regarding them as beardless boys. His friendship with the adventurer Thomas Stukeley—one of the supports of his favour with the pope— earned him many enemies among the English exiles at Rome, shocked by Stukeley's press-gang methods ; so that when Stukeley's expedition, after staggering to Lisbon, was diverted to Africa and Stukeley himself killed at Alcazar in mid-1578, Lewis's reputation suffered. There was, too, the difficulty of running Hospice and College separately. However moribund the former at this time, it still catered for some pilgrims and was an English institution—something which had to be considered when it was suggested that its administration be given to Italian Jesuits. The problems arising from the above factors, added to the racial animosity between Welsh and English, involved Lewis inextricably with the fortunes of the last days of the Hospice. They revealed a strong-minded, somewhat impetuous, prelate, whose overriding interests were Church and country—and 'country' for Lewis certainly included England.

Meanwhile, the College was training priests for the English mission.[27] At the Visitation by Cardinal Barberini in 1657 it

---

[27] The title 'Venerable' was applied to the College in a broadsheet of 1580 giving indulgences to the College church, the first time the title was used in an officially sanctioned document. The Hospice had been given the title in documents since 1395. Cf. *Lib. Inst.* V, 316 ; *Memb.* 24.4.1395.

was stated that 410 priests had been sent on the mission from
the College. More than forty of these had laid down their lives,
130 had suffered imprisonment, while fifty were authors of
books of controversy.[28] The scholars attended the Roman
College, now called the Gregorian University, where the system
of lectures was that introduced by St Ignatius of Loyola, based
on the system at Paris. Throughout its history, except for a
period of some forty or fifty years, the English College has
continued to attend this University, where so many distinguished
professors have held chairs—men like Bellarmine and Suarez,
Perrone and Franzelin, Billot and Vermeersch. Almost from
the beginning the English College was governed by the Jesuits.
Of the training Professor Meyer has said : 'Seldom has education
won a grander triumph over human nature. Among all the
achievements of the counter-reformation which filled the whole
of Christendom with new centres for the diffusion of spiritual
life, nothing grander is to be found than these seminaries of
English priests.'[29] They were training to be martyrs, and they
knew it. When they signed the College oath, declaring themselves ready to return as priests to England 'for the salvation
of souls whenever it shall seem good to the superior of this
College to order me to do so'[30], many of them signed their own
death warrant. The statutes which outlawed the Catholic
religion did not allow for men with a spiritual intent only.
The fact is at last gaining recognition that the seminary priests
were not political agents. This is the verdict of the Oxford
History of England : 'There is no reason to suppose—indeed
the evidence is conclusively against such a supposition—that
political aims entered into Allen's scheme (the founding of
seminaries abroad), or that the priests who enlisted under his
banner were other than they professed to be, crusaders for the
Catholic faith. The *via dolorosa* that led from Douai to Tyburn
could not have been trod by men who were not profoundly
imbued with the spiritual character of their work.'[31] Yet the
English Government of the day thought its laws justifiable
on political and economic grounds.

However successful the Jesuit rule of the Venerabile, their
presence was one of the factors contributing to the famous
'stirs' which disfigure the history of the College. During the

[28] *Scritture* 47, 5, f. 1 v.
[29] A. O. Meyer, *England and the Catholic Church under Queen Elizabeth*, p. 110.
[30] The College oath is given in Tierney's Dodd, II, p. cccxliii ; and in C.R.S., 37, 7.
[31] J. B. Black, *The Reign of Elizabeth* 1558–1603, Oxford 1959, p. 172.

first seventeen years of the Jesuit rule there were three major disturbances and half a dozen minor ones. Even the Jesuits themselves thought it advisable to withdraw, but were retained at the express order of the pope. The discords in the College, arising from an entanglement of motives, were symptomatic of those which divided the Catholic cause in England for generations afterwards. One occasion of revolt against the College superiors was the introduction for reading in the refectory of Persons's book on the English succession, claiming the Spanish Infanta, a descendant of John of Gaunt, as Elizabeth's legitimate heir. The reader, a young divine named Jasper Lobb, flatly refused to accept the book. High-spirited youths these, as we learn from the punishments accorded them for visiting Roman taverns. The 'Sign of the Rose', the 'Spreadeagle' and the 'Sun' seem to have been their favourite haunts.[32] Persons came himself to pacify the College in 1597, but his peace was not decisive. Trouble broke out again, soon accentuated by the refusal of the Cardinal Protector of England to allow the appointment of bishops in England. The secular priests who came to Rome to protest were confined in the College under restraint for some four months before being ordered to leave Rome. That the College produced a succession of martyrs and confessors is all the more marvellous when seen against this stormy background. The heroism of Ralph Sherwin (who had been at Eton and Exeter College) and Robert Southwell, of Kirby and Walpole and Middleton, is typical of the students of their time, many of them Oxford men, all of them strongly patriotic, who cheered Spanish reverses and gladly prayed for their queen even on the scaffold.

The Corte Savella prison next door, the scene of the Cenci episode described by Shelley, was bought by the College in 1643 and rebuilt for College use in 1662. This was the start of the restoration which turned the old Hospice property into the building which stands today. Philip Howard, the 'Cardinal of Norfolk', completed the transformation in 1685. The College was, of course, Jacobite. Cardinal Howard gave a feast on the birth of the Prince of Wales (the Old Pretender) which included an ox 'roasted whole, being stuffed with lambs, fowls and provisions of all kinds'. There was Exposition on the feast of the Annunciation in 1708 for the success of the enterprise which

---

[32] Cf. among other references Westminster Archives, 6, 319.

James III was contemplating in order to regain his throne, and in 1712 for his recovery from smallpox. Pope Clement XI celebrated Mass there before this same James in 1721, adding a special prayer for the queen who was then in her confinement. Records are extant in the Pilgrim Book of people who came to Rome to receive the touch of the exiled James as a cure for the 'King's evil'.[33] When Rome, at long last, recognised the Hanoverian succession in 1766, the Rector of the English College (together with those of the Scots, the Irish Dominicans and the Irish Franciscans) was expelled from the city for continuing to recognise the Jacobite Pretender.[34]

But during the latter part of the seventeenth century the College had experienced a gradual decline. It lost the confidence of the English secular clergy and, later, of the vicars apostolic, who constantly tried to get control of its affairs. The result of the Visitation of 1739 destroyed their hopes, and this, coupled with the continuing effects of the penal laws in England, made it increasingly difficult for the College authorities to find students who had completed their humanities. The Jesuits continued in control until the suppression of the Society in 1773, when Italian secular priests took over. Their rule is noteworthy only for their misunderstanding of the English temperament and the harshness of the discipline they imposed. An archivist can spare them a blessing, however, since their eight careful volumes cataloguing the College archives form the basis of the present reference system. At last, after recommendations by Sir John Coxe Hippisley M.P. and repeated efforts by the vicars apostolic in England, the Prefect of Propaganda consented to place the College under the government of English secular priests.[35] Few priests left the College during these years. Two may be mentioned : Dr John Kirk, the originator of Oscott College near Birmingham, and the Rev Rowland Broomhead, who founded the first three Catholic parishes in Manchester. The French invasion of Rome forced the College to disband in 1798. On its return in 1818 Robert Gradwell was Rector and Nicholas Wiseman one of the first students. The latter's impressions on entering the College have been recorded at the beginning of this article. The English youths again rebelled against the irksome Italian discipline, though they were then, and have

[33] Cf. Pilgrim Book *anno* 1733.
[34] Cf. THE VENERABILE, XV, 269 (May 1952).
[35] Cf. Gasquet, p. 179.

been ever since, under English secular priests. 'They would wish to have the privilege of strolling two and two in the Metropolis', Gradwell writes, 'as they would in the lanes and fields at Ushaw and Old Hall.'[36] But all Rome was astonished at their performance in the public disputations : Wiseman, and later Errington, particularly distinguished themselves. Mr Gladstone, Macaulay and the 'Rector of Lavington'[37] were among the visitors of 1828. Fr Ignatius Spencer C.P. studied at the College and was ordained in the chapel. Newman visited the College during his stay in Italy ; it was on the voyage home that he wrote 'Lead, Kindly Light'. King Edward VII was a visitor when still Prince of Wales.

On the restoration of the Catholic Hierarchy in 1850 Wiseman, who had been both student and Rector of the College, became first archbishop of Westminster. When Garibaldi entered the city in 1870 the College was slightly damaged by cannon fire, while the students took refuge in the cellar. The Collegio Pio (now known as the Beda) shared the English College buildings from 1854 until 1918, although for a number of these years it was without students. The English College benefited greatly under the wise government of Monsignor Hinsley, later cardinal archbishop of Westminster. It was during his rectorship that the College survived the *piano regolatore* mentioned above. The present archbishop of Westminster, Cardinal Godfrey, succeeded Monsignor Hinsley.

In 1940 the College was forced into exile and re-established at Ambleside and soon afterwards at Stonyhurst in Lancashire. The College buildings in Rome were occupied by the Sovereign Order of the Knights of Malta and were known as the *Ospedale del Principe di Piedmonte*. The College returned to Rome in the autumn of 1946. Eighty-eight students, the highest number recorded, are on the College roll today. Cardinal Heard, the Cardinal Protector, who gained his rowing Blue when at Balliol, has his residence in the College buildings.

The Royal Navy still pays its frequent visits as in the 1500's ; the Salve is still chanted every night, as the pilgrims used to sing it in England's Catholic days ; the pilgrims still come, in modern style, taking two hours over a journey which once took as many months. Yet the six hundred years of history

---

[36] W. Ward, *Eve of Catholic Emancipation*, III, 13.
[37] The future Cardinal Manning.

summarised above do not reveal a mere domestic history ; they indicate how strong are England's links with the Continent. As Lord Hailsham has said : 'Being British is only another way of saying that we are part of Europe, culturally and spiritually. Our language, our law, our literature, our religion ; the things which make us what we are, what we have been and what we want to be . . . the very failures which leave us far short of what we would be—all these are European and Christian. Our roots go deep down into the soil of European history and experience.'[38] Conferences may continue about the economic advisibility of 'entering Europe'. In fact, to her own benefit and that of the Continent, England has never been outside ; and the Venerabile, one of the more tangible bonds between the two, entered six hundred years ago.

JOHN ALLEN.

---

[38] In his speech in the House of Lords debate on the Common Market, 3rd August 1961.

THE ORIGIN AND FOUNDATION
OF THE ENGLISH HOSPICE[1]

'... *aureo anello fra Italia e Inghilterra*' (Tommaseo).

THE SCHOLA SAXONUM AND THE HOSPICE

It is not improbable that there is at least a moral continuity in the history of the English national establishments in Rome from the eighth century to the present day. This depends largely on the history of the old church of San Pantaleo, of which, unfortunately, very little is known. There is some likelihood, however, that this church may well provide the link between the earlier Schola Saxonum, supposedly founded by King Ine when he visited Rome in the first half of the eighth century and the Hospital of the Most Holy Trinity and St Thomas, which was founded on the 27th January, six hundred years ago, and which in 1579 became the Venerable English College.

[1] Main Sources : Ven. English College Archives ; Archivio di Stato, Rome : *Archivio Collegio Notarii Capitolini*, 849, an. 1354–1423, ff. 254 v–256 and 310–312 ; W. J. D. Croke, *Dublin Review, The National Establishments of England in Medieval Rome*, July 1898, pp. 94–106, and October 1898, pp. 305–17 ; id. *The National English Institutions in Rome during the Fourteenth Century*, April 1904, pp. 274–92 (also published in *Atti del Congresso Internazionale di Scienze Storiche*, 1903, III, 2, 555–72.) ; Dr Emilio Re, *The English Colony in Rome during the Fourteenth Century*, 4 Transactions of the Royal Historical Society, 6, 85 (April 18th 1923) ; Cardinal Gasquet, *A History of the Venerable English College, Rome.* London 1920 ; H. E. G. Rope, *The Schola Saxonum, The Hospice and The English College in Rome*, Rome, 1951 ; G. B. Parks, *The English Traveler to Italy*, I, Rome 1954 ; Dr Gradwell, *History of Schola, Hospice and College*, iu MS. Z. 68, pp. 1 ss. and 63 ss.

The claim needs substantiating. The foundation of the
Schola is attributed to Ine,[2] who was king of the West Saxons
from 688 to 725. At this latter date, he abandoned his throne
and 'set out for Rome, to exchange a temporal for an eternal
kingdom. On his arrival he built a house with the consent of
Pope Gregory and gave it the name of Schola Anglorum.'[3]
Other authorities[4] add that the Schola was founded for the
support and education of pilgrims coming to Rome, and that
it stood near the Vatican Basilica, between the Leonine City
and the curving bank of the Tiber—on the exact site of the
present-day Hospital of Santo Spirito in Sassia.[5] In spite of
the great fires which devastated most of the Borgo in the ninth
century and threatened St Peter's itself,[6] the Schola continued
to flourish until well into the eleventh century, giving hospitality
to princes and numerous famous people who came from England
to the shrine of St Peter in Rome.[7] It was towards the end of
the eleventh century that the decline of the Schola began,
but it is not at all clear what exactly happened. Baronius
relates that it 'fell to the calamities of the times' and laments
'the deficiencies of its resources' in 1068. The remote causes
of this decline, however, are quite obvious. The Crusades diverted
many pilgrims to the Holy Land and English devotion to Rome
began to wane. The Investiture troubles, the struggles with the
Empire, the ravaging of the Leonine City by Henry IV and
Robert de Guiscard, all hastened the death of the Schola
Anglorum. Callistus II (1119–24), it is true, restored order and
consecrated an altar in the church of S. Maria in Sassia, but
at the same time he counselled intending pilgrims to visit St
David's in Wales for the present, making two journeys there
the equivalent of one to Rome. In 1162–3, Peter, Cardinal
Deacon of St Eustace in Rome, wrote to tell St Thomas of
Canterbury that the Schola had dwindled to a few clerics,[8] and

[2] Though not with certainty. Cf. Rope, op cit., p. 10 ; Croke, op. cit., July 1898, pp. 96–97
and 102–03 ; W. J. Moore, *The Saxon Pilgrims to Rome and the Schola Saxonum*, Fribourg 1937 ;
W. H. Stevenson's edition of *Asser's Life of Alfred*, Oxford 1904.
[3] St Alban's Chronicle.
[4] Wendover and Matthew Paris, *Chron. Maj.* an. 727, i, 330 f. Rolls Series.
[5] The sacristy of the adjoining church has some interesting seventeenth-century frescoes of
its English past painted by order of the distinguished superior of the time, the Tuscan Stephen Vai.
[6] See frescoes of this event by Raphael in the Vatican's *Stanze di Raffaello*.
[7] Among whom, it is interesting to note, were King Alfred in 854 and earlier, and King Macbeth
in 1050.
[8] Ep. ap. *Materials for the History of Archbishop T. Becket*, v. 64, ed. Rolls Series.

finally in 1201, Innocent III took over the building and made it into a hospital, which still exists as the Hospital of S. Spirito.[9]

Yet only fifteen years later, under Innocent's successor Honorius III, we read of a group of English priests serving the church of San Pantaleo.[10] It seems not unlikely that this church was donated by the pope to the English in compensation for the alienated Schola Anglorum, for in substituting the Hospital of S. Spirito for the earlier institution, and in handing over their church to the Hospitallers of Guy of Montpellier,[11] Innocent III must have made provision for the English ecclesiastics, especially since they had always been dependent on the pope.[12] The presence, therefore, of English clerics during the subsequent pontificate at a church which had no previous connection with England, suggests strongly that it was allotted to them in exchange for their previous property in the course of transactions between Innocent and King John for the foundation of the new Hospital.[13] Though Fr Rope[14] and Cardinal Gasquet[15] both prescind from this question, Dr Gradwell in his study of the Hospice, kept in a MS. of the College archives,[16] already hints at this, and Dr Croke, in his scholarly article in the *Dublin Review*,[17] is strongly in favour of this opinion.[18]

If San Pantaleo, then, is to form a possible bridge between the eighth century Schola Saxonum and the English Hospice of 1362, it only remains to show some form of succession between the end of San Pantaleo and the birth of the Hospice. This is a difficult task because we do not know the exact year in which the former ceased to be an English institution. We do know, however, that it continued to be in the hands of the English priests until as late as 1243, because we find the following

[9] *Breve* of 1st December 1201 : in the *Bullarium* of the Ospedale di Santo Spirito, given by Pietro de Angelis, *Innocenzo III e la Fondazione dell'Ospedale di Santo Spirito in Saxia*, Roma 1948, pp. 33–34 ; cf. also *Annals of Waverley*, ad an. 1213 [*sic*], which relates how Innocent founded the hospital '*in loco ubi quondam peregrinantibus de anglia domicilium erat edificatum, et Anglorum Schola dictum*'. Rolls Series, ap. *Annal. Monast.*, II, 280.

[10] Cf. Fonseca, *De Bas. S. Laurent. in Dam.*, Fani MDCCXLV.

[11] Hurter, *Tableau des Institutions de l'église au Moyen Age*, II, 495 ss.

[12] As is attested by a Bull of Leo IV in Arch. Vat. and another of Leo IX, Bullarium. Vatic. I, 23 and in Migne P.L. 143, cols. 704–14.

[13] Ep. vii, 95, 18th June 1204 ; Gesta Inn., n. 144 ; cf. *Annals of Waverley*, loc. cit.

[14] Op. cit.

[15] Op. cit.

[16] Z. 68, f. 63 v.

[17] *Dublin Review*, October 1898, pp. 315–6.

[18] An alternative possibility is that San Pantaleo was one of the four Roman churches which the Schola appears to have possessed when Innocent took over (cf. *Breve* of 1st December 1201 in De Angelis loc. cit.) : in which case the connection between San Pantaleo and the Schola would be even closer.

inscription on one of its bells : '*D. Presbiteri Angli. Anno MCCXLIII*'.[19] Furthermore, Dr Croke significantly points out that it was situated in the Rione del Parione which, together with the Rione Arenula, as it appears from the documents of the English Hospice, was to a great extent an English area. And it is precisely in this area that the Hospice was founded in 1362. An additional fact that throws some light on this issue is that the Hospice was established not so much by the efforts of one individual (which is the impression given by historians when they speak of John Shepherd as the founder) but rather by a guild or society of Englishmen, some of whom had presumably been resident in this quarter for many years. Fr Rope objects that the English body which appears in Rome about the middle of the fourteenth century, and to which we owe the English Hospice, can claim no real continuity with that of the thirteenth ; it was, he says, a new settlement, owing its birth to the Jubilees of 1300 and 1350.[20] With regard to this, we must note, firstly, that it is by no means certain that the English centre of San Pantaleo did not continue much later than 1243, when we last hear of it ; and secondly, that, though it is true that the English colony was greatly increased by the Jubilees and various other social currents in the fourteenth century, the fact that the new immigrants settled in the Parione and Arenula quarter where San Pantaleo was situated, suggests that the new elements were incorporated to an already existing English colony.

This is most certainly Croke's view : 'The Rione Arenula, where the English establishment arose, and where its properties have endured to the present day, is contiguous with the Parione quarter. The topographical relation between the other and the Church of San Pantaleo must now be coupled with the presence of English in the Rione Arenula . . . and while the earlier documents of the Archives of the Holy Trinity mark for a long period the presence of numerous English in the Parione quarter, they also betray a tendency on the part of these to dwell in the Arenula, until, at last, the Church of the Hospital becomes, as it were, the natural successor of San Pantaleo.'[21]

It may be concluded, therefore, that though it is by no means historically certain, it is not unlikely that there is a moral

---

[19] D'Ottavio Panciroli, *I Tesori Nascosti Nell 'Alma Citta di Roma, etc.*, Roma 1600, p. 645.
[20] Rope, op. cit., p. 8.
[21] *Dublin Review*, April 1904, p. 291.

continuity between the Schola Anglorum of the eighth century and the Hospitale Anglorum of the fourteenth ; and that, to say the very least, no categorical statement can be made denying the possibility.

HISTORICAL BACKGROUND

After the loss of the Holy Land, Rome was once more the centre of attraction to pilgrims. In 1300 Pope Boniface VIII instituted, or more probably revived, the Jubilee year to be celebrated every hundred years, and encouraged pilgrims to the 'Holy Places' of Rome. Fifty years later, Clement VI was persuaded to reduce the period to fifty years, on the grounds that many people would never have the chance of taking part in a celebration which only occurred every hundred years. Though the pope was then at Avignon, he issued a Bull proclaiming the jubilee and granting the usual indulgences to those who visited the tombs of the Apostles in Rome. The number of strangers who flocked to Rome in the first and second jubilees of 1300 and 1350 was immense. It is stated by some historians to have exceeded a million people.[22] One of the longest streets of Rome at the time, leading directly to the bridge of Sant' Angelo, was built especially for their benefit and to this day retains the name of Via del Pellegrino. In this neighbourhood, there arose several 'Hospitals' for national pilgrimages, among which can be numbered those of Aragon, Leon, Flanders, Sweden, Germany and France, and it is no surprise that we find in 1362 the foundation there of the Hospital of the English.

But the foundation of the English Hospice and the other national hospices must be seen in a wider context than that of the Jubilees of Boniface and Clement, for there are also more general and more indirect causes which help to give a deeper explanation of the rise of these national institutions.

At first sight the existence of so varied a gathering of different nationalities in the city of Rome may appear as an expression of a European sense of unity. But as Dr Emilio Re has pointed out with great insight in his article on the history of the time, it was rather the reverse that was true : 'Christian

[22] E.g. Matteo Villani in *Istoria* cap. XXIX.

Europe of the fourteenth century was far from possessing the fundamental unity of the past. The great transmigrations, characteristic of the Middle Ages, were over, long residence in the land and antagonistic wars had brought forth and then deepened those differences between the people on which are founded the great divisions and the national struggles characteristic of modern times.'[23] The foundation of the national hospices in Rome in the second half of the fourteenth century corresponds to this general movement of history and is, in fact, an assertion of the national factor : it is significant that the English Hospice first saw the light in Rome at almost the same time as Chaucer was preparing to give England a national literature.

Another reason for the founding of the national hospices can be found by taking a closer look at Rome herself. She was, at this time, a city of very sorry appearance, a city of anarchy, social disintegration, poverty, famine and raging epidemics, and it was necessary for foreign visitors to clan together for their own safety and protection ; but let the pen of a contemporary chronicler tell the story : 'The city of Rome was in great distress. Rulers she had none. Every day there were fights and robberies. Where there was a house of virgins they were abused . . . the labourers, when they are out working, are robbed . . . the pilgrims ill-treated and cheated . . . He only is right who has a sword. There is no safety apart from your family and friends.'[24]

The root cause of this chaos was the eclipse of the papacy and the Empire, the two great authorities which had constituted the meeting point and the symbol of unity in Christian Europe. As Dante writes :

'*Soleva Roma che il buon mondo feo*
Due soli aver, che l'una e l'altra strada
Facean vedere, e del mondo e di Dio' (*Purg.* 16, 36).

'The Papacy had not yet rallied from the insult of Anagni and lay a prisoner at Avignon in what was called by the Italian writers, the Babylonian Captivity, while the Empire had fallen finally with the Great Harry who had come

" . . . *a drizzare Italia*
In prima ch'ella sia disposta" (*Paradiso*, 30, 46)

[23] E. Re, op. cit., p. 79.
[24] Quoted in E. Re, op. cit., pp. 77–78 ; and in Baracconi, *I Rioni di Roma*, Città di Castello 1889, pp. 279–80.

and now slept in his tomb, in the beautiful cathedral of Pisa.'[25] The resulting chaos which spread over the face of Europe reached its climax in Rome—the *caput mundi*. The history of Rome in this century is in great measure the history of the futile and disastrous struggles of the patrician families between themselves and against the trading middle class represented by Cola di Rienzo.

This, then, was the Rome which the pilgrims encountered when they thronged to the shrines of the Apostles for the great Jubilee, and it speaks highly of the faith of these Europeans that they were prepared to face such distressing conditions in their devotion to the 'Holy Places' of the Eternal City, '*patria diversis gentibus una*'.

But there were other less inspiring reasons for the concourse of Englishmen to Rome at this time. Firstly, there was the development of the trading traditions which were for ever to characterise the English nation. Throughout the thirteenth century, England had relied essentially on her agricultural system to provide the raw material for the more advanced industrial and financial organizations of Italy—especially wool destined to be woven in the factories of the Arno and the Po. But towards the middle of the fourteenth century there arose in the south-eastern towns of England a new commercial class and an association of bankers, and so the wool, which had previously been exported, came now to be woven at home. Thus started an industry in which England would never lose her pre-eminence. Consequently, we find the appearance on the Italian market of cloth and merchants from England. In Rome, the statutes of *Gabelle di Ripa* and *Ripetta*[26] distinguish between Italian merchandise and the 'English cloth from Guildford'. And the English names which appear in the early years of the Hospice are mostly connected with trade in one way or another.

The name of John Hawkwood stands for a less desirable connection with Italy : that of the adventurers and mercenaries who eventually found their way to Italy. Giovanni Acuto, as the Italians called him, is the archetype of these bands of Englishmen, and his memory is preserved in the reproaches of St Catherine of Siena, in the painting of the Duomo of Florence

[25] E. Re, op. cit., p. 73, referring to the death of Henry VII on 27th August 1313.
[26] Ed. Malatesta in *Bibl. Accademia Storico-giuridica*, Roma 1886.

and in a novel by Franco Sacchetti. Sacchetti relates a story which reveals the nature and the purpose of these soldiers of fortune. Two friars hailed Hawkwood on a road near Cortona with the usual Franciscan greeting : 'God give you peace'. To which the soldier retorted indignantly : 'Do you not know that I live by war and peace would be my ruin ?' John Hawkwood was by no means the only one of his kind to find his way to Italy. The Hundred Years' War was then raging between England and France and in its brief pauses its surplus mercenaries were discharged to Italian soil. The White Company, though commanded by a German, was mainly composed of Englishmen. It was formed in 1361 as a result of the Treaty of Bretigny, which had left many of these *condottieri* without employment, and Innocent VI could find no better way of getting rid of them than to dispatch them to Italy.[27]

So the breakdown of European unity, the growth of a spirit of nationalism, the decline of the papacy and the Empire with the consequent anarchy in Rome, the discharge into Italy of English mercenaries, and the tide of commerce from England to the Continent, are the context and the remote causes of the foundation of the English Hospice in Rome. The more immediate and concrete cause, however, was, as we have seen, the influx of English pilgrims to Rome in the Jubilee of 1350.

Rome was not ready to receive and accommodate the vast numbers of strangers and the city became grimly overcrowded. Villani[28] tells us that 'the Romans all became innkeepers, giving the houses to pilgrims who came on horse, taking a tournois a day for (the stall of) the horse, and sometimes one and a half, and occasionally two ; the pilgrim having to buy everything for his own and his horse's maintenance, except for the bad bed'. The English pilgrims, having no national hospice of their own in 1350, had to be content with this unsatisfactory accommodation, and they fell victims to the extortion and even violence of the ever-grasping Roman innkeepers. A decree of the Senator Angelo Malabranca says that it had been discovered that 'many of those who dwell in the neighbourhood of the basilica of St Peter force pilgrims and visitors to Rome to take lodgings in their houses. Moreover, what is worse, if the pilgrims and visitors have taken up their abode elsewhere,

---

[27] A. Sautier, *Papst Urban V und die Soldner Kompagnien in Italien in den Jahren* 1362–7.
[28] Op. cit., cap. 56.

these people drag them forth and against their will compel them to lodge in their houses. When they are called to account for such conduct they allege certain evil customs.' The Senator regards this as an offence against the Prince of the Apostles and against God himself and empowers the canons of St Peter's to take measures against it.[29]

A remedy had to be found, and found quickly. The English regarded the great inconveniences they were obliged to endure as a reflection on their nation and an impediment to devotion. The determined and efficient way they set about finding a solution can be seen from the precious documents of the English Hospice of the Blessed Trinity and St Thomas, which are kept in the College archives and which we shall presently consider.

THE LEGENDS

Until recently the history of the foundation of the English Hospice was clouded with confusion and inaccuracy, a muddled mixture of facts and legends ; so that it is difficult to sift the true from the false. The solution, therefore, is to rely solely on the original documents which we possess. These, in fact, more often than not, plainly contradict the stories that have been elaborated through the years concerning the foundation.

The first instance of confusion is the identification made by many authors between the Schola Saxonum and the English Hospice. Harpsfield, for instance, writes : '(The Schola) seems to have stood in that place where is now the so-called hospital for English priests living there, and for other English travellers'.[30] Lappenberg's account agrees with that of Harpsfield: 'In later times it (the Schola) was transformed into the hospital nominally still in existence'.[31] Dodd, according to his editor, also followed Harpsfield, so that he vaguely attributes the origin of the Hospice to the Saxon kings ! 'There was in Rome a small community, called the English Hospital, which had been built and endowed by the kings of our own nation, in the time of the Saxon heptarchy, chiefly for the entertainment of pilgrims and travellers, who constantly visited that

[29] Chartulary of St Peter's, quoted by F. A. Vitale, *Storia diplomatica de' Senatori di Roma*, Rome 1791, I, 98.
[30] *Hist. Angl. Eccl.*, saec. viii, cap. X.
[31] *Hist. of Engl.*, Thorpe's edit., I, 207.

city out of devotion. It continued under this regulation till
the reign of King Henry VIII, when the rupture happening
between England and the see of Rome, several persons, both
laymen and ecclesiastics, who fled out of England were entertained there as to lodging, diet and other conveniences.'[32] It
is difficult to imagine a greater telescoping of events than this.

Piazza also identifies the Schola and the Hospital but
embellishes his account with a touch of romance borrowed
from Fanucci.[33] He relates how an Englishwoman on a procession round the Seven Churches fell behind and eventually
lost her way. At night she was attacked by wolves in a wood[34]
on the site of the Schola Saxonum. 'Her companions, searching
for her, understood, by her garments and (other) signs, to their
infinite sorrow, the misfortune which had befallen her.' One
'Giovanni Scopardo' (see 'John Shepherd' later) 'was so moved
at the fatality that he formed a committee of English prelates,
gentlemen and artisans in Rome and organised the foundation
of a Hospital in 1398.'[35]

This leads us to the other source of confusion : the actual
date of foundation. Piazza, as we see, gives 1398. Donovan gives
1351.[36] Stow says, 'in the yeare of Our Lord 1380 in the Raigne
of King Richard the Second'.[37] But the reader need not fear
that our centenary celebrations this year are based on a fictitious
foundation date, for, as we shall see presently, it is quite clear
from the deed of foundation that the date is 27th January
1362.

Another detail given by some authors is the association of
the Hospice with St Thomas Becket ; but unfortunately the
original documents show that the connection is entirely fanciful.
Stow appears to be responsible for this sentimental touch and
he is worth quoting in full : 'There was no nation of the world
but had some kind of Hospitalite in Rome, save only the people
of England. Certain Englishmen living in Rome, procured
licence of the Pope to build an Hospitall, in place where Thomas
Becket Archbishop of Canterbury, had some time builded a
chapell of the Holy Trinity. In this Hospitall which they
builded, was to be relieuved, a Gentleman three days, Bread,

---

[32] *Church Hist. of Engl.*, II, 168–9.
[33] Camillo Fanucci di Siena, *Trattato di tutte l'opere pie di Roma*, 1601.
[34] This is an unnecessary detail as wolves were a common sight even within the city walls.
[35] Piazza, *Op. Pie di Roma*, edit. of 1679, pp. 93–94.
[36] *Rome, Ancient and Modern*, II, 244–5.
[37] *Annales, etc. by John Stow, Citizen of London*, edit. of 1631, pp. 334 ss.

Wine and Ware ; a commoner, eight days and nights, meat, drink, and lodging . . .'[38]

The acme of confusion is reached by Moroni, who with his usual thoroughness has managed to merge together most of the other existing accounts, omitting not a single detail : 'The English College stands on the exact spot where was formerly the Church of St Thomas, Archbishop of Canterbury. To speak first of the church : this was dedicated to the Most Holy Trinity of the Scots(!), and, according to Vasi (*Itinerario di Roma*, t. ii, p. 500), it was built by Offa, King of England, in the year 630 . . . under Adrian I, and in 793, a second Offa, King of the Mercians, arrived in Rome. He increased the school and the hospice of the English pilgrims which had already been founded by Ine, King of the East Saxons, in 725, in the days of Gregory II. Consequently, we must rather ascribe to Offa the erection of the ancient Church of the Most Holy Trinity, commonly called, according to Panvinio, of the Scots . . . Padre Casimiro da Roma (*Memorie, etc. della Chiesa di Aracoeli*) thinks that it took this designation from a noble Roman family of that name. Certain it is that it was one of the twenty privileged abbeys of Rome, whose abbots assisted the Sovereign Pontiff in solemn ceremonies.[39] Panciroli (*Tesori Nascosti*, p. 794) asserts the existence of a tradition that St Thomas, Archbishop of Canterbury, lived here when he came to Rome to defend himself against the King of England, Henry II, who oppressed the Church in its liberties. And on this account, after his return to England, and his suffering glorious martyrdom, the church was dedicated to him, and according to Vasi, quoted above, there was joined to it a hospice for pilgrims by one John Shepherd, as Piazza describes . . .'[40]

THE FACTS

After such an accumulation of errors it is refreshing to turn to the original documents which are preserved in the archives of the College and which alone can provide a solid basis for a history of the foundation of the Hospice.

[38] Ibid.

[39] There are definite reasons for rejecting this. The church which is today Sta Trinità dei Pellegrini was situated in the same district as the Hospice, the Rione Arenula. It was at that time dedicated to St Benedict and it took the name of 'Scotorum' after the Roman family of the Scoti. It later passed to the Confraternity of the Holy Trinity and hence the confusion with the English Hospice of the Holy Trinity.

[40] Moroni, *Dizionario, Coll. Inglese*, Vol. XIV.

The deed of foundation[41] of the English Hospice begins :[42] 'In the name of the Lord, Amen. In the year of the Nativity of the same, one thousand three hundred and sixty-two ; in the pontificate of the Lord Pope Innocent the sixth ; in the fifteenth indiction ; in the month of January ; on the 27th day. In my presence as notary[43] and (in the presence) of the underwritten witnesses, specially called and summoned for this purpose ; John, (the son) of Peter *Anglicus*, otherwise called John Shepherd,[44] a seller of beads[45] of the Regione Arenula, of his own good and spontaneous will, sold and, under the title of sale, gave, handed over, ceded and conceded to William Chandeler,[46] of York,[47] from England, present, receiving and stipulating for himself, in his own name, and on the part and in the name of the Community and Guild[48] of the English of the City[49] and of those coming to the City, of the poor, infirm, needy and wretched persons from England, and for the convenience and utility of the same . . . for true and clean property, and for personal heredity, free and exempt from every burden of debts, mortgage, return, payment, tax, or tribute ; namely, a certain landed house[50] belonging to the said John, with a garden behind it,[51] with its incomes and expenses, and all its uses, purposes, appurtenances, adjacencies, rights and obligations, from the ground to the top.'[52]

The first point to be noted is of very great interest. We see that the Society or Guild of the English existed prior to the purchase of the house.[53] They now decide to buy a house to provide general accommodation for English pilgrims coming to Rome (*in urbe concurrentium*) and to shelter and care for

[41] *Memb.* 27.1.1362.

[42] For Latin transcription see App. 2.

[43] The notary was 'Francesco, the son of Pietro Rosani, a Roman citizen' (see deed of 28th February 1362).

[44] *Pecorarius*, a latinisation of Shepherd. Until after the first half of the fourteenth century the Roman scribes, as a general rule, tend to translate English names into Latin. But by this time they begin to transliterate them as well (cf. footnote 72 below).

[45] *Paternostrarius*, a seller of beads, so called from the Paternosters counted on these. Shepherd presumably had a shop providing pious objects for the pilgrims who used the neighbouring Via del Pellegrino.

[46] *Ciandelerius*, a phonetic rendering of Chandeler or Chandler.

[47] *de Yercho*, York, or possibly Yarkhill in Herefordshire.

[48] *Universitas*.

[49] Rome.

[50] *Terrinea* ; Dr Croke translates this as 'one-storeyed', but this could not be so as some two-storeyed houses are also referred to as '*terrinea*' ; cf. for example, '*domum terrineam et solaratam*' in *Memb.* 10.10.1364.

[51] The garden is presumably the same as the present College garden.

[52] Even small houses were often divided into two when sold or let.

[53] It must have existed as early as 1358 (see infra, p. 28).

INNOCENTIVS VI· PONT· CCI·
ANNO DOMINI MCCCLII·

Pope Innocent VI

Deed of Foundation, 27th January 1362

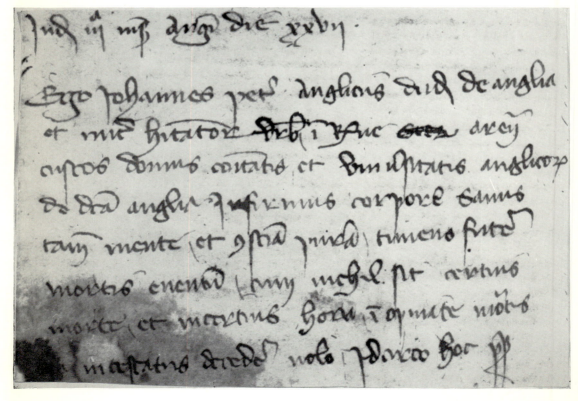

Deed of 14th April, 1362 (*above*), Will of John Shepherd (*below*)

the 'poor, infirm, needy and wretched persons from England'. Now, it is popularly accepted that John Shepherd is the founder of the Hospice, and even recent historians have allowed the claim to go unchallenged. Yet the deed of foundation shows that this is completely false. The Hospice was founded by an already existing guild of Englishmen, and if any individual could claim the honour of founder, it is perhaps William Chandeler, who represented the guild in the transaction and may have been its president. Clearly Shepherd is only the previous owner of the premises.

More conclusive proof of this is furnished by a deed of 14th April 1362,[54] a form of contract by which John Shepherd and his wife Alice, in the presence of William Chandeler and other members of the Guild, 'beholding the works of piety which are performed therein (by Chandeler and the rest) of their own personal and spontaneous wills for the service and attendance of the poor in the aforesaid house, offered themselves, their persons and their works to the above-mentioned William, Robert, John . . . to attend and serve the said poor and needy well and faithfully in the works of piety all the time of their lives, and to anyone of the same in the aforesaid house'. From this we see that the Hospice had been functioning for some time *before* the Shepherds offered their services : indeed, their generous action is prompted by their admiration for the charitable work already going on there.

In one of the later Hospice books,[55] a copyist's error gives the date of this deed as 1360, and it may have been this that led historians to suppose that the Shepherds were the first to give their property towards the foundation of the Hospice. Even the eighteenth-century compilers of the *Indice Generale dell'Archivio* were deceived by this error, and catalogued the deed under this date.

Certainly we are indebted to John Shepherd for his later work in the service of the Hospice, but it is quite evident that to continue to claim him as founder would be tantamount to an historical fraud.

An objection to this may arise from Stow's list of the 'founders' of the Hospice : 'The founders of this Hospital were

---

[54] *Memb.* 14.4.1362. This deed is examined in detail below (cf. infra, pp. 32ss).
[55] *Lib.* 14, f. 81. On the margin is written : '*Donatione di Giovan pecoraro*'. The text, which summarises the contents of our deed, is headed : '*Adi* 14 *d'Aprile* 1360'.

Sir Robert Braybroke, Bishop of London, Thomas Brampton, Bishop of Rochester, Sir John Philpot and his wife, Sir Robert Knowles, Sir Hugh Calveley, Sir John Hawkwood, Sir John Thornham, Knights ; John Twiforde, John Shepherd and Alice his wife, Robert Christall and Agnes his wife, Robert Windleront, Walter Whithers, Robert-at-Pyne, Adam Staple, Henry Line, draper, and other citizens of London . . .'[56]

At least five of those mentioned appear in the early documents of the Hospice, namely the Shepherds, Robert-at-Pyne, and Sir John Philpot and his wife.[57] Could Stow have some documentary evidence for this detailed list of names ? Perhaps ; but we have seen that Stow is not entirely reliable, and the presence of John Hawkwood, who did not arrive in Rome until 1364, two years after the foundation of the Hospice, suggests that these are the names of persons connected with the early history of the institution, but not really the 'founders'.

A more serious difficulty is presented by a reference in a sixteenth-century Hospice book.[58] The book is an inventory of houses owned and rented by the Hospice between the years 1406–1517, but in the middle is inserted a list of books concerning the affairs of the Hospice. This list begins with a book which is dated 1358 and is called *Liber fundationis hospitalis sive registrum fundatorum confratrum et consororum, viz. primo per Johannem petri Anglicum.* This *Liber* does not exist today but it appears to have existed at least as late as 1515 which is the earliest possible date for the compiler of the list. The date of the book shows that it could not have been a book of the foundation of the *hospital* but rather a book concerning the *confraternity* or Guild of the English. The book was simply a register of the members of the Guild in 1358, but the sixteenth-century scribe obviously did not distinguish between the confraternity and the hospital and anachronistically interpreted it as the *Liber fundationis hospitalis;* but he reveals the true nature of the document by adding : '*sive registrum . . . confratrum et consororum*'. Whether the naming of John Shepherd is also an anachronistic addition by the scribe or whether

---

[56] Stow, op. cit., pp. 334 ss.
[57] Cf. *Memb.* 1.5.1350 and then *passim* for Robert de Pinea, syndic; *Memb.* 31.5.1375, 9.9.1375 for Sir John and wife.
[58] *Lib.* 232, f. 34 v.

John Shepherd in fact appeared among the members of the confraternity must remain undecided.[59]

After the opening section which we have already considered, the deed of foundation goes on to give further details about the situation of the house : 'the house which stands opposite to the Church of Saints Mary and Catherine, within these limits : on one side lives one called Matthiotius Velli ; on the other is a house which belonged to the Lateran Church ;[60] on the other side behind lives Cola de Theballescis ;[61] in front is the public road.'

This minute description of the surrounding buildings certainly rules out the theory that there had been a church on the site. For that matter we can confidently exclude all theories connecting the site with St Thomas Becket. For one thing, such an important connection with one of the most revered of English saints would surely be mentioned at least in the deed of foundation. Again, Shepherd had bought the house only a few months before from one 'Antonio Smerucii, formerly of Camerino',[62] and Smerucii in his turn had taken possession of the house as part of the dowry of his wife, the daughter of one Pietro Tannuti.[63] So there is no reason to suppose that the house had any previous English connection at all.[64]

The price paid for the house was forty gold florins : 'for it (William Chandeler gave) by way of price, forty florins of gold, which in the presence of me the notary, and of the undersigned witnesses, he personally counted and from hand to hand received and took from the said William giving and paying for himself, and as above (on behalf of the Guild)'. It is to be noted from the legal structure of the deed that throughout Shepherd

[59] A rather similar error appears in one of the papers which Cardinal Morone collected relating to the College (Vat. Lat. 12159, ff. 206 r–v.). There we are told that the hospital was founded in 1361 and that it was in 1362 that it took the name of 'Smae Trinitatis et Sti Thomae Martyris'. It refers for its evidence to a mysterious 'Lib. Actorum'. But, whatever be the date of this 'Lib. Actorum', it is certainly not a reliable source, for the name of the Blessed Trinity is not given to the Hospice until 1371 (cf. Memb. 25.5.1371), and that of St Thomas not until 1373 (cf. Memb. 1.9.1373).

[60] The vague allusion to this house may be due to its ill-repute ; for in the earlier deed of 1361 (by which John Shepherd bought the house) it is referred to as the house of 'Fina, concupina dni Archipresbiteri dudum (formerly) dictae ecclesiae Sanctarum Mariae et Catharinae'; but the loose-living priest is not named.

[61] Or Tebaldeschi, the name of an important family in that age. Francesco Cardinal Tebaldeschi was the archpriest of St Peter's at the time of the death of Gregory XI in 1378. He was considered eligible for the papacy, and was presented as such to the populace during the flight of the cardinals. Cf. Creighton, Hist. of the Pap., I, 55–59.

[62] Memb. 24.9.1361.

[63] Memb. 8.12.1359.

[64] In a 1320 catalogue of churches in Rome there is no mention of any church existing on the site. Catalogus Tavirnensis given by Huelsen, C., Le Chiese di Roma nel Medio Evo, Firenze ed. Olschki 1927.

appears to be taking part in an actual sale of property, not a disinterested donation as some have described it.[65] This is confirmed from the fact that he actually made a considerable profit on the transaction : he had bought the house only a few months earlier for twenty-seven florins and now sold it for forty ![66]

Before finishing, the deed includes the customary renunciation of rights on the part of Alice Shepherd, and it ends : 'Done at Rome, under the porch of me, the undersigned notary, situated beside St Mary the Round,[67] in the presence of these witnesses ; namely Benedict Sancio, of Florence, the servant of Nero Rosani ; Vanicello Viterbuci and Cecchante, workers from the Region of St Peter's Bridge'.[68]

We can now deal more briefly with three other deeds, beginning with the one we have already mentioned which records Shepherd's purchase of the house. This reads as follows:[69] 'In the name of the Lord, Amen. In the year of the Nativity of the same, one thousand three hundred and sixty-one ; in the pontificate of the Lord Pope Innocent the sixth ; the fifteenth Indiction ; in the month of September ; on the 24th day . . . Antonio Smerucii, wool-stapler,[70] once of Camerino and now a dweller in the City in the Rione Arenula . . . the Lady Laurentia, his wife, renouncing (her claims). . . sold . . . to John, the son of Peter, dealer in beads, formerly of England, and at present a resident in the said Rione Arenula . . . a landed house with garden behind it, situated in the said Rione Arenula, in the parish of the church of Saints Mary and Catharine, within these bounds : on one side is Matthiotius Velli, on the other side is Fina[71]. . . behind is Nicholas Thebaldesci, in front is the public road . . .' The witnesses were : 'Mattia Paccia, of the Rione Arenula ; Symon, the son of John Barber, beads-seller ; John, the son of William, an Englishman, goldsmith ; William Ricciardi,[72] beads-seller, all of the Rione Parione.'

[65] E.g. Fanucci (*Trattato di tutte l'opere pie di Roma*, 1601), quoted by Mgr R. L. Smith in 'A Prologue to the Liber Ruber', THE VENERABILE, XII, 7 (1944).
[66] *Memb.* 24.9.1361, cf. App. 1.
[67] The Pantheon, around which was the legal quarter of Rome. Fortescue (*De Laud. Leg. Angl.*) says that the courts of law closed at noon, so that it was customary for the lawyers to meet their clients after that in the *parvis*, i.e. a portico in front of a church (cf. Chaucer's : 'A serjeant of the lawe ware and wise, that often hadde yben at the parvis'—Prol. Cant. Tales). The huge portico of the Pantheon was the main centre in Rome for such interviews.
[68] This district still bears the name of Rione Ponte.
[69] *Memb.* 24.9.1361. Latin transcription in App. 1.
[70] *Lanarolus*, cf. Italian 'Lanaiuolo'.
[71] See footnote 60.
[72] Richards perhaps—see footnote 44 on the latinising of English names.

The notary for this deed is different from that of the deed of foundation. He is Anthonius Goioli Petri Scopte, who also drew up the deed of 14th April and John Shepherd's own will. He was evidently the confidential solicitor of the English in Rome and particularly of the Hospice. It was his name that gave us the clue to the rediscovery, in the Archivio di Stato, of the will of John Shepherd and other documents concerning the English colony in Rome.

On the same roll of parchment which contains the foundation deed, there are two other deeds signed by the same notary, Francesco Rosani. The first is dated 4th February 1362, eight days after the foundation, and it is a formal confirmation of Alice Shepherd's renunciation of her claims upon the house, already made in the previous deed of sale. It begins with a summary of the contract of the 27th January and then, 'Alice,[73] the wife of the said John, the seller, having been previously informed of the sale made by the same John her husband . . . of her own good and spontaneous will (expressed her consent) to Robert de Pinea, the Syndic,[74] and John the goldsmith, the chamberlain[75] of the Guild and Community of the English, present and receiving for the aforesaid community, and William Chandeler, and me, the notary, as a public person, receiving and stipulating for him.' The deed was drawn up 'in Rome under the aforesaid portico of me, the undersigned notary, in the presence of these witnesses, namely : Pietro Lelli, of Narni, a weigher of the City,[76] and Simone, son of Giovanni Sparo'.

The last deed on the roll is a formal confirmation of the sale and taking possession of the house, according to the usage of the time. It is dated 28th February in the same year. In it 'John, the son of Peter, an Englishman, otherwise called John Shepherd, the principal seller above-mentioned, and Robert de Pinea, acting as procurator for the said seller, (appear as) investing the above-mentioned William, the buyer, on his behalf, and in the capacity described above, with the said house together with the garden, sold by the said John, as in the above

---

[73] Written erroneously *Anixia* for Alixia or Alice.

[74] He is the 'Robert-at-Pyne' mentioned by Stow (op. cit.). He was probably called thus from his residence in the Rione della Pigna, and in his will he chose to be buried in the Church of St Stephen in that district. He was a prominent figure in the Hospice but it is not clear whether the title *Syndic* or Governor refers to his position in the Hospice or in civic administration.

[75] *Camerarius.*

[76] *Ponderator Urbis.*

written deed of sale is more fully stated . . . Of their own good
and spontaneous wills, they invested him with corporal and
free possession, put and placed (therein) the said William and
John, the goldsmith, the chamberlain of the community of the
English, these being present and receiving for themselves and
for the aforesaid association, and me, for notary, as a public
person, receiving and stipulating for it and for them, (namely)
with the same house, by opening, entering, and locking the
door and fastenings of the doors of the said house, and by
standing, sitting down, and remaining, of their own free will,
in the same house. Done in Rome, in the Rione Arenula, in
the presence of these witnesses, namely : Jacobello Cafagii, a
mason ;[77] Paolo Alisii, a notary ; Lello Domini Johannis
Cavalerii[78] of the Rione Arenula. I, Francesco, the son of
Pietro Rosani, a Roman citizen, by the grace of God and by the
authority of the Sacred Prefecture of the Alma Urbs and of
the Imperial authority, because I was present at all and each of
the above-mentioned contracts, wrote and published the
aforesaid, and, being requested, signed it with my customary
sign.'

It is important to observe the occupations of the persons
mentioned in the deed, for they reveal the essential popular
character of the members of the guild, of the transactions in
which they took part, and in consequence of the Hospice itself.
Soon, however, with the growing prosperity of the Hospice,
the case was to be quite different.

The most important deed for the light it throws on the
nature and purpose of the new institution is one which
we have briefly mentioned before but which now needs to
be analysed in detail, namely the contract of 14th April
1362, by which John and Alice Shepherd joined the
Hospice staff :[79] 'In the name of the Lord, Amen. In the
year after the Nativity of the same, one thousand three
hundred and sixty-two ; in the pontificate of the Lord Pope
Innocent the sixth ; in the fifteenth Indiction ; on the fourteenth day of the month of April. In the presence of me, the
notary public, and of the undersigned witnesses, specially
called and summoned for this, John, the son of Peter Shepherd,

---

[77] *Muratore.*
[78] That is, a retainer or servant of the Lord Giovanni Cavalerii.
[79] *Memb.* 14.4.1362. See Latin transcription in Appendix 5.

a beads-seller, formerly of England,[80] and now a resident of the City in the Rione Arenula, with the consent and will of the Lady Alice, his wife ; and the Lady Alice, his wife, with the consent and will of the said John, her husband, and she having first renounced the aid of the Velleian decree,[81] which was introduced in favour of women, she being first informed authentically thus by me, the same notary, of the said help : 'If any woman will have repudiated the other helps in her favour, and will have expressly declined any other of them' ;[82] (both the above-mentioned persons) considering what return they may make to God for the good by Him conferred upon them, and lent to them ; harkening to the word promulgated by the divine mouth : 'Whatsoever you did to one of these my least brethren, you did it to me',[83] wishing, at the sight of the aforesaid good conferred (upon them) by God, to make some return to the needy and poor of Christ ; being enlightened by the fervour of the Holy Spirit to secure heavenly and eternal benefits in exchange for earthly service ; therefore, being personally present before the above-mentioned men, namely, William Chandeler, formerly of York,[84] in England, and now a resident of the City in the Rione Arenula, and Robert de Pinea, Syndic, and John, the son of William, a goldsmith, formerly of Maxigam,[85] and now a resident of the City in the district of the Via Pape[86] and the officials of the Community and Guild of the English of the City,[87] and the wardens and administrators in the aforesaid house, situated and placed in the aforesaid Rione Arenula, in front of, or opposite to, the Church of Saints Mary and Catherine, to which William and the above-mentioned community the aforesaid house is recognised as belonging by full right for the use, and comfort, and service of all and each of the poor, infirm, needy and wretched persons from England. And beholding the works of piety which are performed therein

[80] Though it is Peter, his father, who is called in other documents 'the Englishman' (*Anglicus*) there seems to be an indication here that John too was born in England and came later to Rome.

[81] The Velleianum of the Roman Law ; a measure for the protection of women.

[82] A quotation from the text of the Velleianum.

[83] Croke makes the following comment : 'the democratic note at its loudest, and expressed evangelically'. Cf. *Atti del Congresso*, op. cit., p. 565, footnote 4.

[84] *Dudum de yercho* : see footnote 47.

[85] Massingham in Norfolk ?

[86] This stood near the Church of San Pantaleo. Cf. Fonseca, op. cit., p. 360 and Armellini, *Chiese*, p. 41.

[87] We can, therefore, be certain that the Guild was the only English corporation then in Rome, and that, therefore, the Hospital of Santo Spirito run by the Brothers of Montpellier, though still protected and financially helped by many Englishmen (presumably because of its earlier English connections) was not considered to be an English institution any longer.

(by William, etc.) of their own good, personal and spontaneous wills for the service and attendance of the poor in the aforesaid house ; they offered themselves, their persons and their works to the above-mentioned William, Robert and John, these being present, receiving and stipulating on their own behalf, and on that of the poor, wretched and needy, and sick coming to the said house, and to me, the notary, as a public person, receiving and stipulating for the same, to attend and serve the said poor and needy well and faithfully in the works of piety all the time of their lives, and to anyone of the same in the aforesaid house.'

This shows clearly the genuineness of the Shepherds' charity, and the extent of the sacrifice involved in their decision to devote their lives to the Hospice. But this was not all. They also vowed to leave all their property to the Hospice after their deaths. The deed continues : 'Moreover, now as in the future, and in the future as now, they gave and made over by an act of donation, after the death of both, for the help and succouring of the infirm and poor coming to the said house, to the above-mentioned William, Robert and John present and receiving and stipulating as above stated, and to me, the notary, as a public person, receiving and stipulating for the aforesaid community and the infirm and poor above-mentioned, all and each of the movable and immovable possessions of (themselves), the said man and his wife : the rights, suits and claims, present and future, wherever found, or to be found at the time of their death. Which possessions, rights, suits and claims, immediately after their deaths, the said donors wished freely to pass to the aforesaid house for the use of the said poor, (but) with the proprietorship and usufruct of the same goods and the right (attaching thereto) freely reserved during the lifetime of the said man and wife.'

What was to be the position of John and Alice in the running of the Hospice ? It is commonly held that John Shepherd was its first custos. This may be so if we mean by custos a sort of administrator or director of everyday affairs, but not if we mean it in the sense that the king's ambassadors and Cardinal Pole were later to be *Custodes Hospitalis*. For in this deed it is quite clear that John Shepherd was to have no authority over the general policy and direction of the Hospice. The deed states that Shepherd and his wife shall 'administer in those things which will be required in the house, and diligently arrange for the reception of the poor, do useful things, and pretermit useless things, for the praise of the divine name and his [*sic*] most glorious mother, without any scandalous disturbance ; *and they submitted themselves to the visitation and correction of the aforesaid* (William, Robert, John, etc.) *as their masters and the presiding superiors of the above-mentioned house.*'[88] The position of John Shepherd in the Hospice is, therefore, neatly described by a deed of 1364 where he is called '*oblate and custodian* of the place of the English poor and the Society of the said English'.[89]

John and Alice offered their services 'for the reverence of Our Lord Jesus Christ and His Mother, and all the Saints[90] of God, and for the remission of their own sins'. Their 'masters', William, Robert and John, on their part promised to support the Shepherds 'should they be in need and reduced to poverty, and to maintain them and furnish them with necessary food from the alms coming to the said house, because so it was settled and agreed among them and because, both by divine and human law, a reward is due to those who labour, and the mouth of the ox that treadeth out the corn must not be muzzled.'[91]

The notary is the same as that of the deed of 24th September 1361, Antonio Goioli Scopte.[92] It was drawn up in the house, before William Licciardi,[93] a beads-dealer of the Rione del Parione, Robert, the son of John, an oblate in the church of Santa Maria in Julia,[94] and Henry, the son of John, of the Rione Trastevere.

We have seen how John and Alice Shepherd vowed to leave their property to the Hospice when they died. The will of John Shepherd was discovered in 1923 by Dr Emilio Re in one of the oldest notarial minute-books of the Archivio di Stato of Rome, and he published an abstract of it in the Transactions of the Royal Historical Society.[95] We have recently rediscovered

[88] My own italics.
[89] '*Oblato et guardiano*', cf. *Memb.* 22.10.1364.
[90] *Sanctorum et Sanctarum.*
[91] I Cor. ix, 9.
[92] See p. 31.
[93] Ricciardi or Richards (cf. footnote 72).
[94] *Sancte marie Iniulia.* This church is mentioned in the *Eccl. Urb. Magn. Catal.* of Pannicio, *Spic. Rom.*, XIX, 424. It is there identified with the modern Sant'Anna dei Falegnami. Cf. Fonseca, loc. cit., pp. 371–2 and Armellini, *Chiese*, pp. 447 ss.
[95] 4 *Transactions Royal Historical Society*, VI, 85 (1923). The ref. in the Arch. di Stato is : *Collegio Notarii Capitolini*, 849, an. 1354–1423, ff. 254 v–256.

this valuable document which is fortunately in an excellent state of preservation (see illustration). The book containing it is written in various hands and at various times, but a large part is by the Anthonius Goioli Scopte already referred to. The will is dated 27th August 1365. In it John Shepherd abides by the promise he had made three years before :[96] 'I John Petri, Englishman, once from England and now a resident in the City in the Rione Arenula, custos of the house of the Community and Guild of the English from England, weak in body but sound in mind and with a pure conscience, fearing the approach of death, for there is nothing more certain than death and yet nothing more uncertain than its actual occurrence, because I do not wish to die intestate, I therefore take care to make the following testament . . .' Shepherd continues to leave all his possessions 'for the repair and maintenance of the house of the Guild of the English from England'; except 12d. each to three of Christ's poor ; and to his wife Alice, fifteen gold florins and 10s. sterling (her own marriage dowry), the bed in which he lies (of which all the items are carefully enumerated : mattress, sheets and bolster), three gold florins received on her behalf by him as executor of Alena the Englishwoman, and two gold florins owed to him by Rubeo de Calcararis.

Here we may end the story of the foundation of the English Hospice of the Most Holy Trinity and St Thomas. The aim of this article has been to see this event of 1362 exclusively in the light of the original documents. During the next six hundred years of history the establishment was to pass through many and varied phases. But three fundamental characteristics present in the deed of 27th January 1362 would persist to the present day : the house was to remain planted on the same spot in the heart of ancient papal Rome ; it was always to be Catholic ; and it was always to be English.

BERNARD LINARES.

[96] We are much indebted to Fr Stephen Forte O.P. for the great help he has given us in the difficult task of transcribing this and other documents which we are thereby enabled to publish in full (see App. 6).

APPENDIX 1

JOHN SHEPHERD BUYS HOUSE IN REGIONE ARENULA. 24TH SEPTEMBER 1361

In nomine domini amen. Anno a Nativitate eiusdem Millesimo Trecenthesimo Sexagesimo primo pontificatus domini Innocentii pape Sexti Indictione quintadecima. mensis Septembris die xxiiij. In praesentia mei notarii et testium subscriptorum ad haec specialiter vocatorum et rogatorum. Anthonius Smerucij Lanarolus, dudum de cammerino et nunc habitator in Urbe in Regione Arenule . . . in infrascriptis omnibus et singulis domina Laurentia uxore sua renunptiante et refutante . . . vendidit et titulo venditionis irrevocabiliter dedit cessit et concessit et corporaliter investiens tradidit. Johanni petri paternostrario. dudum de ingriterra et nunc habitatori in Urbe in dicta Regione Arenule praesenti ementi recipienti et legitime stipulanti pro se suosque hereditores et successores in perpetuum. Idest. unam domum terrineam cum orto post se positam in dicta Regione Arenule. in parocchia Ecclesiae Sanctarum marie et catharine. inter hos fines ab uno latere tenet Macthiotius Vellj. ab alio latere tenet fina concupina domini . . . Archipresbiteri dudum dicte ecclesiae Sanctarum marie et catherine. Retro tenet Nicolaus de thebaldescis ante est via publica vel si qui alii ad supradicta omnia et singula sunt plures et veriores confines. cum omnibus introytibus et exitibus suis omnibusque suis usibus utilitatibus pertinentiis et adiacentiis suis spectantibus et pertinentibus ad dictam domum cum orto post se ad veram et mundam proprietatem propriamque hereditatem ab omni nexu obligationis et census exemptam . . . Hanc autem venditionem dationem cessionem et concessionem et omnia et singulaque dicta sunt et infradicentur. dictus venditor. eidem emptorj presenti et recipienti ut supradicitur fecit pro pretio et nomine pretij viginti septem florenorum auri. de quibus presentialiter et manualiter dictus Anthonius venditor recepit et habuit a dicto Johanne viginti quinque florenos auri et alios duos florenos auri residuos usque in dictam quantitatem . . . Actum presentibus hiis testibus. Scilicet. Macthia paccia de Regione arenule. Symone Johannis barberij paternostrario. Johanne guillelmi ingrese. aurifice. et guillelmo Ricciardi. paternostrario omnibus. de Regione parionis ad supradicta vocatis et rogatis. Ego Anthonius goioli petri Scopte. dei gratia Sacre Romane prefecture auctoritate Notarius supradictis omnibus et singulis Interfui. vocatus scribere scripsi et in publicam formam Reddegi Rogatus.

APPENDIX 2

JOHN SHEPHERD SELLS HOUSE TO ENGLISH GUILD FOR THE FOUNDATION
OF THE HOSPICE, 27TH JANUARY 1362

In nomine domini. Amen. Anno Nativitatis Eiusdem Millesimo ccc. lxij⁰. Pontificatus domini Innocentij pape sexti Indictione xvᵃ. mense Januarii die xxvijᵃ. In praesentia mi notarii et testium subscriptorum ad hec specialiter vocatorum et Rogatorum. Johannes petri anglicus dictus aliter Johannes pecorarius paternostrarius de Regione arenule Sua Bona propria et spontanea voluntate Vendidit et Venditionis titulo dedit tradidit cessit et concessit Guillelmo Ciandelerio de yercho de anglia presenti recipienti et stipulanti pro se suo proprio nomine et Vice et nomine comunitatis et Universitatis anglicorum urbis et in urbe concurrentium pauperum Infirmorum Egenorum et miserabilium personarum de Anglia et ad comodum et utilitatem eorumdem . . . ad veram et mundam proprietatem propriamque hereditatem liberam et exemptam ab omni onere debitorum et servitutum ac reddituum pensionis canonis sive census. Idest Quandam domum Terrineam ipsius Johannis cum orto post se cum Introytibus et exitibus suis omnibusque suis usibus utilitatibus pertinentiis et adiacentijs iurisdictionibus et servitutibus Universis a terra usque ad summum. Que domus posita est in oppositum Ecclesiae sanctarum marie et caterine Inter hos fines cui ab Uno latere tenet quidam qui Vocatur Matthiotius Velli ab alio est quedam domus que fuit lateranensis Ecclesiae ab alio latere retro tenet Cola de theballescis ante est Via publica . . . Hanc autem Venditionem dationem cessionem et concessionem et omnia et singula que dicta sunt et infra dicentur prefatus Johannes Venditor prefato guillelmo ciandelerio emptori presenti recipienti et stipulanti pro se et vice et nomine Universitatis et comunitatis anglicorum urbis ut dictum est et mihi notario tamquam publice persone recipienti et stipulanti pro ea fecit propretio [sic] et nomine pretij. Quadraginta florenorum auri quos Inpresentia [sic] mei notarii et infra scriptorum testium personaliter numeraliter et manualiter recepit et habuit a dicto Guillelmo dante et solvente pro se et quo supra nomine et me notario tamquam publica persona stipulante . . . Actum Rome Sub porthicu mei infrascripti notarii posito Justa [sic] sanctam mariam Rotundam presentibus hiis testibus. Scilicet. Benedicto Santii de florentia famulo nerii rosanj. Vanicello viterbucij et Cecchante laboratoribus de Regione pontis sancti petri.

APPENDIX 3

DEED OF 4TH FEBRUARY 1362. ALICE SHEPHERD RENOUNCES HER CLAIMS ON THE HOUSE

Eodem Anno et Indictione mense vero februarii die quarto Inpresentia [sic] mei notarii et testium subscriptorum ad haec specialiter vocatorum et Rogatorum ; Ad haec omnia et singula supradicta Anixia [sic for *Alixia*] uxor dicti Johannis Venditoris certiorata prius (de) quadam venditione facta per eundem Johannem virum eius . . . Sua bona propria et spontanea voluntate . . . Roberto de pinea Syndico et Johanni aurifici camerario Universitatis et comunitatis anglicorum presentibus et recipientibus pro comunitate predicta, et guillelmo ciandelerio et mihi notario . . . consensijt. Actum Rome Sub porthichu predicto mei infrascripti notarij presentibus hijs testibus, Scilicet petro lelli de narnia ponderatore urbis et Symone Johannis sparo.

APPENDIX 4

DEED OF 28TH FEBRUARY 1362.. INVESTITURE OF WILLIAM CHANDELER

Eodem Anno Jndictione et mense februarii die autem xxviij, In praesentia mei notarii et testium subscriptorum adhoc specialiter vocatorum et rogatorum, Johannes petri anglicus dictus alias Johannes pecorarius principalis Venditor predictus Et Robertus de pinea procurator constitutus a dicto Venditore ad investiendum supradictum Guillelmum emptorem pro se et quo supra nomine de dicta domo cum orto Venditam per ipsum Johannem, ut in supra dicta venditione plenius continetur, eorum bonis propriis et spontaneis voluntatibus investierunt et in corporale et vacua possessione induxerunt miserunt et posuerunt Guillelmum predictum et Johannem aurificem camerarium Universitatis et communitatis anglicorum urbis presentes et recipientes prosese ipsis et Universitati prescripta et me notario tamquam publicam personam recipientem et stipulantem pro ea et eis, de domo predicta per hostiam et custanciones ostiorum dictae domus aperiendo intrando et serrando ipsam ostiam, et in ipsa domo stando sedendo et permanendo pro libito voluntatis. Actum Rome in Regione arenule presentibus hijs testibus, Scilicet, Jacobello cafagij muratore, paulo alisij notario, Lello domini Johanis cavalerij de Regione Arenule. Ego Franciscus petri Rosani civis romanus dei gratia almae urbis sacrae prefecturae et Imperiali auctoritate notarius, quia predictis omnibus et singulis contractibus interfui, ideo predicta scripsi et publicavi, omniaque solito singno [sic] singnavi [sic] Rogatus.

APPENDIX 5

DEED OF 14TH APRIL 1362

JOHN AND ALICE SHEPHERD OFFER THEIR SERVICES AND PROPERTY TO THE HOSPICE

In Nomine Domini, Amen. Anno a Nativitate eiusdem Millesimo Trecentesimo Sexagesimo Secundo, pontificatus dominj Innocentij pape Sexti. Indictione quintadecima mensis aprilis. die xiiij⁰. In presentia mei notarij et testium Subscriptorum ad hec Specialiter Vocatorum et Rogatorum Johannes petrj pecorarij paternostrarius dudum de Anglia. et nunc habitator Urbis in Regione arenule cum consensu et Voluntate domine Alixie uxoris eius et dicta domina alixia eius Uxor cum consensu et Voluntate dicti Johannis Viri sui et primo renuptiavit auxilia Velleiani seu consultum quod est pro mulieribus introductum, certiorata primus per me eundem notarium de ipso auxilio autentice : Siqua [sic] mulier ceterisque aliis auxiliis per ea fruentibus renuptiavit et refutavit expresse qualibus eorum uno alteri consentient ; Considerantes quid pro bonis eis a Deo collatis et prestitis eidem retribuere Valeant Attendentes Verbum ore dominico promulgatum quod Uni ex minimis meis fecistis michi fecistis. Volentes intuytu bonorum predictorum collatorum a Deo in egenos et pauperes Christi. aliquid retribuere fervore Sanctj Spiritus. illustratis [sic] et pro terrenjs servitijs eterna bona celestia comparare. Idcirco. personaliter Constituti. coram providis Viris. Silicet [sic] guillelmo ciandelerio dudum de yercho de Anglia et nunc habitatore Urbis in Regione arenule et Roberto de pinea. Scyndico Johanne guillelmi. aurifice olim de maxigam et nunc habitatore Urbis in contra Vie Pape Camerario et officialibus. Communitatis et Universitatis Anglicorum Urbis et custodibus et administratoribus. in domo infrascripta Sita et posita in dicta Regione arenule. ovviam vel in oppositum Ecclesiae Sanctarum marie et catharine ad quem guillelmum et comunitatem predictam. domus predicta. ad Usum et comodum et Utilitatem omnium et Singulorum pauperum anglicorum infirmorum egenorum et miserabilium personarum dicte patrie pleno Jure pertinere dignoscitur et Videntes opera pietatis que exercentur in illa eorum bonis propriis et Spontaneis Voluntatibus ad servitia et ministeria egenorum in dicta domo obtulerunt se se et personas eorum et ipsorum opera predictis guillelmo Roberto et Johanni presentibus recipientibus et Stipulantibus pro se se ipsis et pauperibus et personis miserabilibus et egenis et infirmis concurrentibus ad eandem domum et michi notario ut publice persone recipienti et Stipulanti pro eisdem ad ministrandum serviendum ipsis pauperibus et egenis bene et fideliter in operibus pietatis toto tempore Vite ipsorum et cuiuslibet ipsorum in domo predicta nec non ex nunc prout ex tunc et ex tunc prout ex nunc post mortem amborum ipsorum donaverunt et donationis titulo post mortem amborum ipsorum. in Subsidium et pro Subsidio infirmorum et pauperum occurrentium in domo [sic] predicta. prefatis guillelmo. Roberto et Johanni. presentibus et recipientibus et stipulantibus ut dictum est et mihi notario ut publicae personae recipienti et stipulanti pro dicta comunitate et egenis et pauperibus supradictis, omnia et Singula bona mobilia et immobilia ipsorum Viri et uxoris. Jura actiones et nomina presentia et futura Ubicumque reperirentur et reperiri poterunt tempore mortis ipsorum ; quae bona iura actiones et nomina statim post ipsorum mortem voluerunt dicti donatores ad ipsam domum pro utilitate pauperum predictorum libere prevenire ; dominio et Usu fructu ipsorum bonorum et Jure toto tempore ipsorum Viri et uxoris Vita [sic] eisdem libere Reservatis, . . . (et) quod liceat eis et Successoribus eorum in dicta domo statim post mortem amborum ipsorum. bona omnia et Singula, . . . apprehendere, . . . et in pauperes in domo predicta existentes . . . erogare prout eis melius Visum fuerit pro animabus eorundem et eorum Remissione peccatorum . . . Qui Johannes et domina alixia et eorum quilibet promisit et per Sollepnem et legitimam Stipulationem convenerunt. prefatis guillelmo Roberto et Johanni presentibus et recipientibus ut Supra dictum est. in domo predicta. in servitijs et comodo et Utilitate pauperum predictorum fideliter servire et administrare ea que in domo occurrerit et diligenter disponere pauperes Receptare, et Utilia facere et inutilia pretermictere ad Laudem divinj nominis et eius gloriosissime genetricis absque turbatione aliqua Scandalorum et se se ipsos commiserunt Visitationi et correptioni. predictorum. tanquam dominorum et presidentium domus predicte. Hanc autem oblationem . . . prefati Johannes et alixia . . . prefatis guillelmo. Reberto et Johanni (fecerunt) . . . ob Reverentiam Domini nostri Jesu Christi. et eius matris beate marie Virginis ac omnium Sanctorum et Sanctarum dei et pro Remissione peccatorum ipsorum. Viri et uxoris. et pro eo quod predicti guillelmus Robertus et Johannes et quilibet eorum promisit pro SeSe ipsis et quo Supra nomine. predictis Viro et uxori. presentibus et recipientibus. Si egerent et si ad egestatem pervenirent ipsos alere et competentia tribuere alimenta necessaria eis de elemosinjs occurrentibus in domo predicta. quia Sic Actum et conventum extitit inter eos. Nam laborantibus de Jure divino et humano merces debetur. et Bovj tritulanti [sic] os claudendum non est . . . Actum in domo predicta. presentibus hijs Testibus. Silicet [sic]. guillelmo licciardi paternostrario de Regione parionis. Roberto Johannis oblato Ecclesiae sancte marie Iniulia, et henrico Johannis de Regione transtiberim. ad predicta Vocatis et Rogatis. Ego Anthonius goioli petri Scopte . . . Notarius, . . .

APPENDIX 6

WILL OF JOHN SHEPHERD. 27TH AUGUST 1365

Archivio di Stato, Rome : Collegio Notarii Capitolini. Vol. 849. an. 1354–1423. ff. 254 v–256.

Indictione iii^a mensis augusti die xxvii.

Ego Johannes Petri anglicus, dudum de Anglia et nunc habitator urbis in regione Arenule, custos domus comunitatis et universitatis anglicorum de dicta Anglia, infirmus corpore sanus tamen mente et conscientia pura, timens future mortis eventum, cum nichil sit certius morte, et incertius hora inopinate mortis, quia intestatus decedere nolo, idcirco hoc presentem meum nuncupatum testamentum, quod jure civili dicitur sine scriptis, facere curo, presentibus, volentibus et huic meo testamento et omnibus et singulis in eo contentis mihi consensientibus, Symone Johannis Barberii, Guillelmo Riciardi, Paulino paternostrario et Rogerio Anglico.

In quo quidem meo testamento huiusmodi heredes instituo tres pauperes Christi, quibus et cuilibet ipsorum jure institutionis tabellianice falcidie debiti juris nature et bonorum subsidii et pro omni jure quod a me cum bonis meis petere et exigere possent quocumque modo, jure et titulo sine causa XII denarios provisinorum senatus pro quolibet, et facio ipsos et ipsorum quemlibet contentum (?) etc.

Item relinquo domine Alisye uxori mee dotem suam et jura sua dotalia, scilicet, XV flor. avinionenses in una manu, et X solidos sterlinorum in alia manu, quos habui et recepi ab ea et pro ea tempore contracti matrimonii inter me et ipsam, quos volo et mando eidem Alisie dari et solvi de bonis meis per infrascriptos meos executores.

Item relinquo dicte Alisie uxori mee unum lectum cum uno capitali, unum par linteaminum, unum cultrum in quo jaceo.

Item relinquo eidem uxori mee tres florenos avinionenses, quos recepi et habui pro ea ab Alena Anglica, quo ego tamquam executor testamenti et ultime voluntatis dicte condam Alene dare et solvere debebam eidem Alisie uxori mee.

Item dico, confiteor, recongnosco in iudicio anime mee, me recipere debere a Rubeo de Calcararis duos florenos avinionenses, quos sibi dedi pro arra calcis.

Cetera alia bona mea, mobilia et immobilia, presentia et futura, jura, actiones et nomina (. . .) competentia et competitura quocumque modo, jure, titulo, sine causa, relinquo domui predicte dicte comunitatis et universitatis anglicorum de Anglia de regione Arenule, pro reparatione et actatione dicte domus.

Executores presentis mei testimenti et ultime mee voluntatis facio, constituo, relinquo et ordino, Symonem Johannis Barberii, paternostrarium, presentem et recipientem, cui do et concedo etc.

Hoc est ultimum meum testamentum et ultima mea voluntas etc.

ENGLISHMEN IN ROME AND THE HOSPICE 1362-1474[1]

THE ENGLISH COLONY

A saint, a sinner, and a cardinal—all were among the first neighbours of the Hospice. When John Shepherd, in September 1361, bought the house in the Rione Arenula, which he was to sell four months later to the English Guild, St Bridget of Sweden had already been seven years in the district. Immediately next door lived Fina, *concupina* as the deeds describe her. Behind, on what is now the Via dei Cappellari, stood the house of the noble Roman family of Tebaldeschi, one of whom, Francesco, was raised to the purple in September 1368. Fina and the Tebaldeschi are mentioned in various property deeds connected with the English Hospice. St Bridget herself is not named, but her patroness, Francesca Papazzuri, who gave her house to the Saint, is mentioned at least three times. Bridget died in the house on 23rd July 1373, and ten years later Francesca formally made over the property to the convent Bridget had

---

[1] This article is based mainly on about 140 property deeds and wills covering the years 1333 to 1473, referred to as *Memb.(ranae)*, now in the College Archives. For reference to State Papers and Vatican Registers I am indebted to Fr Anstrüther O.P. Nearly all details of royal envoys are taken from Parks, *The English Traveler to Italy*, Rome 1954, Vol. I.

founded at Vadstena. Thus the English and Swedish Hospices grew up side by side.[2]

It is difficult to calculate the exact number of houses between the two Hospices, but clues in the property deeds indicate that there were at least five. Two of these were acquired by the English Guild, one in 1374 and the other in 1383. In 1406 three houses on the other side of the original house were bought by the Hospice of St Chrysogonus, so that between them the Hospices of St Thomas and St Chrysogonus owned an almost continuous line of property stretching from the Swedish Hospice to the prison of Corte Savella. The houses were by no means uniform in size or appearance. The first one to be bought (27th January 1362) was a simple affair, probably one-storeyed. The next (22nd October 1364) had an upper floor ; the third (9th February 1374) had a tower and its own well, and stood back from the street. The one given by John Palmer, a custos of the Hospice, in his will dated 29th May 1383, was also double-storeyed with similar open frontage. For the first three of these houses the Guild paid out 226 gold florins. Each house had a garden, testimony that the Rome of that time was merely the size of a provincial town.

John Palmer's will is one of some fifteen made between the years 1368 and 1445 by English people resident in Rome. With the other deeds in the College Archives they give a glimpse of the numbers of English then living in the city, as well as their occupations, their families and their wealth. Most of the wills were made when a person was ill : '*infirmus corpore, sanus tamen mente, et conscientia pura per gratiam Jesu Christi*'. One notary put it differently : '*corpore languens*'.[3] The will of Helen, wife of John Clerk, a rosary-seller, is representative of most.[4] It begins with the usual phrase, 'although ill in body, yet well in mind'. The first heirs named are, again as usual, three homeless poor, described as *pauperes Christi*, to whom she leaves twelve denarii. She expresses her desire to be buried in the church of S. Cecilia de Turre Campi, to whose rector she leaves three florins. To the seven major basilicas, as well as to six other Roman churches, she leaves one florin each. To the poor

---

[2] Salvatore Sibilia, *La Casa di S. Brigida in Piazza Farnese*, Rome 1960. The house remained Swedish until the French occupation of Rome ; in 1931 it was given to the refounded Order of St Bridget.

[3] *Memb.* 18.7.1391.

[4] *Memb.* 23.7.1390.

of the Hospice of St Thomas the Martyr, otherwise known as the English Hospice, she leaves three beds to be taken from the best she has ; and each bed is to be furnished with her best pillows, sheets and coverlets. To the same poor she also leaves a necklace. Her house in the Rione Ponte she leaves to Agnes Tayllour, an Englishwoman, as long as she lives ; after Agnes's death it is to belong to the poor of the English Hospice. If Agnes is agreeable, she is to let another Englishwoman, Cecilia Houndene, share the house with her. Other bequests follow, including five bolandini to each of twelve poor people. There are legacies ranging from a bed to a hat of camel's hair, from a ducat to her clothing. To John, Lord Bishop of Derry, she leaves four silver goblets. Another house she owns in the Rione Ponte is to be sold, and the price of it given 'for the souls of the testatrix and of the late John, her husband, and of her parents'. But if the officials of St Thomas's Hospice wish to buy the house, it is to be sold them at ten ducats less than the just price. She appoints as her executors William Richards, rosary-seller, William Holderness, and Sybil Test. The will is valuable in that it gives the names of twenty-six English people then living in Rome. It was made in Helen's house, with seven witnesses (the usual number), and the notary was Anthonius Goioli Petri Scopte, who drew up so many of the deeds connected with English people during the fourteenth century. There was not enough ready money to pay all Helen's bequests, so that in the following March her executors had to sell a house in the Rione Parione which had belonged to her.[5]

One of the executors, William Richards, is worth noting. He first appears as a witness to John Shepherd's purchase of the house in the Rione Arenula on 24th September 1361. He subsequently appears, in different capacities, on no fewer than forty-four deeds, and is last mentioned, as still alive and as *honestus et discretus vir*, on 25th February 1407. He must by then have been the patriarch of the English community. He was a camerarius of the Hospice in 1374, and its custos for some years after 1390. He had a wife, Alice, and one daughter, Palotia. Some time before 1392 the family moved from the Rione Parione to the Arenula, where they seem to have stayed.

In 1375 the Hospice bought a palazzo and four houses in Parione, to the total value of 392½ florins, with money given

[5] *Memb.* 25.3.1391.

by John Philippocti and his wife Joan.[6] This is undoubtedly the Sir John Philpot mentioned by Stow[7] among the list of founders of St Thomas's. Until now it has been thought that this 'list of founders' was entirely legendary, apart from John and Alice Shepherd and Robert de Pyne. This new evidence suggests that, though not founders in the same sense as the members of the English Guild in 1362, the people mentioned by Stow were prominent benefactors of the new institution. There is, indeed, an old tradition that Sir John Hawkwood, whom Stow also mentions, was such a benefactor.[8] The tradition is commemorated in the present College church by a fresco, an imitation in miniature of Uccello's painting in the cathedral at Florence. Croke, too, thought that the members of Hawkwood's White Company aided the Hospice in its early years.[9]

A number of English families are recorded among the deeds. There were, for example, the four Barber brothers : John, James, Symon and Peter. There was Richard Posswych, alias Irlande, the husband of Alice and father of Richard and John. Among the bequests in Richard's will[10] is one 'to the brothers and sisters of St Thomas's Hospice, one ducat for a drink—*ad bibendum*' ! Alice makes a similar bequest in her will.[11] How many English residents in the city were there ? The Hospice records for the period 1333 to 1469 give the names of some three hundred different persons,[12] but this can be by no means a complete list. Of the fifteen English people named by Dr Re[13] as appearing in seven notarial deeds for the year 1365, now preserved in the Archivio di Stato, only four can be definitely identified as being also in Hospice records.[14] Many of those found in these records are mentioned only once and *en passant*, which indicates that the resident English colony was much larger than has been estimated. It must have numbered at least one hundred, especially at the end of the fourteenth and the beginning of the fifteenth century. The majority of the

[6] *Memb.* 31.5.1375 ; 9.9.1375.

[7] J. Stow, *Annales*, 1592 ed., p. 535.

[8] J. Prior, *Discourse on the Centenary of the Re-opening of the Venerabile*, Birkenhead 1919, p. 5.

[9] W. J. D. Croke, *The National English Institutions of Rome*, in *Atti del Congresso Internazionale di Scienze Storiche*, Rome 1903, III, 564.

[10] *Memb.* 18.7.1391.

[11] *Memb.* 10.4.1401.

[12] Appendices 7, 9–11.

[13] Emilio Re, *The English Colony in Rome in the Fourteenth Century*, 4 Transactions Royal Historical Society, 6, 73–92 (1923).

[14] They are John and Alice Shepherd, William, rosary-seller, and John Palmer.

Fifteenth Century Hospice Seals:
from the Lincoln Museum (*above*) and British Museum (*below*)

St Catherine and Sir John Hawkwood

English named lived in Parione or Arenula, though some were also to be found in other Rioni : Ponte, Pigna, Sant'Angelo, Trastevere, Colonna, Campo Marzo, Ripa, Sant'Eustachio.

A document mentioned by Dr Re[15] is worth examining more fully because of the light it throws on a lawless yet Christian aspect of the English colony in Rome in the middle of the fourteenth century. It is a *pacificatio* or solemn contract of peace drawn up between two Englishmen, Roger, son of Nicholas, and John Clerk (not the same as the John Clerk already mentioned). It appears that Roger had murdered a Thomas Clerk. John, the brother and next of kin of the deceased, forgave Roger 'out of reverence for Almighty God and his most glorious mother blessed Mary, and for the remission of the sins of the late Thomas, to whom may God who is the Father of all grant his mercy'. John Clerk and Roger 'gave and returned to each other true and pure peace and perpetual security, expressed with the kiss of peace which they gave to each other . . . remitting to each other all the aforesaid injuries or offences on both sides . . . especially that on the occasion of the death and murder committed, as it is said, by the said Roger against the person of Thomas, cousin-brother of the said John . . .' This peace between the two parties must be preserved for ever by their descendants as well, under penalty of one hundred pounds—'*poena centum librarum provisinorum senatus*'. It may be an indication of the part the Hospice played in English life in Rome that the deed was drawn up there, with John Palmer, custos, as one of the witnesses.

Names which occur time and again in the deeds are John, William, Richard and Robert. Alice was by far the most popular woman's name. There is only one George among the English residents from 1333 to 1469—and even his nationality is doubtful. The occupations of these residents are sometimes given : rosary-sellers, merchants and cobblers are the main classes, although tailors, goldsmiths and carpenters are also found. Dr Croke has written : 'The number of English *Paternostrarii* in Rome during the fourteenth century is nothing short of amazing. They must have monopolized the trade.'[16] This seems an exaggeration, since we know definitely of only about ten English

[15] Re, op. cit., pp. 86 and 91. Arch. di Stato, Rome, *Collegio Notarii Capitolini*, Vol. 849, an. 1354–1423, ff. 310–12.
[16] Croke, *Dublin Review*, 1904, p. 291 note.

rosary-sellers in the fourteenth century ; but there may well have been more who are not named in Hospice deeds. 'Sellers of jewels'—presumably rosaries—are mentioned in the journal of an Englishman who travelled to Rome and the Holy Land in 1344–5. Describing his visit to St Peter's, he writes : 'then we advanced and entered a certain court before the doors of the church, which are sumptuously constructed, and there sit sellers of jewels ; and then lie open the doors to the church which is the largest of all churches in the world . . .'[17]

During the fifteenth century a change is noticeable in the kind of English people resident in Rome, and subsequently in the members of the Hospice confraternity. William Swan, for example, notary at the curia for many years between 1404 and 1429, rented a house from the Hospice. So did Andrew Holes, king's proctor from 1432–44.[18] Two other king's proctors, Nicholas Bildeston and Adam Moleyns, were connected with the Hospice in 1428 and 1436.[19] English members of the Roman Curia are mentioned, though not named, in a Bull of Eugene IV, where they are said to attend the Hospice church 'in large numbers'.[20] In the Hospice, tradesmen are overshadowed by diplomats and lawyers, a movement which culminated at the end of the century in Henry VII's assumption of royal power over the Hospice.

THE HOSPICE PROPER

It is time now to consider the growth of the English Hospice. The English Guild or Community which looked after the Hospice had undoubtedly been in existence for some years before a hospice was actually founded.[21] How many members the Guild numbered it is impossible to say. Probably its members were not many ; most of the English residents were content to give a donation to the good work of the society. At least, this is

[17] Parks, op. cit., pp. 571 ff.
[18] *Lib.* 232, ff. 5 v. and 19 v.
[19] *Memb.* 13.12.1428 ; *Lib.* 232, f. 34 v. Also f. 22 ; reference to a house in 1431 'where once lived the bishop of London'. This was either William Grey (in Rome 1428) or Robert Fitzhugh (1429–32). Cf. Parks, 302.
[20] *Memb.* 25.3.1446.
[21] Cf. e.g. *Lib.* 232, f. 34 v.

indicated by the comparatively small number of people mentioned as officials. The Guild was named in January 1362 *'communitas et universitas Anglicorum urbis et in urbe concurrentium pauperum, infirmorum, egenorum et miserabilium personarum de Anglia'*.[22] These 'poor' were the *raison d'être* of the society. The Hospice is referred to as 'the house of the English poor',[23] and houses were left 'with this express agreement, that all and every income received from the house shall be given and distributed by the camerarii and officials of the confraternity (of St Thomas's) to the poor pilgrims entering the Hospice for their relief'.[24]

The Hospice was dedicated to the Trinity by 1371 at the latest. A deed of this year refers to the *'societas confraternitatis Anglicorum urbis hospitalis sancte Trinitatis'*.[25] St Thomas of Canterbury is also mentioned in the deed, which records a gift of two houses made to the Hospice by William Richards and Robert de Pyne. They make the gift 'out of reverence for Almighty God and the glorious ever-virgin Mary, the Holy Trinity and blessed Thomas of Canterbury, martyr, and for the remission of their sins; and more especially because they acknowledged that the price and florins with which the objects donated were bought had come to their hands from the goods of the aforesaid society'. Two years later St Thomas is mentioned alone as patron of the Hospice.[26] Thenceforth the Trinity (sometimes written as *'Sancta Eternitas'* instead of *'Trinitas'*)[27] and St Thomas are regularly named as its patrons, sometimes together, sometimes alone. It had been called the English Hospice from its foundation—a fact to be remembered when considering the nature of St Edmund's Hospice in Trastevere, which was first called *'hospitale Anglicorum'* in 1406, nearly ten years after its refoundation. St Thomas's undoubtedly grew in prestige as the years passed. Whereas in 1366 it had been merely mentioned as *'quoddam hospitale'*,[28] by 1395 it was 'the venerable hospital founded and built in the city in the Rione Arenula under the name of the Trinity and St Thomas, which is called the Hospice of the English'.[29]

---

[22] *Memb.* 27.1.1362 ; cf. Appendix 2.
[23] Will of John Shepherd, Appendix 6.
[24] *Memb.* 11.1.1376.
[25] *Memb.* 25.5.1371.
[26] *Memb.* 1.9.1373.
[27] E.g. *Memb.* 26.10.1374.
[28] *Memb.* 10.10.1366.
[29] *Memb.* 24.4.1395.

A problem is raised by a folio among Cardinal Morone's papers in the Vatican Archives, headed 'De hospitalis Anglicorum origine et incrementis'.[30] From internal evidence the folio appears to be a report written after Morone's new statutes of 19th January 1556 and before his statutes of 4th February 1577.[31] It gives summaries taken from a Liber Actorum and a Liber Statutorum of events in the early history of the Hospice. The first event recorded is of the year 1361, when, under Pope Innocent VI, the English Hospice was founded 'ad cultum divinum exercendum et ad peregrinos recipiendos'; and in the following year it was called the Hospice of the Most Holy Trinity and St Thomas the Martyr. In the margin is written Liber Actorum, fol. 5–6. This Liber Actorum no longer exists, nor does the Liber Statutorum which is also mentioned. The former is plainly wrong about the date of the foundation, and probably about that of the dedication as well. The Trinity and St Thomas, though mentioned continually after 1371 and 1373, do not appear in the deeds at all before these years. It would therefore seem that absolute reliance cannot be placed on these Libri. We have no idea when they were written, although there is reference in a 1630 inventory of the archives to a Liber Statutorum compiled in 1526 and another in 1553, neither of which is extant.[32]

The Morone paper has this to say about the privileges of the Hospice church. 'In the year 1363 was erected a chapel with several altars. Bernard of Rhodes, the Vicar of Pope Urban V, granted permission for Masses and other divine offices to be celebrated in it by its own priest or priests chosen according to the statute of the Hospice. In 1377 Pope Gregory XI confirmed the rights of the Hospice and granted to any chaplain whatsoever the power of administering the sacraments to the brothers and sisters, to the sick and pilgrims. In 1445 Pope Eugene IV confirmed the same rights.' The first mention of the chapel that I have found in any original deed occurs on 11th January 1376. On that day Gilbert Newman, an English priest living in the Arenula, gave two houses to the English Guild. The donation was effected and the deed drawn up 'in capella hospitalis'. The deed states that when the bell had been rung, 'ut moris est', the brethren of the English confraternity

---

[30] Vat. Lat. 12159, ff. 206 r-v.
[31] Ibid., ff. 98 and 176.
[32] Lib. 277, f. 1 and Index.

assembled in the Hospice chapel and there witnessed Newman's gift.[33]

There may be an oblique reference to the chapel in the will of Richard Posswych.[34] He wished to be buried in his parochial church of St Blaise, and left four florins for candles to be lit around his body on the day of burial. The residue of these candles was then to be divided between the Hospice of St Thomas and the church of St Blaise. Richard's wife, Alice, also wished to be buried in St Blaise's. In her will[35] is a bequest for three series of Gregorian Masses : one in St Peter's, one in St Blaise's, and the third 'in the aforesaid Hospice'. Some twenty-five years later the Hospice church is given in a list of Roman churches made by Signorili, secretary of the senate of Rome at the time of Martin V (1417–31).[36] It is not mentioned again until Eugene IV's Bull, dated 23rd March 1446. This makes no mention of any privileges granted by earlier popes ; it gives permission for the consecration of a cemetery attached to the chapel and grants faculties to the Hospice chaplain to administer the sacraments to pilgrims and Hospice officials.[37] The bull is endorsed : 'chapel with cemetery consecrated 1446'.

Gasquet, following Gradwell, says that the Hospice was rebuilt in 1412.[38] If this is true it will explain the making in that year of the royal coat of arms which hung over the entrance to the Hospice. But Gradwell is so unreliable when writing about this early period that one feels he is not to be trusted unless supported by other evidence. Moreover, in view of the state of Rome at that time, 1412 seems too early a date to assign to the rebuilding of the Hospice. After their return in 1377, the popes found Rome a desolated city. So seldom was it at peace that they often had to live elsewhere. Adam of Usk, writing about 1405, lamented a city 'once full of princes and their palaces, now of hovels, thieves, wolves, worms, and waste-lands'.[39] Even on the feast of SS. Peter and Paul in 1414 no

---

[33] *Memb.* 11.1.1376.

[34] *Memb.* 18.7.1391.

[35] *Memb.* 10.4.1401.

[36] Catalogus Signorili (*c.* 1425), printed in C. Huelsen, *Le Chiese di Roma nel Medio Evo*, Firenze 1927, p. 44. The church is not mentioned in the *Liber Anniversorum* (1461) ; in Flavio Biondo, *Roma Instaurata*, Verona 1481–2 ; or in *De Roma* (varii auctores), Rome 1523.

[37] *Memb.* 25.3.1446. It may be read in full in THE VENERABILE, XIX, 494–5 (May 1960).

[38] Gasquet, p. 46 ; Gradwell, *MS. History of the English College*, 1823, Z. 68, f. 65.

[39] Adam, *Chronicon*, quoted by Parks, 590. Adam himself is mentioned in *Memb.* 8.7.1403, where he is said to owe a lamp, three kettles and an iron spit, to Walter Taylor, an English cobbler of the Rione Parione.

lamp could be lighted before the confession in St Peter's basilica, so extreme was the general poverty.[40] Only under Martin V and his successor, Eugene IV, was Rome rebuilt. Of course this is no proof that the Hospice was not rebuilt earlier. It was English property and concerned with pilgrims ; it did not necessarily share in the general decay of the city. Indeed, in July 1406 the Guild had bought two plots of land adjoining the Hospice and three months later it obtained permission to build on them.[41] This may be an indication that St Thomas's was comparatively unaffected by the disorder surrounding it. In general one is impressed by the orderliness with which business was transacted. Only two Hospice records suggest that all was not well in Rome. The first is in 1406, when a house in the Borgo S. Pietro, owned by the Hospice, is said to be 'almost destroyed by war and men-at-arms'.[42] The second, undated but later, refers to certain property owned by the Hospice of St Chrysogonus, whose 'deeds have been stolen and lost'.[43] Some idea of the Hospice after its rebuilding, whenever this took place, will be obtained from 'Pilgrims and the Hospice' later in this book. Before it was rebuilt, it consisted simply of the four houses which became Hospice property at various times between 1362 and 1383. These were probably joined together in some way to make a larger building. A cloister, porch and refectory are mentioned at different times.[44] The only Hospice inventory we have before the 1490's is a summary of one made in 1445 and copied about 1525.[45] The main items recorded are furnishings for the chapel and pilgrims' rooms. The Hospice owned a bishop's ring and mitre, studded with precious stones and thought to be worth more than a hundred ducats—although a footnote states that the stones were not genuine. There were seven silver chalices, two candlesticks of pure silver, and a silver thurible ; a small cross of beryl mounted in silver ; and a silver monstrance a cubit high. Other chapel furnishings included bronze vases, candlesticks, crosses, bells, a thurible and several pyxes ; thirteen corporals, seven carpets,

[40] Pastor, *Lives of the Popes*, I, 215 ; who here gives a general picture of Rome at this time and under Martin V.

[41] *Memb.* 29.7.1406 ; 10.10.1406.

[42] *Lib.* 232, f. 1. This was the house later occupied by the queen of Cyprus, whom Fr Rope identifies as the Queen Charlotte mentioned by W. Miller, *Essays in the Latin Orient*, Cambridge 1921, pp. 502–07.

[43] *Lib.* 272, f. 9 v.

[44] *Memb.* 10.6.1393 ; 21.12.1396 ; 12.2.1400.

[45] *Lib.* 33, f. 5.

twenty cushions, seven portable altars, sixteen surplices, eleven altar frontals with their curtains, as well as a large number of altar cloths, many given by Richard Ely. Chasubles of silk and velvet of many colours, one the gift of the prior of Canterbury, and two velvet tunicles given by Sir Walter Hungerford, must have enriched many a service in the Hospice. A frontal and two curtains, the gift of Sir Hugh Myddleton, Turcopolier of the Knights of Rhodes, also adorned the chapel. Among the six pairs of candlesticks were two given by Robert Botyl, Prior of the Knights of St John of Jerusalem in England, who in 1447 was sent as envoy by Henry VI to the king of France and the pope. One of eleven tablecloths had been presented by Robert Fitzhugh, a former chancellor of Cambridge University, king's envoy to Rome from 1429 to 1432. He was consecrated bishop of London in 1431.

Building operations were again in progress in 1450. Details are given in *Liber* 17. An agreement was made with the contractor on 26th January 1449. Plans, measurements, estimates and partial payments are recorded, as well as a final reckoning dated 18th June 1453. Four days later the contractor and the Hospice procurators appeared before a notary to attest the justice of the settlement.[46] These operations cost 1918 ducats and 10 bolandini, an enormous sum, and must have involved the rebuilding of much of the Hospice itself. John Capgrave saw the work in progress, for he describes the building of the Pantheon as follows : 'they say there commonly . . . that they made a great hill of earth as broad and as high as they would have the house, and in this hill they buried much money. When the house was made they gave the people leave to carry out the earth, and for their carriage to take the money which they found. In very likeness I saw a vault made at Rome, a full fair house which is a cellar at St Thomas's Hospital, even of this same manner.'[47] Stow says that money was collected in every parish in England to help pay for this new building, 'but that came to small effect, the charges of collecting and conveying was such that there came towardes the worke not past one thousande douckets in one whole yeere'.[48]

[46] A fuller account of this rebuilding, including details of banks and exchange, was given by the late Fr Vincent J. Flynn, *Englishmen in Rome during the Renaissance*, in *Modern Philology*, XXXVI, 129–30 (November 1938). *Lib.* 17, ff. 7–13.

[47] Capgrave, *Ye Solace of Pilgrims*, ed. C. A. Mills, Oxford 1911. The spelling has been modernized.

[48] Stow, op. cit., p. 535.

FINANCE

Stow's reference to collections in England must lead to a consideration of Hospice finance. In its early years the Hospice depended upon the charity of residents in Rome. A more stable income was needed, and gradually property was acquired, sometimes by purchase, sometimes by gift. By 1406 twenty-three houses, one palazzo and various plots of land and vineyards had been acquired. Of these, eight houses and six plots of land had been bought at a cost of 666 florins and 43 ducats. The rest had been donated or left as legacies. The rent from these brought in 243 ducats in 1406. By 1431 the Hospice owned 31 houses and received 280 ducats in rent. In 1445 the income from only 30 houses was 360 ducats—an indication that the cost of living had risen.[49]

Rentals were not the only income. The *firma Angliae*, a collection made throughout England for the Hospice, was in operation during Richard II's reign. In 1398 John Malpas, described as 'proctor-general of the master and brethren of the Hospice of the Holy Trinity and St Thomas the Martyr, Rome', was given protection for one year to collect alms in England on behalf of the Hospice.[50] Whether this was the first collection to be made in England for the Hospice we do not know ; nor do we know if it was an annual collection. Four years later Henry Halum, 'parchemyner', was summoned for not appearing before the justices of the Bench to answer a plea that he render his account to Robert Newton, chaplain and procurator of the Hospice, for the time when he was his receiver.[51] Then there is silence. Hospice records reveal nothing until 1446, when Matthew Crompe of Banbury, Oxfordshire, a bachelor of laws, sent two hundred ducats *de camera* 'for the term of St Michael Archangel'.[52] The sum was repeated twice during the following year, on Lady Day and at Michaelmas, but then records cease. It would seem that the system was already in operation whereby money collected in England and Wales was sent to the Hospice twice a year on the days mentioned. Certainly this system obtained at the close of

---

[49] These details are taken from *Memb.*, *passim*, and from *Lib.* 232. A ducat was worth almost exactly two florins.
[50] *Cal. Pat. Rich. II*, VI, 324 (21.4.1398).
[51] *Cal. Pat. Henry IV*, IV, 79 (3.5.1402).
[52] *Lib.* 16, last two pages.

the fifteenth century. *Liber* 17 also contains copies of a series of letters exchanged between Hospice officials and William Knyghtcote, collector in England, during the years 1450–2. Knyghtcote did not like his position and asked to resign. At various times during the year he sent different sums, but not the full amount due, and he retailed complaints made against the officials by pilgrims returning to England. When the sum promised did not reach Rome the Hospice officials wrote a stern letter on 29th September 1451. They asked Knyghtcote to make good his promises : '*facta querimus et non verba vel litteras*'. But in the accounts dated 20th August 1453 it is recorded that Knyghtcote, although he had sent 1040 ducats, still owed the Hospice 820 ducats. We do not know if the debt was ever paid.[53]

Soon after this period the Hospice was owed money not in England but in Rome itself. John Lax, doctor of law, cleric of Durham, canon and prebendary of Laughton in the diocese of York, and king's proctor at the curia in 1456 and from 1459 to 1462, was camerarius of the Hospice in 1447, 1450 and 1452. He was a *confrater* in 1457, and in this year went to England to represent the Hospice in recovering a legacy. In 1460 he owed the Hospice 300 ducats, half of which Bernard, the cardinal of Spoleto, obliged himself to pay in 1461.[54] In 1463 the house leased to John Lax by the Hospice in 1452 was sold to satisfy his creditors.[55] The Hospice had bought for 300 florins the improvements made in the house by Lax and this led to a dispute with him. We do not know how the affair ended, though Lax was again camerarius in 1466.[56]

Another sort of income was bequests by people in England. Some time before 1450 Sir Thomas Hasley, a member of the Hospice confraternity, had left the institution the sum of thirty ducats yearly. Other heirs refused to recognise the bequest and would not make payment to the Hospice. Letters were sent by the Hospice officials addressed to John Stafford, Archbishop of Canterbury, and his successor John Kemp, asking for their assistance in recovering the debt and petitioning for a share in the estate of Cardinal Beaufort. Later Pope

---

[53] The 1040 ducats may well be the thousand ducats mentioned by Stow. Fr Flynn's account of the Knyghtcote correspondence, op. cit., pp. 131–4, cannot be bettered. The letters are in *Lib.* 17, ff. 2–4.

[54] *Lib.* 17, ff. 2 v. and 4 v ; *Memb.* 25.10.1460 ; 22.3.1461.

[55] *Cal. Pap. Reg.*, X, 615 (16.11.1452) ; XI, 652 (6.11.1463).

[56] *Lib.* 232, f. 35.

Callistus III wrote on behalf of the Hospice to Thomas Bourchier, also archbishop of Canterbury, with a similar request.[57] Among the procurators appointed to help the Hospice regain the bequest were Andrew Holes, Robert Stillington, Robert Botyl, William Saundyrs and Richard Bole. The last was king's envoy in 1459 and a member of St Edmund's confraternity.[58] Botyl we have met already. Robert Stillington was later to be bishop of Bath and Wells and Lord Chancellor. Andrew Holes had been in Rome with Robert Fitzhugh from 1429 to 1432. He represented Henry VI at the curia from 1432 to 1444, though for half that time Eugene IV was compelled through political unrest to hold his court at Florence, where Holes mingled freely with the humanists of the Medici circle.[59] Back in England he became chancellor of Salisbury diocese and in 1449 keeper of the privy seal. Such was his position when appointed procurator for the Hospice. These biographical details give some idea of the kind of friends the Hospice could call upon for aid.

PILGRIMS

We do not have any names of pilgrims for the first hundred years of the Hospice's existence. It is possible that five of the seven witnesses of John Palmer's will, made in the Hospice on 29th May 1383, were pilgrims. Two were priests, three laymen, and they are described in the deed as '*moram trahentes in urbe in regione Arenulae*'. The usual phrase for a person living in the city is simply *de urbe*, followed by the name of the district. However, *moram trahentes* is used on one other occasion, when those so described are certainly residents in Rome, so nothing definite can be deduced from the use of the phrase in Palmer's will.

For the names of pilgrims and their descriptions of Rome at this early period we have to look elsewhere. The fullest

---

[57] Copies of these and other letters, written between 1450 and 1457, are in *Lib.* 17, ff. 1–2 v, 4 v. Again Fr Flynn's account, op. cit., pp. 122–7, cannot be improved upon.

[58] *Lib.* 272, f. 2.

[59] Parks, op. cit., pp. 430–1.

account of the Hospice is given about 1415 by Margery Kempe, the Norfolk mystic. Returning to England from the Holy Land she came by way of Venice and Assisi to Rome. 'Then was this creature received into the Hospital of Saint Thomas of Canterbury in Rome, and she was houselled every Sunday with great weeping, boisterous sobbing, and loud crying, and was highly beloved by the Master of the Hospital and all his brethren. And then, through the stirring of her ghostly enemy, there came a priest, that was held a holy man in the Hospital and also in other places of Rome, who was one of her fellows, and one of her own countrymen. And notwithstanding his holiness, he spoke so evil of this creature and slandered so her name in the Hospital that, through his evil language, she was put out of the Hospital, so that she might no longer be shriven or houselled therein.'[60]

For the next two months she stayed in Rome and won many people to her by her charity. Her fame caused second thoughts among the Hospice officials. 'When the Master and Brother of the Hospital of Saint Thomas, where she was refused beforetime, as is written already, heard it said what love and what favour she had in the city, they prayed her that she would come again to them, and she should be more welcome than ever she was before, for they were right sorry that they had put her away from them. And she thanked them for their charity and did their commandment. When she had come back to them, they made her right good cheer, and were right glad of her coming.

'Then she found there, her that was her maiden beforetime, and, with right, should have been so still, dwelling in the hospital in much wealth and prosperity, for she was keeper of their wine.'[61]

Mention of wine reminds one of Stow's description of hospitality given to pilgrims at St Thomas's : 'In this hospitall . . . was to be releeved, a gentleman three daies, bread, wine, and ware ; a commoner eight daies and nights, meate, drinke, and lodging. And if any woman happen to be nigh hir time of deliverance, so that she dare not take hir journey, she is to be honestly kept till she be purified : and if she be of power, to

[60] *The Book of Margery Kempe*, ed. W. Butler-Bowden, Oxford 1954, p. 102.
[61] Ibid., p. 122.

take hir childe with hir : if not, to be kept there untill it were seaven yeeres olde.'[62]

It has not hitherto been known when the rules regarding provision for pilgrims were introduced. Recently, however, a paper has come to light among the Vatican Registers, where Pius II confirms the ancient statutes of the Hospice.[63] This paper makes it clear that the system described by Stow is as old as the Hospice itself, for a statute said to date from the very foundation of the Hospice commands that all pilgrims in good health coming to the city from England and asking for board and shelter in the Hospice are to be admitted without refusal for three days ; if they are poor, for eight days. Those who are sick are to be kept until their death or recovery. Of the sick the rich are to be supplied with food, doctors and medicine ; the poor are to be given in addition sheets, beds and general hospitality.

The inventory for 1445 mentions twelve quilts in the nobles' chamber, twenty in the *camera pauperum*. The women's chamber had five quilts, and there were others—we are not told where—making a total of 59. There were 63 beds altogether, which means that the Hospice could sleep over a hundred people at once.[64] In the first records of pilgrims available (1479) no distinction is made between rich and poor, nor is any detail given about the length of their stay, unless this was of long duration. In 1504 lists of pilgrims were divided between nobles and poor, and the time limit of three and eight days is mentioned explicitly.[65]

The Hospice would only be full in Jubilee Years. In an ordinary year up to 200 English pilgrims in all might be entertained. Even this total is surprisingly high, but I do not think it extravagant in view of the figures for the years 1479–84.

Pilgrims who arrived at the Hospice in 1450 were not treated with the hospitality they expected. Such at least is the complaint of the collector in England, William Knyghtcote, to the Hospice officials.[66] His work is difficult, partly because of the lack of consideration shown at the Hospice to visitors, both clerical and lay. Many pilgrims, on their return to England,

[62] Stow, op. cit., p. 534.
[63] *Registri Vaticani*, Vol. 510 (Pius II), f. 153 v. The paper is referred to in *Cal. Pap. Reg.*, XI, 651.
[64] *Lib.* 33, f. 5. This presumes the beds were double.
[65] Appendices 12 and 13.
[66] *Lib.* 17, ff. 3 v–4.

accuse the officials in general and the custos in particular of in-hospitality. Consequently they refuse alms. The custos ought to be replaced, as his name suggests : '*Coactus sum dicere maxima culpa imponitur custodi, videlicet Fyge vel Fuge : et ideo fugetur, ne deterius inde contingat*'. It would be better for the Hospice to lose a hundred pounds than to lose in reputation as it has this year (1450). There was only one priest in the place, John Wells, and he was away most of the time. A lot more could be said about the confusion existing at the Hospice, and its bad manage-ment. For the love of God, the welfare of the Hospice, and the honour of England, the collector hopes that matters will be mended. Lest the officials might say they did not know about complaints made against them, he is sending this letter in triplicate.

Fyge was expelled and the officials were able to reply to Knyghtcote that they had done everything he asked of them. They did not deny the charges of inhospitality, but were obviously at pains to remedy the situation.

THE HOSPICE CONFRATERNITY

To close, a word must be said about the confraternity of the Hospice. The paper in the Vatican Registers of 1463 asserts that only those were to be admitted to the confraternity who were of good life and honest character.[67] Upon their admittance they were to swear by the Scriptures to uphold the Hospice statutes. Every year on 3rd May they were to meet and choose officials for the Hospice. A chaplain was to be elected from the number of *confratres* ; an outsider could be chosen were this necessary. Immediately after his election he was to take an oath similar to that taken by the *confratres* ; he would uphold the Hospice statutes, especially that which dated from the foundation of the Hospice and which related to the reception of pilgrims. There is no mention in the paper of the election of custos and camerarii. We know, however, that they too were elected on 3rd May.[68]

---

[67] '. . . *bonae vitae, conversationis honestae*'. Reg. Vat., 510, 153 v.
[68] *Lib.* 17, f. 13 v.

E

One of the statutes of unknown date found in Cardinal Morone's papers[69] lays down that the custos, chaplain and principal sacristan should live in the Hospice and take care of it, helped by other *confratres* who live outside—including no doubt the procurator and two camerarii. These camerarii were both laymen in the early years of the Hospice. We do not have the names of any between 1375 and 1391, but in this latter year a distinction is made between a clerical and a lay camerarius. The distinction is made again in 1401 and continually after this. Perhaps this appointment of a cleric in an official position caused some friction among the *confratres* and the English living in Rome, for in 1403 an Englishman, Walter Taylor, appointed as executor of his will the custos of the English Hospice, 'provided that such a custos or rector is not a priest or cleric . . .'[70]

The confraternity was enriched with indulgences by Martin V. Members were entitled to choose their own confessor, who could give a plenary indulgence at the hour of death. The indult granting this was renewed by Eugene IV in 1445, when it was stated that three-quarters of the brethren and sisters in Rome had died in that year. No doubt this was the cause of Eugene's Bull the following March, granting permission for a cemetery attached to the Hospice church.[71]

People in England could also join the confraternity, and the book containing the names of some hundreds who were members in 1446 is still preserved. The bishop of Chichester, Adam Moleyns, once camerarius 'and always protector of the Hospice', is among those named. A few members were admitted '*ad consilia et suffragia*'. Presumably they had a say in Hospice affairs and in the election of officials.[72]

As the fifteenth century progressed, confraternity members and officials of the Hospice were taken more and more from among English diplomats and lawyers ; so that when the English Crown took control of Hospice affairs it was the final step in a process which had been long developing.

JOHN ALLEN.

---

[69] *Vat. Lat.*, 12159, 206.
[70] *Memb.* 8.7.1403.
[71] *Cal. Pap. Reg.*, VII, 329 (25.4.1421) ; VIII, 130 (16.3.1429) ; IX, 518 (24.10.1445) ; IX, 572 and *Memb.* 22.3.1446.
[72] *Lib.* 16. Appendix 8. A copy of the form of admission for one who joined while in Rome is preserved at St Chad's, Shrewsbury : it was printed in THE VENERABILE, X, 266–8 (May 1942).

APPENDIX 7

CHRONOLOGICAL LIST OF ENGLISH RESIDENTS IN ROME 1333–1469

All persons given in this Appendix are mentioned as English in the collection of property deeds and other documents known as *Membranae* ; most are named as buyers, sellers or witnesses. A question-mark before a person's name means that he is not known definitely to be English ; after a name it signifies an uncertain spelling. Christian names have been translated ; surnames, in nearly every case, have been left as in the original. Sometimes alternative spellings are given in brackets. The date before a name (year, day, month) is that on which a person is first mentioned ; after, the date he is last mentioned alive, or the first time he is mentioned as dead ; this latter is signified by a cross (†). * denotes an official of St Thomas's, ‡ an official of St Edmund's. Dates are usually those of *Membranae* ; where they are taken from *Libri* 17, 232 or 272, these numbers and the folio number are given in brackets. Degrees have usually been abbreviated, albeit anachronistically.

This Appendix should be used in conjunction with Appendices 9–11 to obtain a full list of English residents in Rome who are mentioned in Hospice records of this period.

1333,	15.6.	Henry, servant of monastery of S. Silvestro in Capite. 21.5.1447†.
,, ,	15.6.	Richard, *Anglicus*.
,, ,	15.6.	Symon.
,, ,	15.6.	Rawlins.
,, ,	15.6.	Philip.
1345,	15.9.	Marola, daughter of the late William.
,, ,	15.9.	F. John, camerarius of Hospital of S. Spirito.
1347,	21.5.	Agnes, widow of Henry (above 15.6.1333).
,, ,	21.5.	Robert Adoguardi.
,, ,	21.5.	John de Girlanda.
1350,	1.5.	Joan, widow of William.
,, ,	1.5.	Michael de Pollanda.
,, ,	1.5.	Robert de Pyne (de Pinee)*, son of Robert, *cernitor*, syndic. 26.5.1376†.
,, ,	25.10.	Symon Barber*, son of John. 6.3.1401.
1351,	20.8.	Mabel, widow of Stephen.
,, ,	20.8.	Henry, son of John. 22.12.1387.
1358,	1.1.	(232, 34 v) John Shepherd*, son of John, rosary-seller. 3.8.1365 (Re 91).[1]
1361,	24.9.	John, son of William, goldsmith. 14.4.1362.
,, ,	24.9.	William Richards*, rosary-seller. 25.2.1407.

1362, 27.1. William Chandeler*. 14.4.1362.
  ,, , 4.2. Alice Shepherd, wife of John (above 1.1.1361). 3.8.1365 (Re, 91).[1]
  ,, , 4.2. Symon Sparo (Sparrow ?), son of John.
  ,, , 14.4. Robert, son of John, oblate.
1364, 10.10. William, son of William, de Scotia. 20.4.1377.
  ,, , 22.10. Rowland Dordane (Jordan ?), son of John, rosary-seller. 4.11.1373.
1365, 22.11. John Palmer, alias Ponfret,* (Re, 86).[1] 22.12.1387†.
1367, 27.7. John Alene.
  ,, , 27.9. John Almes, rosary-seller.
  ,, , 27.9. John Barber, son of John. 17.10.1378.
1368, 31.1. Margaret, wife of Robert de Pyne (above 4.2.1362).
1369, 6.6. Richard, son of above. 1.9.1373†.
1371, 25.5. William Mantel*, son of William. 29.5.1383.
  ,, , 25.5. Thomas*, son of Nicholas, rosary-seller. 22.12.1387.
1373, 10.8. John Elvion, son of John, rosary-seller.
  ,, , 1.9. John Thules, priest. 11.1.1376.
  ,, , 1.9. Gilbert Newman, son of William, priest. 8.4.1376.
  ,, , 1.9. Stephany, widow of Richard, son of Roger, later wife of Cola Cole (below 27.2.1399). 25.6.1408†.
  ,, , 1.9. John*, son of Robert. 11.3.1374.
  ,, , 4.11. Richard Test, son of Richard, cobbler. 24.3.1391†.
  ,, , 11.12. James, son of Robert.
  ,, , 11.12. Richard, son of Henry (above 14.4.1362). 24.2.1378.
  ,, , 11.12. Margaret, mother of above. 24.2.1378.
1374, 30.1. John Clerk, son of John, rosary-seller. 23.7.1390†.
  ,, , 21.9. Robert, son of William, a monk, *capellanus domini nostri papae et ordinis apostolici*. 8.4.1376.
  ,, , 30.9. John Champonese,* son of William, of London. 28.12.1381.
1375, 27.5. John Solomon of Salisbury. 1.6.1382.
  ,, , 27.5. Helen, wife of above. 4.7.1379.
  ,, , 31.5. John Philpot. 9.9.1375.
  ,, , 31.5. Joan, wife of above. 9.9.1375.
  ,, , 31.5. (?) John, son of Peter, alias Robin or Riccintus, builder.
  ,, , 19.6. Alice, wife of William Mantel (above 25.5.1371).
1376, 11.1. John Picarinibus (?)*, priest.
  ,, , 11.1. Thomas de Ponte*.
  ,, , 11.1. John, an Englishman. 20.4.1377.
  ,, , 25.6. Alice, maid of Robert (above 4.2.1362). 22.12.1387.
  ,, , 30.12. Helen, wife of John Clerk (above 30.1.1374). 25.3.1391.
1377, 20.4. Beatrice, daughter of John (above 11.1.1376), wife of William (above 10.10.1364).
1378, 24.2. (?) John Elicium.
  ,, , 17.10. Leona, wife of John Barber (above 27.9.1367).

[1] Re, 4 *Transactions Royal Historical Society*, 6, 73–92 (1923).

1378,	17.10.	Peter, their son.
,, ,	17.10.	William, son of Robert. 22.12.1387.
,, ,	17.10.	Felicity, his wife.
,, ,	17.10.	James Barber, son of the late John, labourer.
,, ,	17.10.	(?) Laurence, son of the late William.
,, ,	17.10.	Peter, son of John Barber (brother of above 27.9.1367).
1379,	4.7.	(?) Tutius Alene, carpenter.
,, ,	9.7.	Sybil Knyth, wife of Richard Test (above 4.11.1373). 30.8.1394.
,, ,	9.7.	Reginald Walpoll, cleric, notary, procurator general in Roman curia. 28.10.1384.
,, ,	9.7.	Roger Pannton, priest.
,, ,	9.7.	Thomas Baty, subdeacon.
,, ,	9.7.	John Brygstock.
,, ,	9.7.	John Brown, layman of the dioceses of Norwich, Lincoln, York and Canterbury.
,, ,	9.7.	John Sporier.
,, ,	9.7.	John de Hynkeleye, notary, dioc. of Lincoln.
,, ,	9.7.	Thomas Taylor.
,, ,	14.7.	Richard Posswych, alias Irlande, son of William, *domini nostri papae cursor*. 10.4.1401†.
,, ,	14.7.	Alice, wife of above, daughter of William de Ricchal. 10.4.1401.
1381,	28.12.	Thomas, son of William, of Alton.
1382,	1.6.	Master William, cobbler, *domini nostri papae cursor*.
,, ,	1.6.	Christine, wife of above.
,, ,	1.6.	M. Richard May, notary.
,, ,	1.6.	William Clerk, notary.
,, ,	1.6.	Henry Buycon, canon of Hereford.
1383,	29.5.	Alice, wife of William Richards (above 24.9.1361). 9.4.1402.
,, ,	29.5.	Palotia, their daughter.
,, ,	29.5.	Thomas Janesse.
,, ,	29.5.	D. William, son of Robert de Thrylkacld.
,, ,	29.5.	John, son of John de Buccasale.
,, ,	29.5.	Thomas, son of John Symon Elmund, priest.
,, ,	29.5.	William, son of Symon.
,, ,	29.5.	Benedict, son of Randolph.

Note.—The last five named were probably pilgrims. They appear only in John Palmer's will, made in the Hospice, and are described as 'de Anglia et nunc moram trahentes in Urbe in Regione Arenule'.

1384,	28.10.	Walter Taylor*, alias Synnind, son of Symon, cobbler, *domini nostri papae cursor*. 23.3.1405†.
1387,	22.12.	Thomas, son of John.
,, ,	22.12.	William, son of Roger.

1390,	23.7.	Rudolph, a noble, *miles Thebaldi de civitate Vectoriensi.*
,, ,	23.7.	Agnes Tayllour.
,, ,	23.7.	Cecilia Houndene.
,, ,	23.7.	John Spulier, carpenter.
,, ,	23.7.	John, son of Richard Posswych (above 14.7.1379). 1442 (232, 25).
,, ,	23.7.	Helen, daughter of William cobbler.
,, ,	23.7.	John Sellar.
,, ,	23.7.	John Carpenter.
,, ,	23.7.	Nicholas Baldor.
,, ,	23.7.	Symon and Alice Brugge.
,, ,	23.7.	Agnes Sparcha.
,, ,	23.7.	John, Bishop of Derry.
,, ,	23.7.†	Robert, son of Peter, papal penitentiary.
,, ,	23.7.	William Holderness.* 25.2.1407.†
,, ,	23.7.	John Drax, priest.
,, ,	23.7.	M. John Antingam.
,, ,	23.7.	William Facumer, priest.
,, ,	23.7.	Thomas Guldnyng, priest.
,, ,	23.7.	Thomas Legro.
,, ,	23.7.	Thomas Spaldyng.
,, ,	23.7.	David Urmutand.
1391,	1.3.	John Crosse*. 23.3.1405.
,, ,	1.3.	Philip Nelbun*.
,, ,	24.3.	William, son of William, cobbler.
,, ,	18.7.	D. Richard Yonge, *sacri palatii apostolici causarum auditor.*
,, ,	18.7.	John Teyr, procurator at the Roman curia.
,, ,	18.7.	Anthony de Sancto Tinnterno (?), rector of parish church of Hornsey, York dioc.
,, ,	18.7.	Walter Sporyer.
,, ,	18.7.	William Month, layman of Norwich dioc.
,, ,	18.7.	Richard Posswych, son of Richard (above 14.7.1379). 10.4.1401.
,, ,	18.7.	Peter Nye, priest of Wells dioc., notary.
,, ,	4.9.	Henry Bolvet, doctor of both laws, papal chaplain.
,, ,	4.9.	William, son of John, called Cuper, de Sreenbergio.
,, ,	4.9.	John Deck, priest, dioc. of Leodiensis and Bangor.
1393,	10.6.	D. John Aclinging. 27.12.1395.
1395,	3.4.	Peter Conliffe, cobbler.
,, ,	3.4.	Walter, son of John, *flastorianus.*
1396,	21.9.	David, son of John, a Welshman, *cernitor.* 5.3.1400.
,, ,	21.9.	David Griffi.
,, ,	21.9.	Adam Raynaldi.
,, ,	21.9.	William Covelle, cobbler.
,, ,	21.9.	Philip Adammi, priest.
,, ,	21.9.	John Whyte‡, citizen of London, merchant. 1.11.1404†.

1397, 6.4.   Peter (Baker), commonly called Perrinus, son of William. 7.11.1410.

,, , 6.4.   Mary, wife of above.

,, , 9.9.   Richard, alias John Goldsmith. 1406 (232, 2 v ; 15).

1399, 27.2.   Cola Cole, called Nicholas.

,, , 6.8.   D. John, son of Francis, *litterarum apostolicarum abbreviator et scriptor*. 6.5.1404.

1400, 5.3.   Mary, wife of David (above 21.9.1396).

,, , 5.3.   John Gurgemme.

1401, 25.2.   (?) Raynoldus, son of Peter, cobbler.

,, , 25.2.   (?) Jacobella, his twin sister.

,, , 6.3.   M. John Doneys*.

,, , 6.3.   John Haget (Achet). 1442 (232, 10).

,, , 10.4.   Thomas Weste.

1402, 9.4.   William Trobriogh*.

,, , 9.4.   John Brompton, cleric.

,, , 9.4.   John Grymmsby*. 1435 (232, 34 v).

,, , 9.4.   Margaret, wife of William Holderness (above 23.7.1390), later widow of Rawlins (below 25.2.1407). 25.2.1407.

1403, 8.7.   Robert, *Anglicus*.

,, , 8.7.   John Scruler.

,, , 8.7.   John Yxgoburt.

,, , 8.7.   D. Adamust [Adam of Usk], auditor.

,, , 8.7.   M. John Estcoriet (Escuret). 1406 (232, 11).

1404, 23.10.   D. Nicholas Claypoll.

,, , 23.10.   Roger Burstod, priest.

,, , 23.10.   John Kerkeby, monk.

,, , 23.10.   William, a tailor.

,, , 23.10.   Ricciarda, daughter of Peter (above 6.4.1397), later wife of John Ely (below 11.4.1428). 30.8.1445†.

,, , 23.10.   (?) John Gerrardi, *cernitor*.

1405, 23.3.   John Boyke*.

,, , 23.3.   Robert Dinie, *lartus*.

            (The following eight people are tenants of Hospice houses, mentioned in Liber 232. Folio numbers are given after their names.)

1406   D. Peter de Galfredinis. 2.

,,   The son of Peter Baker (above 6.4.1397). 23 v.

,,   Robert Donne. 2 v.

,,   Robert Kankyn. 17.

,,   M. John Gylman. 2 v.

,,   Henry Faber. 6.

,,   James Scaett. 8.

,,   (?) M. George, *phisicus*. 10.

,, , 13.1.   John Geylot (Giliocti)‡, merchant. 29.9.1406.

1406, 13.1.	William Walter‡.
„ , 13.1.	(?) John Ley. 10.8.1418.
„ , 29.7.	M. William Lovell*. 25.2.1407.
„ , 29.7.	John Thomasson, alias Palmer*. 13.12.1438.
1407, 25.2.†	Raulinus, *Anglicus*.
„ , 25.2.	John Mowter, priest.
„ , 25.2.	John Blyton, alias Lincoln.
„ 25.2.	Thomas Kyrkegat, cleric of Lincoln dioc.
1408, 14.5.	Roger Knecht (Knight)‡, priest. 16.4.1428.
„ , 25.6.	D. Philip Newton*, *capellanus Anglicus et Wallicus*. 20.8.1418.
„ , 25.6.	D. Peter de Ragonia*. 27.6.1408.
„ , 25.6.	John, son of Richard (above 6.6.1369).
1410, 7.11.	John, son of John, cobbler.
1412, 19.2.	Robert Cipeldon* (a Welshman ?).
„ , 30.11.	Philip *de Anglia*.
1415, 28.6.	John Bacwell, priest of Lincoln dioc.
1418, 10.3.	(?) Alexius Ley, son of John (above 13.1.1406).
„ , 20.8.	John Croat*.
c. 1420	M. William Swan, mentioned as past tenant in 1445 (232, 5, v).
1428, 16.4.	John Ely*‡, *domini nostri papae serviens armorum.* 24.8.1445†.
„ , 13.12.	Nicholas Beldeserton, LL.D.
„ , 13.12.	Henry Harburgh, canon of Salisbury
„ , 13.12.	M. Thomas Carpenter.
„ , 13.12.	John*, son of Henry, cleric.

(Note.—Until further notice, names are those of tenants of Hospice houses, mentioned in Liber 232. Folio numbers are given after the names.)

1431.	John Sparham*. 1.
1431–1442.	Thomas Morden*, papal penitentiary. 1 ; 19 v.; 34 v.
1431–1445.	Henry Reynolde. 6 v.
1431–1445.	John Tonor. 7 v.
1431–1445.	Henry Corffe, merchant. 7 v.
1431–1445.	John Satrapoll. 8 v.
1431–1435.	Andrew Glover. 9 v.
1431–1442.	John Godyn. 18.
1431–1435.	Andrew Holys (Holes). 19 v.
1431–1460.	Peter Belholme. 20 v.
1431–1435.	Symon Paynter. 30.
1431.	John Strete*. 34 v.
1431–1435.	D. Robert Sutton*. 9v ; 19 v ; 34 v.
1431–1435.	D. Henry Wyvell. 10.
1431–1442.	John Metus. 10.
1431–1445.	M. Thomas Chapman, LL.B. 3 r–v ; 4.
1431–1445.	John Browne. 6 ; 34 v.

1431–1445.	John Sertor. 5 ; 8 r–v.
1431–1445.	John Smyth. 15 r–v.
1431–1460.	Peter Locksmith. 9.
1434.	John Berbiton. 6 v.
1435.	Maria Powlet. 23.
1436.	Adam Moleyns*. 34 v.
c.1436.	John Burbur, and wife Catherine. 9 v.
1437.	D. Richard Sylveryn*. 34 v. 30.8.1445.
1442.	Thomas Pamator. 15 v.
1442.	Nicholas Forester. 23.
c.1442.	M. Matthew Crompe. 8 v.
,, .	Christopher Frebarke. 10.
,, .	John Selande, and wife Laura. 10.
,, .	John Pursoll (Purssell), priest. 8 v. 7.4.1452.
,, .	John Wallys (Wellis)*, canon regular of Premonstratensians. 8 v. 1445 (34 v).
1445.	Nicholas Sertor. 6 v.
,, .	John Greel. 8 v.
,, .	William Radclyff*, doctor of both laws, *domini nostri papae cubicularius*. 8 v. 22.6.1453 (17, 13).
,, .	D. Robert Clerk*. 34 v. 1466, 35.
c.1445.	John Gunyat. 25. *Scriptor et notarius in penitentiaria.* (End of entries from Liber 232).
1445, 30.8.	Richard Caniton (?), LL.D. *Cameris apostolici clericus.*
1446, 30.2.	John Sandres‡.
,, , 30.2.	William Asculo*†, *domini nostri papae serviens armorum.* 1.2.1451. (17, 10 v).
1449, 26.1.	William Stanley*‡, cleric of Lincoln dioc., *in decretis bacallarius*, notary (17, 11 r–v). 7.4.1452.
1449.	Thomas Cawadower (Caudour)*, *decretorum doctor, domini nostri papae cubicularius* (17, 5). 7.4.1452.
,, .	John Lax*, LL.D., cleric Durham dioc., canon and prebend of Laghton, York dioc. (17, 5). 1466 (232, 35).
1450.	William Fyge* (16, last page).
1451, 1.2.	Thomas Wynchecomb, priest (17, 10 v).
1451, 24.9.	Richard Thwaytes, *armiger.* (17, 2 v). 7.4.1452.
1451, 24.9.	John Kylvyngton*, *nobilis* (17, 2 v). 7.4.1452.
1452, 7.4.	William Gray*, priest, *sacrae paginae professor, domini nostri papae referendarius*, procurator of English king at Roman curia. 18.6.1453 (17, 13).
1452, 7.4.	William Darsett, LL.D. 8.12.1452 (232, 2).
,, , 7.4.	Walter Sandwych, doctor of both laws, papal penitentiary.
,, , 7.4.	William Bynchest (Bynchestere)*, layman (also 17, 7 v).
,, , 7.4.	M. Stephen Close, S.T.B. 8.12.1452.
,, , 7.4.	Baldwin Fulford, *miles.*

1453, 18.6.	Thomas Knight* (17, 13).	
1453, 22.6.	John Bellholt* (17, 13).	
1457, 3.5.	William Shirborn, LL.B. (272, 2). 25.10.1460.	
1458, 7.9.	William Shirwood*, *decretorum doctor*.	
,, , 7.9.	John Lacy*, *canonicus Sothwellie*, York dioc. 25.10.1460.	
1460, 25.10.	Robert Marshall*, priest (also 232, 35).	

(The eight following are Hospice tenants mentioned in Liber 232.)

1460.	M. John Lacy, armiger. f. 3. 9.3.1464 (272, 77).
,, .	Henry Grimond. 6.
,, .	Catherine Wyvett. 7 v.
,, .	Bartholomew Carpenter, 8 v.
,, .	John Meden, bookmaker. 10.
,, .	John Hellyng. 23.
,, .	Matthew Ansell. 25 v.
,, .	John Neyll. 30.
1461.	D. William Lax* (232, 35).
,, .	D. Nicholas Bulwiche* (232, 35).
1466, 1.2.	William Clayton*, cleric (272, 2 v ; 232, 35).
1469.	Edmund Connesburgh*, *decretorum doctor* (232, 35).
,, .	John Burton* (232, 35).
,, .	William Bountayn* (232, 35).

APPENDIX 8

CONFRATERNITY MEMBERS, 1446. LIBER 16, PASSIM.

Note.—The title on the front cover of Liber 16 is 'Liber acquittanciarum de Anglia et fratrum receptorum in Roma'. 'Liber Actorum manualis.'

It is a receipt book, drawn up in 1446 according to English dioceses. Names are those of contributors and of those who were enrolled members of the confraternity of St Thomas's, not the names of actual pilgrims to Rome. A few members were admitted '*ad consilia et suffragia*', having the right to vote at the yearly election of Hospice officials. The original MS. is not paginated : as only a few pages have writing, the numbering has been confined to these. Reading from the back of the MS. there are a few entries under the heading 'Sequuntur copie acquittanciarum de receptis per Matheum Crompe ex emolumentis Hospitalis Sancti Thome in regno Anglie'. These entries are not transcribed here : details have been taken from them to complete the list of Hospice officials in Appendix 28.

Names of brethren from the d. of Canterbury. ff. 1 r–v.

From the parish of Sutton Valens, Kent.

D. Lawrence Goldryng
Robert Donyngbery and
Isabella his wife
Robert Parke and
Benedicta his wife
John Rotyng and
Alice his wife
Richard atte Style and
his wife
John Fordman and
Agnes his wife
William Holynd and
Isabella his wife
John Rede and
Empta his wife
John Haschedowne
and Clemens his wife
Robert Sole and
Margaret his wife
Haymond Elkok and
Elizabeth his wife
William Had and

Christine his wife
Thomas Tiliatte and
Joan his wife
Thomas Turbut and
Juliana his wife
Stephen Goldbryge and
Joan his wife
William at the (?) gate and
Margery his wife
Semain Dawson and
Agnes his wife
Thomas Boneputte and
Agnes his wife
William Parke
Stephen Donyngbury
Robert Kenyugale
Mistress Alexandria Dewerey
John Alby and
Joan his wife
Nicholas Stadam
John Lombcroft
Alice Tiliatte

Parish of Great Chart, Kent.

D. Thomas Goldwell (*anno* 1538).

f. 2 r.

In primis Johannes lofthows civis Eboracensis frater hospitalis beati Thome martyris in urbe Romana qui misit ducatos auri de camera novem bolandinos x. Anno Domini m cccc lmo in partem solucionis xl. solidorum sterlingorum Anglie. quod dictus Johannes transmisit hospitali praedicto in elymosinam sed per Cambium londonijs et Bononij. de dicta summa deficiunt pecuniae in futurum, ut creditur, per eundem restituendae. Receptae fuerunt pecuniae praedicta (in) manus venerabilium Virorum Domini Joannis Diconson, Domini Willelmi Typton, Domini Johannis Wytton, presbyterorum dicta dyocesis Anno ut supra die iij mensis Julij Romae. dicta summa recepta est Romae xiij florenis de Reno et ij bol. antiquis quibus computatis per Bancarium inventum est deficere de summa sex nobilium ut praefertur.

Robertus Clay et
Agnes Vxor eius.

Oxford University

Parish of St John the Baptist

f. 3 r.

Merton College, Oxford

York.

M. John Tygur
M. Walter Hert

Parish of Rycall
John Hampsterley and
Joan his wife
John Hampsterley
Jno Hampsterley
Thomas Hampsterley
Robert Hampsterley
William Hampsterley
Robert Hampsterley
Annie Hampsterley
Margaret Hampsterley
paid ten ducats

M. Roger Kyng, Alice his mother
M. John Woode
M. John Byllyston
M. William Lynham
M. John Wade
M. Richard Longston
M. Roger Kombe
M. Richard Sawbrugh, his parents,
　　brothers and sisters (Scarbrugh?)
M. John Marsthall
M. John Werkwouth (?)
M. John Bradekay
D. John Wymarke
D. Roger Fermon and Joan his
　　mother
D. William Brygham

f. 4 r.

Winchester diocese

Parish of Waltham (*anno* 1538)
D. John Heliaris

f. 6 v.

St John's Hall

Parish of Petersfeld (*anno* 1538)
Henry Pinyns (?)

M. Edmund Mynsty (*or* : Mynsky)
Thomas Therlabye
D. Simon Loftus

f. 5 r.
Durham diocese
M. John Norman
D. John Wynston
D. Richard Forsee (ys ?)
D. John Middilton
D. John Pyrules
D. Richard Byllyngham

f. 7

Wells diocese

Thomas Dryffeld, Cambridge, of
　　the same diocese, 23rd May 1471

f. 7a.

f. 6 r.

Bath diocese

Lincoln diocese

No entry

f. 8.

Norwich diocese

Richard Brome and Elizabeth his wife

The Prioress of Tampsey
Mistress Anne Hasset
Mistress Parnell Fulmerston
Mistress Alice Cook
Mistress Elizabeth Everard   } 16th March 1492
Mistress Elizabeth Jenay
Mistress Elizabeth Norwich
Mistress Margaret Harman
Mistress Anne Bumsted

f. 9.

Salisbury diocese

No entry

Nomina fratrum receptorum in Roma de diocesi Londoniensi. f. 10.

In parochia Sti Swithuni Domina Anna quaedam uxor Roberti Tatsall mercatoris quae legavit hospitali Sancti Thomae martyris Rome ducatos sex. quos Wilhelmus Fige custos eiusdem hospitalis recepit nomine hospitali 1450 prima die julii per manus Thome Drayton familiaris dominae praedictae . . .
    . . . ducati vi
    Item de parochia Ste Mariae Bothall Thomas Scott Aldermannus Londinii Et Bertha uxor eius qui promisunt transmittere Romam hospitali praedicto annuatim durante ipsorum vita quattuor solidorum sterlingorum aut eius valorem sed nihil de praesenti solutum est pro eis . . . iiii l annuatim

    Item anno ab orbe liberato 1491 recepti fuerunt ad suffragia in fratres et sorores hospitalis Iohannes Heron London Mercator et chaterina eius uxor et thomas suus filius et elisabeth et alicia. ricardus frinson (?) dominus thomas thwaytts miles et domina alicia eius uxor. thomas elderton et alicia eius uxor. hi fratres sunt rogatu dicti Iohannis Heron dedit hospitali eodem tempore ducatos de camere quique.

f. 11.

Parish of St Edmund in Lumbardstrete

John Scarburgh
Joanna Scarburgh his wife
Joanna
George
Richard } sons and daughters of the
Alice   aforesaid John and Joanna
John
Richard Giles and his wife.

f. 11 v.
D. William Berwik
D. Stephen Paske
D. John Gaylard
D. William Patnay
D. Thomas Wryght
D. Robert Wryght
D. William Lyndesay
D. George Sortes
D. John Pyrules
D. Thomas Brodane
D. Robert White
John Chiffyn
Nicholas Marshall
D. Robert Denyse
D. John Catby
D. Thomas Smyth
William Cardomaker
Margaret his wife
D. William Wilson
Nicholas Wyfold alderman
George Lily

f. 12.
Willesden

D. William Brompton
Robert Caverlay and his wife
William Attewode
John Harryson
Dynis Skryppe

John Robert
Matilda his wife
Marjory a mother
Roger Frend
Joanna his wife
F. William Goddard junior, professor
    in theology

f. 13.
Worcester diocese

D. James Berkeley soldier and his wife
    Isabella
D. William Berkeley soldier
James Manric Thomas Isabella Margaret
    sons and daughters of the aforesaid
    William
D. Richard Warde
D. Robert Batyn
D. Thomas Kyng
John Thorpe and Margaret his wife
Richard Gleybold and Helen his wife
John Heuby and Agnes his wife
Richard Lec and Alice his wife
Thomas Nelvic and Margaret his wife
John Gryvelle and Juliana his wife

f. 13 v.
John Wakerley and Isabella his wife
D. John Horseley
Richard Ecton and Helen his wife
D. John Tempnot
D. Thomas Jamys
D. William Draper
D. Roger Grenchull
D. John Warmester
William Weley and Alice his wife
Thomas Pardon and Alice Joanna
Henry Wakefeld and Agnes
D. Henry Bolde
Thomas Walker and Agnes his wife
Symond Dawkes and Isabella his wife
Thomas Stanner and Christine his wife

Wat Jonys and Margaret his wife
Richard Lench and Alice his wife
Thomas Fyssher and Elizabeth his wife
John Born and Margaret his wife.
William Saundrys
John Thompnes
John Crevyle and Joanna his wife
Thomas Gadevych and Catherine his wife
John Halle Joanna Walter and Elizabeth
D. Richard Smyth
D. John Wode
William Tracy and Margaret his wife
D. John Gonne
Roger Orchard and Agnes his wife
D. John Stones
William Mylward and Agnes his wife
John Mowle and Matilda his wife
D. John Taunton
D. John Hylle

f. 14.
D. Thomas Avenyng
D. Thomas Lechampton
D. John Monteyn
D. Thomas Tewkysbury
D. Richard Colsborn
D. Richard Walyngton
D. Thomas Elleworth
D. John Croke
D. Robert Wakefeld
D. Thomas Saundrys
D. Thomas Drake
D. John Sodbury
D. Walter Glancefor
D. Thomas Brown
D. Thomas Lane
D. William Wyland
D. Thomas Geldber
D. Thomas Rogers

Henry Garystang and Margaret his wife
William Prelate and Joanna his wife
William Warner and Joanna his wife
Thomas Arnold and Phyllis his wife
John Hont

Thomas Chedworth and Agnes his wife
John Chedworth and Joanna his wife
Stephen Hewys and Agnes his wife
William Compton and Alice his wife
Christopher Woderobe and Agnes his
  wife
William Woderobe and Joanna his wife
William Sawyer and Joanna his wife
Thomas Nayler Joanna his wife

f. 14 v.
John Shaw and Emota
John Conyng and Agnes
John Stervy and Helen wife
William Maynard
John Mayle and Alice his wife
Thomas Wener and Alice his wife
John Leke and Juliana his wife
John Mayle and Joanna his wife
Thomas Paynter and Alice his wife
Richard Lokyer and Helen his wife
William Lokyer and his wife Alice
Richard Compton and Johanna his wife
William Jelyff and Alice his wife
Thomas Lokyer and Helen his wife
Thomas Jenkyns and Margaret his wife
Richard Grete and Agnes his wife
William Webbe and Sibyl his wife
John Gilbert
Robert Obday and Agnes his wife
Thomas Sclatter and Agnes his wife
D. John Wodland
D. Nicholas Salysbury
D. John Tuttebury
D. John Thornbury
M. John Paradyse
Nicholas Daunt and Alice his wife
John Wynter and Johanna his wife
Robert Baker and Edith his wife
Robert Hore and Agnes his wife
John Baylly and Margaret his wife
Edith Blythe
Robert Blakdon and Alice his wife
John Stylle and Margaret his wife
Johanna Cantelowe

f. 15.
Thomas Aleyn and Agnes his wife
Thomas Pakker and Alice his wife
Thomas Roger and Johanna his wife
William Golde and Johanna his wife
D. Walter Honyborn
D. John Lavnder
James Mylle and Elizabeth
Johanna Chagge
Richard Merymon and Cecilia his wife
John Hylle and Margaret
John Pakker and Christina
William Tonley and Johanna
his wife
William Syrr and Agnes
D. John Wakefeld
D. William Monmouth
D. William Cotton
D. John Borway
D. John Lucas
D. Thomas Schawle
D. David Crispy
D. Thomas Dowe
D. Maurice Evenerad
John Sharp and Elizabeth his wife
John Stanley and Johanna wife
Margaret Bolton
John Wytford and Agnes wife
John Palmer and Edith
Walter Nongoll and Isabel wife
Henry Whyte and Elizabeth wife
Thomas Broun and Johanna wife
Walter Jonys and Johanna wife

f. 15 v.
William Philip
D. Thomas Boyer
D. Thomas Welon
D. Robert Chabnor
D. John Semer soldier and Isabella wife
Richard Bayly and Helen his wife
John Montague and Agnes his wife
D. Walter Salkombe
D. Andrew Arthyr

Thomas Holeway and Johanna wife
Richard Haddon and Edith wife
William Raynes and Johanna wife
Agnes Fyler
Nicholas Long and Johanna wife
William Chester and Agnes wife
D. Thomas Mathew
Robert Jake and Elizabeth wife
Richard Walwyn and Johanna wife
John Nancotyn and Agnee his wife
David England and Johanna wife
Thomas Adene and Margaret wife
John Hony
Hans Goldsmith and Agnes wife
William Sampson and Isabella
Richard Bransby and Johanna
William Roter and Johanna wife
Thomas Sharshulle and Christina
Lewis Tapyn and Cecilia wife
John Twyford and Helen wife
D. John Lewys
William Pavy and Johanna wife
William Codyr
John Hawke
Richard Blake and Agnes wife
John Straynsham
William Walshalle and Alice his wife

f. 16.
Aucvista Petw
F. Thomas Holcote
F. John Stoke
F. James Trapstone
F. William Newport
D. Richard Lyttelton
D. John Keynsham
D. Robert Northwich
D. William Abyndon
D. Thomas Sutton
D. Thomas Pylton
D. John Exeter
M. John Galleys
D. Philip Botiller
John Efemouth and Alice wife

John Griffith and Johanna wife
Thomas Watkyn and Juliana
Thomas Assh and Elizabeth wife
John Gossh and Alice wife
Johanna Beremaker
John Davy and Johanna wife
M. John Garland
D. John Oldbury
D. John Carpynter
D. John Heyhamstede
D. John Rawlyns
D. Thomas Akerton
D. William Grene
D. John Elyoth
D. Thomas Colsey
D. William Hoke
D. John Frampton
D. John Deveroe

f. 16 v.
D. Robert Brystowe
D. Robert Hereford
D. William Grove
D. John Baker
D. John Laurens
D. William Philip
D. William West
D. William Tottdus
D. Richard Curteys
D. Henry Predy
D. Richard Wynne
D. William Aston
D. William Evysham
D. John Roger
D. Richard Wynch
D. John Baker
D. William Solas
D. William Halle
William Gyfforth and Margaret wife
D. Nicholas Radland
D. John Porter
M. John Gerves

D. John Permynter
D. John Hylle
D. William Gylbert
D. Richard Barett
D. John Walker
M. John Rows
D. John Byotre
John Marteyn and Agnes his wife
Thomas Kerber and Margaret
Thomas Estope and Margaret wife

f. 17.
John Mayle and Alice wife
William Rudyng
John Donce and Emma wife
William Ford and Alice his wife
John Brovoster and Johanna his wife
Henry Lannasdale
Galford Kaws and Margaret his wife
Thomas Symond and Matilda his wife
John Veel and Alice his wife
D. William Tyler
John Hickys and Helen his wife
Thomas Shepard and Johanna his wife
John Bay and Helen
William Welynton and Agnes his wife
D. John Wyntour
Walter Hawker and Sibyl his wife
John Eycote and Johanna his wife
D. William Wellys
William Clerk and Edith his wife
D. John Wynch
John May and Alice his wife
D. Thomas Pery
William Churchford and Isabel his wife
Robert Benet and Christine his wife
John Asshewalle and Margaret his wife
John Boke
John Botyler and Margaret his wife
D. John Tetbury
D. Thomas Steward
D. William Frebarn

F

f. 17 v.
William Smart and Alice his wife
D. John Roger
Thomas Derehurst and Anne his wife
John Trye and Johanna his wife
D. John Andrew
Robert Bechamp and Johanna wife
Richard Lytylle and Johanna his wife
John Philip and Margaret his wife
D. John Smyth
William Nest and Margaret his wife
Robert Gamelle and Alice his wife
D. John Wodeward
John Fornor and Agnes his wife
John Toky and Marion his wife
John Langher and Alice his wife
D. John Selston
D. William Elys
William Hambury and Christine his
    wife
D. Thomas Lysh
Thomas Mylleward and Agnes his wife
William Drayton and Grace his wife
Thomas Lycherd
Humfrey Saloway
D. Thomas Comley
D. Reginald Cascott
Roger Parker and Juliana
D. Richard Walker
Thomas Perk and Margaret
D. William Yate
John Decon and Johanna
William Decon Burga
F. William Bromyerd
F. John Howell
F. Hugh Fabry
John Beley
William and Agnes parents
Laurence Kech and Margaret
Richard Mychell and Matilda
D. Thomas Byspe
Thomas Laurans and Elizabeth
Margaret Laurans and
daughter of the said
Domina Mary

Thomas Symson
Roger Allebury
D. Richard Freman
Thomas Betrowce and Margaret wife
D. Richard Cowper
D. Robert Rendour

f. 18.
D. John Compton
D. Thomas Massing
Richard Wych & Edith his wife
D. Henry Amys
D. Thomas Ysok
John Cokkys
D. Roger Wheler
D. John Kynsege
D. Thomas Bodylech
William Estyngthon and Joanna his wife
William Stok and Alice his wife
D. Edmund Dovehurst
D. Thomas Asshby
Thomas Helleford and Margaret his wife
Thomas Colard and Margery his wife
D. John Spenser
Richard Kusshedon and Margaret his
    wife
Thomas Mase and Agnes his wife
Richard Personnys and Alice his wife
D. Richard Steward
D. Nicholas Whete
D. Maurice Berkeley soldier & Iora wife
Nicholas Sheldon and Elizabeth his wife
William Vereby and Johanna his wife
Henry Smith
John Wade and Katherine his wife
D. Walter Assheton
D. John Blake
Thomas Bayly and Alionore his wife
John Cramp and Elizabeth his wife
D. Walter Rusgreve
William Wattis and Johanna
Will Walker Ysabel
D. John Wytford
D. Nicholas Ypotone
John Parker Ysabel

D. Roger Horsman
D. Robert Hereford
John Baylly master
Roger Blunte Elizabeth
Thomas Blout Anna
Nicholas Blout master
Reginald ap Evan
D. Thomas Horset
Richard Wallys master
Nicholas Smyth and Denise
John Smyth
Will Morley kt.
John Vurnell
John Pertrych Alice
John Botyller
Thomas Wydington
Walter Marteley Isabel
Walter Yuggram
Richard Marchant Johanna
Roger Pey and Johanna wife
Rys ap David
John Hunt
John Stapull Katherine
John Lyngen Alice
John Ardyng Johanna
D. Hugh Mortymer soldier
John Adamys Isabel

f. 18 v.
John Longdon
D. William Lane
Thomas Pawussote and Margaret wife
Thomas Brassy and Helen his wife
D. Richard Cope
D. Richard May and Johanna mother
John Ywys
D. Thomas Stawnton
Henry Clyfford and Elizabeth his wife
Galford Holleford & Alice his wife
John Stawr and Elizabeth his wife
William Yate and Elizabeth his sister
John Nytor
D. Richard Jenys
D. William Colyvyr
Richard Venables and Johanna his wife
Thomad Framlode and Johanna his wife

Master William Bedenham
John Davy and Isabel his wife
Agnes Baker
Johanna Badam and Alice his wife
John Stow and Alice his wife
Robert Wolworth and Matilda his wife
Henry Pyland and Edith
D. Stephen Laterey
John Hedley and Katherine his wife
Edmund Blount and Margaret his wife
D. John Selwyn
D. John Sparhawk
D. Thomas Baker
Richard Kusselle and Sibyl
William Carter and
    Margaret wife
D. Henry Periton
D. John Herton
D. Thomas Juno
D. Walter Toley
Stephen Fissher and
    Alice wife
Thomas Parker and Alice wife
D. Robert Pery
Walter Frensh & Johanna wife
Richard Smyth & Johanna wife
Thomas Arle and Alice wife
Thomas Bayly and
    Agnes wife
D. John Derby
D. David Rackeway
D. John Combar
D. John Fylde
D. Stephen Garbod
John Hunt
D. Richard Hunte
D. John Monke
Robert Monke & Agnes wife
D. Hugh Roger

f. 19.
Nicholas Poymer & Elizabeth wife
Moryse Denyse & Alice his wife
John Botiller and Margery wife
John Clerk & Agnes wife
Thomas Poynz and Joyce wife

D. Robert Bowlys
D. Henry Newland
D. Nicholas Sukkeley
D. John Lech
D. Richard Morton
D. Walter Tuttebury
D. John Stretford
D. Thomas Sebroke
D. John Grafton
D. John Orchard
D. Richard Poole
D. John Studmore
D. John Standissh
D. Adam Grene
D. Richard Boteler
D. Robert Hylley
Thomas Wener
D. John Wener
D. John Weler
F. Robert Talmer
F. Richard Gilbert
F. Thomas Fleter
D. Charlys
D. Thomas Romondeby
D. Thomas Hewlot
D. John Meryk
Hugh Lyndesay & Elizabeth
Denis Iremonger & Marion
John Porter and Alice
John Wellys and Isabel
Richard Palmer
Thomas Wykyng and Agnes
Margaret Corbette
D. Richard Sondylle
Henry Tayllour Alice Herlyston
Davyd ap Coly ale Radnore
John ap Coly
William Lucy & Helen wife
Agnes Whyte
Robery Newcombe & Agnes
D. John Dekyn
D. John Pynk
William Sambache & Alice
William Hylle & Elizabeth
John Hardyng & Helen
Richard Baldwyn & Margery

Thomas Best & Agnes
Richard Perkyng & Helen//Thomas
    George & Alice
Nicholas George & Alice//
William Austen & Elizabeth
D. Richard Wynchekombe

f. 19 v.
F. John Weke
D. William Sodbery
D. Roger Colme
Thomas Brygge
Henry Deed & Alice wife
John Heskyns & Martina wife
Will Newman & Alice
Will Beneson & Elizabeth
Nicholas Longley & Agnes
Thomas Hyot & Margaret
William Pery & Ida wife
John Morys & Joanna wife
Walter Wyse & Joanna wife
Richard Faver & Marion wife
Richard Tuby & Margaret wife
Robert Spuriour & Katherine wife
David Hopkyns & Anicia wife
William Woddward & Anicia wife
Thomas Horsley & Margaret wife
Thomas Hunte & Margaret wife
Richard Fletcher & Alice wife
John Walsh & Agnes wife
William Bunge & Margery wife
William Alone
Margery Wolaston
Richard Page & Isabella wife
Hugh Goldsmyth & Margaret
William Hope & Johanna
Simon Boyer & Margery wife
John Elyot & Margery
Galford Baker & Cecilia
John Kent & Margery wife
D. Richard Julyane
Robert Barbour & Kosa wife
Margaret Dalby
Richard Coke & Edith
Thomas Peke & Helen
John Herryes & Margaret

Elizabeth Fisher
Richard Defford & Matilda
John Lukenour
Phineas Mungery & Johanna
William Hertland & Sibyl
John Felys & Margery
John Hobby & Agnes
M. Richard Playstow
Laurence Dalemold
Walter & Esibel
William Collynt & Margery
Thomas Colyns & Juliana
D. Simond Brogh
John Vampage and Elizabeth
D. Thomas Staunton
D. John Boklond
D. Thomas Bydford
D. Thomas Maynard
John Crabbe & Alice
Margaret Bleswod
Thomas Charlys & Johanna
D. William Norton
D. Richard Folchardy
D. John Gylford
D. Thomas Mylle
John Folwell & Agnes
D. John Palmer
D. John Salmon
John Balbushe & Elizabeth
John Higford & Matilda

f. 20.
John Hannys & Agnes
D. Robert Bylle
D. Thomas Leveot
D. John Bromwich
D. Thomas Gilberd
D. Thomas Bromwich
D. Richard Harcot
Simon Clare & Isabel wife
Hugh Deken & Alice wife
William Wolaston
Johanna Burdedde
John Pachet & Margaret
Richard Drencher & Margery

John Cole & Elizabeth
Thomas Dollys & Alice wife
D. John Banyster
Thomas Fermour
D. John Saleyway
John Basset & Margaret
Henry Longby
John Newton & Matilda wife
Richard Hampton
D. Will Wele
D. Philip Gyon
Thomas Roger & Agnes wife
John Shepward & Katherine
Richard Alberton & Denise
John Troyt
John Broun & Elizabeth
Roger Peryn & Johanna wife
John Wych
D. Robert London
Robert Colmon & Alice
Will Moret & Agnes
Will Clerk & Johanna
Thomas Uley & Marion
Thomas Grefeth & Edith
Dna Johanna Walys
D. Thomas Tonworth
D. William Pomfret
D. Stephen Russell
D. Richard Ferthing
D. Richard Kingesbury
D. Richard Long
John Robyns and Margaret
John Hokke & Agnes wife
Richard Dekyn & Alice
John Bound & Margery wife
John Shelton & Alice wife
William Wodward & Isabel
Richard Ossenay & Agnes wife
Thomas Sweney & Alice wife
Robert Sheldeslay & Agnes wife
Thomas Wesbury & Sibyl wife
Dna Margaret Baker
D. Elizabeth Stanshaw
Thomas Bache & Agnes wife
John Bradford & Alice wife
D. Thomas Shiphey

D. John Gode
D. Thomas Ede
John Holdon & Christine
Will Saundrys & Elizabeth
John Jelyff & Matilda wife
D. Thomas Vener
John Hayward & Alice
D. John Monmouth
Robert Bentham & Alice
John Danyell & Agnes
D. Thomas Francombe
D. Roger Colyar

f. 20 v.
Robert Albury & Agnes his wife
John Barbour & Isabel
Alice Wesbury
Thomas Partrich
Thomas Newton
Christine Webbe
Robert Poleyn & Margery
John Arche & Edith
D. Nicholas Colmon
D. William Clerk
John Malvern priest
D. John Benet
D. John Lye
D. Roger Holt
D. Richard Lech
Simond Hanley & Katherine
Maurice Waterdene & Agnes wife
Richard Hygdon & Agnes wife
John Hebawde & Elizabeth
D. John Blake
D. John Adamns
Thomas Dynelay & Margery
D. John Hawkyns
D. John Cosnette
Nicholas Jefford & Margery wife
D. William Mere
Henry Follys & Anicia wife
D. Richard Rollys
D. John Wyky
D. Henry Clyffton
D. William Twynnyng

D. John Parcyvalle
D. John Wych
D. John Stoke
D. John Tamworth
Richard Mede & Agnes wife
Edward Tailor frater,
ad concilia et suffragia.
D. Thomas Pery
John Twyfyll & Alice wife
D. John Cardygan
D. William Waryng
D. Thomas North
D. Richard Bradford
D. John Wodeward
D. John Glastynbury
Robert Were & Alice wife
David Delby & Johanna wife
Hamond Husbolston & Johanna
D. Richard Tame
D. John Scotton
Will Scotton & Elizabeth
D. John Cros
D. John Beynam
D. William Demour
D. John Knyght
Roger Poleyn & Agnes wife
D. Thomas Pope
D. John Fythwaren
D. John Chewe
D. John Sampson
Laurence Cros & Alice
D. John Arveys
D. Mylys Jon
D. John Reglyn
Robert Stormy & Helen wife
Nicholas Poynz & Elizabeth
D. John Wath
Thomas Mylle & Margery
D. John Wyke
D. Robert Hereford
D. William Rothewell
D. William Hedy
John Cassy & Elizabeth
Richard Broke
D. Richard Hylonde. May 1467,
ad suffragia et consilia

Dioceses of Exeter, Menevia, Carlisle, Rochester, Bangor and St Asaph (ff. 21, 23, 26–28, 30).

No entry

f. 22.
Lichfield diocese
Ralph Lygh
Robert Worth (*anno* 1466), *ad suffragia et consilia.*

f. 24.
Hereford diocese
Richard Pede, *decretorum doctor*, canon of Hereford

f. 25.
Chicester diocese
First, Reverend in Xt Father Adam Moleyns, bishop of Chicester, formerly camerarius and auditor and always protector of this Hospice. Also D. Laurence Wynchilsey, prior of Mychylham, canon of the city of St Augustine

f. 29.
Llandaff diocese

John Davy
Thomas Lewys of Wales, 23rd May 1471

THE HOSPICE OF ST EDMUND IN TRASTEVERE

On crossing the modern Ponte Garibaldi one looks upon the busy and unattractive square at the head of the Viale di Trastevere. The scene has its redeeming features, however: on the right is the twelfth-century campanile of the church of San Crisogono rising behind a few roadside plane trees, and on the left the restored mediaeval tower of the Palazzo degli Anguillara, generally known as the Casa di Dante. Trastevere used to boast many of these towers. Even today the area retains several reminders of its mediaeval past.

This square in front of the church of San Crisogono was once the site of a hospice dedicated to St Chrysogonus, later to be the English Hospice of St Edmund. St Edmund was the king of East Anglia who was put to death by the Danes in 870 and was thenceforth honoured as a martyr. In England he assumed a position with St Thomas of Canterbury and St Edward the Confessor as a great national saint. Over his shrine, which became one of the great centres of pilgrimage, was built an abbey, second only to that of Westminster in wealth and importance. This foundation, however, was more humble. At the corner of the modern Viale di Trastevere and the Via dei Genovesi there now stands a block of flats and a cinema. Here stood the mediaeval Hospice of St Edmund.

FOUNDATION

We know practically nothing of the history of the Hospice before the year 1396. It had been in existence for forty years or more, offering accommodation to the *pauperes Christi* under the care of the chapter of the church of San Crisogono, which owned the buildings. On 23rd October 1396 John Whyte, a London merchant, appeared before the canons solemnly assembled in choir and put his case to them. The Hospice was falling into disrepair, and Whyte was anxious to offer his services and his money for the rebuilding and extension of the premises. He did not wish to do this without the approval of the canons, nor had he any intention of prejudicing the rights of the poor who were using the Hospice ; on the contrary, it was for their sake and for the love of Christ that he was making the offer. The canons granted his request and gave the lease *in perpetuo* to Whyte and his heirs, though they retained certain rights. The property was not to be sold or put to any other use without their consent. It was to be dedicated to St Chrysogonus, and a picture of the saint was to be painted and placed in the Hospice. Whyte was to pay them 12 denarios a year on the feast of St Chrysogonus, but should he fail in this, he and his successors were not thereby deprived of the possession. To ensure the safe transfer of the property, the canons appointed one of their number, Nicholas Nelli, as procurator. Nelli had already undertaken repairs on the building some years previously, and so he would be the obvious choice for this work. He was to invest Whyte with the property in the name of the chapter.[1]

This intervention by Whyte made it possible for the Hospice to continue its work. As at the Hospice of St Thomas, the institution was supervised by a confraternity, and we have a list of its members in an account book of 1449.[2] At first the members were mainly laymen or clerics of modest description, but these later gave way to major clerics, university graduates, or even diplomats, while a few soldiers are mentioned. All but two of the members are English or Welsh, and so it is no surprise to see the Hospice referred to in 1406 as '*hospitalis Anglicorum*',[3] though its usual designation in the early years is simply 'the

---

[1] *Memb.* 23.10.1396 ; App. 9, p. 92.
[2] *Lib.* 272, ff. 1–2.
[3] *Memb.* 13.1.1406.

Hospice of St Chrysogonus'. At the head of the list of confraternity members, four Englishmen are named as the 'founders' of the Hospice, John Whyte, Peter Baker,[4] Roger Knecht,[5] and John Geylot.[6] All of these figure prominently in the early deeds, but not in a way that justifies the reference to them as the four 'founders' of the Hospice : indeed, the documents seem to indicate that a Roman notary, Paul Stocco, was second only to Whyte in importance, while a German known as Joannes Petri Theotonicus was apparently in charge of the Hospice in 1404, before Knecht and Geylot appeared on the scene. The 1449 list mentions Stocco among the first confraternity members, but does not refer to Theotonicus at all. The other non-English *confrater* mentioned in the list is a Roman doctor of laws, Nicholas Bondy.

Thus it is difficult to see exactly how far the Hospice was under English control in the first decades of the fifteenth century, and there is no clear evidence to settle the question whether it was used mainly for English pilgrims ; certainly this does not appear to have been the intention of the chapter of San Crisogono when it gave the property to Whyte. Two seventeenth-century writers suggest that the Hospice was used for sailors :

'*Eodem fere tempore mercator quidam Anglicus Parvum quiddam et separatum hospitium nautis extruxit in regione Transtiberina.*'[7]

'*Oltre al sudetto Spedale (di S. Toma Cantuariense) ne fu istituto uno in Trastevere . . . ad uso e benefizio in particulare dei Mercanti Inglesi, e Marinari . . .*'[8]

Fr Rope, in his brief history, makes a similar suggestion. He saw the possibility of its use by all who came by water.[9] The Hospice was indeed conveniently situated with regard to the port, which was a little farther downstream in the region of Santa Maria in Cosmedin. Further, Whyte was a merchant and so were one or two other members of the confraternity

[4] Probably the same as the Petrus Guilelmi, commonly known as Perrinus, who occurs so frequently in the early *Membrana* and who is said to have a wife Maria (e.g. 6.4.1397) and a daughter Ricciarda (23.10.1404) : this tallies with the evidence of the account book. He is described sometimes as French (13.1.1406)—the account book refers to him as 'Gallicus'—but more usually as English (29.9.1406).

[5] Almost certainly the Roger Kuyht of *Memb.* 14.5.1408, also referred to in *Memb.* 16.9.1410 as Rogerio Bukuyght, a camerarius and administrator of the Hospice of St Chrysogonus.

[6] Joannes Giliocti, an English merchant.

[7] Amydenus, *De Pietate Romana*, Romae 1625, p. 30.

[8] Piazza, *Enserolagio Romano, ovvero delle Opere Pie di Roma*, 1699, p. 81.

[9] Rope, *The Schola Saxonum, the Hospice, and the English College in Rome*, Rome 1951, p. 22.

about that time. However, there is nothing in contemporary documents to support this theory.[10]

In 1397 Whyte had occasion to return to England. This seems to have been for a period of two years. A deed dated 22nd April 1397 was drawn up in which the revenue of the house in the Arenula district, which had presumably been his home, was made over to the Hospice. It seems fairly certain that this was the house that in future years was to prove a principal source of income for the Hospice. It was eventually sold and demolished to make room for the present Palazzo Farnese. The deed shows the importance of the chapter of San Crisogono, for the arrangement is subject to its approval and the Hospice of St Thomas is named as an alternative beneficiary. Furthermore, the Hospice itself is here described as '. . . *hospitali Ecclesiae sancti grisogoni*'.[11]

In 1401 a new house was bought,[12] and two years later a vineyard beyond Santa Maria del Popolo.[13] In 1406 about 100 ducats were spent on property, and later the same year some houses in Trastevere were bought for 100 florins from Stephen Guarnery,[14] who was in fact the source of most of the property in Trastevere, by purchase or gift.[15] Property contiguous to the Hospice was gradually accumulated; on 1st January 1404 Whyte bought a house for 70 florins,[16] and in 1408 further houses in the same block were acquired.[17]

JOHN WHYTE'S WILL

John Whyte made his will in his own Hospice on 23rd October 1404, just eight years after his meeting with the canons.[18] He is described as '*infirmus corpore, sanus tamen*

[10] It is interesting to note two allusions by W. J. D. Croke (*Dublin Review*, 1904): '. . . another Hospital, generally believed to have been called that of St Edmund the King, and to have been instituted for the benefit of English mariners. My examination of the original documents has rendered a different account' (p. 274, note). 'The situation of St Edmund's leaves little doubt that, in reality, if not in the purpose of its founders, as has been believed hitherto, it was to English seafarers in Rome the principal asylum. Many English came by sea . . .' (p. 292, note).

[11] *Memb.* 22.4.1397.

[12] *Memb.* 25.2.1401.

[13] *Memb.* 17.12.1403.

[14] *Memb.* 29.9.1406.

[15] *Lib.* 272, f. 9 r.

[16] *Memb.* 1.1.1404.

[17] *Memb.* 14.5.1408.

[18] *Memb.* 23.10.1404.

mente', and though this might seem to be a merely legal expression, it seems likely that he died within nine days of making the will, for in a deed of 1st November 1404 the officials of the Hospice of St Thomas petitioned for the possession of a property which Whyte had previously given them, though he had retained the income.[19] Gasquet[20] claims that Whyte was custos of St Thomas's in 1405 and that he died in that year, but I can find nothing to support this.

Whyte was a man of some wealth and his will suggests that he had no natural heirs. We have seen that he had already spent a great deal on the acquisition of property for the Hospice, and in his will he leaves all his goods to its chief officials, Paul Stocco, Perrinus (Peter Baker), and John Theotonicus, for the use and maintenance of the premises, insisting that they should be repaired and enlarged and that they should continue to be used as a hospice.

The will continues with various personal bequests and records Whyte's desire to be buried in the church of San Crisogono, though we cannot discover whether this wish was fulfilled. It is noteworthy that the Hospice of St Thomas does not occur among the legatees : indeed, Whyte points out that this Hospice owes him fifty ducats, and insists that the money be reclaimed, along with various other debts. This may seem surprising in view of the close connection that existed later between the two English institutions. Gasquet[21] wanted to extend this connection back to the foundation of St Chrysogonus's, but this seems most unlikely. On his hypothesis we should expect to see more signs of English influence in the early years. Further, the fact that three houses adjacent to St Thomas's belonged to St Chrysogonus's[22] is an indication that the two were entirely separate. This does not imply, however, that they were not on friendly terms. We have referred to a property given to St Thomas's by Whyte himself,[23] and in 1410 some business concerning St Chrysogonus's Hospice was transacted in St Thomas's and witnessed by an official of the latter Hospice.[24]

Towards the end of the will Whyte deals with the repair of a house in the Via dei Genovesi next to the Hospice and its

---

[19] *Memb.* 1.11.1404.
[20] Gasquet, *A History of the Venerable English College, Rome*, London 1920, pp. 32–33.
[21] Ibid., p. 32.
[22] *Memb.* 13.1.1406.
[23] Cf. sup., footnote 19.
[24] *Memb.* 16.9.1410.

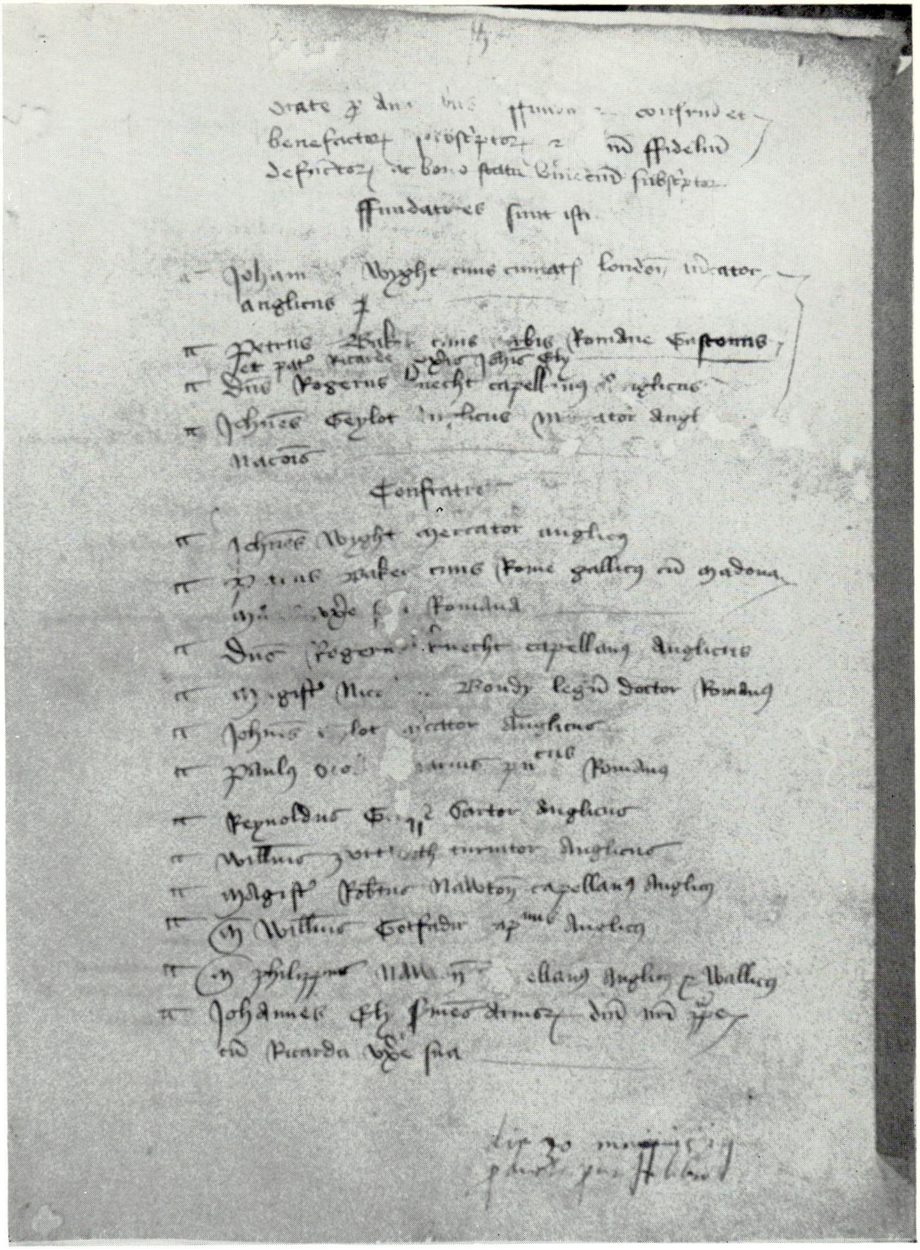

Founders and Members of St Edmund's

Page heading in the account-book of St Edmund's

Union of the two English Hospices

conversion into a chapel, in which the Mass and other divine offices are to be celebrated for the edification of the *pauperes Christi*. Whyte had bought the house on 1st January 1404 and had already begun the work of adaptation. He leaves the house to the three Hospice officials and orders that the chapel be completed and provided with everything necessary for the celebration of the sacred functions, and also that it should be decorated with pictures of the saints.

Gasquet[25] suggests that the erection of the chapel was the occasion for the change of the name of the Hospice to that of St Edmund's, and it has even been indicated that the dedication to St Edmund took place during Whyte's lifetime.[26] But the only reference to a dedication in the will gives the rather general phrase, '*ad laudem et honorem omnipotentis dei et gloriossime virginis marie et omnium sanctorum et sanctarum dei*'. An inventory of 1449[27] mentions a picture of St Edmund which was venerated in the chapel, but this reference comes after an item said to be '*in latere capelle*', which suggests that the picture was not in a prominent position. The first mention of St Edmund in the name of the Hospice appears in 1445, after Our Lady and St Chrysogonus, though the deed adds, '*hospitali sancti Edmundi Anglicorum vulgariter nuncupato*'.[28] The chapel, however, is not explicitly called the chapel of St Edmund until the seventeenth century.[29]

PROPERTY AND INCOME

It is clear that we have only scanty material for our history up to 1449, but the account book begun in that year[30] gives us a clear picture of the state of the Hospice. The institution was now quite definitely English, and it does not appear that the chapter of San Crisogono took any great interest in its affairs.

It would be a mistake to suggest, as some recent writers seem to do, that the Hospice of St Edmund was richly endowed : its wealth was meagre compared with that of St Thomas's

[25] Op cit., p. 35.
[26] Cf. Parks, *The English Traveler to Italy*, Rome 1954, I, 359.
[27] *Lib.* 272, f. 4 r.
[28] *Memb.* 24.8.1445.
[29] *Lib.* 351, f. 78.
[30] *Lib.* 272.

some years later. Yet its income was constant, and commitments seem to have been negligible. The property from which practically all the income was derived had changed little since the days of Whyte. Thus in 1449 there were nine houses and three vineyards, one of which was unproductive and lying in ruins.[31] The next decade saw the acquisition of one or two more houses.

The large house in the Arenula district which seems to have been Whyte's home was the main source of income. This should have realised sixty ducats a year. Among the tenants we find the names of one or two illustrious people, such as William Grey, king's proctor, who occupied the house for six months in 1446.[32] The house was valuable and represented a large part of the income of the Hospice ; it must have been frustrating that it so seldom produced a full rent. From 4th August 1445 until 1st May 1446, it was occupied by the archbishop of Benevento, who was charged no rent because of the help he had given in a recent lawsuit.[33] Andrew de Phano, who succeeded Grey as tenant, was a member of the papal court and is described as a *scutifer*. The papal court was absent from Rome for some time during 1449 and de Phano made a claim for a deduction in his rent according to the pope's instructions to all his courtiers.[34] Later, the same house was occupied by Nicholas Upton until he conveniently vanished in 1452 without paying his rent : the proceeds from the seizure of his belongings were not sufficient to cover the debt.[35]

Property realised about eighty ducats annually. In 1451 the Hospice had 362 ducats to its credit.[36] This included 200 ducats lent to the Hospice of St Thomas the previous year to assist building operations there.[37] The sum was to have been repaid a few months later but after some years the debt was still recorded.[38] A further 100 ducats was put into Grey's hands for safe keeping.[39] Nine and sometimes eleven ducats yearly came from the sale of wine to the Hospice of St Thomas.[40]

As against this income expenditure was low and the sole commitments seem to have been the repair of property and the

[31] Ibid., ff. 8 r–9 v.
[32] Ibid., f. 8 r.
[33] Ibid., f. 14 r.
[34] Ibid., f. 8 r ; f. 24 r.
[35] Ibid., f. 67 r.
[36] Ibid., f. 56.
[37] Ibid., f. 40 r.
[38] Ibid., f. 61 r.
[39] Ibid., f. 52 r.
[40] Ibid., f. 18 r.

payment of employees. No income or expenditure is recorded in connection with pilgrims, but one should not read too much into this fact as such items would be recorded in a separate book, which has not survived. What is worthy of attention, however, is the fact that no expenditure balanced the income which steadily accumulated over the years. The only indications of pilgrims before 1466 are the death of a pilgrim in 1457,[41] the burial of three people in 1458 and the fact that mattresses were repaired in the same year.[42] On the other hand, the inventory of 1449 speaks of about eighteen beds throughout the Hospice, and of these about a third were broken.[43]

GOVERNMENT AND UNION

The Hospice was under the control of the confraternity, but it was administered by a custos and two camerarii, elected annually, and by a procurator. Each year two auditors were appointed to examine the accounts of these various officials.

The annual meetings usually began with the admission of new members : it was not uncommon for these to constitute the majority of those present, as the English community in Rome was very fluid and it was exceptional for a person to remain in Rome for any great length of time. As one would expect, most of the members were also members of the confraternity of St Thomas ; thus the union with the Hospice of St Thomas, which was accomplished in 1464, would seem to be no more than a recognition of a situation that had existed for some years.

At the confraternity meeting in 1457 a move was made towards this amalgamation of the two Hospices. The members present were John Lax and Robert Thornton. The meeting began with the admission of Thomas Burgh, Robert Mason, William Shirborn, and William Holdern as new members. While approving of the old arrangement of two Hospices run independently, they provided for circumstances in which union would be to the greater advantage of both Hospices. In that

41 Ibid., f. 75 r.
42 Ibid., f. 7 r.
43 Ibid., ff. 4 v–5 r.

case the two Hospices were to be governed by the same officials.[44]

Five members were present when the confraternity meeting opened on 9th March 1464, and three days later, on 12th March, the two Hospices were united. The new arrangement was that the two Hospices should retain their own confraternities and that these should continue to function separately. When the new custos and camerarii were elected by the confraternity of St Thomas, the confraternity of St Edmund was to elect the same officials in its Hospice. Furthermore, it was arranged that a man and his wife should be installed as caretakers at St Edmund's. The confraternity expressly ruled at this meeting that these caretakers were not to be Scots or of any other nation unfriendly to the King of England.[45]

SUBSEQUENT HISTORY

In the years that followed the union with the Hospice of St Thomas, St Edmund's lost any importance that it might have had previously. It is not clear for what purpose it was now used. Gradwell said that it acted as an infirmary for the greater Hospice.[46] I have found no evidence for this. It can only be assumed that the Hospice was used to accommodate pilgrims, like the sister establishment. In 1530 a woman was appointed as caretaker and instructed to admit English pilgrims, who were to receive three nights' hospitality.[47]

The confraternity of St Edmund continued to admit new members but this was now a mere formality. Members of the confraternity of St Thomas were automatically admitted to that of St Edmund on payment of an extra ducat.[48] As was provided for at the union of the Hospices, the government was usually in the hands of the officials of St Thomas's. We do know of some exceptions to this rule, however. On occasions, separate custodes were appointed : this may mean that the Hospice was in full use.[49] Chaplains were appointed to serve

---

[44] Ibid., f. 2 r : cf. Appendix 10, pp. 96–7.
[45] Ibid., ff. 77 r–v : cf. Appendix 11, p. 98.
[46] Z. 68, f. 64 v. 'The Hospital of St Edmund besides having care of the English when sick . . .'
[47] *Memb.* 24.4.1530.
[48] E.g. admission of John Whitby. *Lib.* 17, f. 20 v.
[49] John Borobrigg who was also chaplain of both Hospices. *Memb.* 3.5.1523. William Tracy was appointed custos for life. *Memb.* 11.6.1528.

St Edmund's. In 1510, for example, Henry Story held this position and received sixteen ducats annually.[50] With the Reformation the pilgrim traffic from England decreased, so that there was no longer any need for two national Hospices, and St Edmund's ceased to exist as such.

Later, a Roman Archconfraternity of Charity obtained the lease of St Edmund's from the English College, the successor of the old Hospice of St Thomas.[51] This period is hardly our concern, as the Hospice was now maintained for the benefit of Italians. A pilgrim book begun on 1st January 1615 is written in Italian and the names are undoubtedly Italian.[52] It would seem, however, that the chapel of St Edmund was kept open and served by the English College until 1664, when permission was granted for all obligations of Masses at St Edmund's to be transferred to the high altar of the English College church. The old chapel was then closed down.[53]

In 1817 Dr Gradwell returned from England to prepare for the reopening of the English College, which had been forced into exile by the French Revolution. He obviously took some interest in the history of the institutions which preceded the College. The old Hospice building was still standing and he described it as spacious. However, of the church he wrote :

'The church of the original hospital of St Edmund is still visible. The door is No. 22 Via dei Genovesi, in the parish of St Chrysogonus. The picture of St Edmund is still discernible over the door, in fresco. There are arms as follows sculptured on the sill [illustration on right] : in the inside there is a mark where the altar stood. The church was never noble or splendid.'[54]

[50] *Lib.* 13, f. 43 r.

[51] Gasquet speaks of a small tablet to be seen on the site :
'*Domus sub directo dominio Collegii Anglorum Urbis et perpetua locatione Archiconfraternitatis Charitatis Urbis. Anno MDCII Diae XV Octobris.*' Op. cit., p. 35.

[52] *Lib.* 273.

[53] *Lib. Instr.* 9, 29th May 1664.
See also the tablet in the sacristy of the English College :
'*Decreto S. Congregationis Visitationis Apostolicae Edito die xxix Maij MDCLXIV Oratorium S. Edmundi Regis Angliae Transtyberim olim positum suppressum fuit et obligatio illic celebrandi Missas ad summum huius templi altare translata aliis omnibus in pristino suo vigore iuxta mentem S.mam Gregorii XIII permanentibus.*'

[54] Z. 68, f. 77.

Today all that remains to the memory of this Hospice in Trastevere is the altarpiece of the College church, which depicts the Trinity with two saints kneeling below. One is St Thomas of Canterbury, the other St Edmund, King and Martyr. Even this was thought during the last century to be St Edward the Confessor. Such is the oblivion that could overcome a saint known throughout mediaeval Europe. It would be a pity if the Hospice dedicated to him should share the same neglect.

JOSEPH IBBETT.

APPENDIX 9

EXTRACTS FROM THE DEED OF LEASE OF THE HOSPICE OF SAINT CHRYSOGONUS

23RD OCTOBER 1396

In nomine domini amen. Anno domini millesimo CCC LXXXXVI pontificatus domini Bonifatii pape noni, indictione quinta mensis octobris die XXIII, in presentia mei notarii et testium infrascriptorum ad hoc specialiter vocatorum et rogatorum, constitutorum personaliter, discretus vir Johannes Wicht civis Londoniensis de Anglia coram venerabilibus viris domino Cecchi Malgion canonico ecclesie sancti Grisogoni de Regione Transtiberis reverendi in Christo patris et domini domini Johannis Panelle archiepiscopi . . . cui ecclesia sancti Grisogoni predicta cum suis capellis et aliis sibi agnessis in spiritualibus et temporalibus per sedem apostolicum specialiter est commissa vicario generali, et domino Francisco Francisci de Campello de Setia, domino Francisco Turii Andreotii, domino Francisco Turii Velli Versi et domino Laurentio Johannis Laurentii Johannis Canis, canonicis dicte ecclesie sancti Grisogoni cohadunatis in coro dicte ecclesie ad sonum campanelle pro capitulo faciendo, ut moris et in talibus oportunum est, cum reverentia eisdem dominis vicario et canonicis et coram eis dixit, exposuit et narravit, quod cum iam sint quatraginta anni elapsi et ultra quod successive, continue per ipsa tempora usque nunc per pauperes Christi fuerit possessa et retenta pacifice et quiete, prout iam de facto nunc possidetur quedam domus terrinea, solarata et tegulata, que dicitur ac vocatur hospitale sancti Grisogoni posita in regione transtiberis in parrochia dicte ecclesie sancti Grisogoni inter hos fines, . . . ab alio latere est quedam domus terrinea, quam recoperuit seu recoperiri fecit dominus Nicolaus Nelli Johannis Cinthii de Transtibere ad usum et pro usu pauperum Christi . . . et dicta domus que vocatur hospitale, videlicet solarium dicte domus, et dicta domus quam recoperiri fecit dictus dominus Nicolaus Nelli ac etiam domus eidem Johanni donata per dominos de Monterano minentur ruinam, et ipse Johannes conscientia motus velit ipsas domas reparari facere ac in eisdem facere seu fieri facere solaria et de novo parietes domus, quam recoperiri fecit dictus dominus Nicolaus Nelli, et ipsas domos et hospitale ampliare et reparari facere pro recettando et ibidem amore domini nostri Jhesu Christi retinendo et hospitando et hospitari faciendo pauperes Christi, quos eidem Johanni et suis heredibus et successoribus melius pro salute anime sue et suorum videbitur et placuerit pro salute anime sue et suorum mortuorum, et hec nolit facere seu fieri facere sine speciali conscientia, voluntate et consensu ac speciali locatione dictorum canonicorum et capituli dicte ecclesie cum consensu et voluntate eorum superioris, protestatur tamen ipse quod in hiis et omnibus aliis non intendit preiudicare dictis pauperibus, set in omnibus eisdem ad usum et utilitatem ipsorum pauperum intendit proficere, et dicti domini vicarius, canonici et capitulum dicte ecclesie . . .

. . . locaverunt et locationis titulo dederunt, cesserunt et concesserunt ac transtulerunt, et mandaverunt dicto Johanni presenti, recipienti et legitime stipulanti pro se suisque heredibus et successoribus in perpetuum, idest dictam domum que vocatur hospitale sancti Grisogoni et omnia jura . . .
. . . semper tamen salvis et reservatis dicte ecclesie canonicis et capitulo eiusdem ecclesie juribus infrascriptis. Constituentes ipsum Johannem in supradictis rebus et juribus et pertinentiis suis in locum jus et privilegium ipsorum et dicte ecclesie ac dominum et procuratorem ut in rem suam propriam, investientes etiam dominum Johannem de dictis rebus, juribus et pertinentibus suis per presentes scripturas, et ad maiorem cautelam fecerunt, constituerunt, creaverunt et ordinaverunt, eorum et dicte ecclesie syndicum, yconem et procuratorem presbiterum Nicolaum testem infrascriptum ad investiendum et in corporalem vacantium et vacantem tenutam et possessionem dictarum domorum et hospitalis et jurium et pertinentium . . . mictendi et inducendi dictum Johannem . . .

. . . dictus Johannes voluit et promisit dictis capitulo et canonicis . . . pro ipsa ecclesia dare et solvere eisdem annuatim in perpetuum in festo sancti Grisogoni duodecim denarios prov.

Item et pro eo quod dictus Johannes voluit et promisit eisdem . . . signum sancti Grisogoni in dicto hospitali pingere seu pingi facere, et quod semper voluit nominari et quod nominetur hospitale sancti Grisogoni, ac etiam promisit nulli potenti persone nec pio loco ipsum hospitale, et dictas res locatas vendere, dare, donare, alienare nec aliquo alio modo distrahere sine consensu et voluntate capituli et canonicorum predictorum et ipsum semper retinere ad usum et pro usu pauperum Christi . . .

. . . in dicto hospitali et rebus locatis substituere unum vel plures procuratores seu quovis alio nomine censeri voluerit ad manutendum et gubernandum dictum hospitale et res predictas locatas cum jure et pertinentibus suis predictis ad sui voluntatem sine requisitione et voluntate dictorum canonicorum . . . semper salvis et reservatis juribus predictis dicte ecclesie sancti Grisogoni . . .

. . . dictum hospitale et res locate predicte nullatenus reverti seu revolvi possit dicto capitulo et canonicis predictis et dicte ecclesie sancti Grisogoni ratione census non solvendi . . .

. . . set tamen dictis capitulo et canonicis dicte ecclesie licitum sit petere dictum censum et ipsum censum simplicem habere et petere possint et non ultra . . .

APPENDIX 10

LIST OF FOUNDERS AND MEMBERS OF THE CONFRATERNITY

LIBER 272 F. 1 & 2

f. 1 r.

Ihs

Orate pro Animabus ffundatorum confratrum et
benefactorum subscriptorum et omnium ffidelium
defunctorum ac bono statu viventium subscriptorum

ffundatores sunt isti

Johannes Wyght civis civitatis londonensis mercator anglicus
Petrus Baker civis urbis Romane Gastonnis et pater Ricarde uxoris
    Johannis Ely
Dominus Rogerus Knecht capellanus anglicus
Johannes Geylot Anglicus mercator Anglice Nationis

Confratres

Johannes Wyght mercator anglicus
Petrus Baker civis Rome gallicus cum Madona Maria uxore sua Romana
Dominus Rogerus Knecht capellanus Anglicus
Magister Nicolaus Bondy legum doctor Romanus[1]
Johannes Geylot mercator Anglicus
Paulus S. . . .? notarius publicus Romanus[2]
Reynoldus G. . . . sartor Anglicus
Wilhelmus Port . . . th turnitor Anglicus
Magister Robertus Nawton capellanus Anglicus
Magister Wilhelmus Gotfadir capellanus Anglicus
Magister Philippus Nawton capellanus Anglicus et Wallicus
Johannes Ely serviens armorum domini nostri pape cum Ricarda uxore sua[3]

---

[1] Cf. *Memb.* 23.10.1404.
[2] ? Scocco, Paulus Johannis dello—. Executor of John Whyte's will. *Memb.* 23.10.1404.
[3] Camerarius, cf. *Memb.* 16.4.1428.

f. 1 v.

Johannes . . . lingool notarius publicus Apostolicus et Imperialis Anglicus

Thomas Polton Episcopus Cicestrensis[4]

Magister Johannes Yxworth legum doctor

Magister Johannes Blodwell tunc in legibus licentiatus

Magister Ricardus Jurdan in legibus Bacallarius

Magister Johannes Benn in Artibus magister

Magister Henricus Harburgh canonicus Saresburiensis

Lawrentius Benedicti notarius publicus cum uxore sua

Magister Johannes Byldon legum doctor archidiaconus in ecclesia
    Wyntoniensis

Magister Johannes Urry in legibus Bacallarius

Magister Thomas Chapman in legibus Bacallarius

Dominus Thomas Merden domini nostri pape penitentiarius

Magister Henricus Burnham in legibus Bacallarius

Magister Johannes Wellys canonicus Regularis ordinis premonstratensis[5]

Magister Ricardus Caunton legum doctor

Magister Thomas Candouer in decretis Bacallarius

Dominus Johannes Knyvette miles

Magister Matheus Crompe

Magister Andreas Holles[6]

Magister Johannes Pursell

Magister Johannes Bailly

Magister Johannes Saunders

Magister Johannes Lythom

Dominus Johannes Grassonesheed prior de Brynkborne

Magister Walter Sandwych utriusque Juris doctor

Magister Wilhelmus Gray sacre pagine professor prothanotarius apostolicus
    ac sancti domini nostri pape Reverendissimus Archidiaconus et
    serenissimi Domini nostri Regis Anglie in Romana curia procurator[7]

f. 2 r.

Magister Wilhelmus Radclyff utriusque iuris doctor et Sancti Domini
    nostri pape Cubicularius

Magister Henricus Sharpe legum doctor et Sancti Domini nostri pape
    Cubicularius

Magister Nicolaus Saxton Bacallarius in Theologia

[4] Dean of York 23rd July 1416. English Ambassador to the Council of Constance. King's proctor at the Papal court from 8th June 1414. Bp. Hereford 15th July 1420. Remained in Rome. Translated to Chichester 17th November 1421. Returned to England. Translated to Worcester January 1426. Attended the Council of Basle November 1432 and died there 23rd August 1433. DNB.

[5] 'Abbatem monasterii sanctorum quirici et Julitti dicti ordinis Reatensis (Rieti) diocesis'— *Lib.* 272, f. 8 r.

[6] King's proctor in Rome 1432–44.

[7] Rome 1445–54. Bp. Ely 21st June 1454. DNB.

Magister Ricardus Bolle magister in artibus et in decretis Bacallarius
Ricardus Thwaytes armiger
Johannes Lacy armiger
Wilhelmus Astulo serviens armorum Domini nostri pape
Magister Thomas Balscotte decretorum doctor Episcopus Ennachdunensis[8]
Magister Robertus Stillyngton legum doctor
Magister Johannes Wardale
Dominus Wilhelmus Stanley capellanus
Johannes Browne laicus mortuus est
Magister Hugo fforster monachus de Glastonbury
Magister Wilhelmus Symond
Magister Wilhelmus Swan
Magister Adam Moleyns legum doctor Episcopus Cicestrensis[9]
Robertus Roos laicus et questor[10]
Baldewynne ffulford miles
Johannes Kylvyngton scutifer
Nicolaus Upton canonicus Saresburiensis[11]
Johannes Lax legum doctor[12]
Robertus Thorneton Rector ecclesie parochialis de alninsbury Eboracensis
     diocesis
Johannes Kybon in decretis Bacallarius

Nota quod nunc Magister Stephanus Close nunc Magister Johannes Gale nunc Magister Thomas Hope nunc Magister Ricardus Couper nunc Magister Wilhelmus Dorsett sunt fratres in hospitali Sancti Edmundi Scriptum viij decembris mcccclij

M°iiij°lvii° Convocatis omnibus et singulis confratribus huius hospitalis Sancti Edmundi qui in urbe fuerant cum debita forma iuxta antiqua eiusdem hospitalis more et statuta admissi fuerunt in confratres dicti hospitalis venerabiles viri Thomas Burgh de Gaynsburgh Lincolniensis diocesis ac egregius legum doctor Magister Robertus Mason Archidiaconus Northumbrie necnon Magister Wilhelmus Schyrborn in legibus bacallarius ac Dominus Wilhelmus Holdernis Capellanus londonensis diocesis.
Omnes confratres sic ut prefertur congregati laudarunt antiquam consuetudinem et casu quo consuetudo non esset pro maiori securitate ob-

[8] Bp. of Enaghdune or Annadown, a small Irish see four or five miles from Tuam. Brady does not know his surname but indicates that he occupied the see sometime between 1426 and 1428. Brady, *The Episcopal Succession in England, Scotland and Ireland*, Rome 1876, II, 151.

[9] Clerk of the Council 1436–41. In Rome on King's business soon after. Keeper of the Privy Seal 11th February 1444. Commissioned with Suffolk and Robert Roos as ambassador to sue for peace with France. Made Bp. Chichester for his success 6th February 1446. Further mission in France with Roos, January 1448.

[10] Cf. above. It is not clear when Moleyns and Roos can have been to Rome apparently together.

[11] Sent on mission to Rome to sue for the canonization of Bp. Osmund 27th June 1452. DNB.

[12] Official of both Hospices at various times. King's proctor 1456, 1459–62.

servancie fundacionum et hospitalium tam Sancti Thome quam presentis perpetuitate unanimiter concordaverunt et disposuerunt pro quicumque essent Camerarii et custos hospitalis Sancti Thome occuparent et essent Camerarii et custos huius hospitalis Sancti Edmundi Actum Anno mense die et loco praedicto

> Jo. Lax Robertus Mason Tomas Burgh Robertus Thornton
> Wilhelmus Shirburn Wilhelmus Holdernes (signatures)

f. 2 v.

Anno Domini m°cccc°lxvi prima die mensis ffebruarii recepti et admissi erant in fraternitate hospitalis Sanctorum Edmundi et Crisogoni in presencia dominorum   W Clayton

Magister Jacobus Goldwell procurator serenissimi regis Edwardi Anglie et ffrancie[13]

Dominus Johannes Maulynewe miles

Dominus Milo Wylsthorpp

Dominus Nicholaus Lanpytt

Dominus Ricardus Leyland

Dominus Wilhelmus Cowper

Robertus North[14]

SUPPLEMENT TO THE LIST OF CONFRATERNITY MEMBERS

f. 77 r.   1463   Egidius Whittington
                  Johannes Lee
                  Robertus Strete
                  Johannes Lascy
                  Johannes Gerona

f. 77 v.   1464   Symon Wulrigge
                  Johannes Luffyn Wigornensis diocesis Rector ecclesiae
                      sancti martini de marke juxta calisiam
                  Robert Clerke

f. 78 r.   1465   Wilhelmus Clayton Rector de Stannop
                  Ricardus Billyngham monachus et procurator monasterii
                      dunelmensis
                  Johannes Milnerton sacre pagine professor et ordinis
                      Carmelitarum in Regno Anglie provincialis
                  Johannes Barow in artibus magister
           1466   Robertus Newton totius ordinis sancti benedicti
                      magnarum monasteriarum in Anglia procurator
                  Johannes Barton in legibus bacallarius et sancti
                      geroni exoniensis diocesis vicarius

[13] King's proctor 1468–71.
[14] Or Worth cf. *Lib.* 272, f. 78 r.

APPENDIX 11

RECORD OF THE BUSINESS MEETINGS OF THE CONFRATERNITY OF ST EDMUND'S
IN 1464 WHEN THE UNION OF THE HOSPICE WITH THAT OF ST THOMAS
OCCURRED

Lib. 272, f. 77

f. 77 r.

 die ix martii anno a nativitate domini 1464 omnes fratres hospitalis
sanctorum grisogoni et Edmundi martiris transtiberini in urbe presentes
in urbe secundum morem antiquum congregati habita relatione compotis
de annis supraspecificatis eligerunt camerariis dicti hospitalis a dicto ix
martii usque ad primam domenicam mensis februarii et tunc proxime
futurorum magistrum egidium Whitington et Robertum Strete praesentes
tunc ibidem convocati fuerunt
Magister Johannes Lee decretorum doctor
Magister Johannes Lascy
Egidius Whitington
Robertus Strete
Robertus Clerke

Item xii die martii Anno domini praedicto praesentibus Egidio Whityngton
Roberto Strete et Roberto Clerke confratribus dicti hospitalis ut moris
est congregatis electus fuit in confratres dicti hospitalis discretus vir
dominus Symon Wulrigge capellanus qui iuravit secundum formam statutorum. Et tunc consequitur ex habundanti de novo fuerunt electi in
camerarios dicti hospitalis praenominati egidius W et Robertus Strete et
electio eorundem dicto ix die facta per fratres antedictos fuerat commendata

Item omnes fratres tunc ut super congregati sicut alia fuerat ordinatum
statuerunt quod quicumque essent camerarii et custos hospitalis sanctorum
Trinitatis et Thome martiris in urbe essent camerarii et custos hospitalis
sanctorum grisogoni et Edmundi praedicti dummodo in utroque hospitali
sint fratres debito modo electi et tempore congruo ad hoc statutis ordinatis
post electionem camerariorum hospitalis sanctorum Trinitatis et Thome
praedicti fuit electio eisdem camerariis de novo in isto hospitali sanctorum
grisogoni et Edmundi praedicto.

f. 77 v.

 Item eodem die omnes fratres sicut praefertur congregati consenserunt
quidem praenominati Robertus et egidius camerarii ordinarent et dis-
ponerent pro uno viro et uxore sua boni regiminis ad custodiendum hospitale
sanctorum grisogoni et edmundi et quidem in eodem hospitale ad custodiendum illud eosdem imponerent. dummodo talis vir et uxor non sunt de
Scotia aut alterius nationis inimice serenissimo Regi Angliae aut Anglice
nationis.

PILGRIMS AND THE HOSPICE

Some 377 Englishmen came on pilgrimage to Rome in the Holy Year of 1350.[1] Ignorant of language and custom, they fell easy victims to the Roman landlords. Complaints were made, and as a result the English Hospice was founded in 1362. From then until the Reformation, a continuous stream of pilgrims used the Hospice.

Although there is little record of it before the middle of the fifteenth century, it seems to have been a thriving concern. New houses were bought, and a second hospice started in Trastevere. Other property was acquired to endow it. An annual collection was made in England for its needs—known as the *firma Angliae*. The Hospice was taken under royal protection and the royal arms together with an inscription recording the proud claim to sovereignty over France were set up over the entrance.[2] Margery Kempe, the lacrymose mystic from Norfolk, was received at the Hospice in 1416, and praises the kindness with which she was treated, until the accusations of the chaplain of her party turned the authorities against her, and she was forced to leave.[3] (She was invited to return when her

---

NOTE.—This is a reprint of an article in THE VENERABILE, XIX (May 1959).

[1] G. B. Parks, *The English Traveler to Italy*, I, 356. Cf. licences granted to pilgrims and attendants. There are probably others of whom no records survive.

[2] Cf. Gasquet, *History of the Venerable English College*, p. 37. The arms and inscription are still preserved in the College. The latter reads : '*Haec conjuncta duo, successus debita Legi, Anglia dant Regi, Francia signa suo. MCCCCXII. Laurentius Cache me fecit.*' The date indicates that the inscription was made at the end of the reign of Henry IV.

[3] THE VENERABILE, XI, 42–49 (Nov. 1942).

name had been cleared.) In 1446 by a Bull of Eugene IV the chaplains were given licence to administer the sacraments to all Englishmen in Rome, and at the request of the English at the Curia the privilege of right of cemetery for that nation was also granted.[4] There is a bare mention of the Hospital of St Thomas in the account of Rome in 1450 by John Capgrave.[5] But it is only at the end of the fifteenth and beginning of the sixteenth centuries that records are comparatively abundant, and from them we can get some idea of the life of the Hospice and the way in which the pilgrims were treated.

Holy Years were naturally peak periods for pilgrimages. In December 1499 a special meeting of the confraternity of the Hospice was held to prepare for the invasion of the following year, and Edward Scott was asked to assist the custos in the administration on account of the great labours involved.[6] Scott was an efficient administrator, who had already been custos, and was to be again. He was responsible for the careful, painstaking inventory of 1496, when all the goods of the Hospice were listed. Spaldyng, the custos, was ageing and died in the course of the year, and most of the work must have fallen on Scott. In 1500 it is estimated that 750 English pilgrims visited Rome, and in the next Holy Year, 1525, 439.[7] Not all those could have stayed at the Hospice, and the poor were sometimes given money when there was no room left. The number that could be accommodated can be gathered from the inventory of beds and bedding. In 1501 there were thirty-seven bedsteads, of which four were 'running beds' (possibly trundle beds, on wheels), and they were probably all double beds.[8] There were also thirteen feather beds, though it is said that four were 'but feeble'. The

---

[4] *Memb.* 23.3.1446.

[5] Capgrave, *Ye Solace of Pilgrims*, ed. C. A. Mills, Oxford 1911, p. 157. Capgrave describes the building of the Pantheon. The structure was supported on a mound of earth in which money had been buried. When it was complete, people were invited to cart away as much earth as they liked and they were rewarded by the money they found. He says he saw a vault made in the Hospice in the same way.

[6] *Lib.* 17, f. 28 r.

[7] Parks, op. cit., p. 374 sqq.

[8] Ibid., p. 372. *Lib.* 17, f. 45 v. The entry in *Lib.* 17 gives the distribution of beds :
'in the gentylmens chamber vj arynnyng bed j in the yemens chambre xvj in the womens chamber vj arunnyng bed j in the custos chambre j a runyng bed j in the seruants chambre iij arunnyng bed j in the chapellayns chambre j
In the tresor hows a fiate beddstede aftyr italy fascion.' (Vestments and plate were kept in the treasure house.) Parks corrects the sum to 34. He takes the numbers vj in the gentlemen's and women's chambers, and iij in the servants' as *inclusive* of the 'running beds', and brackets in the 'flat bedstead' in the treasure house. But it seems that the 'running beds' should be taken as additional, and the bracket in the MS. does not extend to the treasure house bed : 37 would then be correct.

Hospice could therefore sleep a little over a hundred people.[9] Such a number would only be present during Holy Year, and in Holy Week at that. Normally there would have been ample room.

The size of the tables in Hall is not given, so no estimate can be made of the seating capacity. The greatest number of guests recorded at any one time was on Passion Sunday 1525, when 169 were present.[10] They were not all living at the Hospice.

Amongst the pilgrims there was a distinction between *nobiles*, who paid for their keep, and *pauperes*. The lists of pilgrims from 1504–07[11] give 489 pilgrims, of whom 138 were *nobiles*. In 1514 at least 28 out of 120 were *nobiles*.[12] The *nobiles* included clergy, professional men such as lawyers and doctors, captains of ships, rich merchants and gentry. In 1514 Thomas Cromwell was among their number. Many of them would have come on business, to obtain favours from the Holy See, or to study, but they would normally undertake the pilgrimage at the same time. The poor men were mainly small tradesmen, servants and some sailors. These were treated with less respect, eating and drinking and sleeping apart from the others. In the gentlemen's chamber with six or seven beds there were six chests ; the yeomen's room with sixteen beds had but one chest.[13] The Hospice owned eight pairs of fine Roman sheets for the gentlemen, and sixty-eight pairs of canvas sheets for the others,[14] and in 1502 imported 220 ells of Normandy canvas to make new ones.[15] Similarly in the hall there were three tablecloths of diaper for daily use at the gentlemen's table, besides four others, wrought with crosses, roses and fleurs-de-lis for special occasions. The yeomen's table was covered with two cloths of tyke.[16]

Yet even the gentlemen must have lived in a proximity and familiarity which would be intolerable to us. Perhaps a visiting abbot would be invited to sleep in the custos' chamber, but for the rest one imagines them as a very crowded company
    '*of sondry folk, by aventure y-falle*

[9] Thirty-seven bedsteads (with 36 mattresses !), 13 feather beds, all presumably for two, also 12 'saccons' (which seem to have been some kind of straw mattress), and the bed in the treasure house. The mattresses belonged to the bedsteads, but the saccons may have been used independently for servants of pilgrims, or when the Hospice was crowded.

[10] Parks, p. 371.

[11] *Lib. Inst.*, I, ff. 29r–32r. Cf. App. 13, p. 125.

[12] *Lib.* 13, f. 99–100. Cf. App. 14, p. 141.

[13] *Lib.* 17, f. 47 r.

[14] Ibid., f. 45 v.

[15] Ibid., f. 39 v.

[16] Ibid., f. 46 r.

In felaweship' . . . like Chaucer's Knight and Friar and Shipman : among them merchants, perhaps, and 'men of lawe' who had

'shapen hem to Rome for to wende,
Were it for chapmanhode or for disport', or genuine pilgrims who while in Rome would make for the Hospice, as at Canterbury,

'the holy blisful martir for to seke
That hem hath holpen . . .'

Like its patron St Thomas, the Hospice did not refuse help to its clients *'whan that they were seke'*; in fact the Hospice was at times a hospital in the modern sense. Amongst the items noted as missing in 1499 was a sheet used for Master Lessy's two men, who were hurt at Viterbo when their master was slain, and who came to Rome to the Hospice for help.[17] They were also lent money, twenty-two ducats, which was a large sum, for the custos' salary for the year was only twelve ducats.[18] But they had to leave as pledges 'a grette owche and a little owche off golde', with two rings of gold, one of them having a turquoise set in it.[19] Other sheets were written off as used for Robert Burnham and Robert Soudyer, two sick pilgrims. The day-to-day accounts for 1480 to 1484 frequently note the presence of infirm pilgrims. On one occasion the authorities seem to have been a little inhospitable. A pilgrim suspected of the plague was given a sum of money *'ut citius recederet in partes'*.[20] But there was reason for fear. In 1482 eighteen people died in the Hospice *'ex peste'*,[21] and were buried in the church. Other pilgrims were paid to carry the bier.

The cemetery of the church was certainly in constant use. Not only pilgrims but also notable Englishmen in Rome were buried there. The greatest of these was Cardinal Bainbridge, whose tomb in the present church is the most impressive remaining memorial of the Hospice. The spectacular funeral of John Shirwood, Bishop of Durham, is described by Burchard, the papal Master of Protocol at the time. 'John, Bishop of Durham, ambassador of the king . . . Henry . . . died on the Wednesday evening [14th January 1493–4]. He was borne from his abode to the church of the English Hospice, where he was to

---

[17] *Lib.* 17, f. 26 v. Cf. THE VENERABILE XII, 3–16 (Nov. 1944) : *Prologue to the Liber Ruber*, for other examples of sick pilgrims.
[18] *Lib.* 18, f. 76 r.
[19] *Lib.* 17, f. 31 r. An 'ouch' is a jewelled clasp or buckle.
[20] *Lib.* 18, f. 77 v.
[21] Ibid., f. 147.

be buried, attended by the households of the cardinals of Naples, Recanati, Benevento and Siena, and by the chamberlain of the cardinals. Fifty funeral torches preceded the coffin, which was followed by nine persons in funeral garb, by his chaplains, and by many others in black (though not funeral) clothes.'[22]

Shirwood had been in Rome since 1475, and had been a camerarius of the Hospice since 1476. He must have been a wealthy man, for he rented the most expensive house of the Hospice, paying eighty ducats a year for it, when most house rents were ten to twenty ducats. Another ambassador buried in the Hospice was John Giglis, Bishop of Worcester. He wore when he was buried a pair of bishop's gloves of red cloth belonging to the Hospice. His nephew Sylvester Giglis promised to replace these gloves, but does not appear to have done so.[23]

One of those who died of the plague in 1482 is described as John 'clericus hospitalis'. This may have been some poor English clerk who undertook clerical work for the Hospice while continuing his studies. In the same year a clericus hospitalis was paid a salary of over six ducats.[24] In May 1480 Thomas Oritt, clericus hospitalis, was ordained and given money to return home, and again in September another cleric was given money for the same reason.[25] It is interesting to think that the Hospice may have been undertaking some of the duties of a seminary. Most of the officials had degrees in theology or canon law, and would have been able to teach. In the Middle Ages clerics were often trained in bishops' households, working the while as secretaries, and it is possible that some such system may have obtained at the Hospice.

Few if any of the pilgrims walked all the way ;[26] but even so the journey was not easy. Most travelled in winter, the Hospice being fullest from December to June, and the Alpine passes would have been full of snow. The travellers seem to have preferred to risk the snows rather than the heat of Italy in the summer, when plague and disease spread easily. Moreover, many wished to be in Rome for Easter and this would mean leaving England in January or February, while those going on to Jerusalem would be able to reach Venice by May or June when the galleys left. The two commonest routes were over the Mont

[22] Quoted by Parks, p. 307.
[23] *Lib.* 17, f. 21 r.
[24] *Lib.* 18, f. 100 r.
[25] Ibid., f. 37 r.
[26] Parks, p. 537.

Cenis or through Germany to the Reschen Pass and down to
Venice. Some of the pilgrims may have had to beg, as Margery
Kempe did when she was abandoned by her party. A French
merchant, Boni, travelling from Avignon to Rome in about
1350, gives a list of places to dine, and of places where one could
stay the night. It took him twenty-three days, and he finishes
by dining 'with great joy in old Rome'.[27]

The Hospice food may have lacked variety, but it seems
to have been substantial. Meat was given every day except
Fridays and Saturdays, which were days of abstinence.[28]
Beef and mutton predominated, with pork as an occasional
substitute. In Lent there was fish every day, including Sundays,
and many of the usual kinds appear—tench, eels, tunny, etc.
In fact, Lent seems to have put the kitchen staff on their mettle.
Inventories give us some minor details of the cooking ; 'Item
a lytyll fork of yerne [iron] to make tostys of brede and to roste
appallis withall. Item a chaffyng dish to butter fish withall' can
stimulate the imagination.[29] Bread, flour, salt and oil were
accounted for separately. Food was eaten from vessels of pewter,
trenchers or quaders. In 1502 part of the *firma Angliae* was
received in the form of seventy-two pieces of pewter vessel, sent
out in the royal ship *Sovereign*.[30] The Hospice possessed its own
vineyards near Rome, from which daily supplies of wine were
drawn. For festive occasions, wine was imported from Corsica,
Calabria and Terracina.

In the food accounts, Christmas, Easter and Pentecost pass
unnoticed, but there is a separate entry for the feast of St
Thomas. On this day all the English in Rome were entertained.
In 1481 the feast cost twenty-two ducats, 4 *g*, 4 *bol*, and apart
from the food, there were payments to the archbishop who sang
a solemn Mass, to the singers, to the trumpeters of the king of
Naples and the trumpeters of the pope, and to organists.[31]

[27] Parks, p. 530.
[28] Cf. *Lib*. 18, f. 102. This gives the accounts for the week 7th to 14th May 1481 : '*Domca in
carne bovum iii g in carne multon. ii g iii bol in carne vituliu viii vol in herbis ii q*'. (Monday–Thursday
is much the same.) '*Vend in pisce recente ii g i bol in butiro ii bol ii q in sinapio ii q in ovis ii g*'.
(Saturday's is similar.)
It is somewhat difficult to work out the monetary system used. In *Lib*. 17 the individual units
are ducats, *carleni*, *bolandini* and *quaterini*. Here in *Lib*. 18 '*g*' replaces *carleni*. There were 10 *carleni*
to a ducat *de camera*, and 12½–13 to a ducat of gold. In general there were 8 *bolandini* to one *carl*.,
and 2 *q*. to 1 *bol*., but these ratios seem to vary.
[29] *Lib*. 17, f. 48 v.
[30] Ibid., f. 39 v. The *Sovereign*, weighing 800 tons, was the famous ship built for Henry VII,
and one of the largest then in existence. The king used it both as a warship and for trading. It may
have been a mark of Henry's interest that it should carry the plate for the Hospice.
[31] *Lib*. 18, f. 96.

In 1511 there is mention of incense bought for seven cardinals who were present at the Mass.[32]

We gain an impression of crowds in the church and hall on these occasions. All was bustle and hurry. Guests and visitors were everywhere, and the harassed servants could not keep an eye on everything. Things sometimes disappeared : in 1501 the custos had bought four diaper towels for drying priests' hands in the sacristy, and one was lost on St Thomas's Day.[33] Wine was carried from the kitchen to the hall in great brass pots— not the easiest things to lose, yet one vanished on the feast-day.[34]

Above all, it was in the church that the splendour and colour of the feast would have been most apparent and it is worth trying to recapture the scene.

Although the church survived until after the Napoleonic wars, no picture of the interior exists:[35] there is only a ground-plan dating from 1630,[36] and a description of it in 1662.[37] From the time of the Hospice we have accounts of repairs[38] and inventories of church furnishings ; but there is nothing which shows us exactly what it looked like. It occupied the site of the present church, and a cortile separated it from the dining hall. The present kitchen is on the site of the old hall and probably preserves the actual structure, as it is thought that this part of the College was not rebuilt by Cardinal Howard. All the Hospice buildings were on the eastern side of the church. The present main cortile did not exist ; there were houses owned and rented out by the Hospice in its place. The church seems to have been built mainly of brick and some form of cement, and brick columns, with capitals and bases of tibertine stone, supported the roof.[39] At the end of the nave there was a choir-

[32] *Lib.* 13, f. 106 v.
[33] *Lib.* 17, f. 33 r.
[34] Ibid., f. 26 r.
[35] Contrary to what is often said, the church was in use for a short time after the Napoleonic wars. In 1820 one of the students, William Kavanagh, died, and in *Lib.* 551 it states 'et sepultus ad partem Evangel. Capellae majoris prope locum ubi sedere solebat Vice-Rector.' What happened to his body when the new church was built ? The coffin and tomb would not have been destroyed, as the others are said to have been, by the French. The church was finally condemned as unsafe in 1826.
[36] Cf. THE VENERABILE, XII, 48–50 (Nov. 1944).
[37] Ibid., III, 31–38 (Oct. 1926).
[38] Ibid., V, 177–8 (April 1931) ; *Lib.* 17, f. 20 v.
[39] *Lib.* 17, f. 20 v. gives an account of repairs to the church : 'Item tota ecclesia debet esse strata lateribus planis convenientibus ut moris est. Item debet incolari vel cementari tota ecclesia a parte inferiore solummodo'. Cf. Article 14 : 'Item omnes collune debent esse ex lateribus cum basibus et capitibus ex lapide tibertino'. A cellar was made under the church and repairs were carried out in the roof ; the choir-loft and library were built. The reconstruction work, in which the church was almost entirely rebuilt, cost 1000 ducats. Cf. THE VENERABILE, V, 177–8 (April 1931).

loft, as wide as the nave and about ten feet in depth. Here a
pair of organs stood upon a carved table fixed in the wall.
Here too were four small desks and a table 'to lay all maner
boks a pon', and two long forms, six folding chairs of timber
and one chained stool 'to sytt a pon'.[40] Above the left-hand
aisle was the library. In 1500 there were seven altars,[41] of which
four were dedicated to St Thomas, Our Lady, St Nicholas and
St Catherine. One would imagine that the high altar would be
dedicated to St Thomas, but this is not clear in the inventories
where both are mentioned separately. Moreover, there is a
Bull of Gregory XIII granted to the College in 1579 making
the altar of St Thomas, *'quod maioris non est'*, a privileged
altar. The Lady altar was decorated with a frontal of white
damask with a red cross in the centre. There were several images
of Our Lady in the possession of the Hospice ; they may have
been either pictures or statues. One in the sacristy is described
as being made of alabaster[42] and standing in a tabernacle. The
statue of Our Lady on her altar wore a silver crown ; or rather,
a half-crown, as the inventory ingenuously admits. It was given
by 'Katryn Inglish woman', the wife of Hankyn Stonspall.

Little is said of the other altars. They all seem to have been
flanked by curtains. At one was 'a lytyll ymage of saynt katryne
paynted new . . . and a pon ye auter standys also a old tabyll
with the image of owr lady : saynt John : saynt george : saynt
katryn : and saynt thomas'.[43] The altar of St Nicholas had a
'bankett', which appears to have been a gradine, as it was
used for putting candles on. It was painted with the Trinity
and the twelve Apostles.

The Blessed Sacrament was reserved in the wall, and its
presence indicated by a lamp of latten or brass. Beneath it was
a table covered with a cloth of red baudkyn lined with buckram,
and set in the wall was an iron plate for votive candles.

There were two carved benches in the middle of the nave,
and three plain ones at the side ; at three of the pillars there were
kneeling-desks, and one of them had chained to it a parchment
containing the seven penitential psalms, the Litany, *Placebo*
and *Dirige*. By St Thomas's altar were a stool and desk, to which

[40] *Lib.* 17, f. 43 v.
[41] Ibid., ff. 42 v–43 r.
[42] Ibid., f. 43 v.
[43] Ibid., f. 42 v. Could this be the famous polyptych which once graced the Hospice
(and College) church ? Cf. THE VENERABILE, XX, 127–39 (May 1961).

Hospice Church from a woodcut, *c.* 1580

Fragment of wall from the old Hospice Church

were chained a Life of St Thomas, a 'portose'[44] of Roman use, and a book called '*Manipulus Curatoris*'. A high desk stood in front of the main altar, used for reading the Epistle and chanting the *Salve* daily.[45] Thus the present custom of singing the *Salve* each evening goes back beyond the foundation of the College.

The liturgical colours were rather different from modern usage. Blue was worn, as it still is in Spain; there were no purple vestments—white was the colour for Lent. The vestments were made from splendid materials of oriental origin : baldachin or baudkin, a rich brocade from Baghdad; damask from Damascus, and sarcenet or Saracen cloth (both silks of various kinds with raised patterns). The blue vestments were of camlet, a costly eastern stuff of silk and camel's hair. The Hospice also owned a chasuble of cloth of gold on a blue ground, with alb, amice and maniple to match, but no stole.

The church was a feast of colour in cloth and drapings and in painting. Everything possible was done to add to the glory of the scene on such occasions as the feast of St Thomas. For the celebrant there was 'a rede cheseble braynchyd with gold with a very fyne albe and amese and stole and fanne [maniple]' with tunicles and apparelled amice and alb to match for two other ministers. If a bishop he would wear the Hospice mitre 'set with perlys and counterset stonys estemyed at a 150 doketts'.[46] Hired trumpeters in the organ-loft sounded forth as he entered, and the church in its festive robes of all colours seemed to join in the fanfare. Twenty hangings emblazoned with various coats of arms festooned the walls, while on each side of the church were suspended seven banners bearing the arms of England. Above, the ceiling was ornamented with a regular design.[47] From the beam-ends painted heads of saints looked down, while here and there the arms of England stood out in relief and colour.[48] The congregation too was clad in bright robes. Burchard describes Sir John Kendall, Turcopolier of the Knights of Rhodes and a camerarius of the Hospice, as dressed in 'robes of red taffeta with a white cross in the centre

---

[44] This is spelt variously as 'portose', 'portowse' or 'porthouse' and means a breviary—cf. French '*portehors*', Latin '*portiforium*'.
[45] *Lib.* 17, f. 43 r.
[46] *Lib.* 17, f. 21.
[47] Ibid., f. 20.
[48] The College still possesses four of these beam-ends, which have been placed in the Cardinals Corridor. It is not certain where exactly they were in the church.

before and behind', and accompanied by his pages bearing the banner of his Order—red with a white cross in the centre.[49]

As the bishop walked up the aisle he would see before him the high altar decorated with its own curtains and frontlets. Highest above it hung a red cloth of baldachin with a yellow lining.[50] Below, on the front of the altar, were two cloths of green silk lined with blue, wrought with images of the life of St Thomas.[51] At the foot of the altar stood two great candlesticks, over seven feet high, made of polished latten. On the altar itself were two others of latten about three feet high, and also eight small candles of wood, carved and painted white and gold, with the Trinity on them.[52] The missal rested on a cushion of tawny silk. If John Shirwood, Bishop of Durham and camerarius of the Hospice, was pontificating, he would possibly have used one of the old handwritten Sarum missals, rather than a modern printed one.[53] If so, the Mass itself would have differed a little from ours. It began with the intoning of the 'Veni Creator Spiritus', and the Offertory prayers were reduced in length. There was also a proper sequence for the feast of St Thomas. Shirwood may well have used the costly chalice of silver and gilt, weighing twenty ounces one quarter, presented by the duchess of York.[54] It was not as heavy or valuable as that given by the abbot of Abingdon, but the rank of the donor made it worthy to be used on such occasions.

After Mass on St Thomas's day the whole congregation would retire to the hall. Beakers and glasses stood on a credence just inside the door. The high table was arrayed with the plate of the Hospice, candlesticks of silver, again given by the duchess of York, and also a basin of silver with a rose engraved on the bottom. There was wine from Corsica, Terracina and Calabria ; as the bishop drained his cup he would read on the bottom 'Vinum laetificat cor'.[55] It was the great day of the Hospice, when England's saint, patron of ecclesiastical immunities, was remembered by all Englishmen in Rome.

[49] Cf. Parks, p. 307.
[50] This was replaced in Lent by a cloth with Christus passus est pro nobis embroidered on it.
[51] The Hospice possessed other frontlets for the high altar. One was 'stained' with the Trinity, St Christopher and St George ; another, of gold and velvet, was given by Richard Fenrother, and bore his arms - a rother or rudder - and his name.
[52] Lib. 17, f. 43 r.
[53] Cf. Inventory of Books, Lib. 17, f. 50 r. The Hospice had eleven handwritten Sarum missals and two printed Roman ones.
[54] Lib. 17, f. 21 r.
[55] Lib. 17, f. 21 v.

Such was the Hospice at the turn of the fifteenth century. Everything possible was coloured and painted. A tabernacle of white wood was bought in 1500 for twelve ducats : the Hospice planned to paint it with scenes from the life of St Thomas, and was prepared to pay as much as a hundred ducats for this.[56] There was no stinting in decoration or necessities at this time. Under the wardenship of Hugh Spaldyng, Robert Shirborn and Edward Scott the Hospice was at the height of its prosperity. There was careful management, as the detailed inventories prove, but money was spent freely on repairs and improvements. In 1497 Shirborn spent 1000 ducats in repairing the church which was finally consecrated in 1501. Scott replaced worn-out mattresses, sheets and cutlery, mainly with money given by Shirwood's executors. But with the Reformation the Hospice ceased to be useful. In the sack of Rome in 1527 it lost most of its plate and rich vestments. By 1538 decay had set in, and the pope had to send Cardinal Pole to restore some semblance of order. It was a much impoverished institution that Gregory XIII handed over to Cardinal Allen.

GEORGE HAY.

[56] Ibid., f. 42 v.

APPENDIX 12

D—Dominus   M—Magister   F—Frater   d—diocese

LIST OF PILGRIMS MAY 1479—MAY 1484. LIBER 18, PASSIM

1479
MAY

In the Hospice, 3 servants.
3 John Rynes, Shrewsbury
   Richard Lymster, ibid.
   William Nicolson, Lancaster
4 John Forman, Norwich
5 Thomas Clerk, Sussex
6 Robert Stanley, York
   James Holdeyn, Lancaster
7 Brian Sterkey, Lincolnshire
   John Thomson, ibid.

8 Thomas Spark, Norfolk
   Walter Andrew, London
   Robert Curson, Oxford
9 William Gybson
   Alice his wife
   Thomas Barley, Warwick
   Richard Richardson, Essex
10 F. William Herford and
   F. John Thorlbrand, Oxford
11 D. Philip Molynoux and
   Nicholas Foule and
   Robert Shypley, Kent

12 Thomas Twysett, Cleveland
13 Thomas Herbard, Beverley
17 John Gornay, hermit, Barnett
18 Hugh Botyler, Wales
20 Thomas Durman, Maldon
21 Giles Steynton, Southampton
22 John Water, York
23 William Beslay, London
    William Lyon, Kent
26 Thomas Gybson, Kent
    Richard Mede, Buckingham
    Auditors of the *competus*
28 The aforesaid auditors
29 Thomas Lodge and
    John Andrew, Hull
30 John Flete, Southampton
31 John Browne, Stratford
    David Bailley, Alnwick

JUNE
 6 Marian Haute, Dover (?)
 8 John Gest, hermit, York
    Thomas Chalnor, Warwick
10 M. Thomas Wynchecomb and
    John Thomson, Lincoln
    William Hadwey and
    Reginald Burne and
    John Freman, Sussex
13 William Rose, London
14 John Bernar, Cambridge
    Thomas Johnson, Suffolk
20 John Appley, Wales and
    Anon.
    3 English merchants at supper only.
21 D. John Jesop
    Joanna Horton
    Margaret Lley
    Margaret ap Evan
    William Baxter
    Thomas Lymner
23 Robert Bart, Kent
    John Paynell, Lancaster
24 William Oldburgh, Norfolk
26 Thomas Bothe, Lancashire
    John Gybbs of the same county

27 Mylis (?), of Westminster
28 William Marshal and
    William his son, Boston
    Robert Rogerson, Lancashire
    William Thorp of the same county
29 John Lee, London
    Richard Symmes, Shrewsbury
    John Balle and
    Richard Bate, Yorkshire

JULY
 3 John Niloburgh, Shrewsbury
 8 John Stone, York
    3 sick
11 Thomas of Mirideyn (?), Holland
14 Richard Foderley, Hexham
15 John Lukton, Ripon
    David Ellismera, Shrewsbury
16 Thomas Duffe, Holderness (?)
    M. Thomas Wynchecomb left 2 sick
18 Thomas Marrok, Salisbury
20 John Chambre, Beverley
21 Robert Rogerson died
22 D. Simon Russell, Chester
    William Angners, Suffolk
    Lawrence Stenton, Wakefield
    George Perison, Northants
    William Chiteryng, Norfolk
24 Thomas Walsshall, London
    2 sick
26 John Smyth of the King's house
    hold (?)
    Thomas Dikson, London

AUGUST
 3 Thomas Dryer, Sussex
    John Style, Salisbury
 5 John Moore, Derby
 6 John Southfield, London
    Oswald Bonnd, Paston
    Robert Spendlome, Selby, Lancs.
    2 sick

11 John Flemmyng, Pontefract
2 Sick
15 Gregory of Holyhead, a Welshman
21 William Wylton, Tewkesbury
2 Sick
25 Agnes Marter, Lancs.
26 John Cootys, Lincs.
3 sick
30 John Burton, Lancs

SEPTEMBER
 1 John Hakby, Stratford
 2 Richard Bury, Cambridge
2 Sick
 5 D. John Elys, Stamford
Richard Badby, Suffolk
Richard Folmer, Reading
 6 D. Thomas Wynchecomb came into
the Hospice
2 Sick
14 John Bakk, Norfolk
Robert Kenwyk and
Alice his wife and
Richard Hopkyn, London
Henry Peerson, Durham
15 John Adams, Bristol
Thomas Umfray, Cambridge
16 William Richardson, Yorks
On the same day the grapes were
gathered in St James's vineyard
2 Sick
20 On the same day the grapes were
gathered in the vineyard of the
chalk tower, and D. Thomas
Lymner, canon of Langdon, Kent,
died.
21 D. Thomas Sygge, Ches.
D. John Heron, Staffs.
F. John Donernale of a Northants.
monastery
24 Richard Folmer, Reading, died.
30 D. Robert Stamiton, canon of
Langdon
D. Henry Synger, Wenlock

OCTOBER
 2 David Lloyd and
William Lute from the same place
 3 Thomas Forler, London
 6 Roger Philipp, Sussex
11 John Hervison, Lith
Henry Blakborn, Lekynfeld
12 D. Richard Philipp, London
D. John Furner of the same
F. John Molton of a Northants.
monastery
Thomas Hatley, St Albans
M. William Jones, sick
18 William Thomson, London
20 Nicholas Kychen, Lancs
28 John Awbrey, Wakefield
29 John Northfolk, Suffolk
Joanna Gye, Tonett (Tonell ?)
31 Robert Haycok, Lancs.

NOVEMBER
 3 D. Henry Overyngton and
Richard Overyngton, Sussex
Thomas Alford and
Reginald Story, Cheshire.
 5 Joanna
 7 D. John Hung, Yorks.
Robert Hert, same county
 8 Thomas Lyntbow, Yorks.
 9 D. Abbas
D. Protonotarius
D. Turkepilaris
with two knights of Rhodes
M. John Elys, rector of the pro-
cathedral of St Michael, Stamford,
died.
12 John Clyfton, Yorks
14 William Scales, London
Thomas Pympott, Abingdon
17 John Yate, Scarborough
Robert Neele, Bewlay
24 Thomas Chambre, London
2 Sick
28 F. John Keche, London

DECEMBER

1 F. John Bravue, Oderliel (?)
23 William Millynch, Derbys.
24 John Vincent, London
25 John Morley, Worcs

1480
JANUARY

2 F. Henry Cossey, a Dominican
3 Richard Alyn, Ludlow
12 Maurice Yong, Gloucester.
27 John of Calais
31 D. John Herbard, Prior of
      Threnhath (?)
    D. Hugh Hafildeyn, London d.
    D. Thomas Mason
    D. John Berker
    D. John Porter
    D. John Everard, Suffolk
    Luke Brande, Lamby

FEBRUARY

1 D. Archibald Davy, Shelton
    D. Thomas Pynke, Tikelburgh, (?)
      Suffolk
3 F. John Dunston, Norfolk
    D. Robert Nyker, ibid.
    D. John Chapman, ibid.
16 D. Thomas Raynold, priest,
      Geriswich (?)
    D. Thomas Wait, a canon of the
      same place.
20 Thomas Toker, Bristol
27 Richard Moore, York
28 Anon, who stayed one day
29 Thomas Croft, London

MARCH

1 Thomas Orell, York
10 Richard Bailly, Kent
    Richard Wody, ibid

13 John Chipendale and
    Alice, his wife, Isilton
    William Bradley, Blyth
    Thomas Mylward, Bedford
16 D. Christopher Urswyk, Cambridge
    D. George Smyth, Suffolk
    D. Robert Cravsistre, ibid.
    Robert Johnson, Essex, a layman
21 James Andrewson, Durham
22 John Palmer sen. and
    John Palmer jun. Hadley, Suffolk.
25 John Stevynson and
    Thomas Chapell, Suffolk, p   of
      the hospice
28 Thomas Johnson, Suffolk
30 Thomas ap Rys
    Philip ap Reth
    Henry ap Thomas
    Galfridus ap Evan, Wales

APRIL

1 F. William Bougay and
    Robert, his brother
    Edmund Edy
    Lawrence Yong and
    William Grove, Blackburn
2 Thomas ap Rise, Wales
5 Thomas Grene, Notts
    William Boyge, Lincs.
6 Anon
8 William Bernard, York
12 William Chalmer, London
14 Henry Rose and
    Agnes, his wife, London
    John Grayste, Chester
    John Wilson, Newcastle
    Richard Cromwell, Holderness
16 William Smyth, Grimsby
17 Robert Mason, York
19 John Johnson, Calais
21 D. James Letys, Lincoln d.
    D. Oliver Gatte, Glien (Gloucester ?)
      d.
    John Hewett, London

22 Nicholas Baradow, Derby
Hugh Gimwan (?), York
John Herman, Kent
24 John Rede, servant of the Cardinal
of Canterbury
D. Richard Robert, London
25 Griffeth Nuwburgh and
Geoffrey ap Hasseth, Wales
30 John Brantyng, Suffolk

MAY

1 Thomas Goodhew, London
Margaret Elys, St Neots
2 Matthew Philipp, Cornwall
John Woodcroft, Kent
3 In the Hospice : 6 servants, 5
pilgrims
9 John Higham, Lincs.
10 Henry Lancastre, Suffolk
Agnes Stevynson, London
Katherine Reynold, ibid.
Thomas Twynyng, Worcester
13 M. John Charnok and
D. John Lawe, Kent
John Godehouse and
John Clerk, ibid.
19 Robert Dey, Lancs
20 William Lesyng, York
John Reynold, London
23 Thomas Dunton, Hadley, Suffolk
25 F. John Towett, Beverley
Alexander Robynson, Northumberland
Thomas Lamcute, Glos.
26 John Fevy, Northumberland
James Syde, a hermit, Sitting-
bourne
27 John Long, Richmond
28 D. John Frethby, Lincoln
John ap Howell, Wales
31 D. Thomas Wynawey, London

JUNE

1 John Wynne, London
5 John Downe, Barking
John Langwith, Cornwall
10 D. Walter Lonekyn, Salisbury
Thomas Philip, ibid.
Henry Huret, Ogham, Lincs.
12 Mark Daniel, Canterbury
13 David ap Nefeth ap Griffith, Wales
D. John Woodford, Winchester d.
14 F. William Pauli of a London
monastery
Ralph Coryng, Lancaster
15 Matildus ap Neph ap Grifyn, Wales
17 John Maghton, Chester and
Joanna, his wife
William Atwade, London
27 William Anstyn and
Margaret Nottyngham, Southwell,
York d.

JULY

4 John Brovue, Northumberland
Richard Scotte, Lincs
7 Mark Whyte, Norfolk
8 Richard Papwork, Lincs
John Bamburgh, ibid.
9 F. William Peryth of a York
monastery
10 John Forster, Worcs.
11 George Barlyne, Lincs
18 Thomas Rypon, Yorks.
25 Thomas Florentyne, London
Richard Davson, Boston
Roland Flyndorkyn, Northampton

AUGUST

3 Reginald Merston, Lincs
10 D. Thomas Symson, monk of
Chertsey
14 William Wright, Isle of Man
16 John Tusshew, Milborne Port
Thomas Clerk, York
20 John Forster, London

23   John Midelton, Northumberland
     Thomas Grafton, London
     John William, Plymouth
     1 Sick
29   John Troke and
     Richard, his brother, London—at
        dinner
     1 Sick

SEPTEMBER

3   William Machyne, a servant of D.
        Lawrence White, entered (the
        Hospice).
4   1 Sick   Raynford
     D. Thomas Duffyn and
     D. John White and
     D. Alexander Sympson, Kent
     John Belt, Gravesend
     John Yong, Salop.
5   John Burges, Malling
     John Bocher, London
6   John Tusshew of Milborne Port,
        who stayed for 3 weeks in the
        hospice, died.
8   William Malynerer, Thirsk in Yorks.
9   William Sheffeld, Winchester
     2 Sick
11   D. Richard Peck, Lincs
     Alexander Harelok, ibid.
     Robert Funkell, a hermit, Yorks.
     John Lee, Notts.
12   Joanna Newland, Kent
15   John Midelton, Ches.
     2 Sick
19   Thomas Walsall, London
     Katherine Forster, Chester
     2 Sick
27   Thomas Blakborne, Lancs
     2 Sick

OCTOBER

1   Alan Langreke, Boston
4   D. Reginald ap Evan, Wales
     Nicholas Stordy and
     Thomas Newson, Yorks.

5   John Yong, Chester
     2 Sick
7   Giles, the servant of D. Pro-
        tonotarius, died
11   Nicholas Stordy, Choirmaster of
        York Cathedral, died from the
        plague.
13   William Senettyll, Essex
     Richard Jugelson, Yorks
     1 Sick
15   William Cademay, Lincs
17   Richard Dunowe, Kent
     Robert Bynnyng, Stafford
     1 Sick
22   Robert New, Bristol
     Nicholas Cristofer, Calais
24   William Fulforth, Hallamshire
25   D. John Bravrie, Lancs
26   Thomas Drayton, Lancaster
     1 Sick
29   A sick 'ethicus' (?) Thomas
        Florentyne of London entered
        (the Hospice).

NOVEMBER

1   John Evan, Wales
     William Garnesay, London
     2 Sick
7   William Cornyssh, Bristol
8   Thomas Florentyne of London died.
11   D. William Thrisforth, Norfolk and
     his servant
     1 Sick—William Machyne
13   Thomas Holcott, Norfolk
15   F. John Lambourne, Oxford
     William Machyne not sick but weak
19   William Machyne
26   John Stokes, Lancaster
     John Baghley, Stafford
     John Edward, Somerset
     William Machyne

DECEMBER

5   William Germyn, Norfolk
     William Fytte, ibid.
7   D. Richard William, Hereford d.

9   William Machyne, who had stayed here for 3 months and 2 weeks, departed from the Hospice.

11   Robert Haycok, Lancs

17   2 Englishmen who had been against the Turks stayed in the Hospice to-day and the following days

27   John Morgan, Glos.

1481

JANUARY

21   F. William Kymberley, Norwich

25   M. Christopher Urswik and Thomas Buntyng, Northants.

27   M. William Shirwod and
F. Henry Cossey and
Robert Fuller, Norfolk
John Long, London
John Mytton, Lincs.
Alexander Skatte and
Thomas Orgar, Chichester

FEBRUARY

1   Thomas Buntyng, Northampton

11   John Townley, Pontefract

12   Thomas Byndewyn, Hertfordshire and
Matthew Dewan, his servant

18   John Fermage, Norfolk
Robert Jute, Bristol

21   Anon

24   Anon

25   Robert Saborne and
Robert Machyne, Suffolk

26   D. William Beryfeld
D. Richard Norwich
D. Richard Grene
D. Robert Mannger
D. Peter Fletcher
D. Thomas Morton
D. William Harratt
D. William Sutton
D. Henry Witham, a canon
D. Thomas Sutton
D. William Sampson
D. John Grene
D. John Kempt, all of Suffolk

MARCH

2   John Crosbyde, Durham

7   Thomas Wrynche and
Robert Lang, London

12   D. Richard Harycote, Glastonbury

15   Joanna of Bedleem (? Beadlam)

16   Richard Sendrithe, London
John Browne, Northampton

27   D. John Brown, Notts.
Thomas Rygott, Suffolk
John Wygge, London

31   John Hemmyng, a merchant and
His servant, Bristol

APRIL

1   F. Richard Wyncherley, a Dominican
John Davy, Wales

3   Robert Clerk, Wells

5   M. Thomas Tomgow and
M. John Staunce, Cornwall, students at Bologna
Edward Noreys, Lancs.

7   D. Ralph Stokeslay and
John Bukton, a nobleman, York

8   John Adam
William Gogh
David Dovgan and
John Taillow, Wales

9   Lawrence Herryson, Hants
William Fuller, ibid.

11   Richard Turburvyle
D. John Prenche
Galfridus ap Prys
Thomas Hopkyn
John ap Evan
Robert ap David
David William
David Madok
Evan ap David
Lloyd ap Evan
Edward ap David
John ap Evan
Joanna Welchian
Jankyn ap Gowan
Llowen ap Griffeth

On the same day D. Ralph Stokeslay of Yorks. died of pestilential
fever.

12 Felicia ap Davy
Richard Vaghan
David ap David
Walter Hoxdy

14 Thomas Jakson, Winchester
John Peltane, Kent

15 F. Robert Downebyle of the Order
of a Norwich monastery
D. Roger Warner, Norfolk

16 Thomas Bate, a merchant, London
William Wynkote, ibid.

17 Joanna Shersbury and
Joanna Whyte, Wales

18 2 Knights of Rhodes with 2 servants
were at dinner
Thomas Barrow, Staffs.

19 D. John Frend, Norfolk
Henry Joye, Southsea
David ap Frethe, Wales
John Martyne, Yorks.
Anon (Yorks.)

21 D. John Barow, Sussex
D. Simon Hall and
F. John Bury, Dominicans
Hugh Beck
Alexander Norman and
Thomas Swannie, Suffolk

23 D. John Bartilmew and
D. Richard Eyngett, Lincoln d.

30 William Bugdeyne and
John Coke, London

MAY

2 Robert Hyde
John Monk
Philip Clayton
Evan ap Griffeth
David ap David
David ap Baddy

3 In the Hospice : 7 servants, 8
Pilgrims.

4 Hopkyn ap John

5 Edward Walsshe and
John Kent, London

6 John Hawe and
William Robertson and
William Howell, Wales

8 Richard Herryson

9 John Reynold and
John Warner

11 Hugh Williams, Wales

13 D. William Grislay, Winchester

14 John Brown, London

15 Clement Waryng, London
M. Nicholas Hertt
D. William Randall, London
F. William Rood, a Carmelite of a
London monastery

19 Christopher, London

24 John Godwyn, Lincs.

26 John Rankell, Lancs.

27 Nicholas Brygye, Northumberland

30 James Lyndesay

JUNE

1 Thomas Blikenay, Beverley

3 John Forstre

5 Lawrence Geve, Devon

7 Thomas Kent
Thomas Ward
Anon.

9 D. John Wodbright, Suffolk
Anon.

17 D. John Beke and
John Forster, Dorset

20 James of Lache (?)
John Gerard and
William Harryson, Ches.

23 Thomas Goldsmyth and
Thomas Kyrkby, Somerset

JULY

1 D. Robert

4 John Gwyneth and
Richard Moratt, Hampton

10 John Salmon, Derbys.

16 D. John Stevynson, Suffolk
Paterma Browne, and
John, her son, Middleham
Lawrence Doyle, Wales
20 William Oxon, Yorks
22 Gervase Grenehull, Essex
24 Thomas Shaw, Norfolk
26 D. John Langley, Norwich d.
John Pentuey and
John Thorne, Bury
27 John Roo, Beverley
30 William Sutton, Southampton

AUGUST
1 Elizabeth Hegyns, Bridgnorth
3 D. John Browne, Calais
Lawrence Yong, Yorks
5 Thomas Holme, Yorks.
10 M. John Talbot, Calais
11 John North, London
18 John of the North
20 D. John Sanford, Oxford
John Pedlyven
25 D. John Craksale and
William Metcalf, Southsea
John Parys, Somerset

SEPTEMBER
3 Richard Pone, Bristol
4 John Williamson, Lincs.
5 D. William Rogers
John Cocke
Anon.
15 D. John Mochelney and
William Coker, Mochelney, for 8
days
17 Lucy Mathew, Wales
18 Richard Shephurd, Staffs.
20 Marion Bellynger, Yorks.
21 M. John Talbot, for dinner
22 Thomas Gulford, Winchester
28 John Robson, Newcastle
29 Alice Bedleem, London

OCTOBER
3 Thomas Johnson, Kent
5 D. Christopher Gelett, hermit and
priest of Salisbury d.
Robert Forster, Langley
William Dale, Lancaster
7 John Dokat, Lincs
10 F. Henry Cossey of a Norwich
monastery
Thomas Palmer, Lancs.
12 William Brokshawe, London
15 John Michelson, servant of the Prior
of St John, stayed here for . . .
17 F. Thomas Godwyn of a Norwich
monastery
Matthew Johnson and
John Tawkon, Essex
21 Elizabeth Gowgyn, London

NOVEMBER
1 Margaret Lambard, London
28 William Worsopp, London

DECEMBER
12 John Degre, Cambridge
15 D. John Style, Cambridge
Thomas Fitzwilliam, Essex
21 Agnes, Essex
23 D. John Wellys and
D. John Browne, Kent
Richard Mason and
William Dyer, Lincoln
24 Henry Codle, York
Robert Gray, Hertford
25 Thomas Swayne, London
29 John Warner, Suffolk
31 Isabella Saundres, London

1482
JANUARY
14 Thomas Bitton, Northampton
20 William Selmestre, London
30 John Browne, London

FEBRUARY

7   D. Michael Dulard, Kent
    2 sick
14 Thomas Sefoule and
    Robert Coughlin, Staffs
16 Henry Dalygo, Kent
    2 sick
19 2 merchants from London at dinner
    2 sick
27 Robert Biwgeys, merchant, London
28 Richard Crompett
    1 sick

MARCH

11 Robert Biwgeys, sick, entered with
    2 servants
15 D. Thomas May and
    D. William Gylinen, Suffolk
    D. Robert Carthan, Carlisle
16 Thomas Harlow, Suffolk
17 F. Robert Keche, London
    Thomas Manne, Carlisle
18 Robert Biwgeys died
22 D. Thomas
25 William Bellyncham
28 John Nyott
    Richard Sawyer
    John ap Lloelyn
    1 sick

APRIL

1   John Logan, London
3   D. Robert Molton, Knight of
    Rhodes, at dinner
4   D. William Clerk
    D. William Preston
    Kytto ap Lloellyn
    Morys ap Evan
    Evan Lloellyn
5   D. John
    Jonkyn ap Evan
    Howell Lloyd
    William Baker

    Hean Kennys
    Jonkyn ap Rosser
6   Thomas Cryne
    Louis Chylde
    Richard Avery
    1 sick
11 Thomas Wyker, London
    3 sick
17 F. Henry Cossey and
    F. Thomas Temple, Oxford
    Thomas Cowper and
    John Barton and
    John Taillon, Lancaster
    3 sick
21 John Capeland, Carlisle
22 D. William Gardeyn
    D. Thomas Bynyng
    Robert Lathome
    Henry Honehull
    Anthony Herryson
24 William Aber, Oxford
    3 sick
28 Richard Willeson, Lincs
29 John Chambre
    William Thalangane
    John Jacob
    Robert Lancastre
    Robert Smyth

MAY

2   F. William Skarbrowe of a Lincoln
    monastery
    John Richard
    William Sytorton
3   In the Hospice: 6 servants, 9
    Pilgrims, 3 sick
6   Robert Wylson
    John Smyth
9   John Goldston
    Pauline Wyatt, Kent
11 Martin Myles, London
    3 sick
13 John Nele and
    John Wylton, London

15 John Mason
17 Robert Haycok
    4 sick
20 Thomas Twyninyng
21 D. John Lawe and
    Hugh Robynson, Kent
22 Adam Hardyng
    James Selby
25 D. Richard Rooper
    John Andrew
    John Andrew
    5 sick
28 Richard Mason, Lincs
29 Alexander Johnson
30 D. Robert Potts, Kent
31 D. John Dardan, Oxford
    6 sick

JUNE

6 D. John Carliel, Durham
    Thomas Herrison
    Ralph Blaklogh
    William Cleveland
    John Torner
    William Bolton and
    Margaret Grey, London
    6 sick
9 F. John Makeblythe, York
14 John Browne, Worcestershire
17 Robert Whypenay, London
19 Elizabeth Conyers, Westminster
21 John Corney, Northumberland
22 D. Nicholas Chaffe, monk of Ilford
    3 sick
23 Beatrice Watkyns, London
26 William Robynson, Northumber-
    land
29 D. Lawrence Andrew, Lincoln d.
    D. Thomas Bolinew
    D. John Earpe, York d.
    Thomas Robynson
    4 sick

JULY

1 Robert Curteys
    Richard Hunt
    Stephen Howell
    Thomas de le Launde
6 John Stenton and
    James Leyon, Bristol
    4 sick
10 Robert Catys and
    Ralph Colston, Calais
    John Gyst, York
12 Robert Knyght and
    William Sawer, Northumberland
13 John Thomson
    Thomas Byrde
    John Lythome
    6 sick
14 William Crabford
17 John Brerton died
18 D. Lawrence Andrew, Vicar of
    Cathorp, Lincoln d., died
    5 sick
21 anon
22 Gerard, servant of M. Ralph
    Hethcote, died
24 anon
26 D. William Grave, Chaplain to
    Duchess of York
    D. William, Chaplain of the Staple
    3 sick

AUGUST

1 anon
2 anon (3)
4 4 sick
11 3 sick
21 John cleric of the Hospice died
    of the plague
    2 sick
25 F. Henry Cossey, Dominican of
    Norwich, died
26 D. William Burgeys and
    William Atkynson, Bridlington
28 F. Stephen Badeland, London
    Richard Holte, hermit, Maldon
    3 sick

SEPTEMBER

1   2 sick
8   Lawrence Yong, Windsor
9   Joanna Franke, Chichester
10 Robert Browne, Lincs
11 John Stafford, London
    1 sick
26 Robert Lambert, London
    D. William Hystede, Kent
    John Nyskell, Hounslow

OCTOBER

4   D. Thomas Beverlay, Yorks
    1 sick
6   1 sick
18 F. William Marster, Carmelite, Kent
    D. Thomas Plompton, Knight of
        Rhodes
    Edward Plompton
    John Weston, servant
    1 sick
20 D. William Fox, London
    William Bailly, Lincs
    2 sick
28 William Bailly, Lincs, died from
        plague
    1 sick and 1 poor

NOVEMBER

3   Walter Lathome, Southampton
4   Robert Wodcrosse, Suffolk
8   D. William Cheyne fell ill
9   1 sick
14 John Sendell, Manchester
    2 sick
17 2 sick
24 1 sick

DECEMBER

3   London merchant at dinner today
        and next day
12 D. William Kyldare, Berks
15 Richard Fox and
    Joanna Ogel, London
    John Browne and William Brylle,
        Somerset, stayed in the Hospice
        for 2 weeks, 2 days, with the
        consent of all *confratres*
    1 sick
23 Nicholas Colton and
    John Horsell, Yorks
24 John Torner and
    John Mannsell and
    Thomas Taillonn, Bristol

1483
JANUARY

6   Robert Horne
    Robert Belle
    William Kendall
8   Thomas Warde
13 D. William Bowman, Barnewell
    F. Henry, Augustinian, London
    Margaret Grene, Canterbury
20 William Akers and
    William Partriche and
    Thomas Walsall, London
27 William Godbolt and
    Hugh Candwell, Notts
28 Thomas Machbourne, Cambridge

FEBRUARY

7   D. William Chapman, Suffolk
    D. Thomas Skypwith, London
    Edmund Hedon, Yorks
15 William Power, hermit and
    Edward Coke, Suffolk

20 D. Peter Fletcher
   D. John Playford
   D. John Gybson
   D. Edmund Southwell
   D. Hugh Whytehed
   Robert Cowper
   Edward Pristland
   Oswald Bend
   John Mason, all of Suffolk
21 Agnes Rowell, London
28 D. Richard Wilforth
   D. John Porter
   D. William
   John Parker, Suffolk

MARCH
 1 F. Thomas Temple, London
 6 Richard Taillonn, Yorks
13 William Skelton, Yorks
15 D. George Smyth
   John Nele
   Thomas Berne
   Richard Newman
   Galfridus Robert
18 F. Brynley, Boston
   Robert Houghton, London
19 D. William Marshall, Prior of York
   John Baker, his servant
   D. Thomas Lincoln
   D. Richard Spitlesby, Lincoln
22 F. John Makeblyth
   D. John Monmoth
   Edward ap Jankyn
   Evan ap Predith
   David ap Howell
   Evan ap Meredith
   John Evan
   John ap Peroryn, Wales
23 D. John Hulles, Salisbury
   John Decka
   Evan ap David
   Lewis John
   Philip ap Thomas
   John Morys
   Margaret Berth
   Thomas, Wales

24 D. Grifeth Llewburgh
   D. Maurice Lloyd
   Maurice ap Howell
   Evan Googh
   David ap Evan
   Evan ap Agoo
   Llalley, Wales
   William Pittersley, Devon
27 F. William Mawutefeld, Stamford
   James Scott

APRIL
 5 Robert Tomson, Yorks
   William Walshman
 6 D. Thomas Staynborn, Canon of
     Shap
 7 D. Marmaduke Lomley, Knight of
     Rhodes
   D. William Bykerton
   John Walcot
   Richard Stylman
11 Robert Spakeman, Derbyshire
13 William Silnestre, Lincs
14 William Person, Yorks
19 Howell ap Evan
   David ap Howell, Wales
24 Galfridus Lewan
   John Doode
   Thomas Smyth
27 John Hemgyng and
   Janicote, merchants, Bristol

MAY
 1 William Pery
 4 William More
   Walter Blak
   William Harper
   John Mede
 6 Walter Williams and
   D. Thomas Hertbury and
   Robert Pene, Wales
 9 John Poole
11 Hugh ap Evan
   David ap Howell
   William Cristyan and
   Margaret Lindlow, Wales

12   Richard Bayon
      William Colt
      Henry Dutton
18   Robert Delf, Yorks
22   Robert Katermayn, Oxfordshire
23   Matthew David, Wales
29   William Tonstell
30   Robert Wilkyns
31   William Gyles

JUNE
 1   John Halle and
      Robert Caster, Northumberland
 7   Thomas Coke
      Alice and
      2 companions
10   Robert Sewyn
12   Alice Melton, washerwoman, died,
         R.I.P.
      her 2 companions
25   Thomas Deverous, Gloucestershire
27   D. John Edmund, Bradford
28   F. John Hundeyn, Suffolk
      Richard Fenby
29   D. Thomas Tomgow
30   Thomas Elstan

JULY
 2   John ap Howell
      John Richard
      John Saltern
 3   Jóhn Sygon and
      John Curten, Yorks
      William Oxe, with one companion
 6   John Ambrose, Lincs
10   Richard Morys, Lancs
      2 sick with 2 companions
19   Thomas Lamley and
      John Carliel, Worcestershire
      2 sick with 2 companions
20   Edmund Clapton, Knight of Rhodes
      John Andrew, Suffolk
      Roger
      2 sick with 2 companions

27   F. James Wright, Prior of a
         Canterbury monastery
      William Camberton, Yorks
29   William Dykson, Staffs
31   3 merchants, London
      3 sick with 3 companions

AUGUST
 5   William Griffyn, Bucks
 8   John Berton, Lincs
21   John Mathan, Northampton
      Joanna
22   John Wynkersell, London
      Tomson, Beverley
24   Thomas Cliffe, London
27   William Taillonn, Cambs
30   M. Robert Midelton, student at
         Bologna

SEPTEMBER
 1   George Chadworth, Sandwich
 5   Richard Russell
 6   Robert Porte
      John Olys
      2 sick
 9   William Rolleston, Staffs
12   D. John Warburton and
      John Clerk, Northumberland
      3 sick
22   John Clerk and
      Hugh Tomkyns, Northumberland
24   F. Edmund Pery, Carmelite
26   M. Edmund Martyn, doctor of laws
      his servant
      1 sick
30   Richard Chamberleyn, Kent
      1 sick

OCTOBER
 8   M. William Nycke
      M. Richard Nycke
      Richard Hulton, doctors
 9   John Clerk, Worcestershire
11   John Boucher, Middleham
      1 sick
12   M. William Jonys, sick

17 Henry Hakystow, Derby
John Ryngwod, Hants
2 sick
20 John Doverale, Dominican, Oxford
21 John Ryngwod, who came last
Friday, died from plague
22 M. William Jonys, Welshman, died
11 days after entering Hospice
1 sick
29 William Foller, Bath
30 Richard Fawcose
Andrew Lovage
William Alman, merchant, London

NOVEMBER

1 Lawrence Percedale, Minehead
1 sick
6 Edmund Burne, London
7 Henry Grant, Northants
8 Thomas Hewett, St Ives
1 sick
13 D. Alan Thomson, Newcastle
1 sick
17 D. Prior, Essex
21 2 sick with one companion
22 John Faron, Hospice cook, died
from plague, R.I.P.
24 M. John Whelpedale, Cambridge
25 John of Calais
James Browne and
William Spencer, Hull
1 sick
30 M. John Whelpedale, Cambridge

DECEMBER

3 Thomas John, Wales
1 sick
8 D. John Farby, Lincoln d.
13 D. John Warburton, who had
stayed in Hospice for 13 weeks
and 1 day left today. He had
lived here all autumn at the
expense of the Hospice, was
completely healed and when he
left he gave nothing.

1484
JANUARY

9 John Carve, Bristol
13 M. John Clement
Thomas Tedyr
William Olynge
14 John Hewys
16 John Forster
Andrew Crake
23 Edmund Crathorn, Yorks

FEBRUARY

4 D. Robert Webbe and
D. John Grene, Bury St Edmunds,
Suffolk
6 Herny Goldfinyth, Kent
8 Peter Otley, London
17 anon
19 anon
24 William Clerk
John Kendale, Hexham
Lawrence Pecox
Reginald Platte
25 Thomas Graunge, Lincs

MARCH

5 D. Richard Allerton, London
6 D. Thomas Gregge
D. John Preston
D. Reginald ap David, Wales
9 D. John Wodehell, London
Thomas Lanerok, Yorks
14 William Corper, Walsingham
15 D. Thomas Halywell
D. Richard Amott
F. John Hayward
William Southwell
John Russell
John Swale
17 D. Nicholas Williams
D. Thomas Blandryll
D. John Herman
D. Richard Hydon
D. John Danby

I

D. Robert Nyker
William Morton
Robert Depying, Lincs
22 D. Robert Wodroff
24 Stephen Samford and
Stephen Downe, Devon
25 M. John Talbott and
D. William Lolindede, Calais
27 D. Simon Eston, Thanet, Kent
31 D. Hugh Whitched, London

APRIL

1 John Sampson, Winchester
4 John Walter, Wales
5 D. Louis Henry and
D. Thomas Wenlok, Wales
6 D. John Jankyn
F. John Saule
F. John Watson with
4 substar. (?)
F. Bartholomew Lucas
7 Evan Pyper
Thomas Crondew
Richard Power and
John Williamson, Wales
8 Hugh Geffrey
John Dykett
Thomas Wychow, Wales
9 John Neelson
10 John Browne

11 11 pilgrims whose names are in the margin. [The names are not given.]
12 anon (3)
13 anon (12)
14 anon (6)
15 anon (11)
16 Thomas Shawe, York
17 Welthcan Morgan and
Henry Taillonn, York
18 Thomas Nevyll, Sherburn
21 William Mason
William Johnson
23 Alexander Pilkyngton, Lancs, died from plague
24 Thomas Holcott
25 Thomas Williamson
26 John Frost and
John Browne, Northumberland
27 John Symson
John Nelson
P. Stirett
Peter Clerk
John Herst
William Melle
28 anon

MAY

1 John Browne died

Summary of the numbers of persons mentioned above :

Year	Jan.	Feb.	Mar.	Apr.	May	Jun.	July	Aug.	Sep.	Oct.	Nov.	Dec.	Total
1479					37	36	17	12	19	16	19	4	160
							(7)	(9)	(6)	(1)	(2)		(25)
1480	11	11	21	30	26	17	12	11	19	16	10	7	191
							(2)		(9)	(5)	(3)		(19)
1481	10	23	12	61	27	15	16	12	14	13	2	13	218
1482	3	8	13	35	24	19	21	8	7	9	3	11	161
(Plague)		(7)	(1)	(10)	(18)	(13)	(18)	(12)	(3)	(6)	(7)	(1)	(96)
1483	13	19	40	17	22	13	29	9	13	12	12	2	201
							(9)		(7)	(5)	(6)	(1)	(28)
1484	8	11	28	81	1								129

The figures for sick pilgrims are given in brackets. They are greater than the actual number of sick, because they were included every week they stayed in the Hospice, and names are not usually given.

APPENDIX 13

LIST OF PILGRIMS FROM 4TH NOVEMBER 1504 TO 4TH MAY 1507

In forma nobilium 4.11.1504—4.5.1505

DECEMBER
8   D. John Vaughane, priest, chaplain (*ut dixit*) of D. John Williams, Knight, Bangor d.
9   D. Thomas Halsey, student at Bologna, Lincoln d.
30 D. William, rector of Witcombe, priest of York d., but living in Glos.

JANUARY
8   D. Theodoric, Dominican brother, born in Cambridge
12 William Skyl, *sensalis urbis*, then coming from England, admitted for 4 days
D. William Fackenham, canon regular of St Augustine, of the monastery of Hempton, Norfolk, Norwich d.
D. William Oxforde, canon regular, living (*ex licentia*) in Hoo, Rochester d.

FEBRUARY
13 M. John Bende, *praepositus* of the college of St John the Evangelist, Rushborn, Norwich d.
D. Martin, priest, a chaplain, for 3 days, though his servant Richard Thurmode stayed 8 days
D. John Person, vicar of St Mary, Stratton, Norfolk
D. John Treygonavel, vicar of the cathedral church of Exeter
D. Thomas Legate, vicar of Sporsey, Norfolk, but born at Chiviton, Bath d.
14 D. William Layfild, priest, Faham
D. William Wais, priest, Hotley, Suffolk
D. Nicholas Benyngham, Benedictine monk, from the monastery of Norwich
D. William Attkynson, priest, Norwich
D. John Heddone, priest, ibid.
D. Richard Fox, Myddilsam, ibid.
D. John Hayward, Hokold, ibid.
18 M. Robert Fisher and
M. William Tate, students at Bologna
William, servant of the same Master Robert

MARCH
11   William Heyrone, London merchant
13   D. Richard Hangemer, priest
      D. David Guinneg, also a priest
      D. Richard Abrome : all of Bangor d.
      D. Thomas Hopkyn, living at Calais
23   Master Game, Hereford d.

APRIL
 1   D. John Poltone . . . Bath d., but at the time living in the Isle of Wight
      William Gase, Southington
      F. John Houssmane, Carmelite, London d.
15   D. Thomas Halsey
      D. Robert Osborne, Carmelite, from a London house

In forma pauperum 4.11.1504—4.5.1505

NOVEMBER
25   John Dauson, scholar, Lancs., Lichfield d.

DECEMBER
 8   William of Confilde, Sussex, layman
16   John Lambarde, scholar, Lincoln d.
      Thomas Walter, scholar, Hecvilsal, Staffs, Chester d.
19   John Flemmyng, layman, Sussex, Winchester d.
21   Robert Motley, *unietarius* (?), Bristol
22   George Madescome, Wylbey, scholar, Lincoln d.
      John Hedwel, scholar, Granthorpe, ibid.
      Thomas Barbar, scholar, Louth, ibid.

JANUARY
 5   Thomas Barley, Hirsam, Kent
      John Butler, Hemsam, Gloucestershire
12   William Clifforde, cleric of the parish church of St Nicholas in Strata
      Antique Piscium, London
      Thomas Pepin of Great Harwood, Buckinghamshire. Erat puer in-
         nocens xii annorum propter iniuriam quia erat semimortuus qui
         venit mansit in hospitale usque initium Maii.
15   William Wake, born in London, layman
21   Thomas Brenstrete, tiler, Rye
22   Thomas Broker, *vir sun* (?), born in London

23 John David, Romsey in the county of Southampton
29 John Nevin, cobbler, London
30 Richard Hugsone, Carlisle
    Henry de Vice, scholar, born in Gonerby, Lincoln d.

FEBRUARY

6 Thomas Laurentii, born at Brentwood, Essex
15 James Browne, Norwich, Norfolk, born in Rothwelhithe, York d.

MARCH

5 William Ganil, scholar, Lincoln d.
   Nicholas Sarote, scholar, ibid.
   Thomas Douse, London
6 John Raulyn, sailor, born in Ludlow, who was brought in half dead,
   having been wounded by thieves, and stayed in the Hospice for
   36 days until restored to perfect health at the great expense and
   trouble of the Hospice.
8 William Springe, scholar, born in the parish of St Giles, London
15 Martin Nicholes, Hey, Suffolk
    Henry Peyne, scholar, Exeter d.

MARCH

16 William Bensone, scholar, Lincoln d.
    Robert Webster, scholar, York d.
    Evan ap Jhone, Oswestry
    Evan ap David.
    Henry ap David, Carmarthen
20 William Recol, Winchester, scholar of York d.
    John Luset, soldier, Calais
    William Pepersone, scholar, Calais
    Thomas Hardy, scholar, Lincoln d.
23 John Massye, merchants' apprentice, London
    David ap Thomas, Mahautley, Wales, scholar
    Llewellyn ap Jhone, Toven, Wales

APRIL

6 Thomas Butteler, Great Harwood
7 Thomas Farnysh, cleric, Southampton
15 Petronilla Chissey, Montgomery, Wales
19 Thomas Hoppie, dealer in spices, Wulbrige, Dorset

20   Thomas Williams, Steeple Aston, Wilts. Died in Hospice on 24th, quia ante adventum fluxu ventris insanabili ad fores mortis venerat.
22   William Cocke, Canterbury
29   Humphrey Weymer, scholar, Wurwell, Salop
30   William Langtone, Tattersall, Lincoln d.

In forma nobilium 4.5.1505—4.5.1506

MAY

4   John Hoptone, captain of 2 ships (?), Shropshire
     D. Thomas Grene, rector of the parish church of Wodmonstorne, Winchester d.
     D. William Argoll, priest living at Lambeth, near London.
11   F. Richard Clarke, Carmelite, London
     Hugh Cloptone, London merchant
     William Dyne, merchant, ibid
14   Richard Whighte, Dominican
     F. Robert Smithe, Dominican

JUNE

14   John Schepard, master and first sailor of the ship 'St Ann'
     D. Thomas Skynner, Bury St Edmunds
     D. Robert Higgis, Coventry
     D. William Wilsone, Augustinian canon, from the abbey of Dale, near Derby
19   F. Robert Shrogge, Dominican, Canterbury
     F. Richard Backester, same Order, Worcester d.
     Nicholas Waryng, captain of the ship 'Sovereign'

JULY

29   D. Richard David, priest of Morshalte, Pembrokeshire

SEPTEMBER

15   D. Richard Riches, hermit, Grantham, Lincs

OCTOBER

17   D. Nicholas Harpesfilde, student at Bologna
20   John Romlyns, singer or musician, Llandaff d.

NOVEMBER

12 D. Robert Lytelmane, Maldon
15 F. William Dores, Franciscan, London

DECEMBER

17 John Purnay, recently *canucuarius* (?) of the Hospice

JANUARY

 4 D. Richard Hilley, treasurer of Salisbury
30 John Mortimer, *nuncius* of the king
31 F. Robert Duram and
    F. John House, Franciscans, London

FEBRUARY

19 John Clerke, Hampton

MARCH

 9 D. Robert Wingefelde, noble, Suffolk, *hostiarius camerae regis*
    Doctor Wilkockes
    M. Richard Tylnham
    M. Richard Wingefelde, brother of the aforesaid Robert
11 (?) Richard Bray, *frater spurius eiusdem*.
    D. John Larke
    D. Robert Touris
    D. Henry Roberti
    D. Edmund Evertone
    D. John Highham
    D. Nicholas Saunders
    D. John Tauternayhte
    D. William Faryntone
    D. John Foutre
    D. William Tacy
    D. Henry Halley
    D. Thomas Undrewode, all priests of Norfolk and Suffolk
22 D. Anthony Calver
23 D. William Alene, vicar of Bristone, Norwich d.
25 D. Robert Rysone and
    D. William Taylor, London
    D. Thomas Wilsone, Louth, Lincs
    D. Richard Bromeley, Cistercian, of Valle Crucis, Llandaff d.

APRIL
1 D. Thomas Fouler and
2 D. William Taylebushe, Fotheringham, Lincs
4 D. David ap Thomas, priest, Llandaff
5 D. Reginald Mynsterworthe
   D. Thomas Luddam, vicar of Wulle, Salisbury d.

In forma pauperum 4.5.1505—4.5.1506

MAY
5 John Turpyn and
   Robert Claxby, Feversham, Canterbury d.
   Richard Griffyn, London
7 Robert Graunte, scholar of Oxford
8 John Wilsone, Hackney, near London
   John Bevy
   William Wilson
11 John Jacksone
   William Fisher
   John Clerke
   William Graunte
   Nicholas Edingtone
   John Kenworthe
   William Cloughe
   William Osyngton. The last ten all sailors of the ship 'Anna Clerke'
12 William Wrighte, parish cleric of Lynn—stayed 16 days
14 William Jonson, born in Holdernesse

JUNE
15 James Watkyn, servant of the Hospice at Calais
19 James Radman and
   William Clerke, sailors of the Southampton ship 'Ly Jesus'
   John Leneryn, Combe, Devon
   William Hegge, Stow, ibid.
21 Robert Broughtone, of the abbey of Holme
22 Thomas Borletone, Shepnel, Shropshire—stayed 17 days
   Simon Robynson, Concolde, York d.
   Nicholas Harysone, Hermyngtone, Oxfordshire
   Richard Aphouel, Arundel
29 Annes (?) Bungay and
   James, son of above, London
   Matilda Abel, arriving with them
   John a Bourtone, London

JULY

5   Richard Jakesone, Brentone, in the county of Richmond
11 John Pucocke, Calais
12 Wilfrid Martyne, fisherman, Sandwich
14 James Lovel, sailor, Dover
    Philip Stephani, Basingstoke, Winchester
24 William Jaaquessone, Lincoln
    Thomas Spense, scholar, ibid.
29 Nicholas Cochet, born in Derby

AUGUST

3   Thomas Waller, North Colyngham, Notts.
    John Algoode, weaver, ibid.
5   Thomas Manyerde and
    Robert Stephan, Tysaw, Sussex
12 Richard Daly, brewer, London
24 Robert Dycy, weaver, Newmarket
    Richard Alby, ibid, who died in the Hospice
    John Hogg, scholar, Camelford, Cornwall
25 Andrew Hosborne, Yfercombe (Ilfracombe ?), Devon
27 John Hudson, Suynerfelde, Kent
    Robert Cuteler, tanner, Sudbury, Suffolk
29 Lucy Mason, Carmarthen
30 Elizabeth Kithin, Oswestry, Welsh Marches
31 Richard Cabald, Lincoln

SEPTEMBER

1   William Halyday, Kegworth, Leicestershire
4   John Baker, Badby, ibid
5   John Bakone, York
30 Richard de Le, Ipswich, sailor in the ship 'Sovereign'

OCTOBER

2   John Creswel, serving-man, Southwark, London
12 John Fuller, Hungerford, Berkshire
    William Stondeley, Newcastle, sailor
16 Milo Faber
    John Biby
    Thomas Gam
    Edward Write
    John Tego, all five sailors of the king's ship
    Margaret Beket, Canfold, Lancs.
17 John Coke
    Joan, his wife, Calais

NOVEMBER

12 John Brederwike, York
31 Nicholas Morgan, Bristol

DECEMBER

17 Richard Hill
    Edward Alen
    William Preste, sailors in the ship 'Thomas' of London

JANUARY

 5 James Jonhson, Whitby, Yorks.
 6 Hugh of Knaresborough
    John Alene, London
 8 Thomas Smyth, Carpenter.
15 Henry Perot, sailor in the ship 'Margaret' of Southampton
18 John Sparke, Bath d.
    Joan Sparke
28 George Wellis, Neapolitan Knight

FEBRUARY

19 William Coke
    John Sprusemane
    Roger Hunte
    John Dounyngharte
    William Fovy
    Walter Griffyn
    Richard Dyckeman
    Matthew Dickeman
    Thomas Justise
    Thomas Morice, all ten sailors of the ship 'Margaret' of Southampton
    Evan ap Thomas, Rye
23 William Howe, Ripon, Yorks.

MARCH

 8 Richard Griffyn, Lincoln
    Thomas Grene, Bury St Edmunds
10 Robert de Lever, Bolton, Lancs
12 Robert Hill, Dartford, Kent
13 David Cenith, Poyselond, Wales
14 John Oley, Horsely, Derbys, who remained 32 days because of illness
15 Robert Borow, London
22 Thomas Skeler, scholar of Oxford, remained 14 days

23 Thomas Widought, Premonstratensian canon, Langdon.
24 David ap Howel ap Evan
    John Galfride
    Evan ap Ennow
    Morgan ap Ennow
25 Thomas Topclefe of the college in Fotheringay
    John Emlyne, Denbigh, Wales
30 John Anglicus, Southampton.

APRIL

 1 Robert Woode, Dartmouth, Devon
    Harry Tudre, Denbigh, Wales
    John Coke, scholar of Boxly,
 2 William Grome, scholar of Barton upon Humber, Lincoln d.
    Henry Dey, scholar of Skidbroke, Lincs.
 4 Wilfred Hugh
    Hugo ap Evan
    Rhys ap Mad
    David ap Houel ap Evan
    Philip Ricard
    Philip ap Rice
    John Thomas
    Gryffith ap Kynbyn
 5 David ap Gryffin
    Philip ap Evan
    Llewellyn William
    Morus ap Evan, all Welshmen, Llandaff d.
    Morus London, qui egrotavit in hospitali per xvj dies et quia nescivit
        loqui nisi Wallice habuit secum tot dies ad hospitalis onus unum
        alium Wallicum qui servaret eum.
    Oweth ap Evedo, Mulier
    Howoth ap Morod
    John Mater, scholar of Crokehorne, Bath d.
    John Swan, Shipton, Suffolk
    Philip Sartor, Denbigh
 8 William Baker and
    David Guynueyth, Denbigh
 9 John Asseveryn, Marteley, Worcs.
    Richard Esteby, London
12 Henry Jonson, Welsh hermit
    John Hoskynson, Wellock, Salop
    John Kinghston, Westmorland
    Thomas Smyth, London
15 Richard Forlone, S. Salvator, Yorks
    Edward Ynghsby, Pangbourne, Devon

23   William of Framlingham, Suffolk
      John Leger, Durham
      John Job, Hastings
24   Lambert Moton, St Martin's
27   Thomas Benson, London

In forma nobilium 4.5.1506—4.5.1507

MAY

14   F. Henry Standish, *Sacrae Paginae Doctor*, Provincial of the Friars
          Minor in England, Coventry d.
      F. Thomas Draper, of the same Order, doctor, Hereford d.
      F. John Warner, of the same Order, prior of the House of St Francis,
          Bedfordshire
19   F. William Garden, Carmelite, Newcastle
20   F. John Holen, Franciscan

JUNE

12   D. John Evan, Rector of St Mary de Ax, London
17   D. John Breynford, monk of the monastery of Bury St Edmunds
      D. Robert Jury, Vicar of Thurston, Suffolk
27   F. Richard Koy, Augustinian, from the monastery of the Augustinians,
          London

JULY

16   D. Thomas Ephani, *vicarius choralis* of the church of Mek (?)
      D. Hugh Daniel, Knight of the Order of St John of Jerusalem, coming
          from Rhodes on his way to England
21   F. William Derian, Carmelite, London

AUGUST

      No *nobiles* came

SEPTEMBER

21   D. Richard Bushe, Carmelite
24   D. John Chambre, doctor of medicine and arts, Durham
25   D. John Coton, priest from London

OCTOBER

      F. Robert More, Carmelite, London

(NOVEMBER)

D. Robert Barker, Vicar of Tederyng, Norfolk : *venit* 28 oct. [*sic*]
D. William Knyghte, doctor of laws, London, *eodem die*
D. Thomas, of Yfish, Norfolk, *eodem die*
F. John Stanley of the Augustinian friars, London, 29 *die*
(It is not clear whether these entries refer to October or November.)

DECEMBER and
JANUARY

No *nobiles* came

FEBRUARY

16 D. Henry Roberti
D. William Bevet
Master Richard Jaqueson, Rector of Wethnesham
D. Richard Date, Rector of Coton
D. William Basse. All five priests of Norwich d.
18 Thomas Grantham, merchant, who had come to Rome from the Holy
Land
19 F. William Kymbery, Dominican, Rector of Suelands, Norwich d.
D. Robert Bramford, canon of the Order of St Augustine, Vicar of
Rishmer, Norwich d.

MARCH

14 D. Christopher Fisher, London, Rector of Toucetur (Towcester ?)
15 M. Robert Duffyng, Rector of the parish church of Wikem, Norwich d.
D. John ap D., priest, born at Chalyan, Bangor d.
D. Peter Croche, professed canon of Taunton, Bath d., residing in
Suffolk
25 D. Morgan applln (ap Llewellyn ?) ap Rice, priest, Menevia d.
28 D. John Conwey, Abbot of the Monastery of the Blessed Virgin in
the Island of Bassey (Bardsey ?), Bangor d.
D. Robert Bethum   ⎫ priests of the same diocese
D. Robert Lewis *nante* (??) ⎭
30 D. Thomas Asteley, priest, Durham diocese

APRIL

3   Robert Bolte, of Worstede, Norwich diocese
William Claxton, of Norwich
(two London merchants)
16 D. William Buttre, priest, Llandaff diocese, coming from Bath

20   Master Stint, student, Lincoln diocese
     D. David Flemyng, Rector of Ostyng Hanger and of St Peter near
     Calais
     George Effamat, London
22   D. William Wode, monk of Thame, Cistercian
     D. Robert Taylor, monk of Stanlake, of the same Order
29   D. William Roger, Rector of Kingisdon, Canterbury or Rochester d.
     John Clerk, Gravesend, Rochester d. (Both noted at *March* 29th.)
30   D. Robert Grene, Welby, Lincoln d.

MAY

1   D. James Partrich, monk of the Order of St Barnardine, Ruley, Oxford

In forma pauperum 4.5.1506—4.5.1507

MAY

5   Nicholas Wurseley, scholar, Eglem, Lancs.
7   Thomas Lenke, London
    Richard Neykilhode,
8   Richard Alway, Colorne, Bath :
    Richard Higon, Carmarthen : both stayed 24 days because of sickness
    Walter Russell, Hanley, Ches.
9   William Nisoll, Cardiff
14 Robert Broune, scholar, Southam, Devon : stayed 30 days because
       of sickness
    Thomas Morynge, scholar, Winchester d.
    John Rakison, Venerley, Norwich d.
    Robert Morel, scholar, Lancaster
    Robert Tuynond, servant of Dr Standish, provincial of the Friars
       Minor
23 John Whight, rustic, Lifon, Devon
24 Edmund Harte, scholar, Hemsley, York d.
27 Hugh Grant, Taunton
    John Ruthbey, Malmesbury,
29 William Wrigth, scholar, Byland Abbey, York
30 Richard Bryght, tailor, Sandwich, Canterbury d.
    Thomas Ponfret, London
    Richard Whitbye, London

JUNE

- 2 Robert Grene, Maldon, Essex
- 7 William Broke, servant of William Buttre, London merchant
    John Povyne, Beverley, York d.
- 9 Elizabeth Wellis, Norwich, widow
- 12 Henry Hannad, scholar, Godalming
- 17 Robert Graymyngton, Gisborne Abbey, York d. : servant of the prior
    of Gisborne who died at Jerusalem with Richard Omtford, Knight
    of the Garter
    William and Agnes Bloker, Norwich
- 29 (19 ?) Thomas Corbet, Pensbury, Salop.
- 25 Christopher and Agnes Venables, Bungay Abbey, Suffolk
- 27 Richard Hoskynson, Brym Stapliforth, Ches.
    John Sterissenger, scholar, York
    Michael Marton, scholar, York
- 28 Matthew Conwey, Wrexham, scholar

JULY

- 2 Thomas Eymyl and John Chanin, Shepton Mallet, Somerset
- 3 William Debet, Wallingford, Berks.
    William Chesterton, Missenden
- 11 Alicia Bythin, Gloucester
- 16 William Smyth, *tonsor pannorum*, Shepton Mallet, Bath d.
    Henry Edwardi, scholar, Rammysbury, Lincoln
    Servant of D. Daniel
- 21 Louis Purde, *tabernarius vini*, Bristol
- 23 Thomas Crofte, scholar, once an apprentice, London
    Thomas Wode, apprentice of Master Eglesfild, *tonsoris pannorum*,
    London
- 24 Richard Drywre, *sonatorum in tubiis* (trumpeter ?), who remained sick
    in the Hospice until 24th August, his son serving him the whole time
    John Dryvre, son of Richard, Ramsey
    Thomas Smythe, scholar, Ramsey
- 27 John Richardeson, York
- 29 Peter Warme, Drayton, Norfolk

AUGUST

- 13 William Arpes, scholar, Vrome, York d.
- 18 John Smyth, *factor stringarum*, London
- 19 Juliana Dutt, London
- 26 John Chidley, sailor, Dartmouth

SEPTEMBER

19   Edwardus, barber, of the parish of St Peter in Comel, London
     John Smyth, scholar, Cherton, Norfolk
     F. Thomas Cooke, Dominican, London
22   John Hill, weaver, Upton Smeyllysbury, Norfolk

OCTOBER

3   William Case, cobbler, Southampton, coming from Naples
12   John Teper, Swyneshed Abbey, Lincoln d.
23   Lionel Holden, monk, Malmesbury
     Henry Wulley, Amesbury, Salisbury d.

DECEMBER

3   Christopher Foxe, of the parish of Lynn, Norfolk
19   A certain Thomas, servant of D. Nuporte, Knight of the Order of
     St John of Jerusalem and treasurer of the Order, coming from
     Rhodes to England

JANUARY

1   A hermit of Kent, whose name was unknown because of the shortage
     of servants

FEBRUARY

24   William Brekestnete, cleric, Norwich d.

MARCH

1   Margaret Birchnata, Glovernie, Worcester d.
3   Richard King, born at Anste, London d.
     John Leper
10   Thomas Wright, Uterton, Suffolk
13   Matthew Conwey, a poor young scholar of Wrexham, Coventry d.,
     who was here in June of this year but returned after a long illness
     and was admitted for 3 days only for motives of charity
     George Knollis, Porton, York d.
     Robert Cathy, Bisborne, ibid.

MARCH

14 Edward Curtes, Eusterton, Norwich d.
    Robert Wode, Warwick, Lichfield d.
16 Richard Tege, Carmardyn, St Asaph d.
    A servant of D. Christopher Fisher
22 John ap David
    John Poole
    Thomas Lewyl
    David Carte
    Henry Adamo
    John ap Evan
    Griffin Storke
    John ap Griffyn, all of Karleyn
    William Furchey, Aylesbury
23 John Swan, Shipton
    Robert Prety, Eya, of Suffolk, Norwich d.
24 John Edde, Southampton, Winchester d.
    Hugh ap Gryffyn
    Griffyn ap Evan
    John ap Evan, of Wolshiphm (?), Llandaff d.
    Maurice Hathy, Knyghton
    David Cornil, Caernarvon
25 Richard ap Thomas
    John ap Rice
    William ap Rice
    Jenkyn ap Evan, Menevia d.
    Llewellyn ap David, St Asaph d.
    Yngerarde, wife of Evan
    Guervil, wife of Rice
    Guervil, wife of Hugh, 3 women of St Asaph d.
26 Morgan ap David
    Galfrid ap Meredid
    David Meredid, Bangor d.
27 David Galfridi
    Galfridus Dickon
    Galfridus ap Llewelyn
    John Mocke
    Howel ap David
    David Debnant
    Galfridus Mervice
    David Deicus
    Galfridus David
    Ygerin Hayle
    Margaret, wife of Llewelyn

K

Ledo ap Griffyn
Henry ap Griffyn, all of Bangor d.
29 John de Cantia, Stockland, Suffolk
William Pason, Carlisle, Cumberland
Robert ap Robyn
Olwyn ap Gittyn
Thomlewis, wife of Meredith, Bangor d.
William Bowon, Norpole, Lincoln d.
30 William Gilson, Ripon, York d.
John Clappon, Skipton, ibid.
Robert Aerth, Teweyn, Norwich d.

APRIL

1 Raulinus Harison, London d.
Roger Hanson, ibid.
3 Thomas Porter, Stone, Lichfield d.
John Gebil, servant of Robert Bolte, merchant of London
6 Robert Marshal, Bromeley
John Tegnar, both Winchester d.
Heliseus Harte, Leighth, Lichfield d.
John Cokeson, Lynn, Norwich d.
Henry de Landynthorpe, Lincoln d.
10 John Ken, Higham, Lincoln d.
John Layns, Alerton, York d.
16 Richard Burdon, Southwark, London
Oliver Jonson, ibid.
John King, Flecbor, Lichfield d.
Robert Vullyng, Norwich
William Harteford, Spelber, Lincoln d.
John Parmonson, Parmonson, Exeter d.
22 Thomas Nirte, Eglondsh, Lincoln d.
Gilbert Mason, Birchley
John Jonson, Birkeby, both Winchester d.
23 John Rede, Dunwich, Norwich d.
27 Thomas Carleton, Northallerton, York d.
28 Robert Bocbery, Sarum Cuothetarius
29 John Marys, (? . . .) tesbury, Salisbury d.

MAY

1 John Sanderson, Dalton, Furness Fells
John Synose, Egrimond, York d.

3 John Aphiwel, Northern, St Asaph d.
John Kingestone, Hatefield, York d.
4.11.1504—4.5.1505

Nobles	34
Poor	48
Total	82

4.5.1505—4.5.1506

Nobles	55
Poor	147
Total	202

Total of pilgrims 4.11.1504—4.5.1507
489

4.5.1506—4.5.1507

Nobles	49
Poor	156
Total	205

APPENDIX 14

LIST OF PILGRIMS FOR 1514. *Liber* 13, ff. 99–101

APRIL

In forma nobilium

The Lord Abbot of St Augustine of Canterbury
The Lord Prior of St Gregory, 3 days
The Lord Abbot of Tynbi, 1 day
The Chaplain of the Abbot of St Augustine
D. Dunstan Petlay, Chaplain of the Prior of St Gregory
D. Martin, Canterbury, with a servant
John Wolff, Calais, 3 days
A Canon with one Priest from Rowforth Abbey
    (these two were poor and so stayed for 8 days)
The Chaplain of the Abbot of Tynbi, Wiltshire
D. up David Flood, Wales
D. Walter Powell

D. Robert Wylson, York d., who came from Germany
Andrew Wodcok, merchant, Canterbury
D. Michael Wawan, London
D. Wm. Smith, York, for 8 days because he is poor

In forma pauperum

Wm. Goyghe, Somersetshire
Robert Pernell, Norwich
Robert Farnell, hermit, Norwich
Thomas Battyn, Warwickshire
Robert Lyn, York
John Ben, Dorsetshire
John Lambert, Wiltshire
Robert Wylson, Northumberland
Robert Wolrych, Dorsetshire
Thomas Holsted, Canterbury
Two hermits, Westmorland
John Husthawayt, Westmorland
Morgan Thewelli, Welshman
Trahar up William, Welshman
Hugh Gryffith, Welshman
Robert Hart, Canterbury
John Hart, Canterbury
John Hallan, Suffolk
John Selli, Suffolk
John Bernaed, Calais

MAY

(From this month the distinction between *nobiles* and *pauperes* is
not recorded.)

Robert Pernell, Norwich
W. Smith, priest
Robert Farnell, hermit
W. Wreith, Lynn, Norfolk
John Byrd, Cambridge
Thomas Whyte, Boston, Lincoln
D. W. Stoide, *frater*
Richard Painter
John Grenlay, Ludlow
John Monicor, Hull, York d.
Harry Debeni, Sidmouth, Devonshire
Andrew Carter, Sydberry, ibid.

JUNE

Thomas Crumwell, London d.
Richard Garland, Isle of Wight
John Garret, Devonshire (?)
Brother John Hyston, Franciscan, Norwich d.
Brother John Howys, Franciscan
D. Robert Rychmonde, Canterbury
Edward Dawson, Norumbrus (?)
Humphrey Gowgg, Welshman

JULY

Thomas Hawkis
3   D. John Smyth
David Johan, Welshman
John Regent

SEPTEMBER

3   W. Smyth, Huntingdonshire
Thomas Stewyn
W. Nubi, Durham d.
John Apy, Hertfordshire
Richard Fyllypis
D. W. Oxffurd
Gilbert Pilson, Bedfordshire
W. Brown
Augustine Pakyngton
W. Paynter, Somersetshire
17   D. John, Sudbury, Suffolk
The Sub-Prior of Standlay, Wiltshire
Master Knight, London d.
W. Atkynson, Somerset
18   Richard Page
Thomas Porich, Master Knight's servant
W. Wicarris
25   John Diccons, Lincoln
Richard Smyth, Somersetshire
28   Antony Gardner, Kent
30   Joan Phelyp, Welsh, Glamorgan

OCTOBER

2 Richard Cly
3 Nicholas Harfford, Westchester
Stephen Bryan, Winchester d.
Richard Dani, Chester
W. Perkyn, Rotherham
Thomas Hynam, Hertfordshire
4 Robert Huddelston, Derbyshire
7 D. Manni
8 D. Sharkher, London d.
An unnamed Welshman with Joan David, Welsh
A young man *ex campo espanorum*
John Gretham, Wiltshire
David Johns, Kirkowell, Welshman
W. Danyell, Hampton
10 Richard Morgan, Brecknock
W. Cotte, Suffolk
11 David Clark, Yorkshire
James de Calisie, Furness Fell
19 Edmund Lyll, Northumberland
23 4 servants of M. Gryffith Down
22 Allan's butler, Kendal
26 Thomas Sadler, Cheshire
John Thynkyll, Yorkshire
27 W. Priarman, Canterbury
John Parman, Canterbury

NOVEMBER

1 Joan Buges, Welsh
8 Joan Raw, London
M. a David
Richard Dod, Salisbury
W., Cardiff
John Surray, Manchester
Thomas Berret, Mawmsfelde in Sherwood
John Smith, Northumberland

THE HOSPICE OF ST THOMAS
AND THE ENGLISH CROWN 1474—1538

The Hospice of the Blessed Trinity and of St Thomas was founded in Rome in 1362, as a refuge for English pilgrims, by a guild of Englishmen then living in the city. These men acted on their own initiative and in a private capacity. But as the Hospice flourished and became known in England, it came to be considered as belonging to the English nation and to the Crown. Royal interest in the affairs of the Hospice reached a peak with Henry VII's interventions in its government, which brought it under royal control. The connection between the Hospice and the English Crown was finally broken (apart from a brief resumption during the reign of Queen Mary) by Henry VIII's repudiation of papal authority. The popes seldom intervened in the running of the Hospice, but in 1538 Pope Paul III secured the replacement of Henry VIII's custos by Reginald Cardinal Pole, and the period of royal control came to an end.

We are here concerned with the last sixty years of the Hospice's connection with the Crown, but a brief examination of the earlier years of the Hospice is necessary to understand what happened between 1474 and 1538. It is also necessary to give a brief account of the constitution of the Hospice, to understand the form taken by the royal interventions.

THE GOVERNMENT OF THE HOSPICE

The members of the Hospice, called *confratres*, were admitted to the confraternity on payment of one or two ducats. We know of many admitted in Rome[1] but it was also possible to join without leaving England.[2] The *confratres* actually residing in Rome met every year on 3rd May, always in the same room of the Hospice, and elected the officers to govern the Hospice for the following year. These were the custos, or warden, and two camerarii, or chamberlains. They served for a year, but were often re-elected several times. Two auditors were also elected at this time, to check the accounts of the custos from the previous year. A chaplain was elected when necessary, but this office was more permanent than the others. It must be remembered that most if not all of the Hospice officers had other business to attend to in Rome. Most of them in this period had taken law degrees, usually at one of the Italian universities, and were engaged in legal business at the Roman Curia, often as procurators for bishops and monasteries in England.[3] The custos was paid twelve ducats a year and the chaplain sixteen, but the other officers received no salary.[4]

Of course, this system did not always work perfectly. There seem to have been few *confratres* living in Rome at any given time ; consequently it sometimes happened that one man held two offices, custos and auditor or camerarius and auditor. In 1475 only one camerarius was elected because there was no *confrater* available for election as second camerarius. Again, in 1504 one reason given for the king's decision to appoint the custos henceforth was the fewness of *confratres* in Rome at that time.[5] From 1517 onwards it was difficult or impossible to find anyone fit to serve as custos.

The camerarii were usually associated with the custos in the yearly *computus* or accounts, and when there was no custos they took control of Hospice affairs. They were usually men of some eminence, who did not live in the Hospice, were not paid,

---

[1] Cf. App. 26, p. 188.
[2] Cf. Gasquet, *History of the Venerable English College, Rome*, London 1920, pp. 40–41.
[3] E.g. Richard Belyngham, auditor in 1472, was procurator of the monastery of Durham. In the notes on Appendix 26, p. 188. we give details of *confratres* who had studied at Italian universities.
[4] *Lib.* 18, f. 100 v. But v. inf., p. 172.
[5] *Lib.* 1, f. 12 r. Cf. App. 20, p. 182.

and had more important work to do elsewhere. But their position was not merely nominal, because the *confratres* took the trouble to elect a new camerarius if one left Rome before his term of office was ended. The part played by the camerarii no doubt varied with the men who held office ; some would concern themselves more than others with the running of the Hospice. The *confratres* themselves were the supreme governing body of the Hospice, and their consent was necessary when matters of importance had to be decided. Even men of authority in Church and State such as Cardinal Bainbridge had to secure their agreement in order to act effectively in Hospice affairs. Not all their power was delegated to the officers of the Hospice.[6]

The Hospice existed to serve English pilgrims, particularly those who were poor or sick. It could house about a hundred people, and when there was no room the poor were given money instead of accommodation. A distinction was made between pilgrims *in forma nobilium*, who paid for their keep, and those *in forma pauperum*, who did not. Between two-thirds and four-fifths of the pilgrims were reckoned as poor.[7]

Financially, the Hospice was dependent upon the rents from the property it owned, especially from its houses, which numbered between thirty-five and forty.[8] There was also an annual collection made for it in England, known as the *firma Angliae*, but the proceeds of this varied considerably, depending upon conditions in England and the qualities of the *firmarius*, the Hospice's procurator in England. Miscellaneous sources, legacies, and the payments of newly admitted *confratres* also brought in money. The inventories of goods show that the Hospice owned a considerable amount of plate and other valuables, which must have been worth a great deal.[9]

Pilgrims returning to England from Rome would soon make known the existence of the Hospice ; news would also be brought by royal envoys, since there was considerable diplomatic activity between the English Crown and the papacy, particularly after the beginning of the Great Schism in 1378 when Richard II supported Urban VI against the French anti-pope, Clement

---

[6] As can be seen from John Clerk's appointment in 1523, *Lib.* 22, f. 3 v (Prefatory letter). Cf. App. 22, p. 183.

[7] Cf. supra, p. 101.

[8] Cf. Rentals, *Lib.* 18 *passim* and *Lib.* 1, ff. 14, 24, 41.

[9] Inventories of goods exist in *Lib.* 33 for 1445, 1491, 1496, 1515, 1525, 1538, and also in *Lib.* 1 and *Lib.* 22.

VII.[10] However, we do not know for certain when the kings of England began to interest themselves in the Hospice.

Houses belonging to the Hospices of St Thomas and St Edmund had signs outside them, either of the Trinity, in the case of St Thomas's Hospice, or of St Edmund ; with the signs were the words *'haec est domus hospitalis nationis anglorum'*. At least two houses, mentioned in leases for 1510 and 1514, had the arms of the king of England as well.[11] The Hospice building itself had a shield outside above the main door, which exists to this day in the English College. It bears the arms of England and France, quartered in the style first adopted by Edward III. A Latin verse beneath records the claim of the English kings to the French Crown, and also gives the name of the shield's maker, Lawrence Cache, and the date, 1412. The shield and its inscription were still in position outside the door of the Hospice in 1630.[12] If the Hospice was rebuilt in 1412,[13] we may reasonably connect this rebuilding with the shield displaying the royal arms. But we do not know whether Henry IV, then reigning, took any interest in the Hospice, even though this evidence suggests that he may well have done. The seal of the Hospice which now exists at the British Museum also bears the Royal Arms, though an otherwise similar seal in Lincoln Museum does not.[14]

Further evidence of royal interest in the Hospice is found in the inventories of 1491 and 1496, which mention plate given by the duchess of York, the mother of Edward IV and Richard III ; this included a magnificent chalice and silver candlesticks. It must have been given after 1445, since the plate is not mentioned in the 1445 inventory. In connection with Edward IV, it is worth noting that his brother-in-law, Anthony Woodville, Earl Rivers, was admitted to the confraternity of the Hospice, together with his companions, when the earl and his party came to Rome on pilgrimage in 1475.

[10] Parks, *The English Traveler to Italy*, Rome 1954, I, 290–1. Unless otherwise stated, all details on diplomatic activity are taken from this book.
[11] *Lib*. 14.
[12] *Lib*. 277, f. 1 r.
[13] Gradwell (Z. 68, f. 65 r.) suggests this, but there is no other evidence.
[14] THE VENERABILE, XVI, 115 (May 1953) and cf. illustration, p. 46.

Royal Coat of Arms once over the entrance of the Hospice

Frontispiece of John Clerk's account-book

THE ROYAL ENVOYS

Some indication has been given of the general connection between the Crown and the Hospice in the first century of its existence. It is now time to examine the most important link between the two, the men who were servants of the king and of the Hospice at one and the same time. These must be carefully distinguished into two classes, according to where their primary loyalty lay, even though in particular cases it is often difficult to do so. On the one hand, there were men living in Rome, with some business to occupy them. Such men would be elected to office in the Hospice and the king of England would often make use of them to handle routine English business with the Holy See. Their official title was *procurator* in the fifteenth century and *solicitator* in the early sixteenth. On the other hand, the king would at times send men to Rome on a special mission, which might involve their staying in Rome some years. They were usually elected to be camerarii of the Hospice, and no doubt served it well, but they were primarily royal civil servants and diplomats. They were called *oratores* and were in effect temporary ambassadors, ranking above the *procuratores*. Unfortunately the position is slightly more complicated, because neither the king nor the pope liked the term *orator*, and envoys were supposed to revert to the rank of *procurator* after six months as *oratores*. But the tendency was for the term *orator* to become permanent, as official diplomacy became the rule, and diplomatic contacts and business increased. Diplomatic representation in the modern sense developed at Rome in the early sixteenth century, while elsewhere the mediaeval system of special embassies still prevailed.

We are not here concerned with the evolution of diplomatic relations between the English kings and the papacy, except in so far as it throws light on the history of the English Hospice. The first royal envoy we know to have been connected with either of the Hospices was Thomas Polton, later bishop of Chichester. He was sent to Rome in 1414, went from there to the Council of Constance in 1416, and was then resident envoy in Rome from 1418 until about 1426. He was a member of the confraternity of St Edmund's Hospice,[15] but we do not know the date of his admission, nor whether he was a member of St

---

[15] *Lib.* 272, f. 1 v. The references to the confraternities of St Edmund's and St Thomas's Hospices immediately following are taken from *Lib.* 272 and *Lib.* 17 respectively.

Thomas's Hospice. Andrew Holes, resident envoy at the Curia from 1432 to 1444, and later Keeper of the Privy Seal in England, was associated with the Hospice of St Thomas in 1450. His successor as resident envoy, William Grey, later bishop of Ely, was king's proctor at Rome from 1445 to 1452, and rented a house from the Hospice of St Edmund. He was associated with St Thomas's Hospice in 1452-3, and both Holes and Grey were members of the St Edmund's confraternity. John Lax was king's procurator in 1456, and from 1459 to 1462 : he was also papal secretary, and camerarius of St Thomas's in 1447, 1450 and 1452, and again in 1466, besides being a member of the confraternities of both Hospices. Other royal envoys associated with the Hospice of St Thomas were Richard Bole, royal envoy in 1459, and Robert Botyl, Prior of the Order of St John of Jerusalem in England, who was an envoy to the king of France and to the pope in 1447.[16] In 1463 Peter Courtney, later bishop of Exeter, and of Winchester, was camerarius of St Thomas's Hospice, and in 1466 James Goldwell, later bishop of Norwich, was admitted to the confraternity of St Edmund's. The two Hospices were united in 1464.[17]

We are now in a position to see the events between 1474 and 1538 in their historical context. During the first part of this period, up to 1496, we merely find the same state of affairs as has already been outlined. Royal envoys are associated with the Hospice and serve as camerarii. From 1496 to the end of Henry VII's reign we find the Crown in control of the Hospice. But in the years that followed, Henry VIII and Wolsey were not interested in the Hospice, and royal control was dependent on the personal efforts of three envoys : Christopher Bainbridge, Cardinal Archbishop of York, Sylvester Giglis, Bishop of Worcester, and John Clerk, Bishop of Bath and Wells. Royal control comes to an end in 1538 with the intervention of Pope Paul III and Cardinal Pole.

[16] English Knights of the Order of St John of Jerusalem figure prominently in the history of the Hospice in the second half of the fifteenth century. The inventory of 1445 records gifts to the Hospice from Robert Botyl, Prior, and Hugh Myddleton, Turcopolier, of the Order.

[17] *Lib.* 272, f. 77 r. Cf. supra, p. 89.

THE YORKIST KINGS AND THE HOSPICE 1474–85

There are three reasons for beginning a detailed study from about the year 1474 onwards. From 1474 Hugh Spaldying held office in the Hospice for over twenty years, with scarcely a break. For most of the time he was custos, and this continuity is in sharp contrast to the frequent changes in custodes before and after his time. In 1476 John Shirwood became camerarius ; he was orator to the pope for some years, representing Edward IV, Richard III, and Henry VII, and was important both as a royal envoy and as a link between the Crown and the Hospice. Also from 1474 we have almost complete records of elections to offices and of admissions to the confraternity of St Thomas's Hospice.[18]

Spaldyng was camerarius from 1474 to 1478, and custos of the Hospice from 1477 to 1491, again from 1492 to 1496, and finally from October 1499 till his death at the end of August in 1500. We know little about him ; his doctorate in law suggests that he was the permanent representative in Rome of some monastery or diocese. Henry VII appointed him royal procurator in 1486, together with two royal envoys, to deal with provisions to benefices in English cathedral churches, and in 1487, as resident royal procurator, he joined the large embassy sent by Henry VII to thank Pope Innocent VIII for the dispensation permitting his marriage to Elizabeth of York. He is clearly distinct from the class of orators or procurators sent specially from England.

Edward IV sent many envoys to Rome, some of whom we have already mentioned. John Sant, Abbot of Abingdon, represented the English king at Rome from 1474 till 1479. He was admitted to the confraternity of the Hospice in 1475, and is described as orator in the record of his admission. The term *orator* becomes more common from now on, though the distinction of *orator* from *procurator* is still not always made clear. Sant held no office in the Hospice but the election of 1476 was held in his house, owing to the fear of plague in the Hospice, where someone had recently died. Abbot John also gave to the Hospice a large and valuable chalice.[19]

---

[18] Cf. App. 26, p. 188, and App. 28, p. 266. All details of elections to offices and admissions to the confraternity up to 1511 are taken from *Lib.* 17.

[19] *Lib.* 33, inventory of 1496.

Another royal envoy of Edward IV, John Shirwood, Archdeacon of Richmond, was admitted to the confraternity in 1476 ; elected camerarius in the same year, he held this office continuously till 1486. He was a royal *orator* in 1478, again in 1483 and 1484, and again in 1492 ; the term seems to have been restricted to particular occasions still. As we know from rentals of the Hospice, he paid eighty ducats annually for the most expensive of the Hospice's houses (with a stable) from 1480, and possibly earlier, until 1486.

John Dunmow was a royal envoy from 1476 to 1488, but was not admitted to the confraternity of the Hospice till 1482, when he is described as royal *nuntius*, a special envoy ; he was also a royal chaplain and a prebend of Windsor. Another Shirwood, William, was admitted to the confraternity in 1478, where he is described as chaplain to the duke of York, the second son of Edward IV. He may have been John Shirwood's brother. In 1479 he served as auditor, then from 1481 till 1483 he was camerarius. But in 1484 he was sent to England to dispatch Hospice business with Richard III ; the Hospice accounts mention the horse which was bought for him for this mission. He was dean of Acland in the Durham diocese, and papal penitentiary, and when he died in 1497 he was buried in the Hospice church.[20]

Though Edward IV sent many diplomatic missions to Rome, we get the impression that Richard III took a greater interest in the Hospice. Certainly he took a great interest in John Shirwood. At his coronation, John Shirwood walked beside him and the king asked Pope Sixtus IV to make him bishop of Durham, and to raise him to the cardinalate. More surprisingly, he wrote to the cardinals with the same requests. John Shirwood was in fact consecrated bishop in the church of Sant'Onofrio, Rome,[21] in May 1484, only two months after Richard III's request, but he did not receive the red hat. Before his consecration, in April, the king wrote to Pope Sixtus and to the cardinals asking for a remission of the tax due on the first year's income of the new bishop, on the grounds that the bishop of Durham had to maintain large garrisons against the

---

[20] For William Shirwood, cf. Parks, op. cit., pp. 361, 456 ; *Lib.* 17, f. 16 r. ; and his memorial slab in the College church.

[21] Cf. Brady, *The Episcopal Succession in England, Scotland and Ireland*, Rome 1876, I, xxi. For Richard III's letters to the pope and cardinals, cf. Rymer's *Foedera*, 1741 edition, Vol. V.

Scots. Richard was always alive to the problems of the defence of northern England.

Edward IV's resident envoys, John Shirwood and John Dunmow, kept their position during Richard's brief reign and Thomas Langton, Bishop of Menevia, was sent out to join them with the title of orator. The two bishops ranked higher than Dunmow, who is called procurator, and who was a royal chaplain and prebend of Windsor. His prebendship may well account for his presence in Rome, since in 1484 one of the subjects of negotiation with the papacy was that of privileges for the new royal chapel at Windsor, begun by Edward IV.

Another of Richard III's envoys fits into neither of our categories. John Kendall was camerarius of the Hospice from 1486 till 1492, but he was resident in Rome from 1480, as representative of the Grand Prior of the Order of St John of Jerusalem for England, France and Italy. John Kendall and John Shirwood were members of the guard over the conclave which elected Innocent VIII, and Kendall walked in the new pope's coronation procession as representative of the Grand Prior.[22] But the king also made use of Kendall, for in December 1484, Shirwood, Langton and Kendall were appointed royal orators to give the king's obedience to Innocent VIII, a routine procedure on the election of a new pope.

Short as Richard's reign was, we find that it marked an advance in the evolution of relations between the Crown and the Hospice. He is the first king of England who is explicitly recorded as having direct business with the Hospice.[23] The importance he attached to relations with Rome is shown by the fact that he employed two bishops as his permanent representatives in Rome, Shirwood and Langton. Shirwood and Dunmow were both camerarii of the Hospice throughout his reign. Royal interest in Rome and in the English Hospice was evidently growing, and it reached a climax in the reign of Richard III's successor, King Henry VII.

[22] Parks, op. cit., p. 307.
[23] Lib. 18, f. 172 r.

HENRY VII AND THE HOSPICE 1485–1509

The change of dynasty made no immediate difference to the Hospice and Henry VII continued to employ as his envoys men who had been loyal servants of his Yorkist predecessors, though he also employed new men. His first important business with Rome was to secure a dispensation for his marriage with Elizabeth of York, together with diplomatic recognition. Christopher Urswick, King Henry's chaplain and confessor from the days when he was merely the duke of Richmond, an exile in Brittany, was sent to Rome early in the reign to secure recognition and the dispensation. He was admitted to the confraternity of the Hospice in June 1486. He succeeded brilliantly in his mission, obtaining not only the dispensation but also a Bull excommunicating anyone who rebelled against Henry VII. But he was too valuable a man to leave in Rome ; in November 1486 he was occupied in quieting discontent in Lancashire.[24] He was orator again to the pope and to the king of Sicily in 1493.

In February 1486, Henry VII appointed three procurators to deal with the provisions to benefices attached to English cathedrals. They were Shirwood, Dunmow, and Hugh Spaldyng, the Hospice custos. Dunmow was elected to the see of Limerick in November 1486 ; he was camerarius of the Hospice from 1483 till 1485 and again from 1486 till 1489, in which year he died at Rome. In May 1487 Pope Innocent VIII received in audience an embassy sent by King Henry to thank the pope for the marriage dispensation. The ten members of this group —the most imposing English diplomatic mission to Rome of the period—were the following : the bishops of Durham, Hereford, and Limerick ; the dean of Salisbury ; William Selling, Prior of Canterbury ; John Weston, Prior of the English Province of the Knights of St John ; and John Kendall, Hugh Spaldyng, and two lay knights. Four of them—Shirwood, Dunmow, Kendall and Spaldyng—were already resident in Rome and joined the party when it arrived there. These four at least were members of the Hospice and past or present officers. When the business of this embassy was concluded, Shirwood returned to England and was employed by Henry VII later in 1487 in enquiring into the causes of the rebellion

---

[24] Cf. article *Christopher Urswick* in DNB.

of that year.[25] Presumably Dunmow replaced him as senior English resident envoy, for we find the bishop of Limerick called orator for the first time in 1488.[26]

A new orator, David William, Archdeacon of St David's and Master of the Rolls,[27] was admitted to the confraternity of the Hospice in November 1490 ; the following May he was elected as camerarius and is described as procurator, which suggests that he was a resident envoy, perhaps intended to replace Dunmow, who died in 1489. But David William himself died not long after this and was buried in the church of San Crisogono, opposite the St Edmund Hospice. Another orator, John Englis, was admitted to the confraternity in May 1491, but nothing more is known of him. About this time we find many Englishmen of rank admitted to the confraternity, including the future archbishops of Canterbury and York, William Warham and Christopher Bainbridge. The latter rented a house from the Hospice in 1493 and was camerarius of the Hospice in that year.[28]

Another interesting embassy arrived in 1492, when John Shirwood returned to Rome and, with John Giglis, conveyed Henry VII's obedience to the new pope, Alexander VI. The interest of this embassy from the point of view of the Hospice lies in the combination of the old and the new. Shirwood had been connected with the Hospice since 1476 in the days of Edward IV. This was his last mission to Rome ; he died there in 1494 and was buried in the Hospice church. John Giglis on the other hand represents the future trend of the history of the Hospice. He had been a papal collector in England from the days of Edward IV, but Henry VII sent him to Rome some time between 1489 and 1492 as his orator, the first of a series of Italian agents employed by the English Crown. Perhaps the new dynasty felt that foreigners were more trustworthy than Englishmen with possible Yorkist sympathies, but it may merely be that the Italians knew the ways of the Curia better than the English. John Giglis' nationality did not prevent his becoming closely connected with the English Hospice. There is no record of his being admitted to the confraternity but he was camerarius in 1494, with Robert Morton, Bishop of Worcester,

[25] Cf. article *John Shirwood* in DNB.
[26] *Lib.* 17, f. 18 v.
[27] Mackie, *The Earlier Tudors*, O.U.P. 1957, p. 648 ; and also Parks, op. cit., pp. 302–08.
[28] *Lib.* 232, f. 19 v.

and again in 1496, a crucial year in the history of the Hospice. He succeeded Morton as bishop of Worcester in 1497, the first of a series of three successive Italian bishops of that see. In 1498 he died and was buried in the Hospice church. Henry VII, in his letter to the Hospice of 1497, mentions his orator John Giglis as one of his informants on the state of the Hospice.

So far in the history of the Hospice there is no evidence for direct royal intervention in its affairs. Royal officials and envoys held office in the Hospice and rented houses from it. Doubtless they were influential in the running of the institution, and we know that the king was kept informed. But in 1496 we find the custos replaced by a royal envoy, and in 1504 the king decided that henceforth he would appoint the custos himself. For the rest of the reign of Henry VII elections cease and the custos is appointed for a term of years or perhaps indefinitely. His accounts are sent to England for examination by the king. Because of the lack of evidence, these momentous changes are not easily explained but there seem to have been two principal reasons for them. The first and more important was the genuine interest and concern felt by Henry VII for 'his' Hospice ; the second was the *confratres*' request to Robert Shirborn, royal orator in 1496, to take over the administration from the custos Hugh Spaldyng. Alexander VI took the Hospice and its inhabitants under the protection of the Holy See in 1493,[29] but it is doubtful whether this meant very much, and there is no reason to suppose that this caused Henry VII's assumption of control. Nor is there any evidence to support the theory that the Hospice sheltered a band of Yorkist rebels, and that Henry VII acted to bring the Hospice under the control of his own supporters.

Robert Shirborn, Archdeacon of Buckingham and King Henry's secretary,[30] was sent to Rome, to tell the pope that the English king was prepared to join the Holy League, to keep the French out of Italy. He arrived in Rome in June and was escorted to the house of John Giglis, Henry VII's resident envoy and camerarius of the Hospice. Shirborn was admitted to the confraternity of the Hospice on 21st August. The usual election had been held in May 1496 when the officers for the coming year were elected, with Spaldyng as custos. But

[29] Cf. App. 15, p. 176.
[30] Cf. article *Robert Shirborn* in DNB.

Spaldyng's administration ended on 30th September following, and Robert Shirborn took over the next day, at the request of all the *confratres*. An instrument of conditions was drawn up, which unfortunately no longer exists. The entry in *Liber* 17 describing the change says nothing of the duration of Shirborn's term of office, but an insertion in the margin says that it was to last until 1st October 1499 ; it therefore seems probable that a three-year term of office was agreed upon. Shirborn named Edward Scott, who was admitted as a *confrater* on 8th November, as his substitute to deal with Hospice business.[31] That Shirborn took over control of the Hospice at the request of the *confratres* is confirmed elsewhere in *Liber* 17, at the beginning of an inventory of the Hospice made early in October, where it says 'at what season the brethren of the sayd hospitall requiryd master shyrborn to take the reule of yt in hys handys *ad meliorem finem*'.[32]

When Shirborn began his term of office, he found that there was no money in the Hospice chest. He therefore lent rather more than thirty-seven ducats for the care of pilgrims, 100 ducats to buy necessities for the Hospice, including food, and a further 100 ducats towards the rebuilding of the Hospice church. The work on the church began in 1497, '*studio et ingenio domini roberti shyrborn*', and was completed in 1501, when the church was reconsecrated. A new wine-cellar was also built.[33] The sums lent by Shirborn were repaid at the end of his administration,[34] and a total of 1000 ducats was spent on the rebuilding of the church ; so it would seem that the destitution which Shirborn found on taking over was only temporary.

It is evident, however, that the immediate initiative in securing the change of control came from the *confratres*, not from the king. Hugh Spaldyng was now an old man, and probably his administrative skill was declining. So far as we know he governed the Hospice well during his long wardenship. Detailed accounts survive only for the years from 1479 till 1483,[35] but judging from these, from the regularity of the annual elections, from his long tenure of office, and from the confusion which we find in the next century, the last independent *custos* deserved well of the Hospice. The reasons for his replacement

[31] Cf. App. 16, p. 177.
[32] *Lib.* 17, f. 21 r.
[33] Ibid., f. 20 v.
[34] Ibid., f. 20 r.
[35] *Lib.* 18, *passim*.

by Shirborn remain obscure, but his old age, financial difficulties of the Hospice, and possibly a desire on the part of the *confratres* to secure royal help may all have played a part.

King Henry soon learnt of these developments. He wrote to the *confratres* on 29th January 1497 (new style), and the letter was received on 10th March.[36] The king describes the Hospice as *noster hospitalis*, and goes on to say that he has heard from the Cardinal Protector of England[37] and from John Giglis, his orator, that the Hospice is well enough endowed to support more people than it does. It is interesting to note these sources of Henry's information. He tells the *confratres* to observe all that has been decreed by Shirborn in consultation with them, regarding the existing statutes and the hospitality they are to exercise towards the king's orator. He also shows concern that provision be made for English students in Rome. In connection with this, it should be noted that Thomas Linacre, William Lily, and John Colet all became members of the Hospice not long before 1496, and that during this period many Englishmen were admitted to the confraternity of the Hospice at the end of their studies at Italian universities. The letter shows King Henry's interest in the Hospice, which he clearly regarded as a national institution subject to him, and it concludes with the command to copy out the letter into the Hospice statute-book, so that no one in future can pretend ignorance of the royal commands.

Shirborn did not stay long in Rome, for in 1498 he was appointed to fine those of the clergy guilty of supporting Perkin Warbeck. He was sent to Rome as orator again in 1502 and in 1504. Meanwhile, Edward Scott, his substitute, was in charge of the Hospice with the rank of camerarius. The election held in May 1497 merely confirmed the existing officers in their respective positions, without giving their names. There is no record of an election in 1498, but in 1499 the existing officers were confirmed as before. In addition, however, new officers were elected as well to take over the administration when Shirborn's three-year term expired at the end of September 1499. The new custos was to be Hugh Spaldyng, now re-elected after three years out of office.

Henry VII wrote again to the *confratres* and camerarii on 28th September 1498, and his letter arrived probably at the

---

[36] Cf. App. 17, p. 178.
[37] Cardinal Francesco Piccolomini, Archbishop of Siena, later Pope Pius III.

end of the year.[38] He has heard that they have obeyed his previous instructions and that things at the Hospice have improved, so now he thanks them and encourages them to persevere. This letter speaks of Shirborn as the originator of whatever reforms were made ; presumably the phrase in the earlier letter suggesting that the *confratres* had a share in it was largely politeness. The *confratres* replied to the king's two letters the following January, 1499, and speak of the Hospice as '*tuum hospitale*'. They stress their unanimous agreement with the steps taken by Shirborn, and add a flattering eulogy of Henry himself.[39]

Shortly before the end of Shirborn's term of office, in July 1499, two new orators were admitted to the confraternity—Sylvester Giglis, Bishop of Worcester, and Adrian Castelli, both Italians. Castelli was a valuable agent, as he was Alexander VI's secretary ; he was made a cardinal in 1503, having become bishop of Hereford in 1502. In 1504 he was translated to Bath and Wells. After the death of Alexander VI his influence declined and he was on bad terms with Sylvester Giglis. We are not concerned with his career here, fascinating as it is, as he had little connection with the Hospice.[40] Sylvester Giglis, on the other hand, was closely linked with its fortunes until his death in 1521 ; he was John Giglis' nephew, and succeeded his uncle both as bishop of Worcester and as Henry VII's resident orator.[41]

Spaldyng returned as custos on 1st October 1499, at the end of Robert Shirborn's period of office. But Edward Scott, having returned from Bologna where he took the degree of Doctor of Law some time in 1499,[42] was made camerarius in December, with the provision that he should live in the Hospice and help Hugh Spaldyng with the administration, in view of the extra business involved in the Jubilee Year of 1500. There is a similar provision in the election of May 1500, again because of the Jubilee and because of Spaldyng's old age. This was the last time Hugh Spaldyng was elected as custos : he died the following August.

[38] Cf. App. 18, p. 180.
[39] Cf. App. 19, p. 180.
[40] Cf. article *Adrian Castelli* in DNB ; Parks, op. cit., p. 309.
[41] Cf. article *Sylvester Giglis* in DNB.
[42] Cf. Parks, op. cit., p. 627. All details about Englishmen studying at Italian universities are taken from this book.

The Hospice was now under the control of the two camerarii, Sylvester Giglis and Edward Scott, both of whom were connected rather with the Crown than with the Hospice, for Sylvester Giglis was resident orator, while Scott had been Shirborn's deputy, and on his tomb in the Hospice church was described as a royal *solicitator*. On this occasion Giglis took the initiative, and in January 1501 called an extraordinary meeting of the *confratres* to deal with the situation. The solution, which was approved by the *confratres* but initiated by Sylvester, was to make Scott custos. He was succeeded by Thomas Cabold, papal penitentiary, as camerarius.[43]

In the next three elections (1501–03) Scott was re-elected custos each time and Giglis continued as camerarius, living in a house rented from the Hospice, the same house as that rented by John Shirwood fifteen years before.[44] It is interesting to note, in 1502, what may have been a sign of further royal interest in the Hospice ; some of the *firma Angliae*, the proceeds of the annual collection in England for the Hospice, was brought out in Henry VII's large warship, the *Sovereign*. This instalment consisted, not of money, but of pewter vessels and Normandy canvas, to make sheets for the beds of the poor pilgrims.[45]

The year 1504 brought a new crisis and a further substantial step in the establishment of royal control. Henry VII sent a delegation to convey his obedience to the new pope, Julius II. It was composed of Richard Beere, Abbot of Glastonbury, Gilbert Talbot, Earl of Shrewsbury, and Robert Shirborn, now dean of St Paul's. Edward Scott rode to Florence to join the delegation there ; it arrived in Rome in May and was met there by Sylvester Giglis. The Hospice officers were involved in the business of the embassy, and consequently the customary audit and election could not take place at the usual time. When the envoys left Rome it was evidently hoped to hold the election in June, but Edward Scott fell ill of a fever, and died on 24th July, being scarcely forty-two years old. He was buried in the Hospice church.

---

[43] *Lib.* 17, ff. 29 r–v ; this account of the extraordinary meeting was written by Sylvester Giglis himself.
[44] *Lib.* 232, f. 27 r.
[45] *Lib.* 17, f. 39 v. App. 25, p. 187.

The Hospice was again without a custos, and John Allen, chaplain of the Hospice since 1502, governed the Hospice until 4th November. King Henry must have learnt very quickly of the state of affairs, perhaps from the returning delegates. He decided that the present system, by which the custos was elected by the *confratres* in Rome, could lead to many evils— especially when, as now, there were few *confratres* in the city. So he called together many of the most noble and knowledgeable *confratres* of the Hospice then in England, and decreed that henceforth the custos would be nominated by the king. He then wrote to Robert Shirborn, still orator in Rome, and named Hugh Inge as custos, with the agreement of the English *confratres*.[46] Hugh Inge's administration began on 4th November 1504.

Inge was at New College, Oxford, till 1496; in that year one of the Hospice books[47] describes him as custos. There is no supporting evidence for this, and although it is theoretically possible that he was custos in that year, it seems far more likely that it is a mistake. In 1504 he was English penitentiary in Rome, and in October of that year was appointed *solicitator* by Henry VII to receive the obedience of Cardinal Adrian Castelli, on the occasion of the latter's translation from the see of Hereford to that of Bath and Wells. Shirborn and Giglis were also named to represent the king in this matter.[48] At the end of 1504, Sylvester was sent to England by Pope Julius II on a mission to the king. So his advice and assistance were not available to the Hospice until his return, when Henry VIII sent him back to Rome as orator and as his representative at the Fifth Lateran Council.

Inge's term of office lasted just over three years, ending on 1st January 1508. Some of his accounts exist, but there is no reference to any elections in his period of office, nor to any camerarii or auditors. It seems likely that the king appointed him for a definite three-year term, perhaps recalling the precedent of Shirborn's administration from 1496 to 1499. During Inge's administration, the accounts of the Hospice were sent to England every six months for inspection by King Henry. This was at any rate done for the first and the last six months of his term, and presumably in between. This final innovation

---

[46] *Lib.* 1, f. 12 r. ; *Lib.* 17, f. 25 v. App. 20, p. 181.
[47] *Lib.* 33, inventory of 1496.
[48] Cf. article *Hugh Inge* in DNB.

marks the high-water mark of royal control : the king not only appoints the custos, but also checks the accounts.[49] We do not know whether the practice continued under Inge's successor, but it certainly came to an end with the death of Henry VII in 1509. Yet ironically enough, Hugh Inge is the first of a series of custodes who fell into debt to the Hospice ; he owed 193 ducats, which were still unpaid in 1523 when he was archbishop of Dublin.[50]

Little is known about Inge's successor as custos, Christopher Fisher, who succeeded him on 1st January 1508 and held office until 1st May 1510.[51] He was a royal *solicitator* during this period. There are the usual yearly accounts, and at the end of Fisher's administration it was found that he was in debt to the Hospice, owing over 990 ducats, a large sum.

King Henry VII died in 1509, and with him died much of the Crown's concern for the Hospice. Henry VIII, unlike his father, had no personal interest in the Hospice, and neither had Wolsey. But the changes of Henry VII's reign had made the Hospice more or less dependent on royal support, and when this was not forthcoming its fortunes tended to vary with the interest and initiative of the resident royal envoys. The king himself is the dominating figure in the history of the Hospice in Henry VII's reign ; in that of Henry VIII, Bainbridge, Sylvester Giglis and John Clerk stand out far more than the king or Wolsey.

THE HOSPICE UNDER CARDINAL BAINBRIDGE
1510–1514

Christopher Bainbridge, Archbishop of York, was sent to Rome early in the new reign as royal orator to Julius II. Since the reign of Richard III the rank of envoys sent to Rome had been rising steadily, and with Bainbridge this tendency reached its peak. He arrived in Rome in November 1509, and was welcome, for Louis XII of France had invaded Italy, and English support was valuable to the papacy. Bainbridge represented England in Italy till his death in 1514, and was made a cardinal

[49] *Lib.* 1, f. 13 v. ; *Lib.* 13, ff. 184 v., 187 r.
[50] *Lib.* 22, f. 8 r.
[51] Christopher Fisher arrived as a pilgrim *in forma nobilium* in March 1507. *Lib.* 1, f. 29 v.

by Julius II in 1511. This soldier-pope also employed him with the papal troops as his legate, and as a military commander.

But Bainbridge also found time to introduce a new regime at the Hospice, of which he had been camerarius in 1493, and a *confrater* since 1492. He called a meeting of the *confratres* on 3rd May 1510, the usual election day, and eight new *confratres* were admitted, the first we have record of since 1503. Five of these were employed as officers of the Hospice in 1510 and 1511. No audit of the yearly accounts had taken place in the Hospice since 1504, presumably because the accounts had been sent home to Henry VII ; so five auditors were appointed to examine the administration of Inge and Fisher. Of these, two were long-standing members of the Hospice and the remaining three had just been admitted and belonged to Bainbridge's entourage. The first two were William Fell, vicar of Newcastle-on-Tyne, a *confrater* since 1490 and an auditor in 1491, and John Allen, in Rome on business for the see of Canterbury, chaplain and *confrater* since 1502, and temporarily in charge on Scott's death in 1504. The three new men were Thomas Halsey, English penitentiary, William Styntt, a scholar of Thomas Langton (Bishop of Winchester and Bainbridge's uncle), and William Burbanke, Bainbridge's *servitor familiaris* and secretary. All three were closely connected with Bainbridge ; the archbishop had been present at Halsey's examination in law at Bologna in this year, and later obtained for him the Irish bishopric of Leighlin.[52]

Besides the five auditors, two camerarii were elected, John Allen and William Styntt. Again we note that the old and the new were represented. No custos was elected ; instead William Burbanke was appointed by Bainbridge to manage the Hospice.

A further seven *confratres* were admitted in April 1511, but the only one of any importance for the history of the Hospice was Richard Pace. He was Bainbridge's other secretary, and like many others, was admitted to the Hospice soon after finishing his course of studies at Italian universities. He later became dean of St Paul's and king's secretary, and one of the leading English diplomats of the period.[53] Pace was elected custos of the Hospice in 1511 on the usual day, 3rd May, but the list of salaries for the year 1510–11 indicates that Burbanke

---

[52] For Bainbridge's intervention cf. App. 21, p. 182.
[53] Cf. Parks, op. cit., p. 317, for a good summary of Pace's career.

served for only four months as vice-custos till 1st September 1510, and that Pace was vice-custos for the remaining eight months of the year.[54] The camerarii elected with Pace were William Fell and John Wolfe, the latter having been made a *confrater* with Bainbridge's first group in 1510. We have no mention of elections after 1511, and the names of officers have to be gathered from the yearly accounts and from other sources.

Bainbridge, a cardinal from 1511, was said to be a quarrelsome, contentious man. In view of this, and the difficult situation of the Hospice with its old and new *confratres*, it is not surprising that dissension developed. According to the account we have, drawn up by Bainbridge and signed by himself and by Sylvester Giglis, a general meeting of the *confratres* was called by Bainbridge to deal with John Allen.[55] Allen was expelled from the Hospice confraternity as a contentious and useless member, whose intrigues and troublesome conduct were harming the Hospice. It appears that he had failed to mend his ways despite the cardinal's written and spoken admonition, and in the very meeting here described had argued against the views of Bainbridge and the *confratres*. Unfortunately we have no other source for this, so it is impossible to say whether John Allen merited expulsion or whether this was merely Bainbridge's way of overcoming opposition. The expelled *confrater* returned to England, where he entered Wolsey's service and rose to become archbishop of Dublin in 1528.[56] We have no date for this meeting of the *confratres*, but it must be between 1511 and 1514, as Bainbridge is recorded as a cardinal, and Sylvester Giglis was back in Rome. From what we know of John Allen's life, 1511 is the most likely year. Also Bainbridge and Sylvester Giglis were not on good terms for most of the time; so it is likely that Sylvester's co-operation in this matter occurred earlier in their acquaintance rather than later.

Richard Pace was custos again in 1512–13, but the camerarii were Thomas Halsey and John Clerk. The latter took a degree in canon law at Bologna in 1510 and then came to join the Bainbridge circle at Rome. He was camerarius again in 1514, and no doubt his experience of the Hospice proved useful when he came to reform it in 1523.[57]

---

[54] *Lib.* 13, f. 43 r.
[55] *Lib.* 17, f. 59 r.
[56] Cf. article *John Allen* in DNB.
[57] Cf. App. 22, p. 183, and article *John Clerk* in DNB. Cf. infra, p. 170.

In August 1512 the enquiry into Christopher Fisher's administration was complete, and it was found that he owed the Hospice a little over 990 ducats, as we have seen.[58] Fisher was now bishop-elect of Elphin, in Ireland. It was decided that he should repay this sum at the rate of one hundred ducats per year and he signed his agreement to this. Other signatories were Bainbridge himself, Richard Pace, custos, and the two camerarii, Clerk and Halsey. The debt was never paid and was finally written off in 1523.

In 1513 Thomas Halsey replaced Pace as custos. Pace went home to England, though he was back the following year. In 1514 John Clifton was custos, and the camerarii were John Wolfe and John Clerk. We know nothing of Clifton, but the others are all familiar members of Bainbridge's entourage. But the cardinal's death, on 7th July 1514, brought this period of the Hospice's history to an end, and revealed how dependent the Hospice had now become on the patronage of some dominant figure. It was believed by some that Bainbridge had been poisoned by an Italian chaplain acting on behalf of Sylvester Giglis. Pace and Clerk were anxious to press the case against Sylvester. The two envoys had quarrelled, and Leo X preferred Sylvester to the cardinal, who had been a favourite of Julius II. In the event, Sylvester Giglis was exonerated by the pope, and worked for the Hospice during the next few difficult years; the cardinal was buried in the Hospice church.

A month after the cardinal's death, on 8th August, what seems almost like a winding-up meeting of the *confratres* was held.[59] Two camerarii, William Fell and John Wolfe, had their accounts approved, and reference is made to their long and faithful administration. Then the approval of the *confratres* was given to all administration, of every sort, performed by William Burbanke, Richard Pace, John Clerk, John Newman and Christopher Wilson. These measures were evidently to indemnify them from any further proceedings arising from their government of the Hospice, and were a preliminary to their leaving Rome. The document was signed by nine *confratres*: John Clerk (camerarius), John Buckley (religious), John Newman, John Bell, John Wolfe, John Clifton (custos), Thomas Halsey, Richard Pace and William Fell. Of these only

---

[58] *Lib.* 13, ff. 209 r–v.: cf. supra, p. 162.
[59] *Lib.* 17, f. 57 v.

John Bell and Thomas Halsey play any part in the future of the Hospice, except for John Clerk who came back as a royal envoy in 1523.

SYLVESTER GIGLIS AND THE HOSPICE 1515–21

Sylvester Giglis now resumed the dominating position in the Hospice which he had held from 1500 to 1504. John Clifton, the last custos to be appointed under Bainbridge's regime, either died or left towards the end of 1514, so for the first four months of 1515 John Bell was in charge. Bell was one of Sylvester's adherents and had come to Rome with him when he was sent as envoy to the Lateran Council, probably in 1511.[60] Before long, however, Sylvester Giglis made John Bell his vicar general and chancellor for his bishopric of Worcester, and Bell pursued his career in England, where he became a royal chaplain and a diplomat.

What happened in May 1515, when John Bell ceased to be custos, is far from clear. A new man, John Pennande, arrived about this time from Perugia, at which university he had matriculated in 1513. In one of the Hospice account books there is a page set out to receive the usual yearly accounts under the name of John Pennande, custos, from August 1515 to May 1516. But none of the details has been entered and what is written has been lightly crossed out.[61] Elsewhere[62] there is no mention of a custos but Pennande and Halsey are described as camerarii. Halsey was now bishop of Leighlin in Ireland; he had been made a bishop through Bainbridge's influence. It is clear that these two, Halsey and Pennande, were now in control of the Hospice.

In the following year, 1516, Thomas Colman arrived from Bologna and was made custos. Halsey remained camerarius but Pennande was replaced by John Blyth. In October 1516 Colman wrote to Wolsey, whose scholar and servant he was, to inform him of his election to the wardenship of the Hospice.

---

[60] For John Bell, cf. article *John Bell* in DNB. Giglis had been sent to England by Julius II on a mission to Henry VII late in 1504. He was popular at the English court and remained there for some years, until Henry VIII sent him back to Rome as ambassador to the Fifth Lateran Council.

[61] *Lib*. 13, ff. 125 v–126 r.

[62] *Lib*. 4, f. 4. They are also called auditors : *Lib*. 33, inventory for 1515.

He adds that Cardinal Adrian Castelli was sheltering Halsey and Pennande in his house. The two men owed the Hospice 288 crowns and had abused Colman for demanding payment.[63] But Colman died in February 1517, and the Hospice was once more without a custos. Sylvester Giglis wrote to Wolsey, telling him of Colman's death and saying that he knew of no one in Rome worthy to succeed him.[64] Writing to Ammonius, Henry VIII's Latin secretary, Giglis describes Colman as Wolsey's scholar and servant, and says that he had died suddenly of the sweating sickness.[65] In this letter and in another to Ammonius of the previous day—8th February[66]—he gives a clear picture of the Hospice at this time. The Hospice was in a very evil plight, and the few Englishmen there did nothing but eat, drink, run riot, and abuse each other. Unless Wolsey had compassion on it the Hospice would go to ruin. There was no one fit to succeed Colman, for the bishop of Leighlin, Thomas Halsey, was an idle voluptuary, and John Pennande a fool. Other Englishmen are mentioned as unsuitable, and the only positive suggestion Sylvester Giglis makes for custos is Bell, Dean of the Arches, presumably his own vicar general, who had been custos in the first four months of 1515.

The situation justified the bishop of Worcester's gloom. There were few *confratres*, particularly after Bainbridge's retinue had left Rome on their master's death. The Hospice had little attraction for the wealthy pluralists of the time. The administration was inevitably bad, considering the difficulty in finding custodes, and the brevity of their periods in office. The accounts of this period, when any were made, were written not in a book but on loose paper, which was later bound by John Clerk in 1523, without any orderly arrangement or sequence, to form *Liber* 13. This compares most unfavourably with the account books of Edward Scott and John Clerk, both of whom bought large, well bound books for their accounts and records.[67]

The *confratres* were incapable of running the Hospice and there was no one to run it for them. Cardinal Bainbridge, Edward Scott and Robert Shirborn were Englishmen, with the

---

[63] *Letters and Papers of Henry VIII*, II, 2446. All references to these (L. & P.) are taken from summaries by Fr Anstruther o.p.

[64] Ibid., 2887.

[65] Ibid., 2895.

[66] Ibid., 2888.

[67] *Lib.* 1, *Lib.* 22, *Lib.* 33.

authority of the Crown behind them. Bainbridge had great personal authority as a cardinal archbishop, besides being a royal envoy and a favourite of the pope. Henry VII's personal interest in the Hospice supported the efforts of Shirborn, Scott, Inge, and Sylvester Giglis himself. Bainbridge possessed the added advantage of a large retinue, which he could employ in the Hospice. Compared with these men Sylvester Giglis was in a difficult position. He was a bishop and a royal orator, but he had no support from England. Henry VIII seems to have had no interest in the Hospice, and Wolsey did not answer Giglis' letters about it.[68] As an Italian, Giglis perhaps lacked both confidence and prestige in dealing with the confratres, all of them English. An additional difficulty was his relationship with Cardinal Adrian Castelli, with whom he had been admitted to the confraternity in 1498. Castelli had returned to Rome after his exile in 1513, and still worked in the interest of Henry VIII. But the two men were on bad terms, and Castelli was soon to be disgraced through being implicated in the conspiracy against Leo X in 1517. The pope was disposed to be lenient, but Henry and Wolsey were determined on Castelli's ruin, and Leo X gave way. In 1516 both Halsey and Pennande, after their period in control of the Hospice, were sheltered by Castelli. It looks as if there were two parties in the Hospice, one supported by Castelli and the other by Giglis.[69] All these factors must be taken into account when assessing the situation between 1514 and 1523. But despite all the difficulties, Sylvester seems to have done his best for the Hospice without seeking any personal advantage from its troubles.

The immediate problem of finding a new custos to replace Colman was solved by the appointment of Edward Bassett, who had graduated in canon law at Ferrara in 1516 and then come to Rome. Giglis made him his chaplain, and had apparently known him for twenty-five years. The appointment was only temporary, and in January 1518 Bassett was sent to England by Sylvester and the other officers of the Hospice to give Wolsey an account of its affairs. They had written without effect to various confratres in England. In a letter to Wolsey written at this time Sylvester gives another description of the state of the Hospice, as well as some information about Bassett. It is

[68] L. & P. III, 840 (p. 291).
[69] Parks, op. cit., p. 364.

not rich as is thought but in great distress, and the insatiable appetites of an increasing number of pilgrims must be provided for. The custos ought to be appointed for life, not merely for a year, and a church ought to be built suitable to the honour of England.[70] In a second letter of the same date he recommends Bassett for the post of custos, and asks for a reply by 3rd May, the election date, so that he can show it to the *confratres*.[71] If all had gone according to Giglis' wishes, Bassett would have been made permanent custos in 1518, but Wolsey seems to have taken no action whatsoever.

The disgrace of Cardinal Castelli and his flight from Rome in 1517 helped to bring to an end the dissension within the Hospice. John Pennande was camerarius in 1517 and played an important part in the administration of the Hospice later on under John Clerk. Thomas Halsey and Sylvester were now on good terms, and in January 1518 the latter wrote to England saying that the bishop of Leighlin (Halsey) was destitute, since neither Bainbridge nor Castelli had done anything for him. He had not enough to live on as English penitentiary, and his Irish bishopric was worth nothing.[72] With his rival out of the way Giglis could afford to be generous. Halsey returned to England, where we find him in July 1518 assisting at the reception of Cardinal Campeggio.[73] He died about the year 1521 and was buried in the Savoy Chapel, London.[74]

On the departure of Edward Bassett for England early in 1518 the Hospice was once again without a custos. One of the camerarii, Elias Bodley, took over the administration, but now Sylvester Giglis took an even greater part in the management of the Hospice. In several deeds Bodley and Giglis are named as camerarii.[75] Bodley, however, was in charge of daily affairs. In May 1520 Sylvester wrote again to Wolsey, on behalf of John Borobrigg, chaplain of the Hospice, who was leaving Rome on account of its great poverty. He said that he had often written about the Hospice but had received no answer, and that since Bassett's departure a young man named Elias Bodley had administered the Hospice diligently, but that his

[70] L. & P. II, 3875.
[71] Ibid., 3876.
[72] Brady, op. cit., I, 385.
[73] Brady, *Anglo-Roman Papers*, p. 34.
[74] Brady, *Episcopal Succession*, I, 385.
[75] Cf. *Lib.* 14.

accounts needed looking into.[76] A deed dated 4th January
1521 names Richard Shurley as custos, with two camerarii,
John Grygg and John Huyes ;[77] Shurley is prominent in the
Hospice for the next six years. Sylvester Giglis died in Rome
in April 1521, leaving the king without a resident envoy and
the Hospice without a protector. But in that same month John
Clerk, camerarius of the Hospice in Bainbridge's day and now
dean of Windsor, arrived in Rome to present the '*Assertio
Septem Sacramentorum*' of Henry VIII to the pope. He stayed
in Rome just over a year, and seems not to have intervened
in Hospice affairs ; but when he went home he would have taken
with him first-hand information about conditions there. Another
royal orator, Thomas Hannibal, wrote to Wolsey from Rome
in September 1522, saying that he had visited the Hospice and
had found it well governed.[78]

JOHN CLERK'S REFORMATION 1523–25

In June 1523 John Clerk returned to Rome as royal orator.
He was now bishop-elect of Bath and Wells, the see formerly
held by Cardinal Castelli. On 1st July there took place the last
large-scale intervention of the Crown in Hospice affairs. The
confratres of the Hospice met, together with John Clerk and
Thomas Hannibal, the two royal orators, and first of all Hannibal
was admitted to the confraternity. Then, at the command of
the orators and of the other *confratres*, John Pennande read
aloud a letter from Wolsey, written in the name of the king,
to the custos, Richard Shurley, and the camerarii of the
Hospice.[79] In this letter the king, '*utpote eiusdem hospitalis
curam intimam gerens*', required the camerarii, custos, and
confratres, for the better maintenance and reformation of the
Hospice, to hand over to the bishop-elect of Bath its rule and
administration. Moreover, John Clerk was to be given greater
authority and power than previous rectors had enjoyed. When
the letter had been read, the custos and camerarii resigned
their offices into the hands of the *confratres*, and the *confratres*

[76] L. & P. III, 840 (p. 291).
[77] *Lib.* 1, f. 84 v.
[78] L. & P. III, 2521.
[79] For Clerk's intervention cf. App. 22, p. 183.

handed over the administration and rule of the Hospice to Clerk, giving him full authority. The former custos, Shurley, was instructed to draw up the accounts for his period of administration within a certain time, and John Pennande and John Borobrigg were appointed to audit them. Two camerarii were elected: John Nase, English penitentiary, and Robert Coket. John Clerk appointed Richard Shurley and John Pennande as his commissaries to deal with Hospice business.

John Clerk's reforms were thorough and, as far as can be judged, effective. One good indication of their effectiveness is that enough evidence of them has survived for us to describe them. Their one weakness was that they were dependent on his presence in Rome. When he left in November 1525 the standard of accounting immediately declined. Clerk gave two new account-books, one of which contains the daily living expenses and a yearly *computus*; into the other were copied inventories of goods made from the year 1445 onwards.[80] He also had the loose accounts from 1505 bound together.[81] For two or three years after 1523 we have more information on Hospice administration than for any previous period in its history. A picture of the patrons of the two Hospices—the Blessed Trinity, St Thomas of Canterbury, and St Edmund— was painted as a frontispiece in the books of accounts and inventories, and in his account-book Clerk wrote instructions on how the *computus* was to be kept.[82]

Probably Clerk's first task was to deal with the problems left by the maladministration of recent years. The debts of three former custodes, Fisher, Halsey and Colman, which totalled well over a thousand ducats, were written off as irrecoverable.[83] Hugh Inge's debt was not written off for he was now archbishop of Dublin and they hoped to recover the money he owed. It was estimated that the Hospice had lost well over fifteen hundred ducats through debts and bad administration.[84] Besides this, the *firma Angliae*, the annual collection for the Hospice in England, owed over four thousand ducats to the Hospice. The binding together of the accounts for 1505–19 illustrates Clerk's efforts to remedy bad administration in the past.

[80] *Lib.* 22 and *Lib.* 33.
[81] *Lib.* 13.
[82] *Lib.* 22, f. 4 v.
[83] Ibid., f. 8 r.
[84] Ibid., f. 8 r.

M

For the future, he evidently pinned his faith on more detailed book-keeping, which in turn depended upon the efficiency and industry of the custos and auditors. The salary of the custos had risen from twelve ducats, which it was till 1511, to thirty-six in 1517.[85] In 1523–4 it looks as if Shurley received thirty-six ducats.[86] John Clerk's account-book tells us for the first time who actually ate in the Hospice. These *commensales* numbered eight to begin with—Richard Shurley (custos), Nase and Borobrigg (chaplains), the cook, the butler, two servants of Shurley, and a notary. This was for 1523–4, when Shurley was not really custos, but rather Clerk's deputy with John Pennande.[87] But after six months Clerk reduced the number of *commensales*.[88]

The *computus* for the first year after Clerk's intervention was compiled by his commissaries, Shurley and Pennande, and audited by Borobrigg and Walter Cretyng. Pennande alone was in charge in the following year, and his *computus* was audited by Shurley and Cretyng. Clerk left Rome for England in November 1525, and in that month Shurley replaced Pennande as custos. Possibly Pennande went home with Clerk. The standard of accounting fell at once. Among the new names we find one, Nicholas Wotton, destined to become famous. Wotton had studied at Perugia and came on to Rome, where he was admitted to the confraternity. He ended his career as secretary of state and dean of Canterbury.[89]

THE LAST YEARS OF THE CONNECTION WITH THE CROWN 1526–38

Like the rest of Rome, the Hospice suffered severely in the sack of Rome at the hands of the Imperial troops in 1527. A comparison of inventories made before and after the sack shows that it had lost all its plate and many other goods.[90] A

---

[85] *Lib.* 13, f. 261 v.
[86] *Lib.* 22, f. 47 v.
[87] Ibid., f. 3 v.
[88] Ibid., f. 9 v.
[89] Cf. article *Nicholas Wotton* in DNB.
[90] *Lib.* 33, inventories of 1525 and 1538. The first was made at John Clerk's orders and the second at the orders of Cardinal Pole.

Bull issued in 1530 described the losses of the Hospice in the sack of 1527, and promises indulgences for all who enter the confraternity of the Hospice, paying the required fee, and visiting the Hospice church on certain feasts.[91] Nicholas Wotton was custos from June 1527 till May 1528, and in his *computus* we learn that many of the tenants of Hospice houses had fled from Rome and not yet returned. Richard Shurley had died without making a *computus*, and some of the necessary books were missing.[92] The Bull of 1530 speaks of writings being lost in the sack. Evidently, therefore, the gap between November 1526 and June 1527 is due to the loss of the relevant papers. It is possible that Shurley was killed in the sack, since Wotton's term begins in June 1527. Besides the loss of plate and goods, and of the rents of the departed tenants, the Hospice also suffered from damage to its houses, and perhaps to the Hospice building itself.

William Whyte was custos from May 1528 till November of that year, after which all formal records cease until 1538. Fortunately we can reconstruct the last years of the Hospice under the English Crown from other sources. Various deeds, ranging in date from March 1529 till February 1538, name John Borobrigg as custos.[93] On 21st August 1532 he was made custos for life by Henry VIII.[94] It is ironic that at this stage of the history of the Hospice when the English Crown was on the point of separating itself from the Catholic Church, we have this unique royal grant of the wardenship of the Hospice, given directly without mention of orators or camerarii, and for life. It represents the culmination of the whole movement towards royal control of the Hospice, at a moment when the connection of the Hospice with the English Crown was doomed.

John Borobrigg had served the Hospice well. We met him in 1520 when he was chaplain of the Hospice and went home to England, but he was back in Rome, still chaplain, in 1523, when he helped John Clerk with his reformation. In May 1525 John Clerk and the other officers of the Hospice describe his service as long and faithful. In particular he had thrice ridden to England at awkward times on Hospice business. Therefore, because he wished to end his days at the Hospice

[91] *Memb.* 3.3.1530.
[92] *Lib.* 22, f. 163 r.
[93] *Lib.* 14, *passim.*
[94] Rymer, op. cit., Vol. VI. App. 23, p. 185.

and also because a man of his experience was likely to be useful, they made him permanent chaplain of St Thomas's and St Edmund's Hospices. Besides the normal salary of two large ducats every month they added a third ducat, because the ordinary salary seemed too little for his needs, considering his age.[95]

It is rather surprising, after this, to find that Borobrigg was expelled from the Hospice at a general meeting of the *confratres* on 25th October 1528. The record of this meeting[96] explains that he owed the Hospice slightly more than 642 ducats. He was asked to assist the Hospice with money, in view of its great need, and to attend the meeting to discuss some business which concerned him. Borobrigg not only refused, but claimed to be *dominus et patronus* of the Hospice. So the custos and camerarii, on the day before the meeting, conveyed to him an ultimatum from the *confratres*, demanding his presence. The *confratres* awaited his arrival and on his failure to appear declared him contumacious and expelled him from the confraternity. Besides describing him as a useless and harmful brother they call him a contemner of the Hospice's and the king's statutes. The phrases applied to him contrast most vividly with those used in 1525 when Borobrigg was made chaplain of both Hospices for life.

Borobrigg's expulsion is not mentioned elsewhere in the Hospice records, and we have no further information about it. We do not know what grounds he had for his claim to be master and patron of the Hospice, nor what precisely is meant by the term. But henceforth, until March 1538, he alone is mentioned in the property deeds, the only records which survive, as custos of the Hospice *regia auctoritate*. Some of the deeds add the saving clause *ut asserit* or *se asserens*, which implies that Borobrigg was not necessarily recognised as undisputed custos at Rome. But evidently no one was able to displace him, and Henry VIII's grant of the custody of the Hospice for life to him in 1532 shows that his claim had an objective basis.

Borobrigg's survival in Rome as a tiny bulwark of royal authority until 1538 can only be explained by the reluctance of Clement VII and Paul III to recognize the Henrician schism as more than temporary. For both Borobrigg and the Italian

95 *Memb.* 3.5.1525.
96 *Lib.* 4, 25.10.1528.

bishop of Worcester, Ghinucci, continued to work for the interests of Henry VIII. This is shown by a letter from Borobrigg to Thomas Cromwell, written on 26th May 1535,[97] which mentions the elevation of Ghinucci to the cardinalate at the same time as St John Fisher. It goes on to say that when Ghinucci learnt that his *intrate*[98] was taken from him, he sent for Borobrigg and the English penitentiary and said that he was content, since it was the king's pleasure, and promised to do anything in his power for them and for the Hospice. An Englishman who had spoken treasonably against the king in the Hospice was sent to prison by Borobrigg, and then, with the co-operation of Ghinucci, to the galleys. Also in this letter he mentions a scrivener, James Holywell, who said in the Hospice that when every man was sworn to the king, he was not, nor would be. Borobrigg put him out of the Hospice and he left Rome. The custos adds that if he could have found him the next morning he too would have gone to the galleys. The letter concludes with his prayer for the preservation of the king, the queen and Cromwell.

Such a situation could not continue, and in 1538 Pope Paul brought it to an end. The Hospice passed into the hands of the English exiles under Cardinal Pole, and the change is summarised in a *motu proprio* issued by Paul to confirm it. Only one *confrater* remained at the Hospice and he is described as decrepit. This can only refer to Borobrigg. The document goes on to say that he exercised all the offices which were formerly assigned to different *confratres* yearly, and applied the income of the Hospice to himself. Cardinal Pole and the other Englishmen in Rome feared that the Hospice, lacking *confratres*, might be occupied by others, and England deprived of it. So the pope decreed that Pole and his companions be admitted to the confraternity by the old custos, in whom alone the confraternity resided, and this was done. Then the custos resigned, Pole was elected in his place, and the other officials were elected. These proceedings were all confirmed by Paul III in this *motu proprio*, dated 8th March 1538.[99]

We can add some details to this from other sources. One of the new *confratres* admitted to the Hospice with Pole was John Legh, who in 1540 was a prisoner in the Tower of London

[97] L. & P. VIII, 763.
[98] I.e., his licence to enter England.
[99] *Lib*. 4, 8.3.1538. App. 24, p. 185.

and gave an account of Pole's activities in Rome.[100] From this we learn that Borobrigg was promised a pension before he resigned ; this was paid in April,[101] and he is in the list of *commensales* for March.[102] Also on record is a gift of one hundred ducats which he made to the Hospice.[103] It would seem that matters were arranged amicably between him and Cardinal Pole.

So ended the long connection of the Hospice with the English Crown. It was now in the hands of the English exiles, whose primary loyalty was to the See of Peter. They were indicted in England on 3rd December 1538 'for betaking themselves to the Roman pontiff in parts beyond the sea, and renouncing their true prince'.[104] We may close by recalling the dedication of the Hospice—to the Blessed Trinity and St Thomas of Canterbury. After the admission of the new *confratres* in March 1538, Cardinal Pole, John Borobrigg and John Legh dined together and talked of the Hospice, and after dinner the cardinal remarked that the Hospice was founded in the name of Thomas of Canterbury, whom the king had pulled out of his shrine.[105] The shrine at Canterbury could indeed be pillaged and destroyed ; but St Thomas's Hospice and College still exists in Rome after six hundred years.

BRIAN NEWNS.

APPENDIX 15

BULL OF POPE ALEXANDER VI TAKING THE HOSPICE UNDER HIS PROTECTION
DECEMBER 1493[1]

Alexander episcopus servus servorum Dei. Dilectis filiis Camerariis Custodi et confratribus hospitalis pauperum sancte Trinitatis et sancti Thomae Martiris de Urbe Anglicorum nuncupati, Salutem et apostolicam benedictionem.

Cum a nobis petitur quod iustum est et honestum, tam vigor equitatis quam ordo exigit rationis, ut id per solicitudinem officii nostri ad debitum perducatur effectum. Ea propter, dilecti in Domino filii, vestris iustis postulationibus grato concurrentes assensu, personas vestras et locum in

---

[100] L. & P. XV, 721.
[101] *Lib.* 22, f. 176 r.
[102] Ibid., f. 170 r.
[103] Ibid., f. 169 r.
[104] L. & P. XIII, part II, 979.
[105] Ibid., XV, 721.
[1] *Memb.* 7.12.1493.

quo divino estis obsequio mancipati, cum omnibus bonis quae in presen-
tiarum rationabiliter possidetis aut in futurum iustis mediis praestante
Domino poteritis adipisci sub beati Petri protectione suscipimus, atque
nostra omnes quoque libertates et immunitates a predecessoribus nostris
Romanis pontificibus, sive per privilegia vel alia Indulta vobis et hospitali
predicto concessas, necnon libertates et exemptiones saecularium exac-
tionum a regibus et principibus ac aliis christifidelibus, vobis et eidem
hospitali rationabiliter indultas, specialiter autem oblationes census fructus
redditus proventus domos agros possessiones prata nemora silvas casalia
iura iurisdictiones et alia mobilia et immobilia bona ad hospitale predictum
spectantia, sicuti ea apostolica confirmamus et praesentis scripti patrocinio
communimus. Nulli ergo omnino hominum liceat hanc paginam nostrae
confirmationis et communitionis infringere vel ausus temerario contra ire.
Si quis autem hoc attemptare praesumpserit, indignationem omnipotentis
Dei ac beatorum Petri et Pauli apostolorum eius se noverit incursurum.
Data Viterbi, Anno Incarnationis Domini 1493, 7 Ides Decembris, pontificatus nostri Anno 2ndo.

APPENDIX 16

ROBERT SHIRBORN UNDERTAKES THE ADMINISTRATION OF THE HOSPICE AT THE REQUEST OF THE CONFRATRES, OCTOBER 1496[1]

Die ultimo Septembris 1496 cessavit Dominus Hugo Spaldyng, consensu omnium confratrum tunc temporis in Urbe existentium, ab officio
administrationis hospitalis Sanctae Trinitatis et Thomae martyris in
regione Arenule in Urbe, necnon Sancti Edmundi Trans-tiberim. Et
Dominus Robertus Shyrborn, tunc temporis serenissimi regis Angliae
specialis in Urbe orator, consensu et omnium confratrum dicti hospitalis
in Urbe rogitu primo die Octobris 1496 hospitalium predictorum curam et
adminstrationem in suas manus accepit :[2] cum conditionibus et pactis in
magnam predictorum hospitalium utilitatem resultantibus ; de quibus
articulis in instrumento publico inter hospitalia predicta et dictum dominum
oratorem confecto plenissime constat : Quod quidem instrumentum in
trium clavium capsa in hospitale Sanctae Trinitatis supradicto ad perpetuam
memoriam depositum fuit. Et Edwardum Scott eius substitutum ad negotia
et causas dictorum hospitalium administrandas in Urbe ordinavit, et
praesentibus eorumdem hospitalium confratribus publice in hospitale
affirmavit.

[1] *Lib.* 17, f. 19 v–20 r.
[2] The words 'usque ad primum octobris 1499' are here inserted in the margin.

Et notandum est primo quod dominus Robertus Shyrborn serenissimi regis Angliae et Franciae specialis in curia Romana orator, nihil pecuniarum in trium clavium capsa hospitalis in principio quo hospitale praedictum in suas manus ad meliorem ipsius hospitalis reformationem, rogitu fratrum dicti hospitalis, pro triennio accepit, inveniens ; volensque eidem hospitali et peregrinis pauperibus morem gerege ; ex sua liberalite et pietate dicto hospitali tunc temporis in maxima paupertate laborante, ducatos in carlenis xxxvii k. 8 b. 6 q. 3 mutuavit, ut patet in libro computus hospitalis primi anni eius administrationis a die primo Octobris proxime sequentis.

Item, dictus dominus Robertus Shyrborn etiam eodem anno proxime suprascripto mutuavit eidem hospitali pro principio fabricae ecclesiae dicti hospitalis ducatos in carlinis centum ad rationem x carlenorum pro singulo ducato. Que quidem ecclesia fuit fabricata in primo anno suae administrationis ; ut haec omnia patent in computu primi anni suae administrationis.

Item, dictus dominus Robertus Shyrborn, regius tunc orator, mutuavit dicto hospitali etiam alios centum ducatos in carlinos similes pro necessariis rebus et victu hospitalis primi sui introitus, et illos ducatos posuit in trium clavium capsa, ut quando opus esset exponerentur, ut in in libro primi anni sui computus clarius apparet.

Qua quidem[3] summa suprascripta est domino Roberto Shyrborn suprascripto satisfacta, ut apparet in libro computus hospitalis in fine computus supradictorum trium annorum, quo anno doctor Trappe, Papae penitentiarius pro natione anglicana, et dominus Johannes Tong, Rhodii miles, erant auditores computus huius hospitalis.

APPENDIX 17

FIRST LETTER OF KING HENRY VII TO THE HOSPICE, JANUARY, 1497[1]

1497 die vero decimo Martii.

Copia litterarum regiarum quas Henricus Dei gratia rex Angliae et Franciae ac dominus Hiberniae dispensatoribus hospitalis Sanctae Trinitatis et martyris in Urbe Rome eiusque loci confratribus misit, easque in hoc libro Ordinationum nos confratres infrascripti ad perpetuam rei memoriam registrari fecimus die suprascripto quo illas recepimus.[2]

Honorandis viris dispensatoribus bonorum hospitalis nostri Sancti Thomae martyris in Urbe Roma eiusdemque confratribus quamplurimum dilectis.

[3] This paragraph, in a new hand, was added later.
[1] *Lib.* 17, f. 20 r.
[2] I.e. 10th March 1497.

Henricus Dei gratia rex Angliae et Franciae ac dominus Hiberniae, honorandis viris dispensatoribus bonorum nostri hospitalis Sancti Thomae martyris in Urbe Romana, eiusdemque loci confratribus, salutem.

Intelleximus iamdudum tam ex litteris reverendissimi domini Senensis, regni nostri protectoris,[3] quam ex domino Johanne de Giglis oratore nostro, hospitale Anglicorum in Urbe Romana adeo splendide et honorifice dotatum ut una cum consuetis omnibus nonnullas personas quae divinis obsequiis ac litterarum studiis incumbunt (modo recte gubernetur) ad Dei gloriam et nostrum ac regni nostri decus et commodum sustinere possit, quemadmodum in hospitalibus aliorum regnorum Romae existentibus factum est, quorum dos longe inferior dignoscitur.

Nos igitur, cupientes cultum Dei, a quo bona cuncta procedunt, ubique et praesertim in ista alma Urbe augeri et crescere, Vos omnes praesentes et futuros et quemlibet vestrum hortamus pariter et requiramus, ut illa, quae pro illius felici preservatione per dominum Robertum Shyrborn oratorem nuper istic nostrum, cum matura confratrum deliberatione, tam circa Ordinationes factas quam pro hospitio pro Oratore nostro perpetuis futuris temporibus duraturo, edita sunt, Inviolabiliter observatis ac ab aliis observari faciatis.

Et ne nostra mandata (quid nollemus) intelligantur irrita, praesenter litteras nostras in libro Ordinationum hospitalis praedicti quamprimum scribi faciatis, ne posteri huius nostri mandati ignorantiam aliquando pretendere valeant. Si quem impugnantem intellexeritis, illius nomen nobis referatis, in quo quidem ad Dei et nostram quoque non parvam complacentiam indubie facietis.

Ex palatio nostro iuxta Westmonasterium Januarii die xxix, mcccclxxxvi[4]

(signed) Jo de Giglis regius orator

Edwardus Scott, praedicti hospitalis camerarius manu propria

Frater Franciscus eiusdem hospitalis capellanus manu propria

Thomas Lasenby confrater hospitalis supradicti manu propria.

---

[3] Cardinal Francesco Piccolomini, Archbishop of Sienna, later Pope Pius III, 1503.

[4] This is an obvious mistake for 1496. The old style of dating is here employed, so the correct date is 29th January 1497.

APPENDIX 18

SECOND LETTER OF KING HENRY VII TO THE HOSPICE, SEPTEMBER 1498[1]

Sequitur copia litterarum regiarum ad confratres hospitalis scriptarum.

Henricus Dei gratia rex angliae et franciae ac dominus hiberniae, venerandis camerariis et confratribus hospitalis nostri anglorum in urbe Roma nostris quamplurimum dilectis, Salutem et prospera incrementa.

Scripsimus alias ad vos ut ea, quae ad Dei omnipotentis laudem et nostrum ac regni nostri honorem et decus per dominum Robertum Shirborn, nostrum nuper istic oratorem, in isto nostro hospitali constituta et ordinata essent, non modo registris et vestrarum ordinationum libris inscriberentur, sed inconcussa et inviolata prorsus a vobis observentur. Ceterum fide digna relatione certiores reddimur, nostrum huiusmodi mandatum plene atque integre in hunc usque diem esse a vobis executum, et interea res hospitalis non mediocriter crevisse, quod non modo est nobis vehementer gratum. Sed etiam gratias proinde habemus vobis quamplurimas, rogantes ut sicuti cepistis ita quoque constanter velitis perseverare in bene de nobis et de ipso nostro hospitali merendo. In quo et Deo primum, deinde nobis ipsis, magnopere complacebitis.

Ex oppido nostro de Wodstok, die xxviiii septembris, 1498.

APPENDIX 19

LETTER OF THE HOSPICE TO KING HENRY VII, JANUARY 1499[2]

Copia litterarum quas camerarii et confratres hospitalis anglicorum in urbe ad illustrissimum Henricum anglorum regem scripserunt duplicatas : primas xx die Januarii 1499, secundas ultimo die eiusdem mensis.

Serenissimo Henrico anglorum regi Camerarii una cum confratres hospitalis tui in urbe cum omni subiectionis obsequio salutem plurimam dant. Dedisti ad nos binas suavissimas litteras, princeps illustrissime, quibus maiestatem tuam velle intelleximus ut ea, quae in hospitali tuo per ingeniosissimum virum dominum Robertum Shyrborn, tuum olim hic in urbe oratorem, confratribus uno ore unaque animi sententia convenientibus, constituta decreta essent, diligenter custodiri inviolateque servari debeant. Tum praeterea quod tam recepta quam in rem eiusdem conversa in libris rationum sint praescripta ac demum apud nostra monimenta recondita postremo, ut omnia inspiceremus ita accurate regamus atque administremus ita moderate ac sapienter quod proventus atque facultates tui hospitalis, quas regia tua maiestas miro incremento iam pridem auctas intellexerat, magis ac magis reddantur auctiores.

[1] *Lib.* 17, f. 27 r.
[2] *Lib.* 17, f. 27 v.

Tua enim praecepta, rex pienissime, quasi beata admiranda imitanda non inviti audivimus atque probavimus. Praeterea curabimus, ut iussisti, quae tui A(nglicorum) hospitalis huic uni studebimus, huic invigilabimus, ad huius incrementum et dignitatem omnes denique cogitatus nostros referremus. Quid enim isto nostro hospitali imo tuo aut iucundius aut beatius unquam contingere potuit quam eidem te afferri admirabili prudentia principem, cuius divina quadam ope felicique ductu omnia bene beateque nobis successerint semper et successura sint. Non possumus, te rege munificentissimo ac felicissimo regnante, nisi quae volumus pro sententia nostra fauste et fortunate consequere omnia. Non possit profecto satis narrari quanta es in omnes facilitate humanitate clementia mansuetudine denique ac munificentia praeditus. Quid enim loquamur de iustitia tua mirifica quadam comiseratione condita. Quid de invicto animi robore atque magnitudine. Nihil sane iustum aut laude ulla dignum estimas quod a fide religione pietateque sit alienum. Tanta est certe tuarum rerum gestarum gloria atque magnitudo quod optimo iure et habendus et dicendus sis omnium saeculorum omniumque gentium omnis memoriae facile princeps. Nihil enim cogitas, nihil meditaris, nihil agis, nisi quod divinarum rerum representat imaginem. Faveat tibi Deus favet certe auxilio est semper iustis tuis ceptis salutiferis quas cogitabis. Omnia quippe ad eum refers itaque omnia tibi sunt laeta, omnia secunda et ad votum omnia.

Quare qui te non amat, non colit, non ex animi sententia veneratur, profecto inhumanus est ac plane impius. Pro tuo itaque, rex Henrice, tam magnifico tam excelso erga nos, non quod tandem referremus quod pollicentur aliud, certe nihil habemus quam nosmetipsos, quos una cum nostris quotidianis divinisque orationibus tibi ac sacrae tuae familiae et vivos et mortuas dedicavimus ac perpetus devovimus.

Vale principum decus, et tuum hospitale omnium sane tuorum anglicorum dulce praesidium atque refugium singulare tibi commendatum habe, ut facis. Dominum Robertum Shyrborn, cui propter tot tantaque sua erga hospitale nostrum meritum plurimum debemus, maiestati tuae non vulgari commendatione commendamus.

Ex urbe, xx die Januarii, 1499.

APPENDIX 20

KING HENRY VII NOMINATES THE CUSTOS OF THE HOSPICE. 1504[1]

A 4to Novembris A.D. 1504 ad 4to diem ejusdem mensis anni sequentis.

Nota quod hoc anno in mense Maii venerunt ad Urbem legati missi ab illustrissimo rege nostro Henrico septimo ad praestandum obedientiam

[1] *Lib.* 1, f. 12 v.

S.D. nostro Julio Divina providentia Papae 2⁰. Propter cujus legationis varia negotia commissa officiariis Hospitalis auditus ratiocinii et electis Custodis fieri congruis & solitis temporibus non potuit usque discessum Oratorum. Quibus discedentibus, dominus Edwardus Scot maxima febre correptus continuo aegrotavit usque ad 24 Julii, quo die e saeculo ad Deum migravit, & vacavit domus ista sive Hospitale sine custode usque iiij^m. Novembris, interim tamen gubernata per D. Johannem Alen, capellanum Hospitalis. Quo tempore Serenissimus rex clare perspiciens plurima mala contingere posse ex electione custodum per Anglicos in Urbe existentes, quoniam saepe, sicut nunc contingit, paucissimi sunt, vocatis multis confratibus, eisdemque nobilissimis et melius cognoscentibus quid Hospitali commodius foret, statuit quod de cetero Custos sive Gubernator Hospitalis per Majestatem suam deputaretur ac nominaretur. Qua deliberatione habita, litteras ad D. Robertum Shirborne, tunc decanum S. Pauli ac Oratorem suum in Urbe scripsit ut interea, ne locus ipse detrimentum pateretur, doctor Ynge, S.D.N. Poenitentiarius, pro natione Anglicana vices ipsius Custodis susciperet, quem postea Majestas sua, una cum consensu & consilio confratrum praedictorum in Anglia per suas litteras confirmavit. Recepto igitur compoto pro tempore administratiensis domini Johannis Alen, videlicet a 4⁰ Maii 1504 usque 4^m Novembris sequentem, quem idem dominus Johannes tanquam executor supramemorati D. Edwardi integre computavit pro vj. mensibus. Ad ipsum igitur 4^m Novembris, supramemoratus Hugo gubernationis onus subiit, cujus gubernationis tempore ista negotia Hospitalis sequentia facta sunt.

APPENDIX 21

CARDINAL BAINBRIDGE TAKES CONTROL OF THE HOSPICE, MAY 1510[1]

Iuxta tenorem formam et essentiam statutorum huius hospitalis Sanctae Trinitatis et Sancti Thomae martiris in urbe, tertio die Maii videlicet festo Inventionis Sanctae Crucis, Anno Domini 1510, coram Reverendissimo in Christo patri et domino Domino Christophero Dei et apostolice sedis gratia Ebor Archiepiscopo Angliae primate et eiusdem apostolicae sedis legato, eiusdem hospitalis confratre et ad tunc Serenissimi Regis Angliae Henrici Octavi in dicta urbe Romana Oratore, et eius speciali mandato omnes alii et singuli confratres huius hospitalis in dicta urbe ad tunc commorantes in dicto hospitali loco et more solitis capitaliter congregati, quosdem venerabiles et discretos viros, quorum nomina praesentibus inferius inseruntur, in confratres eiusdem hospitali acceptarunt et admiserunt iuratos in forma statutorum consueta.

[1] *Lib.* 17, f. 56 r.

Et demum Sancti Spiritus gratia primitus invocata, idem Reverendissimus pater et confratres eorum unanimo consensu pariter et assensu (quia non constat nec apparet de aliquo Computo sive Ratiocinio super redditis et proventis dictorum hospitalium et onerum eorundem facto a tertio die Maii Anno Domini 1504 usque in presentem diem iuxta formam statutorum) ad acceptandos computos omnium Custodum interim in eodem hospitali ministrantium, eligerunt in auditores providos et discretos viros, dominos Willelmum ffell veritatum professorem ac Vicarium Novi Castri super Tynam, Johannem Alyn legum doctorem, Thomam Halsey penitentiarum Domini Nostri Papae pro Natione Anglorum, Willelmum Styntt et Willelmum Burbanke in legibus Baccalaureos, deputandos singulos eorum pro singulis annis, providendoque quod idem Willelmus Burbanke sit semper unus. Quorum quaedam Computorum particularia apud acta in libros eorundem plenius apparent. ffines vero et visus Computorum praesentibus loco suo intendimus inserendos.

Camerarios vero pro statu hospitalium praedictorum in anno iam proxime et immediate sequenti consilibus assensu et consensu idem Reverendissimus pater et confratres eligerunt dominos Johannem Alyn praedictum, Capellanum Reverendissimi patris Cantuariensis Archiepiscopi, et Willelmum Styntt Reverendissimi patris Wintoniensis Episcopi scolarem.

Tandem certis causis tam Iuri quam Rationi ac Utilitati eorundem hospitalium consonis idem Reverendissimus pater cum consensu fratrum ab electione eiusque Custodis usque alias distulit. Et interim dictum Domimum Willelmum Burbanke servitorem dicti Reverendissimi Dominationis suae familiarem non Custodem sed loco Custodis pro debito ordine iuxta consuetum morem in ipso hospitali conservando deputavit . . .

APPENDIX 22

JOHN CLERK TAKES CONTROL OF THE HOSPICE, JULY 1523[1]

Anno Domini 1523, Indictione ii, Die vero primo mensis Julii, Pontificatus Sanctissimi Domini Nostri Adriani Papae VI, Anno primo.

In hospitale Sanctissime Trinitatis Nationis Anglorum de Urbe, Ad infrascripta faciendum et peragendum convocatis et congregatis Reverendo in Christo Patre ac Domino, Domino Johanne Clerch electo Bathoniensis, Nec non praeclarissimo Iuris Utriusque Doctore, Domino Thomaso Hanybal, serenissimi Henrici VIII Angliae et Franciae Regis apud praefatum Sanctissimum Dominum Nostrum oratoribus, ceterisque omnibus et singulis confratribus praefati hospitalis tunc Romae praesentibus.

Primo et ante omnia admissus est in confraternitatem supranominatus egregius Vir, Dominus Thomas Hanybal, orator antedictus. Deinde ac

---

[1] *Lib.* 22, f. 3 v.

consequenter in eadem congregatione personaliter constitutus Venerabilis
Vir Dominus Johannes Pennande, Decretum Doctor, eiusdem hospitalis
confrater, ex mandato eorundem oratorum et ceterorum confratrum,
quasdam litteras sub nomine praefate Majestatis Regiae, a Reverendissimo
in Christo Patre et Domino, Domino Thomaso Ulceyo,[2] Cardinali Eborace
ac Regni Angliae a latere Legato Cancellerioque, ad Camerarios et Venera-
bilem Virum Dominum Richardum Shurley, dicta hospitalis Custodem,
necnon eiusdem confratres scriptas, publice legit. In quibus antedictus
Serenissimus Rex, utpote eiusdem hospitalis curam intimam gerens, eosdem
Camerarios Custodem et Confratres requirebat et obnixe adhortabatur,
ut pro meliore ipsius manutentione conservatione ac reformatione, curam
regimen et administrationem eiusdem Electo Bathoniense praefato committere et tradere velint, cum amplioribus auctoritate et potestate quibus
aliquis ante hac dicti hospitalis rector uti consuevit.

Quibus quidem litteris perlectis et publicatis, ac Camerariis Dominoque
Custode praefato ex tali earum requisitione sese huiusmodi officio et administratione ibi palam abdicantibus, hospitaleque praefatum in manus
confraternitatum cedentibus et consignantibus, omnes et singuli confratres dicti hospitalis ibidem tunc praesentes iuste petitioni et dicti
Serenissimi Regis pie requisitione unanimiter, nemine quidem contradicente,
assenserunt, et quilibet eorum expresse assensit. Et eundem Dominum
Richardum sponte cedentem et tunc in antea omni huiusmodi officio et
administratione penitus exuentes, dicto Domino Electo Bathoniense
oratori praefato praesenti et acceptandi ac onus in se assumenti,
ut praefertur, plenarie in futurum commiserunt ampliore via modo et
forma quibus id facere potuerunt.

Quo facto, assignatus est terminus dicto Domino Rychardo Custodi
praefato intra quem de perceptis et levatis in administratione bonorum
antedicti hospitalis iustum ac verum calculum sive computum reddere
debeat et teneatur Auditoribus ac id deputatis, videlicet Domino Johanne
Pennande supranominato ac cognito, super conscientias suas fidelem inde
faciant relationem.

Deinde Camerarii electi sunt Dominus Johannes Nase, nationis
Anglicorum in Basilica Sancti Petri penitentiarius, et Dominus Robertus
Coket, presbyter. Praesterea commissarios suos in negotiis hospitalis ex
consensu fratrum constituit idem Bathoniensis Dominum Richardum
Shurley ac Dominum Johannem Pennandum praenominatos, quibus et
Camerarii vices suas cesserunt quandocumque eos abesse contingeret.
Itaque soluta est congregatio.

Acta sunt haec Anno die et loce praenominatus.

[2] Cardinal Wolsey.

APPENDIX 23

HENRY VIII APPOINTS JOHN BOROBRIGG AS CUSTOS OF THE HOSPICE FOR LIFE,
AUGUST 1532[1]

Rex omnibus ad quos &c Salutem.

Sciatis quod Nos, de Gratia nostra speciali ac ex certa Scientia & mero Motu nostris, Dedimus et Concedimus Dilecto Nobis Johanni Borobryge Clerico Custodiam Domus sive Hospitalis Sancti Thomae Martiris in Alma Urbe Romae, Habendam Tenendam et Occupandum Custodiam praedictam, cum omnibus Juribus Debitis ac Commoditatibus eidem Custodiae qualitercumque spectantibus sive pertinentibus, praefato Johanni ad Terminum Vitae suae, in tam amplis modo et forma prout aliqua alia Persona eandem Custodiam ante haec tempora habuit et occupavit.

In cuius &c

Teste rege apud Westmonasterium 21⁰ Augusti.

Per ipsum Regem.

APPENDIX 24

POPE PAUL III CONFIRMS CARDINAL POLE AND THE OTHER ENGLISH EXILES
AS MEMBERS AND ADMINISTRATORS OF THE HOSPICE, MARCH 1538[2]

1538   8 Mar./1537 8 Id. Mar.

Forma administrationis Hospitalis Anglicorum per Sanctissimum Dominum Nostrum Paulum Pp. 111 motu proprio.

Cum nuper intellexerimus Hospitale Sanctissimae Trinitatis et Sancti Thomae martyris Anglicorum nuncupatum de urbe adeo confratribus defecisse ut vix unus tum supervivescet, et ille decrepitus qui omnia officia diversis confratribus eiusdem Hospitalis dari annuatim solita, ipse solus exerceret, fructusque dicti Hospitalis capiens non in usum pauperum eiusdem nationis prout constitutionibus cavetur eiusdem, cum nulli Anglici in urbe essent, sed in proprios exponebat : et cum ex Dei Domini Nostri benignitate hodie dilectus filius noster Reginaldus Polus S. R. E. diaconus Cardinalis cum plerisque aliis eiusdem nationis in urbe existant, verentes ne Hospitale praedictum omnino confratribus carens ab aliquibus occuparetur aut impetraretur, sicque natio illa hospitali et hospitalitate privaretur, volentes quantum cum Deo possumus utilitati et honori bonorum virorum illius nationis providere, venerabili fratri nostro Paulo Capisucco Romano Episcopo Neocastrensis Almae Urbis Vicario Nostro dedimus in mandatis

---

[1] Rhymer's 'Foedera', Vol. VI (1741 edition).
[2] *Lib.* 4, f. 370.

ut praefatum Reginaldum Cardinalem et alios Anglicos in Urbe existentes secundum statuta et constitutiones in confratres recipi curaret. Qui Paulus Vicarius mandata nostra exequens dictum Reginaldum Cardinalem et fratrem Robertum Buknam penitentiarium, Joannem Heliare, Thomam Golduellum, Michaelem Throkmertonum, Georgium Lilium, Henricum Piningum, ac eundem vicarium nostrum Romae existentem per dictum antiquum custodem, in quem solum confratria residebat, in confratres recipi fecit.

Qua receptione facta ac aliis solennitatibus requisitis observatis : volentem ut par erat, quae per constitutiones mandantur adimplere dicto antiquo custode officio custodiae renuntiante de unanimi consensu, confratres presenti eundem Reginaldum Cardinalem in custodem et administratorem elegerunt, aliosque officiales iuxta formam statutorum eiusdem hospitalis deputaverunt, aliaque fecerunt, prout in instrumento desuper confecto, cuius tenorem haberi volumus pro expresso, latius continetur. Nos admissionem in confatres, renunciationem electionem et deputationem, praefatas ratas et gratas habentes, ea omnia motu proprio et ex certa scientia approbamus et confirmamus et praesentis motus proprii patrocinio communimus. Dantes authoritatem et pietatem eidem Reginaldo Cardinali per se alium omnia gerere et exercere quae ad eiusdem custodis seu administratoris officium pertinet. Volentes quod tam dictus Reginaldus Cardinalis dicti hospitalis de fructibus et bonis dicti hospitalis nihil omnino, exceptis quae per constitutiones eis conceduntur, in proprios usus convertere possint. Sed de omnibus administratis fidelem computum aliis confratribus et futuris officialibus reddere omnino teneantur. Ita tamen quod semper hospitalitas pro infirmis et peregrinis iuxta formam et tenorem constitutionem omnino teneantur, et divinis cultus non negligatur. Et quia evenire posset, quod ob mortem (quod absit) vel carentia confratrum hospitale omnino vacuum remaneat, sicque, ut iam diximus, hospitale illud ab aliis occuparetur, vel de facili ut beneficium impetraretur, huic inconvenienti providere volentes decrevimus et declaramur, quod dilectus filius vicarius urbis pro tempore existens de eadem confratria esse censeatur, etiam si de natione Anglicana non fuerit. Quem ex nunc ad effectum infrascriptum in confratrem creamus et deputamus perpetuis futuris temporibus, tunc et eo casu omnibus deficientibus in custodem et administratorem dicti hospitalis et bonorum eiusdem elegimus creamus et deputamus. Ita quod omnia quae ad administratoris et custodis officium pertinent, exercere possit et debeat, donec et quousque aliquis de natione ad hoc idoneus venerit, cui administrationem omnem et rationem administrationis, cum reliquorum restitutione reddere teneatur. Et quia ex varietate temporum, personarum et rerum convenire videtur, quod statuta etiam varientur humana, volumus et eadem authoritate concedimus praedicto Reginaldo Cardinali de cuius conscientia bonitate et maturo consilio plurimum in Domino confidimus ut de consensu aliorum confratrum possit de antiquis statutis mutare, addere et abolere, prout utilitati dicti hospitalis et pauperum peregrinorum et infirmorum quantum eum Deo poterit, noverit expedire. Dummodo quae ad substantiam hospitalitatis et conservationem bonorum pertinent, non mutentur. Non obstantibus constitutionibus et ordinationibus apostolicis dicti hospitalis et confirmatis statutis ceterisque contrariis quibuscumque.

Datum Rome apud S.tum Petrum octavo id. martii, anno quarto.

APPENDIX 25

THE FIRMA ANGLIAE

Except for three references at the back of Liber 16, when a total of 600 ducats was sent to the Hospice in the years 1446 and 1447, these are the only details of the *Firma Angliae* to be found in the Hospice account books. They give an indication of the general income from this source. Sources: 1497–4.5.1505, Lib. 17. 4.5.1506–1514, Lib. 13. 1523–4, Lib. 22.

Date	Collector	Sum
Jan. 1497	John Plumpton	182 ducats de camera
24.8.1500	John Plumpton & Walter Smyth	120 ducats de camera
21.4.1501	ibid.	80 ducats de camera
26.6.1501	ibid.	114 ducats de camera
2.2.1502	ibid.	180 ducats de camera
1.4.1502	ibid.	35 ducats, 6 carlini, also 72 pewter vessels and 220 ells of Normandy canvas to make sheets for pilgrims in the Hospice, brought out in the royal ship 'Sovereign'.
3.5.1504–4.11.1504		365 ducats, 9 carlini
4.11.1504–4.5.1505		324 ducats, 2 carlini
(No date, *c.* 1506)		393 ducats, 2 bol.,
4.5.1506–4.5.1507		400 duc., 1 carl, 1 bol.
4.5.1507–1.1.1508		208 duc., 1 carl, 5 bol.
1.1.1508–1.1.1509		88 ducats, 9 carlini
1.1.1509–1.1.1510		Nil
1.1.1510–1.5.1510		130 ducats
1.5.1510–1.5.1511		Nil
1.5.1511–1.5.1512		Nil
1.5.1512–1.1.1513		Nil
1.1.1513–1.5.1513		5,055 ducats
		Remanent in manibus firmariorum
1.5.1514–1.10.1514	Walter Smyth	3,988 ducats, 4 carlini.
1523	Walter Smyth	820 ducats
	John Freer, 'modernus collector' owed	917 ducats, 60 bolandini
1524	John Freer owed	1,261 ducats.

'Integra firma erit nec plus nec minus quam ducati de carl. 552.'

APPENDIX 26

LIST OF *Confratres* ADMITTED TO THE HOSPICE[1]

Liber 17	Date	Name	Description
f. 13	29.12.1474	M. William Walwyn	Abbot of Eynsham
		D. Robert Welles[2]	Bishop-elect
		D. Thomas de la Mare	Knight
		M. Doctor Thomas Matyn	Doctor of decretals
		Robert Hyll	Armiger
		M. Robert Slymbrygge[3]	Bachelor of both laws
f. 14	25.5.1475	Richard Wayye	Armiger ; *nobilis vir*
f. 15	16.7.1475	D. John Sant[4]	Abbot of Abingdon
		M. Richard Warburton	Bachelor of Theology
		M. Richard Rede	Bachelor of Theology
		D. Hugh Bradbury	Chaplain
		John Wakefield[5]	Layman
	25.12.1475	D. Anthony (Woodville), Earl Rivers[6]	
		D. John, Earl of Ormonde	
		D. John, Lord Scrope	
		D. William Yonge	Knight
		Robert Poynes	Armiger
		Edmund Geddyng	
		Thomas Brexton	Armiger
		Thomas Shukburgh	Armiger
		William Brerton	Gyan King of Arms
	2.5.1476	D. John Shirwode*	Archdeacon of Richmond
		D. John Gerona[7]	
		John Mower	
		Richard Joce	Priests
		Robert Rogger (?) *alias* Walker	
		William Maudesley	

[1] This list is compiled from *Liber* 17 *passim*. It should be used in conjunction with the list of officers of the Hospice in Appendix 28. The details of Italian university degrees and residence are taken from the lists in the appendix to Parks, *The English Traveler to Italy*, Rome 1954. Names marked with an asterisk are dealt with more fully in the article entitled, 'The Hospice of St Thomas and the English Crown', pp. 145–176.

[2] Robert Welles, a Franciscan, provided to the see of Achonry in Ireland by Sixtus IV in July 1473, and consecrated in the Hospice church in 1475. He was chaplain of the Hospice 1474–5 and auditor 1475–6. He died before 1488. Cf. Brady, *The Episcopal Succession in England, Scotland and Ireland*, Rome 1876, Vol. II.

[3] Robert Slymbrygge took a degree in canon law at Bologna in 1474.

[4] John Sant, royal orator 1475–9.

[5] John Wakefield, the only lay custos of this period.

[6] Woodville and his eight companions were on pilgrimage and had been to Bari.

[7] John Gerona, member of St Edmund's confraternity from about 1461 onwards. He left a house to the Hospice of St Thomas.

Liber 17	Date	Name	Description
		William Graystoke	
		Richard More	
		William Balcomb	
		William Lee	Laymen
		Thomas Orton	
		William Walker	
		William Redchednor	
f. 16	3.5.1477	D. John Merbek	Cleric, York diocese
	14.9.1478	D. Thomas Asshby	Professor of Theology ; Rector of St Peter's, Cornhill, London
		D. William Shirwode*	Doctor of Decretals ; chaplain of the Duke of York
		D. William Knight	Vicar-perpetual of Aylysbeare, Exeter diocese
	10.1.1479	D. William Raygord	Prior of Luffield, Lincoln diocese
		D. William Cokys	M.A.
		D. John Sabrisford	Monk of Walden, London d.
		M. Robert Hagurston	Notary, Coventry and Lichfield diocese
	19.4.1479	D. Robert Fenton[8]	Doctor of Theology
		Thomas Fenton	Laymen, York diocese
		John Brerton	
	3.5.1482	William Oxe	Layman, York diocese
	25.5.1482	F. Henry Coney	Dominican, Professor of Theology
	10.7.1482	D. John Dunmowe*	Royal chaplain and *nuntius ; licentiatus in legibus ;* prebend of Windsor
		Ralph Hethcote	Chancellor of Hereford ; master or warden of free chapel of St Laurence, Poltney, London.
	28.8.1482	D. William Grave	Rector of Sanderton, Lincoln diocese
f. 18	3.5.1483	D. John	Bishop of Waterford and Lismore
	3.5.1484	D. Thomas Tomyow[9]	Doctor of both laws
		M. John Lucas	

[8] Robert Fenton, penitentiary in St Peter's.
[9] Thomas Tomyow, Doctor of Civil Law, Bologna, 1483.

Liber 17	Date	Name	Description
	4.12.1484	D. William Shaldo	M.A. ; chaplain of merchants of Calais staple
	3.5.1485	M. Robert Shirwyne	B.C.L.
		Ralph Bryd	Coventry and Lichfield dioc.
		William Partrych	London diocese
		John Lee	York diocese
	3.5.1486	Peter of Proceria	
		Joan (his wife)	
	11.6.1486	M. Christopher Urswik*	Almoner of Henry VII ; archdeacon of Salisbury
	3.5.1487	Thomas Thwaites	
		D. William Smythson	
		Thomas Yorke	York city
		Thomas Lasenby	
	3.5.1488	D. Thomas Alcok[10]	Archdeacon of Worcester
	4.11.1488	D. Peter Huse	Archdeacon of Northampton
	3.5.1489	D. John Cloos	LL.D., dean of Chichester
		D. Richard Trappe	Bachelor of theology
		D. Thomas Newport	Knight of St John of Rhodes
		D. John Toun	Knight of St John of Rhodes
	3.5.1490	D. William Warham[11]	LL.D.
		D. David William*	Doctor of Decretals ; king's orator
		D. William Fell	M.A.
		D. Thomas Linacre[12]	
		D. William Lilly[13]	
	23.4.1491	M. Tarlokes	Master of theology ; Chancellor of Exeter
		M. Ralph Esceying	Alderman of London
		D. John Thornton	Archdeacon of St Albans
		M. Charles Bogthe	
f. 19	3.5.1491	D. John Englis*	King's orator
	20.5.1492	D. Ralph Scrope[14]	
	30.1.1493	D. Christopher Baynbrigge*	Doctor of both laws
		D. Thomas Galston	Monk of Canterbury
		D. William Cosyn	Prebendary of Sarum

---

[10] Thomas Alcock was at the university of Bologna in 1488 and 1489 ; he took degrees in both laws there in 1489.

[11] William Warham, later archbishop of Canterbury.

[12] Thomas Linacre M.D. at Padua 1496. King's physician 1509. Founded the Royal College of Physicians 1518. Custos of the Hospice 1491–2.

[13] William Lily, later first headmaster of St Paul's School.

[14] Ralph Scrope, 8th Baron of Masham.

Liber 17	Date	Name	Description
	3.5.1493	D. Humphrey Talbot[15]	Knight ; Marshal of Calais
		D. John Colett[16]	Cleric, London diocese
		John Water, *alias* Yorke	King's herald
	3.5.1494	D. William Lovel[17]	Bachelor of Laws
		Richard Wyndson	Bachelor of Laws
	3.5.1496	F. John Francis[18]	Professor of theology
		Fr John Tynemouth	Professor of theology
		D. John Mortemer	
	21.8.1496	Robert Shirborne*	King's orator
		D. Richard West	
	8.11.1496	D. Edward Scott*	
f/20	7.5.1497	D. John Whitby[19]	Prior of Gisborne
f. 27	7.1.1499	D. William Barons[20]	
	15.1.1499	D. John Haryngton	Doctor of both laws
	10.5.1499	D. John Prous	Prior of Taunton ; Augustinian canon
	16.7.1499	D. Sylvester Giglis*	Bishop of Worcester
		D. Adrian Castelli*	} orators and procurators of Henry VII
	30.9.1499	D. William Throgmerton	LL.D.
f. 29	10.10.1500	D. Thomas Cabold[21]	Doctor of both laws ; Norwich diocese
		D. Thomas Bowden[22]	Hospice chaplain
f. 39	3.5.1501	D. Richard Charnoke[23]	Prior of Christ Church, London
f. 40	2.2.1502	D. John Taylar[24]	Doctor of Canon Law, Sarum diocese
	3.5.1502	D. John Yong[25]	LL.D., Chichester diocese
f. 41	9.6.1502	D. George Cromer	M.A.
		D. John Alan[26]	M.A.

[15] Talbot was on a diplomatic mission to Rome and Naples, with Christopher Urswick and John Water (*alias* Yorke), a royal herald.

[16] John Colet, founder of St Paul's School, 1509, and later dean of St Paul's.

[17] William Lovel, civil law degree, Bologna, 1495.

[18] John Francis O.F.M., appointed chaplain to the Hospice, 3rd May 1496.

[19] This is probably the prior of Gisborne who died at Jerusalem later, cf. sup., p. 137.

[20] William Barons took the degree of D.C.L. at Bologna in 1499, and is probably to be identified with the Master Barons or Barnes who was made Master of the Rolls in 1502 and bishop of London in 1504. Cf. DNB.

[21] Thomas Cabold, papal penitentiary. He died in 1503 and was buried in the Hospice church.

[22] Thomas Bowden D.C.L., Bologna, 1502.

[23] Richard Charnock, English humanist, friend of Erasmus and Colet. An Augustinian canon.

[24] John Taylar, at Ferrara University in 1500.

[25] John Young, at Ferrara University in 1500.

[26] John Allen, probably to be identified with the John Alan who became archbishop of Dublin in 1528. Cf. DNB.

Liber 17	Date	Name	Description
f. 52	18.8.1503	William Clark	London merchant, born Newport, Salop.
	25.11.1503	D. Thomas Metcalf[27]	Doctor of theology, York dioc.
f. 56	3.5.1510	(name left out)	Prior of Browrton, Bath dioc.
		Thomas Waleshe	Prior of Bradstoke, Sarum diocese, Augustinian
		(John) Wulf	LL.D.
		John Docwra	Nephew of the *Magnus Prior Angliae*[28]
		D. Thomas Halsey*	Bachelor of laws
		William Styntt	Bachelor of laws, Lincoln d.
		John Landaph *alias* John . . .	Bachelor of laws
		William Burbanks*	Carlisle diocese
f. 57	22.4.1511	Richard Wyott	Professor of theology
		William Latymer[29]	Doctor of Arts
		Lanslottus Colyns	Nephew of the Cardinal of England[30]
		Joachim Bretonar[31]	Bachelor of theology
		William Hatclyffe[32]	Bachelor of theology
		Christopher Wylson	Bachelor of laws
		Richard Pace*[33]	*Alter secretarius* of the Cardinal of England
	3.5.1511	. . . Colett	

[27] Thomas Metcalf, died 1503, buried in the Hospice church.

[28] The *magnus prior Angliae* was the English prior of the Order of St John of Jerusalem, Thomas Docwra, who succeeded John Kendall as prior in 1502.

[29] William Latimer, English humanist, fellow of All Souls and tutor to Reginald Pole. Friend of Linacre. At Padua University in 1498 and Ferrara University in 1502.

[30] Bainbridge.

[31] Joachim Bretonar was at Turin University in 1511.

[32] William Hatclyffe was at Turin University in 1511.

[33] Richard Pace, a protégé of Thomas Langton, bishop of Winchester and Bainbridge's uncle, who sent him to study in Italy (at Padua, Bologna, and Ferrara) in 1498–1509.

THE REFORMATION AND THE HOSPICE 1514-59*

RESTLESS YEARS : 1514–21

The prestige which the Hospice must have enjoyed while an English cardinal was, for the first time in more than a century, resident in Rome, doubtless dwindled after the death of Bainbridge. For the seven years from 1514 to 1521 no Englishman of high station came to Rome, and English ambitions were entrusted to Italian prelates : the new Cardinal Medici, Protector of the English nation from February 1514 ; Cardinal Adriano Castelli of Corneto, whom the English called Cardinal Hadrian, papal collector for England until his disgrace and departure from Rome in 1517 ; Sylvester Giglis, Bishop of Worcester, English ambassador until his death in 1521 ; and Cardinal Campeggio, who took on English commissions in Rome after returning from his legation to England in 1518. The authority of the king of England was represented by the palace which Cardinal Hadrian had presented to him in 1505, the graceful building which Bramante is thought to have built in the Borgo Nuovo on the way to St Peter's ; now the Palazzo Giraud-Torlonia, it has been brought out from its quiet square and fountain to the glare of the Via Conciliazione, where it is but

---

* Professor Parks, the writer of this chapter, is Professor of English at Queens College, Flushing, New York, and author of *The English Traveler to Italy*.

one pale unit in a row of robust barracks, now faded but still distinguished.

We do not know who lived in the Castelli palace, but we suppose it to have been the cardinal who built it. After his departure from Rome in 1517 it was given by the king in 1519 to Cardinal Campeggio, probably because it needed much repair.[1] So this symbol of English power ceased to be English, though at least one later ambassador stayed there with Campeggio in 1522.[2]

It was left to the official spokesman for England, the ambassador Bishop Giglis, to concern himself with the Hospice. Not at first, as it happened, because he was accused of procuring by poison the death of Cardinal Bainbridge,[3] and it was six months before the pope exonerated him. The cardinal's servants, Clerk and Pace, former custodes of the Hospice, had accused Giglis, and we can imagine the dismay in the Via Monserrato. The cardinal was buried there in the church of St Thomas, and his retinue departed for home ; Bishop Giglis was in the end reconciled to his accusers.

Before they left in August 1514, a special audit was made of the Hospice books, not by the usual two persons but by a committee of five, three of whom were Bainbridge's servants and former custodes : Burbanke, Clerk, and Pace. The minute-book was signed in addition by the officials of the Hospice and by four more members of the confraternity, presumably all those who could be gathered up for a new start. In this August 1514 we thus have the names of eleven members.[4]

The record shows that there was no longer an English resident in Rome to take over the Hospice, and control went to whatever student, almost always in law, stayed in Rome for a time after taking his degree. Thomas Halsey stayed from 1510 to 1518, and achieved a bishopric. Henry Story, priest, was collector from 1510 to 1519. Otherwise, newcomers seem to have served. I do not know the John Clifton who was elected custos in Bainbridge's last year ; but after the Bainbridge retinue left, John Pennande arrived from Perugia to be custos in 1515, and became a fixture. In 1516 Thomas Colman arrived

---

[1] *Letters and Papers*, III, 38, 45, 217.
[2] Ibid., III, ii, 1068.
[3] Ibid., I 843, 844, 866, 868, 938, II 4, 54.
[4] John Clifton (custos), John Clerk and John Wolfe (camerarii), William Burbanke, Richard Pace, John Newman, Christopher Wilson, John Buckley, John Bell, Thomas Halsey and William Fell.

from Bologna, and was taken up by Bishop Giglis, but he died
within the year. In 1517 Edward Bassett appeared with his
degree from Ferrara, but went home within the year. I do not
know where Elias Bodley came from, but according to Bishop
Giglis, he took over, a young man, from Bassett and served
for at least two years (1518 to 1520). Meantime the rent collector
Story had died in 1519, and our records disappear for several
years.

We observe Italian rivalries affecting the Hospice. Bainbridge had been at odds with both Hadrian and Giglis. Later,
Giglis made cutting remarks about Cardinal Hadrian, whom
he called, in writing to the king's Italian secretary Ammonius,
'ribaldo'.[5] Giglis wanted and got more effective commissions
from Wolsey, and aspired to the cardinalate himself. He welcomed Thomas Colman from Bologna, and may have been
responsible for Colman's election : probably he knew that
Colman claimed Wolsey's patronage. When Colman wrote to
Wolsey in the summer of 1516 to report his election as 'Master
of the Hospital', he complained that Cardinal Hadrian was
sheltering Halsey and Pennande, who owed money to the
Hospice which they would not pay to Colman.[6] Giglis continued
to complain about Hadrian, and may have been girding at him
when he reported on the hopeless situation of the Hospice
after Colman's death.

Giglis then announced to Wolsey that he knew no Englishman in Rome worthy to succeed him.[7] He added details in
writing to Ammonius :[8] that Halsey was an idle voluptuary,
Pennande a fool, John Grygg stupid, the suffragan of London
unfit because ignorant of Italian : but Master Bell, Dean of
the Arches, might be suitable. The next day he modified some
of his judgements :[9] Grygg was 'beastly and mad', Pennande
worthless, the suffragan had some knowledge of the language
and was active ; but the Hospice was 'in evil plight, and the
few English do nothing but eat and drink, run riot and abuse
one another'.

A year later, in January 1518, he sent Edward Bassett,
whom he called temporary custos, home with recommendations
to Wolsey. Giglis reported the hospital in distress, and the

[5] L. & P., II, 509.
[6] Ibid., 58, 166, 527, 764.
[7] Ibid., 928.
[8] Ibid., 929.
[9] Ibid., 934.

pilgrims gifted with insatiable appetites. He recommended a permanent custos, together with a new church which would match the facilities of other nations. He had now changed his mind, it seems, about Halsey, who had apparently made his peace since the flight of Cardinal Hadrian. Halsey knew Italian perfectly, and was a good prelate ; he had only his office of penitentiary in St Peter's to live on. If made custos and obedient to Giglis, he would exercise some surveillance over the pilgrims, especially the evil-disposed clerks who came yearly from England to be made priests, obtaining clandestine 'false tittyls'.[10]

Bishop Giglis' proposals seem to have brought no results. Bassett did not return to Rome, and Halsey in his turn left for home. Young Bodley took over, and at some time John Borobrigg became chaplain. In May 1520 the bishop sent the latter to England for instructions and money, though to what end we do not know ;[11] at least the chaplain returned to Rome, and remained for twenty years. The Hospice records are now blank for more than two years ; at length, in July 1522, the new English ambassador John Clerk began to set its affairs in order.

After 1514 we have no information about pilgrims, the list of registrants for that year[12] being the last existing for the Hospice : not until the College replaced the Hospice in 1579 was the complete record again kept of visitors. The accounts of the Collector might leave some inference concerning their increase or decrease, but we have no reason to suspect other than a steady flow of pilgrims in these years.

FROM CLERK TO POLE : 1521–38

The seven years from 1521 to 1528 are the last in which we have a documented history of the Hospice as in fact a centre for pilgrims. The institution survived the sack of Rome in 1527, and we have entries for another year : then virtual silence for ten years, during which England broke with Rome. In 1538 the English cardinal in exile, Reginald Pole, was given custody of the Hospice, and the last stage in its history began.

[10] Ibid., 1213.
[11] Ibid., III, 291.
[12] Appendix 14, p. 141.

In April 1521 an English envoy returned to Rome in the person of John Clerk, former camerarius of the Hospice and now dean of Windsor. He was sent to present to the pope and the cardinals the king's book against Luther, copies of which remain in the Vatican Library. Clerk was speedily followed by Richard Pace, another former custos and now dean of St Paul's, his mission being to promote the election of Wolsey to the papacy in the conclave at the end of 1521. Actually he did not arrive until 27th January 1522, eighteen days after the election of Adrian VI. Both envoys departed in the summer of 1522.

Clerk's place was filled at the end of August 1522 by Thomas Hannibal, English envoy to Spain, who accompanied the new pope to Rome. He reported that the Hospice was well governed,[13] the custos being Richard Shurley.[14] In June of 1523 Clerk returned, and Pace later, for the conclave in which the candidacy of Wolsey for the papacy was actively promoted, but in which Cardinal Medici was elected instead as Clement VII. Cardinal Campeggio was appointed Protector of the English in 1524. Pace left to promote anti-French action elsewhere, Hannibal went home in the summer, but Clerk remained to present to the pope Wolsey's grandiose plans for alliances and threats of war. In the English documents, indeed, Wolsey's instructions to the envoys in these seven years indicate the man who would be arbiter of the affairs of Italy and of Europe : who tried to become pope, and was told by Clerk that he would need to come to Rome to do so, and who offered to bring the king of England to Rome too, to make head against the common enemy France ; and who then argued war against France and the Empire in turn in order to keep the balance of power. How much his power counted in Rome and buoyed up the English pilgrims we cannot tell.

It was certainly surprising that in October 1524 Sir John Russell arrived with 100,000 crowns of gold which he had brought to pay an anti-French army. In February 1525 the French danger vanished with the imperial victory at Pavia. In November 1525 Clerk went home, again leaving only Italian agents for England.

[13] L. & P., III, 1068.
[14] Ibid., 1020.

In February 1527 Russell returned for three months with his young kinsman Thomas Wyatt the poet ; Russell declined to stay in the Vatican, but went instead to the house of a Bolognese agent of England, Gregorio Casali.[15] The mission was to stiffen resistance to the new danger from the emperor's army. The hope was vain, and Russell had barely left Rome when in June 1527 the imperial army sacked the city. We have no direct report of the pillage of the Hospice, or of danger to the English. Though England gave money (25,000 ducats) to the pope, and Wolsey offered to be acting pope, operating from Avignon, the English attempt to play a strong hand in Italy was in fact over. Moreover, even while the pope took refuge in the Castel Sant'Angelo, an English envoy arrived to broach the annulment of the king's marriage, Casali presenting the request. Many special envoys followed rapidly for the next seven years, but their stay in Rome was usually brief, and their probable authority over the Hospice limited. The effective English agent in Rome after the departure of Clerk in 1525 was Casali, and with his death in 1536 England retained no agent in Italy outside of Venice. Casali's name does not appear in the Hospice records, which indeed vanish after 1528. The Act of Supremacy in England in November 1534, and the excommunication of the king in August 1535, finally cut off the Hospice from England.

Apart from the presence of English envoys at the conclaves of 1521 and 1523, over the first of which John Clerk as senior ambassador kept guard, we do not know how the English in Rome were affected ; certainly if Wolsey had had the chance of election which Pole was to have later, the Hospice would have needed protection against the customary rioting, as it did in fact have in 1549. The history of the Hospice records only two noteworthy events. The first was the shake-up by John Clerk ; the second was the Holy Year of 1525, which brought pilgrims in droves. Our first record of the Hospice since Elias Bodley was in acting charge in May 1520 is of the election as custos of Richard Shurley, presumably in May 1522, and presumably under the aegis of Clerk.[16] Shurley had taken a degree in canon law at the University of Turin in 1511 : otherwise

---

[15] Ibid., IV, 2875.
[16] Our record is contained in Shurley's report of his post to Wolsey on 1st August. (L. & P., III, 1020.)

we do not know what he did in Rome. Clerk went home in the summer of 1522. Hannibal arrived in August and reported the Hospice well governed.

Returning in June 1523, and staying for two and a half years, Clerk, now bishop of Bath and Wells, continued the shake-up which gives us our first news of the members of the Hospice since Bainbridge. He donated a large blank paper volume bound in vellum and labelled *Liber Rationarius*.[17] The inner cover, also vellum, was adorned with an illumination showing the Blessed Trinity, St Thomas Becket, and St Edmund the Confessor, with the caption *Jo : Clerk Bathoniensis*. On the reverse of the first page of this account-book and minute-book is copied a report of a meeting at which was read a letter written by Cardinal Wolsey in the king's name to the custos Shurley, giving custody of the Hospice to the bishop. As before, auditors were appointed of Shurley's accounts in the persons of Dr John Pennande and Dr John Borobrigg, chaplain. As camerarii were elected John Nase, English protonotary, and Robert Coket. Clerk chose Shurley and Pennande as his deputies to deal with the routine business with the consent of the *confratres*. Evidently a special meeting had been called on Clerk's arrival and on Wolsey's order.

The accounts were now kept for two years and five months, from May 1523 to October 1525 ; annual summaries follow for November 1525 (when a change of custos occurred) to October 1526 ; from June 1527 to June 1528 ; and from May to November 1528.

In 1525 John Borobrigg was named chaplain of both hospices.[18] In October 1528 he was expelled by vote of the *confratres* for refusing to attend their meeting, and for refusing to aid the Hospice with money when he owed it 642 ducats, 45 *baiocchi*.[19] He was made custos for life by Henry VIII in 1532.[20] In 1535 and 1536 Borobrigg wrote to Cromwell, calling himself governor of the Hospice.[21] In 1538, when Cardinal Pole took over, he was the sole survivor.

[17] Now *Lib.* 22.
[18] *Memb.* 3.5.1525.
[19] *Lib.* 4, 283.
[20] 1.8.1532 : Rymer, VI, 173.
[21] L. & P., VIII, 287–88, X, 275.

To return to 1523 : we now for the first time have a record of the regular staff, so to speak, of the Hospice.[22] The *commensales* then listed were the custos, Dr Shurley ; the two chaplains, Nase and Borobrigg ; and the servants : the cook, the butler, and the two servants of the custos ; also the notary and proctor William Bryton, and the collector of rents Master Isaac, 'who supplied the wines, and for his services received his meals'. This pattern was noted before the intervention of the bishop, for the latter reduced this list of eight *commensales* after the first semester, that is probably in the winter ; who had to go is not specified. The camerarii are not mentioned.

We are now given a regular balance sheet of the Hospice, which may be compared with the accounts of Henry Story in the 1510s. The daily number of guests at the Hospice is given, but not their names nor the duration of their stay.[23]

Comments in the record indicate the number of pilgrims for 1523–24 (May to April) at 75 : 12 nobles, 63 poor ; 1524–25 (May to April) at 530, '*ex quibus multi receperunt pecuniam et non intraverunt hospitale*'.[24] The year 1525 was Holy Year, and this accounts for the notable influx beginning in March, four weeks before Easter (16th April), and rising to a startling number during all of Holy Week. A normal capacity of 100 guests has been calculated for the Hospice ;[25] an increase to a maximum of 169 on Palm Sunday eve and to 167 on Good Friday is a surprising expansion, and must have required the commandeering of lodgings all about. The fact of war seems not to have deterred these bold pilgrims, who probably came by way of Venice. Perhaps the danger from the victorious imperial army, first in Lombardy and then in the papal states, was greater after the battle of Pavia in February than before it. Unfortunately we do not have the final figures for 1525, and cannot compare them with the figures for 1500.[26]

We might here note the monthly figures of reception of guests at the Hospice from the years in this century in which

[22] *Lib.* 22, f. 9 v.

[23] I complete and correct my lists in *The English Traveler to Italy*, I, 370–1. The list there given for October 1524, should be headed March 1524 ; now I add October 1523 ; January to April, August to October 1524 ; August 1525. The figures are in *Lib.* 13, ff. 10–41, 65 v–87, 107–120 v. For the lists, see Appendix 27, p. 216.

[24] *Lib.* 13, f. 87.

[25] Cf. supra, p. 101.

[26] My estimate for 1500 was 750 guests, for 1525, 439 : op. cit., I, 374.

we have them or can guess at them, as we must do with the daily figures in 1523 to 1525.[27]

If the climax of the pilgrim year was Easter, the climax of the Hospice year may well have been the celebration of the feast of St Thomas on the 29th December. Special meaning attaches to the feast in 1524, opening the last Holy Year which England would officially acknowledge. At this feast were present Bishop Clerk ; the current bishop of Worcester, Jeronimo Ghinucci, his title dating from 1522, who was soon to go to England and then to Spain on English affairs ; Sir John Russell, special envoy ; Richard Fermer, merchant of the staple of London, with an office in Florence ; the Knight of Jerusalem, ex-Rhodes, Clement Wigt as written, presumably Clement West, a new member of the Knights who were now centred at Viterbo before going to Malta.[28] In addition 24 other Englishmen were present, that is 28 altogether. Nine guests were recorded for that day at the Hospice, leaving 19 English residents or transients in Rome, beginning with Bishop Clerk and Russell who came in for dinner. This is a rather larger number of Englishmen than we might expect to find here, and we suppose that most of them were followers of the envoys Clerk and Russell, or perhaps religious from Roman houses, or perhaps other Knights of Rhodes down from Viterbo.

This celebration, together with the influx of pilgrims in the following Easter and throughout the Holy Year, must mark the climax of our history. In 1526 the census of Rome mentions ten residents at the 'Hospital de li Inglesi', but does

[27] From *The English Traveler*, I, 370.

	1504	1505	1506	1507	1512*	1513*	1514	1523*	1524*	1525*
January		15	12	1						11
February		18	13	9					8	32
March		25	39	61					16	65
April		13	44	34		62	39		7	170
May		25	24		13		12	13		37
June		21	18		27		8	8		35
July		9	20		22		4	11		13
August		14	4		13		5			13
September		5	8		13		21	10		23
October		13	4		17		29	6		40
November	1	4	4				8		10	
December	11	4	2						26	
		166	188				121			439

* Estimated from the daily figures.

[28] H. P. Scicluna ed. *The Book of Deliberations of the Venerable Tongue of England 1523–67*, Malta 1949, 38.

not provide us with any names.[29] In June 1527 the sack of Rome robbed the Hospice of its gold and silver ware, as well as goods and writings, as we learn from the Bull of Clement VII in 1530 which offered indulgences to all who should come to the aid of the church of St Thomas.[30] What other harm was done by the imperial troops we do not know, though we note that regular elections of officers were held in the next year. We may guess that the *commensales* continued to live at the Hospice, and the collector to gather in the rents of the Roman properties : and that pilgrims still came from England. Before or after the Act of Supremacy, the revenues from England must have ceased. Six months before, John Borobrigg wrote to Cromwell to protest his loyalty ; he noted a kind of English triumvirate in Rome, Bishop Ghinucci of Worcester, who had just been deprived, himself and a penitentiary unnamed. He himself kept on the watch for 'non-true' Englishmen, whom with the bishop's aid he sent to prison, and one of whom had been sent to the galleys for life by the Governor of Rome. He represented to Cromwell the harm done by 'many Englishmen' come there without passports and bringing unlicensed coin out of the realm.[31] He wrote again a year later,[32] but we doubt that he received a reply. Two years later, in March 1538, the pope in effect took over the Hospice.

THE HOSPICE AND POLE

On 8th March 1538 Pope Paul III addressed a *motu proprio* to the Vicar of Rome concerning the English Hospital of the Holy Trinity and St Thomas the Martyr, called *de Urbe*. His Holiness had learned that only one *confrater* remained, and he decrepit and unable to perform alone the offices of the Hospital. In order to re-establish the institution, he now decreed that the Vicar arrange for the election of new *confratres* : Cardinal Pole, Robert Peckham, John Heliar (penitentiary), Thomas Goldwell, Michael Throckmorton, George Lily, Henry Penning

---

[29] Gnoli, *Descriptio Urbis*, Archivio della R. Societa Romana di Storia Patria 17 (1894), 471.
[30] *Memb.* 3.3.1530.
[31] L. & P., VIII, 287–8.
[32] Ibid., X, 275.

Tomb of Cardinal Bainbridge

Cardinal Pole

and the Vicar himself (the bishop of Nicastro). The confraternity thus revived, the members would proceed to elect Pole custos, plus other officials ; they would then carry out the duties laid down in the statutes, giving hospitality to the sick and to travellers, and performing the divine offices. The accounts would be kept accurately, and no money accrue to private use, except as the *confratres* might live at the Hospital. If the membership shrank again the Vicar would have authority to rebuild it. The custos would have authority to modify the statutes to meet new charitable needs, though not to alienate the Hospital property.[33]

Seven of the eight persons named were English, and of these all but one (Robert Peckham) were in the Pole entourage. The same six Englishmen were then duly admitted as *confratres* (the cardinal, Heliar, Goldwell, Throckmorton, Lily and Penning), together with two other Englishmen (Robert Buckenham and John Legh) ; on the occasion, the surviving member, John Borobrigg, gave 100 ducats to match their eight ducats.[34] As of this same March 1538, eight *commensales* were then listed : omitting Pole and Legh and Throckmorton, but including the other five new members plus Borobrigg, and adding Anthonius Trovatus, who was later listed as sacristan, and Henry Hartwell ;[35] Throckmorton's name was added later,[36] to make nine. All were put on salary, as was the cook, and we are thus back to the number of ten residents as in 1526.

So Cardinal Pole, the one English ecclesiastic of high rank in Italy (Cardinals Campeggio and Ghinucci had lost their English bishoprics at the schism), was given control of the English Hospice, and the English members of his *famiglia* were housed there. It will appear presently that the actual operation of the Hospice was to be parcelled out principally to them in turn. They should first be identified.

Reginald Pole had been brought to Rome from Venice and created cardinal in December 1536. He travelled a great deal for a time, spending at best only some of the winter months in Rome. He had returned in the autumn of 1537 from a mission which took him as far as Liège, and in March 1538 he was about to depart in the pope's retinue for the meeting at Nice with

[33] Cf. Appendix 24. The *motu proprio* is copied in *Lib.* 4, f. 370 ; a draft is in the Vatican Secret Archives, Armarium II, tom. 67 (formerly 66), fol. 242 r–v.
[34] *Lib.* 22, f. 169.
[35] Ibid., f. 170.
[36] Ibid., f. 176.

O

the emperor and the king of France. He was further to be absent
on mission for most of 1539, 1545 and 1546. From 1541 to 1550,
it is true, he was stationed at Viterbo as legate to the Patrimony,
and was thus easily able to come to Rome for the consistory.
Moreover, he began to spend his summers in the hills near
Rome, at Capranica or Civitella. From 1550 to his final departure
from Italy in 1553 his duties were entirely curial, and he must
have lived in Rome.

The papal mandate regarding the Hospice named, after
Pole and the Vicar of Rome, five of Pole's suite. The one English
outsider was Robert Peckham (1515–69). The appearance
in Rome at this time of this young gentleman from
Buckinghamshire is a surprise, and is not mentioned elsewhere
as far as I know. Actually his presence was highly dangerous, for
his father Sir Edmund Peckham was a trusted civil servant,
and if it had been known that his son had 'gone to Pole' as
the phrase was, that is to the arch-rebel in Rome, the king
would have struck at the Peckham family as he struck at the
Pole family. Since Peckham is not named in the list of actual
admissions to the confraternity, I infer that he avoided further
indiscretion, and went home quietly. He was to return to Rome
twenty-six years later as Sir Robert, an exile for religion. He
died in 1569 and was buried in the cloister of San Gregorio
Magno, where his epitaph records only his exile without
mentioning the earlier visit.

Another young gentleman on his travels was John Legh,
who in a sense took Peckham's place in the confraternity. He
did not become a resident (*commensalis*), and I do not know
how long he stayed in Rome. A year later, in the spring of 1539,
he was in Venice, and remained for some time. When he went
home from there in April 1540 he spent a month or so in the
Tower on the king's suspicion of him. He asserted that he had
stood up to Cardinal Pole, and, whether or not he was believed,
he was at length released.[37] I do not know of any further
connection with Rome.

The rest of the company had followed Pole. Michael
Throckmorton was of a prominent Warwickshire family, and
had come to Venice with Pole after 1532 : he had been with
him since. George Lily, son of the grammarian William Lily,
had likewise come to Padua as a student, and lived all his life
in Pole's household, dying in 1559 a canon of Canterbury.

[37] L. & P., XV, 358, 369, 468, 697, 721.

Thomas Goldwell, Oxonian, had come to Padua in 1532, but gone back home to take the B.D. degree in 1534. In 1536 he matriculated at Louvain,[38] but in 1538 he went on to Padua and Rome.[39] Evidently Pole expected him, because Goldwell had not reached Rome when his name was put down in the Hospice list. Goldwell was to be in and out of Rome after he joined the Theatines in 1548. He left with Pole for England in 1553, was elected bishop of St Asaph in 1555, and returning to Rome in 1560 was the senior English prelate there until his death in 1585.

John Heliar was also an Oxonian, taking the degree of B.D. in 1532, who held a living in the town where Pole's mother lived. He had left England for Paris after taking his degree, and had then passed several years at Louvain.[40] When Pole came to the Low Countries in 1537, and his brother Sir Geoffrey was thought to have seen Heliar in Louvain on the way to visit the cardinal, Heliar was at once suspect, and was attainted with Pole, Throckmorton, Goldwell and Peto in 1539.[41] The Hospice records now show that he must have accompanied Pole on the latter's return to Rome in autumn of 1537, since by the following March he had obtained the post of papal penitentiary, doubtless on Pole's request. Heliar was not to live long, for in December 1541 Pole approved of his successor to the post.[42] His notebook for 1534–37 survives[43] containing among other things the transcript of an early Latin version of the Spiritual Exercises of St Ignatius.

Henry Penning is first found in 1535 as Heliar's servant, though he was evidently an educated man. He came into Pole's *famiglia*, and remained until Pole's death, being described in the cardinal's will as '*meus fidelis & carissimus Cubicularius, & proventuum receptor generalis*'.[44]

To these five members of Pole's *famiglia* in 1538 (Heliar and Goldwell clerics, and Throckmorton, Lily and Penning laymen) we add a further *commensalis*, the cleric Robert Buckenham ; D.D. Cambridge 1531 and prior of Blackfriars there, he went into exile at the time of the Act of Supremacy, first to

[38] Henri de Vocht, *Monumenta Humanistica Lovanensia* (1934), 604, n.
[39] L. & P., XIII, i, 851, 935.
[40] De Vocht, 583–605.
[41] L. & P., XIV, i, 867.
[42] *Poli Epistolae*, III, 41.
[43] Vatican MS. Regina Lat. 2004.
[44] *Poli Epistolae*, V, 185.

Scotland and then to Louvain. Here his story has stopped.[45] Now the Hospice records place him in Rome in 1538 and 1539. Then he drops from sight, and he was of course no longer a young man. The further name of Henry Hartwell I do not identify, and I do not find it again.

The cardinal's *famiglia* henceforth rotates the roles of the direction of the Hospice.[46] We identify some of the later officials after 1538. John Fisher, who appears for one and a half years (1540–41), was perhaps the Oxonian chaplain with two law degrees (1528, 1532). Antonio Trovati, later described as a Sicilian and called sacristan and chaplain, died in 1548–49, leaving a bequest to buy a chalice. The two Italian collectors, Palumbi and Bolognino, are not otherwise identified.

In 1543 appeared two further English clerics. Richard Hiliard, elsewhere called doctor and here named penitentiary, may have been a new arrival in Rome when he was made auditor of the accounts in December 1543. He had escaped from England in 1540,[47] and presumably Pole obtained for him the post of penitentiary. He became a fixture at the Hospice until 1552, and he may then have followed Pole to England. Hiliard and Throckmorton and one other had meanwhile travelled to the Low Countries in 1549 to present Pole's invitation to the Protector Somerset to return England to the Roman faith.[48]

A more important person was William Peto, Franciscan Provincial for England, who had gone abroad in 1533. He had followed Pole from the Low Countries in 1537 or 1538 to Venice, where his order kept him for a time.[49] In March 1543 he was appointed bishop of Salisbury, doubtless on Pole's initiative. For some years from the beginning of 1544, as is evident, he alternated with Goldwell as *locum tenens* of the Hospice.

One Englishman in Pole's orbit who does not seem to have taken an interest in the Hospice was Walter Pate, former ambassador, who 'went to Pole' early in 1541, leaving his post as envoy to the Low Countries. In that summer he was appointed by the pope as bishop of Worcester, again undoubtedly on Pole's recommendation. Pate had travelled up and down Italy earlier as envoy to the emperor, accompanying the latter

---

[45] DNB, art. by C. T. Martin.
[46] Cf. Appendix 28, p. 269.
[47] L. & P ., XV, 747.
[48] *Calendar State Papers Venetian*, V, 560, 563, 567, 570.
[49] L. & P., XIII, ii, 724.

homeward from the African expedition of 1535, and stopping off with him in Rome. He may well have had acquaintance there therefore, and need not like Bishop Peto have resorted to the Hospice. The first record of his being there is in November 1549, when he stopped there for two months with his chaplain and four servants at the expense of Cardinal Pole.[50] His chaplain Seth Holland had previously served as auditor in September. The bishop was a guest again in May 1554.[51] When the Pole company went back to England after 1554, Holland like Penning was attached to the cardinal, was made dean of Worcester, and witnessed the cardinal's will in 1558. Bishop Pate was imprisoned by Elizabeth, and, though released, never returned to Rome. Incidentally Bishop Pate was the only English bishop at the first sessions of the Council of Trent in 1547 and in 1552, as Bishop Goldwell was to be the only one there in 1561 and 1563.

This history of the administration of the Hospice somewhat pathetically reflects Cardinal Pole's worldly situation. He seems not to have had much to live on in Italy, being dependent on a pension from the emperor and later a Venetian living; I do not know if his appointment as legate to the Patrimony at Viterbo (1541–50) carried a stipend. We read in the report of a guest at Viterbo in 1541–42 that three Englishmen lived in his *famiglia* there: Goldwell, Lily and Throckmorton.[52] Yet these three Englishmen were at the same time *commensales* at the Hospice in Rome, not only then but for as long as Pole remained in Italy. It looks as if the cardinal could not always afford to look after his own, but imposed them on the Hospice. We know that he did not himself live there, though he visited it with his retinue for dinner on St Thomas's day, 29th December 1550 and 1552, and probably at other times as well. I do not know where he lived in Rome: perhaps in the pope's and Cardinal Farnese's great new palace, perhaps with some other patron who could accommodate his Italian suite: Alvise Priuli the Venetian patrician, Flaminio the poet, and many more.

Other dependents of Pole were also put up at the Hospice. A relative Gerald Fitzgerald, son of the lately executed ninth earl of Kildare, had fled Ireland at the beginning of 1540, when he was fifteen, and being harried in France and the Low

[50] *Lib.* 23, ff. 78, 124.
[51] Ibid., f. 190.
[52] Pietro Carnesecchi, as reported in his Holy Office Processo, ed. Girolamo Manzoni in R. Deputazione di Storia Patria, X (Torino 1870), 254–55.

Countries by English diplomatic protests, made his way to Pole. He lived in the Viterbo household in 1541–42 ; then for some months in 1543 his living was at the charge of the Hospice,[53] as if his rank prevented his living there. Perhaps since Pole was at Trent for early 1543, his kinsman had to be taken care of, and his servant was carried as a *salariatus* at the Hospice, and presumably lived there. Kildare was thereafter in and out of Pole's company, going with him to Trent for the Council in 1545, but returning to England in 1547.

Another dependent was James Griffith ap Howell, a Welsh exile since 1533. He had passed through Venice in 1538 on the way to Rome, though Pole suspected him then of being a royal agent or spy.[54] He is next found in Vienna in 1542 with a papal letter recommending him for a command of troops against the Turk.[55] In 1543 he and a servant were living as *salariati* at the Hospice.[56] In 1549 he was the third messenger with Hiliard and Throckmorton taking a letter for Pole to the Protector, and it may be that he did not come back to Rome with them.

Still another dependent was the cardinal's younger brother Sir Geoffrey, who stopped at the Hospice in 1549 with three servants, at the same time as Bishop Pate with five :[57] all, however, was at the cardinal's expense. This was at the time of the death of Paul III, when presumably lodgings were scarce in Rome. Moreover, Sir Geoffrey remained only a week, as any traveller was presumably entitled to do. Again it is surprising that the cardinal, wherever he lived when he came down from Viterbo for the funeral and the conclave, had no room for his brother. Perhaps he had later, since Sir Geoffrey's name does not recur until August 1552, when the cardinal was presumably absent from Rome. I do not mean by this long list of dependents whom the Hospice sheltered to suggest that it was merely the lengthened shadow of the cardinal of England. It is clear however that it began to be used to eke out the scanty resources of exiles, though in nothing like the thorough fashion of the refuge it was later so exclusively to become.

Edward VI died in July 1553, and Cardinal Pole left for England from Lake Garda in September. In the Hospice there

---

[53] *Lib.* 21, f. 54.
[54] L. & P., XIII, ii, 508.
[55] Ibid., XVII, 583.
[56] *Lib.* 21, f. 40.
[57] *Lib.* 23, f. 77.

were then twelve *commensales*,[58] and though we do not have the list, we suppose it to include the vice-custos Simon Belost (otherwise unidentified), the steward Robert Talcarne, the cook and the butler and certain servants, and such of Pole's followers as were not with him at Maguzzano. Throckmorton had departed in January, perhaps not to return. Abbot Parpaglia —Pole's chief of household, as the Hospice thought him— —appeared at the Hospice on 16th August and left on 4th September. George Lily and Thomas Rice (a new arrival, whom I do not otherwise identify) departed on 2nd September. Thomas Goldwell came on 7th September and left on 13th September. Bishop Peto departed on 19th September. For some reason the number of *commensales* remained at twelve despite these departures. On 10th October the vice-custos made up his accounts and departed, giving place to Talcarne. The latter may have been the Cornishman who took two degrees at Oxford in 1545 and 1547–8 ; I do not know how he came to Rome. He was to be the business director of the Hospice for the next twenty-five years.

So the followers of Cardinal Pole left the Hospice behind, though ironically the number of pilgrims to be cared for took a sudden leap. The cardinal's agents continued to stop at the Hospice when in Rome : Ormanetto and his staff in 1554 ;[59] one sent from Dilingen in November 1554 ;[60] a courier from England in 1555.[61] The cardinal's last interest was marked by his charge to Henry Penning, whom he sent to Rome in 1557 with dispatches, to inspect the Hospice. So the Venetian envoy in London reported at least, and Penning proceeded to audit Talcarne's accounts for the last three years. The cardinal died in November 1558 ; in the following March the pope assigned the wardenship of the English College, as the Bull now called it, to Sir Edward Carne, English ambassador to the Holy See, who had been recalled by the Privy Council. A year later the appointment was revoked, and the charge given to Bishop Goldwell, who returned in the spring of 1560. Since the bishop was to be away a great deal, the Hospice continued under the effective management of Robert Talcarne. Incidentally, the office of camerarius seems to have dwindled away by then,

[58] Ibid., f. 195 v.
[59] Ibid., f. 212 v.
[60] Ibid., f. 200.
[61] Ibid., f. 229 v.

and the deputy custos and the collector seem to have run the institution.

Before leaving Cardinal Pole's administration, we may try to discover the nature of the changes which he was obliged to recognize after 1538 in the functions of the Hospice. In 1546 he laid down a *Reformatio statutorum*.[62] This document lists a series of changes in the existing statutes of Bishop Clerk, rather than a new set, but since we do not have the earlier ones, we cannot always understand the changes. At least it is clear from the document that the custos can no longer be required to possess an English living worth at least twenty marks by the year, just as it is clear that the *confratres* need no longer be English born, and accounted loyal to the king. Pilgrims from an England in schism may no longer be received without a warrant from the cardinal; priests and religious may now be given money (4 *carlini*) instead of three days' lodging, and the poor likewise (10 *carlini*) instead of ten days' lodging. For religious observances, Masses are now, because of the shortage of priests, to be said rather than sung; at St Edmund's, only one altar is to be served by the custos or at his order.

In addition to the *Reformatio*, the document includes a statement apparently made to the later Protector Cardinal Morone of the unwritten tradition of Cardinal Pole's administration. It was emphasized that none was elected or received, and none performed an office, without Pole's approval. It was his idea that *confratres* might be both laymen and priests (as before were the camerarii) in order that the priests should not concern themselves with secular affairs. Moreover, he agreed to a stipend for laymen as well as (it is inferred) for priests; and a list of payments indicates five ducats per month for Goldwell as custos, and two ducats each for Throckmorton, Lily, Penning, and later Talcarne, intended for the purchase of clothes and other necessaries.

DOMESTIC AFFAIRS

We have come to the finances of the Hospice. In the absence of records we do not know when the receipt of money from England ceased, nor when therefore the apparent annual

---

[62] MS. Vat. Lat. 12159 (formerly Secret Archives, Armarium XI, tom. 94), ff. 116–17.

receipts of 4269 ducats (1527–28) shrank to the 1300 ducats of 1541.[63] From 1546 on to 1559 the books are neatly kept, the total receipts varying from some 900 ducats a year to some 1700, principally from rentals. Arrears account for the variations, since the rental lists of 1548[64] add up a total receipt of 1405 ducats per year, whereas arrears have accumulated to a total of 967 ducats.

This varying income was still adequate for the uses of the residents and the pilgrims, or at least the accounts show a larger or smaller surplus at the end of all but one year. This result is the more surprising because the annual expenditures vary from 922 ducats in 1551–52, when the income was only 921 ducats (of which 896 in rents instead of the expected 1405), to 1507 ducats in the next year 1552–53, when the receipts were 1519 and the rents 1219. Again, in 1554–55 the receipts were 1177 ducats (of which rents were 1008), and the expenditures 1067 : while in 1555–56 the receipts were 1564 ducats (of which rents were 1309), and the expenditures 1359. One wonders if the collector adjusted his diligence to the needs of the Hospice, and collected only as much rent money as was needed.

The expenditures were made principally for subsistence and 'salaries' or expenses for residents (*commensales*), and for subsistence for guests. The accounts specify the exact amounts purchased of food, candles, firewood, etc., and give the daily number of residents and guests on hand ; they do not show how long a given guest stayed, and we can only guess at their total number. We can note the relative rarity of guests, and the corresponding slow increase in the average number of residents.[65]

[63] *Lib.* 22, f. 228.
[64] *Lib.* 23, ff. 5–7 v.
[65]

	Rentals ducats	Total Receipts ducats	Total Spent ducats	Average number of daily :		Maximum daily (est.) no. of guests
				Commensales	Guests	
1549–50	918	1079	1065	9	3	16
1550–51	1100	1241	1241	15 (7 mo.)	2 (7 mo.)	9
1551–52	896	921	922	14	?	?
1552–53	1219	1519	1507	12	6	10
1553–54	1125	1522	1356	12	6	12
1554–55	1008	1177	1067	10	8	13
1555–56	1309	1564	1359	7 (5 mo.)	6 (5 mo.)	24
1556–57		1249	1238			
1557–58		1710	1664			
1558–59 (11 mo.)		1041	995			

The record fails us, and we cannot tell where all the money went in the later years of Queen Mary's reign. Presumably there was a resurgence of either residents or pilgrims or both.

The Hospice property consisted in 1548 of no fewer than forty-five houses and five vineyards.[66] The houses varied in obvious value. Seven of them, mostly in Trastevere, rented for less than six ducats a year ; fifteen rented for forty ducats or more, up to sixty-six and a half ducats. Four shops were included, in the Ripa region south of the Aventine. Most of the house property was in the substantial part of Rome, in the immediate regions of Arenula, Parione and Ponte, and altogether in six regions commanded a total rental of 1405 ducats. Two property changes are noted : in 1553 the Hospice spent 245 ducats on a *nova fabrica* ;[67] this was in the Via Nuova near the Via del Pellegrino, and was paid for by the sale of the vineyard outside the Porta del Popolo.[68] One has the impression that the wine bill increased at once. In principle, however, the property had dininished only slightly since 1523. Then forty-six houses brought in 1593 ducats per year ; in 1548 forty-five houses brought in 1405 ducats.

We have some evidence now of the losses, if not the damage, due to the sack of Rome by imperial troops in 1527. The inventory of 1525 listed in the church six silver chalices with five gilt patens, four silver candelabra and nineteen bronze candelabra, four silver fonts, one silver censer, one silver cross, two silver vases, and one silver pyx.[69] The 1538 inventory records only two chalices and four patens now lacking gilt, one silver cross, one silver pyx—and instead of the nineteen bronze candelabra, only two, with six more of wood.[70] The original nineteen silver pieces had shrunk to four : this was the obvious serious loss in the pillage of 1527. In 1543 there were again sixteen bronze candelabra.[71] In 1551 a bequest of the late sacristan Antonio Trovati provided for a third silver chalice with gilt paten.[72]

---

[66] *Lib.* 23, ff. 5–7 v.
[67] *Lib.* 23, f. 197.
[68] Ibid., f. 188.
[69] *Lib.* 33, ff. 8 v–9.
[70] Ibid., f. 16.
[71] Ibid., f. 20.
[72] Ibid., f. 24.

POLE, THE PAPACY AND QUEEN MARY

For the impact finally of the outside world upon the Hospice, we may suppose first a considerable satisfaction there in the rebuilding of an English hierarchy with the appointment of Bishop Pate in 1541 and Bishop Peto in 1543 ; the appointment of Cardinal Pole as one of the three legates to preside over the Council of Trent in 1545–46 ; the mounting hopes of his election to the papacy in the conclave of 1549, when only his *nolo episcopari* in effect lost him the choice ; the glorious opportunity of the accession of Queen Mary in July 1553, dimmed though it was by the emperor's caution in retarding for a year the cardinal's return home ; the appearance in 1555 of the first formal English embassy since Bishop Clerk (if we discount the feverish whirl of the special envoys sent by Henry VIII for his annulment suit) ; the recall to Rome in 1557 of Cardinal Pole (though the queen refused to let him go), and the naming of Bishop Peto as Cardinal Legate ; the desperate news of the death in November of both the queen and Cardinal Pole, and the gradual filtering back to Rome of an occasional colleague and of new refugees.

Few of these events are marked in the extant records of the Hospice. Bishop Pate is not mentioned there until he came to stay during the conclave of 1549. Bishop Peto is noted, it is true, almost at once at the start of 1544, and it is likely that he had lived at the Hospice before his elevation. He lived there at any rate to the end of 1549, and perhaps longer ; the last entry concerning him is of 19th September 1553, when he departed as did others for England. Perhaps he had stayed at the Hospice all this time.

In the conclave at the end of 1549, Cardinal Pole called in as his conclavist Thomas Goldwell, whose record of the votes taken is preserved in the archives of the English College.[73] Much excitement is to be inferred in the minds of the handful of English at the Hospice—Bishop Peto, Throckmorton, Lily, Penning, and Hiliard, and perhaps Bishop Pate, but we have only one outward visible sign. This is the record of the assignment of a guard of soldiers to protect the house from the pillage which the Roman mob was licensed to undertake of the property of a favoured candidate for the papacy. We note the sequence of events.

[73] *Lib. Rub.*, ff. C–D. Cf. THE VENERABILE, I, 231–4 (Oct. 1923).

On 10th November Pope Paul III died ; the account-book of the Hospice reads ; 'the pope died, and everything became dearer in the city, and there arrived in the Hospital Master Geoffrey Pole with three servants, and the Bishop of Worcester with five, at the expense for food of the Reverend Cardinal'.[74] On 14th November Geoffrey Pole, the cardinal's younger brother, left, but returned for dinner the next day. On 18th November it is noted that the bishop of Worcester (Pate) with five servants stayed at the Hospice. Their departure is not specified, nor their expenses.

The more important notations follow. On 3rd December the bishop of Salisbury, ill, went to the Hospice of St Bridget next door 'on account of the beginning of the conclave',[75] that is in fear of the disorders apprehended ; his food was furnished by the English Hospice. On 5th December 'we were compelled to receive many soldiers for the defence of the house because of the rumours of the election of a pope, and we paid their expenses'.[76] The new pope, Julius III, was elected on 7th February, but presumably the soldiers were withdrawn well before that date, when it became clear that the English cardinal was not to be elected. At any rate, it is only December that shows a sudden jump in the expenses of board at the Hospice, from fifteen ducats a month in October and November to twenty-nine ducats in December, and back to seventeen and sixteen each in January and February.[77]

No such excitement appears in the solid accounts at the time of the death of Edward VI in the summer of 1553, except for the rushing in and out of the Pole following on the way to England. It is true that there was an influx of visitors in that August, usually a dull month, and the irritated accountant wrote of 'now eight, now ten, now twelve *foresteri*'.[78] The date is 16th August, and the king had been buried only on 8th August though he had died on 6th July : we can hardly trace the influx to travellers from home, since the journey from London to Rome took six or seven weeks. Perhaps it was the exiles on the way home who crowded in.

[74] *Lib.* 23, f. 77.
[75] Ibid., f. 80.
[76] Ibid., f. 80 v.
[77] Ibid., ff. 76–87.
[78] Ibid., f. 194 v.

One other high point of excitement is to be noted. In the spring of 1555 an English mission appeared in Rome, the first and the last since the Act of Supremacy. The three envoys were Bishop Thirlby of Ely, Anthony Browne Viscount Montagu, and Sir Edward Carne, lawyer, and they were to present the formal obedience of England to the Roman church. Having set out in February, they found on arrival in May that a new pope, Paul IV, had been elected. In Rome for two weeks,[79] the mission entered on 6th June ; it was housed in the palace of Margaret of Austria (the emperor's daughter and duchess of Parma), now the Palazzo Madama, at papal expense. The obedience was rendered by the bishop in consistory on 10th June, and on the 16th a thanksgiving Mass was held in S. Maria in Aracoeli, followed by dinner with the pope in the Palazzo San Marco. Lord Montagu and the bishop departed at separate times, leaving Sir Edward Carne as 'lieger' or resident ambassador.

The Hospice accounts keep some slight record of this last English official spectacle in Rome. On 31st May, while the main body of the mission was awaiting instructions in Spoleto, 'a part of the *famiglia* of the ambassadors' came to the Hospice,[80] and the next day twenty-four guests were recorded, as if they had stayed overnight. On the 5th is recorded the official entry (Massarelli names the 6th). On the 6th one ambassador called at the Hospice, though he is not named. On the 9th, which was Trinity Sunday, many English were invited, but no further details are given. On the 21st, eight guests were received. But the June expenditures of the Hospice rose to fifty ducats, as compared with twenty-eight for May and thirty-two for July.

Sir Edward remained as a very active ambassador for three and a half years. On the death of Queen Mary, news of which took an exact month to arrive in Rome on 17th December 1558, he asked for recall ; he received it on 10th March 1559, but on the 31st the pope ordered him to stay and take charge of the English College.[81] It was supposed then that he preferred staying, being no longer young. He was maintained with four

---

[79] An account of the journey is in B. M. Harleian MS. 252, ff. 49–73 ; the major part, on the outward travel and the sojourn in Rome, was printed in the (Hardwicke) *Miscellaneous State Papers*, I (1778), 62–102. Diary VII of Angelo Massarelli notes the public appearances of the embassy : *Concilium Tridentinum* (Goerres-Gesellschaft), II, 273–5.

[80] *Lib.* 23, f. 236.

[81] *C.S.P. Foreign, Elizabeth* 1558–9, 469, 789.

servants by the Hospice,[82] but presumably remained in the house he had taken in Trastevere.[83] About the time of the return of Bishop Goldwell from England, Carne was relieved of the wardenship ; (20th April 1560) he died on 18th January 1561 and was buried in San Gregorio Magno. Bishop Goldwell and Robert Talcarne were left to link the old exile and the new.

GEORGE B. PARKS.

APPENDIX 27

DAILY NUMBERS OF PILGRIMS, MAY 1523—OCTOBER 1525

	1523						1524					
	May	June	July	Aug.	Sept.	Oct.	Jan.	Feb.	Mar.	April	July	Aug.
1	5	3	1		2	2				2		8
2	5	4		1	3					2		
3	6	4		1	1	2				3		2
4	9	6	2		1	2				2		3
5	9	7	3		3	2				4		1
6	6	5	3		3	2		1		4		
7	7	5	3	1	3	2		1		4		
8	4	3	4	1	3			4	2	6		
9	4	3	4	1	3			1		5		
10	4	3	4	1	3			1		5	6	
11	3		4	1	2			1		4		
12			4	1	2			1	3	3		
13			4	1	2			1	3	1		
14				1				2	3			
15				4					3	1		1
16				4	1			1	3	1		1
17				4	3				4			
18			1	4	3	1		3		1		1
19			1	3	2	3		3	7	2		1
20	1		1	3	2			3	9	2		
21	1		1	1	3			3	9	2		
22	2		1	1	3	2	1	3	9	3		
23	2	1	7	1	3	2		3	10	2		
24	2	1	1		3	2		3	12	2		
25	1	1	1		3	1		2	11	1		
26	1	1	1		3	1		2	13	1		
27	1	1	1	2	3	1		3	10	2		
28	1	1		2	2	1		3	8	1		
29	1	1		1	2	1		3	10	1		
30	1	1		2	2	1			8	1		
31	3			2		1			4			

[82] *Lib.* 30, f. 1.
[83] *C.S.P. Foreign, Mary*, 589, 664.

	1524				1525									
	Sept.	Oct.	Nov.	Dec.	Jan.	Feb.	Mar.	April	May	June	July	Aug.	Sept.	Oct.
1	2			2	3	2	10	34	19	2	2	3	1	3
2	2			2	5	2	9	32	22	2	2	3	2	5
3				2	5	2	6	29	14	1	2	1		3
4				2	5	2	6	29	12	4	2	1	3	1
5				5	5	3	3	30	15		2	3	1	
6				2	5	3	2	36	7		3	3		
7				2	6	3	4	40	8	15	2	3	4	14
8				4	6	3	3	61	6	23	3		6	16
9		4		4	7	5	5	169	11	22	3	3	4	13
10	2	5	4	4	8	6	5	150	12	18	3	4	10	5
11		5		2	3	15	5	162	12	19	4	3	12	6
12		5	1	2	1	12	9	155	13		4	2	8	4
13	2	5	2		2	16	8	147	12	7	5	4	10	2
14	2		4	3	2	12	7	167	10	11	3	4	4	4
15			2	3	2	7	8	162	9	15	3	3		3
16			3	3	2	5	5	151	14	6	2	3	2	3
17			4	4	2	7	4	50	11	5	2	4	4	5
18			4	4	2	3	21	60	11	5	3			7
19			4	4	2	3	21	32	4	5	3	1		4
20		3	2	7	2	2	21	25	7	4	3	3	2	4
21			2	7	5	4	31	20	3	5	1	2	6	2
22			2	12	7	3	26	30	3	7	2	1	5	5
23			2	5	5	5	41	18	3	5	2	3	5	2
24			1	6	9		9	9			2	3	5	
25			1	7	1	10	41	5	5		2	3	4	3
26			1	7	1	12	39	4	4	6	1	2		3
27			1	10	1	14	22	4	4	6	1	5		2
28			1	6	2	10	22	3	5	4	1			
29			2	9	2		36	10	4	3	1	2		
30			2	5	2			7	3		6			11
31				5							3			

FROM HOSPICE TO COLLEGE[1]

A REFUGE FOR EXILES

At the accession of Queen Elizabeth I in 1558 the mediaeval English Hospice in Rome came to the end of its useful existence. It was a handsome building in the fashionable quarter of the city, well endowed with the profits of four vineyards and the rents of some thirty houses. The houses stood mainly in the Via di Corte Savella (now Via Monserrato), the Via dei Cappellari, the Via del Pellegrino, the Via dei Macellari and in Trastevere; each house bore over its door an image of the Trinity as a token of its ownership.[2] The Hospice appears to have been governed still, in theory, by the mediaeval statutes, with slight modifi-

---

[1] NOTE: This article appeared in THE VENERABILE, XIX–XX (May 1960–Nov. 1961), and is now reprinted here in reduced form.

Historians of the College have not greatly interested themselves in events prior to 1579. The earliest accounts of the foundations of the College are (i) the *Brevis Narratio de Origine ac progressu Collegii Anglicani in Civitate Romana* written in 1582, preserved in MS. in the Roman archives of the Society of Jesus (A.R.S.I.), Romana 156, 21ff, and in the Vatican (Vat. Lat. 3494); this was apparently composed from two separate sources which give quite different reasons for the foundation of the College; (ii) *Initia et progressus Collegii Anglicani de Urbe*, written in 1587 and largely dependent on the Brevis Narratio: this has been printed from a copy at Stonyhurst in Volume II of the Catholic Record Society's publications (C.R.S.), pp. 89–101, with variants from another version in A.R.S.I. Rom. 156, 101ff; (iii) Fr Persons's account in the *Storie of Domesticall Difficulties*, C.R.S. ii, 48ff. All three of these accounts are demonstrably inaccurate and betray an animus against Owen Lewis; early as they are they are not to be trusted except when confirmed by strictly contemporary sources. The best published account of the foundation of the College is that in Fr Pollen's *The English Catholics in the Reign of Queen Elizabeth*, 271–82. The chapter in Cardinal Gasquet's history is somewhat inadequate and not without inaccuracies. The present article is based mainly on the unpublished papers of Cardinal Morone in the Vatican (Vat. Lat. 12159, 98ff; abbreviated in notes to VL), recently discovered by Fr Godfrey Anstruther O.P., to whom I here record my indebtedness. Use has also been made of the volumes of the Calendar of State Papers, Roman (C.S.P.).

[2] VL, 193; C.R.S. 9, 51.

cations made in the reign of Pope Paul III by Cardinal Pole.[3]
There does not seem to have been any general agreement where
the supreme authority over the Hospice lay. Cardinal Morone,
who became Protector of England after the death of Cardinal
Pole, claimed jurisdiction over the Hospice, but his claims
were not immediately accepted. There was a College of five
priests, and also a wider confraternity which included some
non-residents. There was also a custos, in theory but not always
in practice elected by the *confratres*. In 1559 the custos was
Sir Edward Carne LL.D., the English Ambassador in Rome :
the following year he was replaced by Bishop Goldwell.[4]

After the Elizabethan settlement of religion it soon became
obvious that henceforth few genuine English pilgrims would
visit Rome. In these circumstances, it was not long before a
proposal was made to turn the Hospice into a College for émigré
students. In about 1560 an anonymous memorialist wrote :
'There are, outside the kingdom [of England] many Catholic
prelates and priests who have been deprived of their churches
and benefices because they were unwilling to follow the new
religion. If his Holiness wishes, the order could be given that
the revenues of the English hospital in Rome should be administered by these priests and prelates, instead of by laymen, and
used to bring up those young Englishmen who wish to learn
Christian doctrine and ecclesiastical ceremonies, so that when
the time comes they will be able, God willing, to serve the
Church in England.'[5]

Sixteen years were to pass before any of the funds of the
Hospice were used for the education of young Englishmen ;
but there was no lack of priests and prelates willing and anxious
to administer the revenues. During the early 'sixties Rome
filled with refugee clerics who had left England rather than
conform to the Elizabethan settlement. Some of them had
been imprisoned for their religion ; but few, if any, of them
appear to have been saintly men. Rather, they were experienced
benefice-hunters with a keen eye for a cosy sinecure such as a
fellowship in the Hospice had now become. For instance, there
was Henry Henshaw S.T.L., a priest of the Lincoln diocese,

---

[3] Pole's modifications were designed to cope with the conditions of the Henrician schism,
e.g. the requirement that a *confrater* must be a loyal subject of the king was withdrawn (VL, 173).
The statutes drawn up by Bishop Clerk in 1526 had remained a dead letter (ibid.).

[4] *Memb.* 20.4.1560 : cf. Appendix 30, p. 269.

[5] Meyer, *England and the Catholic Church under Queen Elizabeth*, Appendix I.

P

Rector of Lincoln College at Oxford until 1599, and also canon of Wolverhampton, rector of the parish church of Twyford, and rector of a chapel in Buckinghamshire. There was Edmund Daniel PH.D., once of Merton College, then sub-dean of the Chapel Royal, dean of Hereford, canon of Worcester, canon of Hereford, and rector of Kingsland. There was Edward Taylor PH.D., a former schoolmaster from Eton. All these men, with a former chaplain to the countess of Feria named Henry Alwaye, acquired chaplaincies in the Hospice before the first half of the decade concluded. Sir Edward Carne died in 1561 ; he had been relieved of the office of custos in April 1560, but had enjoyed a pension from the Hospice until his death, and presented to it a white damask chasuble. In his place Thomas Goldwell, who had twice been custos during the earlier schism, and had been made bishop of St Asaph by Queen Mary, came from the Theatine house in Naples to govern the Hospice. During his absences at the Council of Trent, the house was supervised by a vice-custos.[6]

Other exiled pluralists found other benefices in Rome. John Seton S.T.D., poet and preacher, canon of York and canon of Winchester, provost of the Hospital of St Mary Major and rector of Alresford, became chaplain of the chantry which Cardinal Morone had attached to the Hospice in memory of Cardinal Pole. Dr Nicholas Morton, a former fellow of Trinity College, Cambridge, rector of Plukeley and vicar of Milton, became English penitentiary at St Peter's. With him, at the college of the penitentiaries, lived Dr Charles Parker, rector of Swanton, Folsham and Faringdon, the brother of Lord Morley.[7]

The names of Goldwell and the five chaplains, along with those of Morton and Seton, appear among the signatures to a testimonial drawn up in the Hospice on 19th January 1564 in favour of Thomas Sackville. Sackville, who later became Earl of Dorset, was a young English nobleman on a tour of

---

[6] The details are taken from a paper entitled *Nomina cognomina et beneficia Presbiterorum Anglicorum qui modo sunt Romae*, VL, 113.

[7] Other refugees were not so fortunate. Oliver Starchey, who describes himself as 'to the last degree indigent', wrote from Malta in April 1562 begging for a pension from Hospice funds. The Cardinal Protector replied that such relief could be given only to residents in the Hospice. Starchey renewed his request in July, pointing out that with the diminished number of pilgrims there must be funds to spare ; so that to refuse his request was to defeat the intention of the founders of the institution. It was not of his own choice that he was absent from Rome, in Malta of all places ! (C.S.P., I, 78 and 96).

Europe, who, after being entertained in the Hospice, had been arrested on suspicion of being a dangerous heretic. Among those who signed the testimonial were also the Welshman Gruffydd Robert (the grammarian, who lived in the Hospice before becoming chaplain to St Charles Borromeo in 1565) and Morus Clynnog.[8]

Clynnog had had a more distinguished career than any of the other exiles. During twelve years of study at Oxford he had become D.D. and B.C.L. ; he had lectured for six years in various Colleges and Halls on civil law. He had studied law for a further eight years at Louvain, Bologna and Padua. During Mary's reign he had enjoyed the confidence of Cardinal Pole and had held responsible positions both in the archdiocese of Canterbury and in the legatine court. He had been chancellor of the prerogative court of the province of Canterbury, and dean of peculiar jurisdiction in Canterbury itself ; he had been auditor of the legate and confessor to the cardinal's *famiglia*, frequently acting also as almoner and personal secretary. Shortly before Mary's death he had been nominated bishop of Bangor, but learning of the change of religion while seeking confirmation in Rome, had decided not to be consecrated to an empty title. He had accompanied the papal diplomat Parpaglia on his mission to Queen Elizabeth in 1560, and since then had studied theology in Louvain. It was probably in 1563 that he returned to Rome and began to take an interest in the affairs of the Hospice.[9]

In 1565 Bishop Goldwell went to live at the Theatine house at San Silvestro, and Clynnog became custos of the Hospice. In that year there were living in the Hospice, besides the chaplains mentioned above, William Knott and William Giblet, both former fellows of New College, Oxford, and William Grescop PH.D., once a fellow of Corpus Christi College in the same university. There were also three laymen, Robert Talcarne, Edward Alport and George Neville. The camerarii for the year were Henry Alwaye, one of the chaplains, and Dr Morton, who did not reside in the Hospice.[10]

For some reason which is not entirely clear, the new custos became very unpopular with a number of the *confratres*. Certainly

[8] C.R.S., 2, 3ff.
[9] These details are taken from Clynnog's autobiography, VL, 137.
[10] *Lib.* 33, 40 v.

Clynnog, a Welshman, an Oxford man, and a jurist, proved himself consistently unable to agree with Morton, who was an Englishman, a Cambridge man, and a theologian. Moreover, Clynnog was a friend of the Protector, Cardinal Morone, whose authority over the Hospice had been contested by the brethren only two years previously. It is perhaps significant that it is not until Clynnog's wardenship that we have any record of Morone's taking an effective part in the government of the Hospice. Certainly, Clynnog later bore the reputation of having unjustly sided with the cardinal against the Hospice confraternity.[11]

However the quarrel began, it became public through a rather trivial affair in the autumn of 1565. Cardinal Morone was at this time absent in Lombardy. Dr Morton, with some other *confratres* resident outside the Hospice, approached Clynnog with a view to buying some of the wine which had been bought for the Hospice at the Ripetta. Clynnog replied that such a sale was forbidden by a papal edict under pain of excommunication. Greatly annoyed, the three outsiders conspired with three of the resident fellows to have Clynnog deposed. Late one night the six plotters, unknown to the custos and the other fellows, met together in the presence of a notary and drew up an act of deposition. The pretext given was that Clynnog had given alms to some Englishmen without the consent of the camerarii, and that he had bought wine and wood for the Hospice in their absence.

Next morning, when the news became public, Girolamo Pareseti (Cardinal Morone's auditor) and Vincenzo Parpaglia (Clynnog's companion of 1560) came to the Hospice and quashed the proceedings in the name of the Protector. Morone, on his return, took statements in writing from both sides, confirmed Clynnog in office, and made the interested parties agree to a new set of statutes.[12]

These statutes, which were confirmed by Morone on the 19th January 1566, are still extant.[13] The first provides that

---

[11] In 1563 Morone wrote from Trent to order the Hospice to entertain a client of his. The vice-custos replied that the fellows did not accept any authority but that of Bishop Goldwell (C.S.P., I, 146).

[12] This is Clynnog's account of the quarrel, written in 1579 (VL, 137ff). His enemies—the first students of the College—said : '*praeteritis annis dum custos hospitalis . . . esset, ita se gessit ut cum totius nationis consensu illo munere depositus tanquam dissipator bonorum communium hospitalis pronunciatus fuerit.*' (C.R.S., 2, 108) But Clynnog's account bears the marks of truth and is confirmed by what contemporary evidence we possess.

[13] VL, 98.

Clynnog is to remain custos until 3rd May 1566. The second forbids the custos to receive any guest without the consent of a majority of the *confratres*. The third provides that each year a new custos is to be elected, in holy orders, and '*unus ex Collegio, iuxta vetera statuta*'. The fourth rules that to the College of five priests there should be added four other *confratres* now living in the Hospice.[14] The sixth instituted offices of major chaplain, sacristan, and chaplain of St Edmund, for which elections were to be held yearly. It also insisted that on feasts the chaplains and their associates should attend the High Mass, as also a monthly Requiem for benefactors. The seventh provided that the chaplain of the Pole chantry should have a room provided in the Hospice, if of English nationality. Others provided that important decisions needed a majority vote of the *confratres*, and that doubts of interpretation were to be settled by the *congregatio*, which appears to have been an assembly of all the English in Rome.

The statutes clearly represent a compromise between custos and *confratres* ; they also mark a victory for the Cardinal Protector, whose authority was not further questioned. In 1566 Bishop Goldwell returned to the Hospice, and Henry Henshaw became custos in Clynnog's place while Dr Morton remained camerarius. In 1567 Clynnog was elected custos again, but refused ; Edward Tayler was elected in his place. Henshaw and Clynnog together became camerarii, thus breaking an earlier tradition that at least one of these officers should be a non-resident. During the next few years the handful of priests in the Hospice circulated its offices and benefices between themselves. In 1565 three laymen had been among the four new members of the *collegium* ; but as their places fell vacant they were filled up by clerics. Alport and Neville disappear in the years before 1572 ; the third layman, Talcarne, appointed rent-collector, remained on the staff until the very end, occupying both a room in the Hospice and a private house, and growing steadily richer by speculations in *luoghi di monte* which brought him into ill-repute. Into the vacancies moved Edward Bromborough, yet another fellow of New College, and

---

[14] This is surprising, since there were at least six others living in the Hospice besides the five chaplains. We know that three of the four new members were laymen : they must therefore have been Talcarne, Neville and Alport, the only laymen resident. The fourth new member may have been Knott, Giblet or Grescop.

a priest named Thomas Crayne. Alwaye returned to England after 1566 and was imprisoned in the Tower; Knott left for Louvain, it seems, in 1569, though a room was reserved for him at the Hospice in 1570. Tayler and Kirton disappear from the lists of residents in 1569 and 1570 respectively, some years after the Protector had first tried to eject them to make room for others. The gaps were filled in 1572 by the appearance of a priest named Richard Bernard, and John Bavand, a tutor of St John's College, Oxford. During the 'seventies the Hospice can have resembled nothing more than an Oxford senior common room. The nine clerics resident there included two fellows of New College, one of All Souls, and an ex-president of Lincoln. The one Cambridge man concerned, Dr Morton, steadily lost influence. It was not surprising that Sir Richard Shelley, English Grand Prior of the Knights of Malta, wrote to complain to the pope that the Hospice had become 'the exclusive preserve of Oxford men of plebeian origin . . . who remain there for ten, twelve, or even fourteen years, and are but benefice hunters'.[15]

From time to time attempts were made to break into this closed ring of refugee dons. Impoverished Englishmen with a

---

[15] C.S.P., II, 244. Shelley was an aristocrat with small respect for the academic life : he had broken off his own university studies to travel abroad.

It would be tedious to describe in the text the changes of internal government in the Hospice, but for the convenience of researchers I list below what information I have about the *confratres* between 1565 and 1578.

Clynnog : Had rooms in the Hospice 1565–78. Custos in 1565, 1576 and 1577. Camerarius in 1569–71 and 1573.

Morton : Camerarius in 1565, 1566 and 1568.

Alwaye : Had rooms 1565–6 ; Camerarius in 1565. In Tower, 1572 (C.R.S., 2, 3).

Tayler : Had rooms 1565–8 ; Custos in 1567.

Seton : Had rooms 1565–67 ; died 20.7.67.

Neville : Had rooms 1565–7 and 1569–71. (Sir John Neville had a room in 1572.)

Giblet : Had rooms 1565–78. Custos in 1572, Camerarius in 1576.

Henshaw : Had rooms 1565–78 ; Custos in 1566, 1571, 1578 ; Camerarius in 1567, 1572–5.

Alport : Had a room in 1565.

Talcarne : Had rooms 1565–78.

Daniel : Had rooms 1565–76.

Grescop : Had rooms 1565–67.

Knott : Had rooms 1565–70 ; matriculated Louvain 8.4.69 (C.R.S., 26, 9).

Kirton : Had rooms 1565–71 ; Custos in 1568 and 1570 ; Camerarius in 1569 ; had a servant, Nathan Sheppard, who had rooms 1568, 1570.

Goldwell : Had rooms 1566–78.

Crayne : Had rooms 1569–78.

Bromborough : Had rooms 1569–78 ; Custos in 1573 ; Camerarius 1574.

Bernard : Had rooms 1573–6 ; Camerarius 1572, 1575 : Custos 1574.

Bavand : Had rooms 1572–8 ; Custos 1575 ; Camerarius 1576.

From 1572–78 the chaplains were : Clynnog, Henshaw, Giblet, Daniel, Bernard, Crane, Bavand and Bromborough.

Most of the above information was supplied from *Lib.* 33 in the College archives.

mind to study would present themselves, armed with an injunction from the Protector, or a *motu proprio* from the pope, granting them permission to reside in the Hospice ; but all to no avail. Year after year the same caucus remained, thwarting all attempts, however high-powered, to have them dislodged. In 1568 and in the early fifteen-seventies, as in 1560, suggestions were made in vain that the Hospice should be turned into a College ; it was even alleged that it had been Cardinal Pole's intention to make the building a school for young Englishmen of noble family. The example of Douai, founded in 1568, was ignored ; young Englishmen who wished to study in Rome, such as John Gibbon or Thomas Cotton, had to seek admission to the Germanicum.[16]

The question obviously arises : what did the *confratres* of the Hospice *do* all this time ? They were certainly not overwhelmed with the work of entertaining pilgrims. It is difficult to know exactly how many genuine pilgrims visited Rome during these years : it was suggested at the time that the fellows of the Hospice deliberately kept the number secret.[17] We know for certain that no women pilgrims came during Elizabeth's reign, though a room was still set apart for them ; and as for the men, even at the most generous estimate there was never more than a daily average of three in the Hospice.[18] The liturgical commitments of the *confratres* were not heavy : the sung Masses for benefactors had been commuted into low Masses by Cardinal Pole. In any case, they were not observed ; outsiders noticed that the lay *confratres* would not even get up to serve Mass.[19] During this period, the penurious English exiles in Flanders wrote volume after volume of apologetics, spiritual reading, church history. Their comfortable compatriots in Rome, for all their academic distinction, produced scarcely a book between them. How, then, did they occupy their time ?

In dissipation and faction, say the contemporary sources. A memorial of 1568 alleges that the *confratres* spend their days in card-playing and drinking, in speculating with Hospice funds, in patronising brothels, in entertaining concubines and in

[16] See, for example, the disregarded injunction of the Protector to admit Ralph Egerton and to expel Tayler and Kirton (probably 1566, VL, 119) ; the complaints of Shelley about the twice disregarded *motu proprio* (C.S.P., II, 224) ; and the memorial in C.R.S., 9, 51ff.

[17] C.R.S., 9, 51.

[18] This estimate was made in a list of expenses necessary for the Hospice in 1578. (VL, 151) It seems to have been based on the figures for 1575—a Jubilee Year ! (Tierney, ii, cccxliv)

[19] VL, 173 ; C.R.S., 9, loc. cit.

quarrelling with one another. This last detail is amply confirmed : we are not surprised to be told that the public meetings
of the confraternity were marked by raucous shouting, banging
of feet, waving of arms, and physical violence. The atmosphere
was so charged with hostility that it was impossible to attend
to the Divine Office. The only virtue of these men—according
to the memorialist, who regarded it as a vice—was tolerance.
They entertained heretics to meals in the Hospice and connived
at their changing their lodging nightly to avoid the Inquisition.
They even welcomed as a guest John Dee the astrologer, 'a
married priest, given to magic and curious arts'.[20]

It is impossible to be sure how true these charges are :
certainly other observers agreed that the condition of the
Hospice at this period was a scandal.[21] But two, at least, of
the English colony in Rome seem to be innocent of the general
idleness : Clynnog and his rival Dr Morton. Clynnog, in spite
of his age, continued his studies and attended the lectures of
Emmanuel Sa, Toletus, and other Jesuit theologians ; he
produced a simple introduction to Christian doctrine in Welsh,
Athravaeth Gristnogavl, which was published at Milan in 1568.
Morton, in connection with his work as penitentiary at St
Peter's, took the doctorate which, in his younger days, he
had failed to obtain at the Sapienza. Unkind people said that
it was awarded not for any learning, but out of commiseration
for his age and banishment.[22]

However that may be, it was not in letters but in politics
that Clynnog and Morton attempted to leave their mark on
history. By a strange quirk of fate, the foundation of the
English College came about as a by-product of their energetic
but misguided attempts in these fields.

---

[20] C.R.S., 9, 51ff. For the quarrels, see, for example, the disputed election of Roger FitzWilliam in 1570 (VL, 99).
[21] Shelley : C.S.P., loc. cit. ; and an undated visitation, VL, 157.
[22] So VL, 155 ; which says of the former occasion : '*reiectus olim . . . in examine solemni, unde cum lachrimis, re infecta rediit, prandio amicis frustra parato*'.

POLITICAL ACTIVITY

The one serious interest of the English exiles in Rome in the 1570's was the reconversion of England by force of arms. Morus Clynnog, while still at Louvain in 1561, had written to Cardinal Morone, the Cardinal Protector of England, urging that the king of Spain should intervene to dethrone Elizabeth and replace her by Mary of Scotland. It was, he maintained, quite untrue that the English could not abide a foreign monarch : better to go to heaven under foreign leadership than be dragged to hell by an enemy at home.[23] Clynnog's rival, Dr Morton, was no less insistent that the pope should attempt the 'reduction' of England by force. In 1569 he travelled to England with papal letters of credit to report on the possibility of excommunicating the queen. He left England shortly before the rebellion of the Northern Earls in November of that year, and on his return to Rome Pope Pius V instituted proceedings against Elizabeth. Most of the residents of the Hospice—Goldwell, Clynnog, Henshaw, Daniel, Kirton and Bromborough—turned out to give evidence with him during the excommunication process. On 25th February 1570 the queen was placed under the ban of the Church by the bull *Regnans in Excelsis*.[24] Thereafter the English exiles constantly urged Pius V and his successor Gregory XIII to give effect to the excommunication by force of arms.[25]

In 1574 there arrived in Rome Dr Owen Lewis, Archdeacon of Hainault, sent to prosecute a lawsuit for the diocese of Cambrai. At this time he was forty-two years old. Like Giblet and Bromborough, he had been a fellow of New College ; shortly before the change of religion he had taken his B.C.L. Skilled in both the theory and practice of law, he had since been professor of canon law in the newly-founded University of Douai, and *officialis* of the court of Cambrai. More talented and more energetic than any other Briton then in Rome, he soon acquired great influence in the Curia. In a short time he was made referendary of the Segnatura, and became undisputed leader of the English colony in Rome.[26]

[23] C.S.P. 1, 60 ; Meyer, op. cit., 241.
[24] Pollen, op. cit., 142–59.
[25] C.S.P. II, 39, 45, 53, 134–5 ; C.R.S. 26, 13.
[26] On his influence at this period see, for example, C.S.P. II, 242.

Lewis, abetted by his compatriot Clynnog, threw himself into plans of political action. Early in 1575 the two of them joined forces with another English exile, Thomas Stukeley, ex-pirate and veteran of Lepanto.[27] In the early months of 1575 Clynnog submitted to the Vatican a detailed project for the conquest of England. According to this plan the pope, under the pretext of an expedition against the Turks, was to fit out a fleet in a Mediterranean port and man it with 6,000 assorted Italian soldiers at his own expense. This fleet, under the command of Marcantonio Colonna, was to sail through the straits of Gibraltar, and then collect a further 4,000 French and Spanish troops and surplus armaments as it coasted from one Biscayan port to another. It was to embark not only soldiers, but also a legate *a latere*, a papal nephew, Don John of Austria, a set of brand-new English bishops culled from the clerical exiles, and scions of every royal house of Europe to be enriched with dukedoms from the spoils of the English heretic nobility. On landing in the Menai straits, the legate was to publish Pius V's sentence on Queen Elizabeth and offer a plenary indulgence to all who joined the papal army. The English Catholics were to be armed, and the heretics overthrown ; the Anglican clergy were to be imprisoned, the queen dethroned, and Mary Queen of Scots proclaimed sovereign of England, Scotland and Ireland. The English exiles were to be rewarded with riches to be confiscated from the heretics. In particular, Stukeley, 'a man most skilled in naval warfare, sent hither by God for the solace of the afflicted church', was to be awarded an Irish dukedom with revenues to match. So perfect was the scheme that it could hardly fail.[28]

Gregory XIII and his cardinal Secretary of State lent eager ears to these rash proposals. King Philip of Spain was more difficult to convince. He sent Sir Francis Englefield from his court to advise the pope about the practicability of the project, and Dr Allen too was summoned from Douai to the same end. They arrived in February 1576 and drew up a modified plan for the invasion. Reluctantly, King Philip promised financial support. But before he had completed paying his subsidy, a rebellion broke out among his subjects in Flanders, and the project was therefore shelved.[29]

[27] C.R.S. 2, 186.
[28] Arch. Vat., arm. lxiv, 28. I am greatly indebted to Mr J. H. Cleary for permission to make use of his copy of this paper.
[29] C.S.P. II, 196–260 ; C.R.S., 2, 64.

The Council of War of 1576, however, had one positive and lasting effect. For it seems beyond doubt that it was at this gathering of Englishmen in Rome that it was at last decided to give effect to the scheme to turn the Hospice into a College to train students for the priesthood.[30] This was a project on which each of the three parties among the refugees was likely to agree. Prior Shelley had already suggested that the idle and factious chaplains should be turned out to make room for a school of English nobles. Dr Allen, as president of the overflowing seminary at Douai, was presumably enthusiastic for the project. But it appears to have been Owen Lewis, relying on his influential connections in the papal court, and the temporary kudos brought by his association with Stukeley, who persuaded Pope Gregory to carry out the plan which had already been thrice proposed in vain.[31]

For some time, it appears, the plan was kept secret : but events moved swiftly. On 26th May 1576 Clynnog was elected custos of the Hospice for the second time. At about the same time Allen left Rome with instructions to send students from Douai to continue their studies in Rome. Just a month later Cesare Spetiano, acting on instructions from Cardinal Alciati, the Vice-Protector of England, carried out a visitation of the Hospice (24th–26th June 1576). On 16th August, one month after Allen's return to Douai, the first batch of students left for Rome.[32]

Spetiano's visitation gives us a glimpse of the Hospice at the end of its long history. He visited the church on 24th June, and reported that the Blessed Sacrament was kept at the high altar in a tabernacle of gilded wood. On the right of the high altar, looking towards it, was the altar of Our Lady, at which Solemn Mass was sung every Saturday ; next to that was the altar of St Edmund, King and Martyr. By the main door there

---

[30] The only explicit evidence is Fr Persons's : 'In the yeare of Jubiley aforesaid when there mett in Rome the aforesaid Mr D. Allen afterwards Cardinal, D. Saunders, D. Lewes, Sir Francis Inglefield and others above mentioned, considering with them of the best means of setting forward the cause of England, and namely by Seminaries, some speech was, that if the English Hospitell in Rome (wherein there were at that tyme some ten or twelve chaplaynes), might helpe that way to maintayne some schollers also, or be turned into a Colledge, it would be great furtherance to the cause' (C.R.S. 2, 83). This is supported by a weight of circumstantial evidence.

[31] So much is agreed even by the sources hostile to Lewis (e.g. C.R.S. 2, 284 and 2, 90). The *Brevis Narratio* states : '*primo creditur propositum fuisse ab Archidiacono, Ill. Dno. Contarello Datario, ut iuniores aliquot studiosi praesbiteris veteranis in hospitii domo coniungerentur*' (A.R.S.I. Rom 156, 21). But the date (1578) and the motive (to spite the chaplains for refusing to elect his friend Price) which these sources attribute to Lewis cannot be correct.

[32] Douai Diaries, 25, 110 ; VL, 137. Spetiano's visitation is VL, 180.

was the altar of St John the Evangelist, which had been endowed by Cardinal Morone in memory of Cardinal Pole ; Mass was said there each morning by the chaplain, Mr Thomas More, who received fifty gold scudi from the rent of a house by St Peter's tenanted by the *famiglia* of the *maestro di camera*.

The Visitor ordered that a picture of the Trinity should be erected behind the high altar, which was then bare ; that Cardinal Bainbridge's tomb should be moved from its present position in front of the high altar to the wall on the road side, by the Lady altar ; that the side altars should be railed off and covered over with wooden canopies ; and that a confessional should be installed on the pattern of those used in San Girolamo.[33]

Two days after visiting the church, Spetiano returned for the visitation of the Hospice itself. He assembled in the Hall seven of the resident *confratres* : Clynnog, Henshaw, Giblet, Crayne, Bernard, Bromborough and Bavand. (Daniel and Talcarne were absent.) He noted that many English people outside the Hospice complained that its present state was contrary to the statutes, and very wasteful, being burdened with the salaries of so many men. At one time, it was complained, all the English nobles who lived in the city were admitted to the confraternity ; now the nine residents kept the government in their own hands, 'with much murmuring of the said noblemen'. The *confratres* replied that the statutes were faithfully administered. All guests were asked about their religion, and required to produce letters of recommendation ; those who were ignorant of the truths of faith were instructed by the *maior capellanus*. For the present, the Visitor contented himself with ordering that the ten beds in the Hospice, which had been worn out by the influx of pilgrims for the Jubilee of 1575, should be repaired.[34]

[33] In the sacristy there were *inter alia*, five chalices (one the gift of Bishop Goldwell, another presented by Robert Talcarne) and two pyxes (one again given by Goldwell) ; a crimson pall bearing the arms of England ; a red silk pall with a fringe of gold and green silk, given by Lewis ; another pall given by Cardinal Pole ; two palls containing the history of St Thomas Becket ; a chasuble of crimson satin given by Dr Morton ; 3 copes, 26 albs, 18 amices and 11 surplices ; tabernacle covers given by Goldwell, Prior Shelley, Lewis and Brombrough ; a thurible and boat ; a die for making hosts ; and many liturgical books, both Roman and Sarum, including a *Breviarium novum Plantini in 4°* and a *Missale pulchrum in folio in extypis eiusdem Plantini*, the gift of Sir Francis Englefield.

[34] Earlier, it was alleged that the good beds from the pilgrims' rooms had been taken by the *confratres* and replaced with foul and worn ones (C.R.S. 9, 51).

Nothing was said yet about the possibility of admitting students into the Hospice. But the Visitor made a careful report of the revenues of the house, with a view to seeing how many more men they could support. The annual income was 1450 scudi, all derived from rents on houses, with the exception of a gift of ten scudi a year from Morone, and the profits on four vineyards. The custos received about twelve scudi a month, in victuals and cash ; he had a servant whose keep and salary amounted to four scudi monthly. Each of the chaplains received his board, valued at four scudi a month, and one scudo monthly in cash. Besides the custos' servant there were four others, one to serve in church and read at table, one butler, one cook and one under-cook : these cost the Hospice 192 scudi a year. 108 scudi a year, it was alleged, were spent on the board of pilgrims visiting the Hospice. Altogether about 900 scudi were spent annually on the board and salaries of the inmates. Another 400 went on the expenses of the church, repairs to Hospice property, and salaries to non-resident officials such as the procurator, the doctor, the notary and the laundress. A further 140 crowns had been spent on extraordinary alms to pilgrims, and on entertaining the English colony, especially to the feasts on Trinity Sunday, St Thomas's Day and St Edmund's Day. It is an interesting commentary on the way the Hospice was managed in these last years of its life that less than ten per cent of its income was spent on the purpose for which the institution had been founded ; and that it took eight priests, one layman, four servants and four other employees to cater for an average of three pilgrims a day ![35]

The Visitor recommended that the 140 crowns spent on non-statutory alms and feasts should be saved, and added to the present annual surplus of $53\frac{1}{2}$ crowns, to provide for the upkeep of a greater number of persons. No further steps were taken until the students began to arrive from Douai.

---

[35] Some of these details are taken from a paper printed by Tierney, ii, cccxliv. I am assuming, as seems probable, that this paper was drawn up in connection with the Visitation. Certainly it dates from the same period.

FIRST STUDENTS

On 16th August 1576 Ralph Standish, William Holt, and two others named Madder and Hunt, left Douai for Rome. The reason given at the time for their departure was to gain the indulgences recently granted by Gregory XIII at Allen's request ; but later the diarist noted that Holt, at least, had been sent to await a place in the College which had not yet been founded in Rome.[36] This group fared badly on its journey : they met plague on the way and had to winter on the wrong side of the Alps. They did not arrive until the following spring. Four others who set out in the following weeks also encountered plague and were forced to return. Later parties were more fortunate. On 1st October John Gower, Thomas Bell, John Mush, John Askew and William Lowe left for Rome, followed on 9th December by a distinguished party consisting of Drs Stapleton and White, Gregory Martin, William Sheprey and Blessed John Shert, then a deacon.[37]

Stapleton's party must have arrived in January or earlier, since Dr White was safely back at Douai by 13th February. Gregory Martin was received into the Hospice and, now or later, became a *confrater*. This, as Fr Persons noted, 'was thought secretly to prepare some entrance for schollers also there, and so proved the sequell'. John Shert also took up residence ; and by February the other party of five students had arrived as well. At Lewis's instigation, Pope Gregory decreed that these six scholars should live and study in the Hospice at the Hospice's expense.[38]

To achieve this aim, it was necessary to break the monopoly of government which the chaplains had hitherto enjoyed. This Cardinal Morone did by drawing up a new set of statutes, acting on the complaints made at the Visitation of the previous year. Henceforth, all English noblemen and Doctors resident in Rome were to be admitted to the confraternity, subject to the procurator's approval. They were to attend all *congregationes*, supervise the keeping of the statutes, and be particularly vigilant to see that no outsider was enriched directly or indirectly from

[36] '. . . ut locum expectaret in . . . Collegio . . . nondum quidem constituto ; sed statuerat iam Gregorius . . . antiquum Hospitale in Seminarium convertere. De eo etiam admonuerat Alanum' (D.D. 25).
[37] D.D. 109, 111, 113.
[38] D.D. 119.

Hospice funds. For the next two years the Protector was to be informed of every *congregatio* so that he could send a representative. Votes at these *congregationes* were to be by secret ballot. The present camerarii, Giblet and Bavand, were deposed; in future, it was decreed, camerarii should be elected from non-residents, and for this year Alan Cope D.D. (a canon of St Peter's), and John Sanderson—two men who had not hitherto been connected with the Hospice—were chosen. Since Clynnog, the custos, was in favour of the seminary project, there was now little danger of the chaplains' opposition being effective.

It was ruled that henceforth no outsider was to be admitted to meals in the Hospice, or to drinks with the fellows. Nobody was to be given any alms over ten julies without the express approval of the protector, not even after a majority vote of the *confratres*.

Scholares convictores approved by the Protector are to be provided gratis with food and necessaries. Each person is to have his own room, with a bed to himself and modest furniture. Each chaplain and scholar, on entry into the Hospice, must take the Profession of Faith of Pius IV at the hands of the custos; he must then, if a priest, celebrate Mass in the Hospice church or, if a layman, receive Communion from the custos. All the scholars are to wear the same uniform.

Morone noted that the present Hospice chaplains would have been much more useful if they had known Italian. They could then have been given posts outside the Hospice and left room for younger men to complete their studies and seek employment in Rome or elsewhere. To prevent the present blockage from recurring, the young men now in the Hospice are to learn Italian: to this end an Italian spiritual reading book is to be read at table every day.[39]

These statutes are interesting in two ways. First of all, they show that at this time Morone—and presumably Owen Lewis—did not consider that they were founding a specifically missionary College like Douai. The students, having finished their studies, were to find posts 'in Rome or elsewhere'. Secondly, they make it clear that Morone felt that there was no hope of the College taking root if the government of the Hospice was left in the hands of the chaplains. These aged dons, so long isolated in comfortable security, cannot have been expected to welcome the influx of young seminarists with alarmingly post-Tridentine

[39] VL, 176.

ideals. It was as if All Souls had been ordered to remodel itself on the lines of Maynooth.

This decree of Morone's is the first official document establishing the Hospice as a house of studies. Its date, therefore —4th February 1577—has as good a claim as any other day to be considered the date of the foundation of the English College. But two years and many troubles were yet to pass before the Bull of Foundation could be issued.

The first six scholars of the College, all sent from Douai by Dr Allen, were John Shert, Thomas Bell, John Gower, John Mush, John Askew and William Lowe. Except for Shert, who had left Douai as a deacon, they were all laymen, not far advanced in their studies ; their average age was twenty-eight. With them was Gregory Martin, the future translator of the New Testament, who supervised their studies. In the spring four more Douai scholars sought admission : Ralph Standish, William Holt, and two others named Hunt and Madder. The first, a twenty-year-old metaphysician, and the second, a theologian who had taken priest's orders on his way to Rome, were admitted without difficulty. But Madder and Hunt were older, and the Hospice had no further funds to spare. Owen Lewis asked for a papal subsidy, but was refused by the Datary ; such longbeards, Cardinal Protector Morone told Clynnog, were of an age to be teaching, not learning. So Madder returned to Douai, and Hunt became a Jesuit. At the same time the custos' nephew, Morgan Clynnog, a promising youth of nineteen, was admitted to the seminary.[40]

News of the new College quickly spread across Europe. Owen Lewis wrote to Dr Allen to inform him of the safe arrival of his scholars and the foundation of the seminary. His letters were read publicly at Douai on 6th May 1577 amid general rejoicing. From Milan, St Charles Borromeo wrote to his agent in Rome, Mgr Spetiano, instructing him to use his influence in favour of the new College.[41]

Cardinal Morone drew up rules for the scholars. Every applicant for admission was to be examined by the Protector's deputy. The custos of the Hospice was to be Rector also of the scholars, removable at the Protector's discretion ; the scholars were to obey him and reverence the chaplains and fellows of

---

[40] VL, 135ff ; D.D. for 1576-7. Each of the scholars was given a room to himself ; there is an inventory of their furniture in the College Archives, Lib. 33.

[41] Pollen, op. cit., 276.

the Hospice. Each day the scholars were to go, class by class, to lectures at the Roman College. They must not wander unescorted through the streets, nor leave the College without the custos' leave. Every scholar was to be enrolled in a sodality of the Annunciation, and perform the prescribed exercises. One of the older scholars, or another priest from the Hospice, was to be appointed *praepositus seu observator scholarum*, to inform the Rector about the scholars' behaviour. Week by week, a scholar was to be appointed to read in Hall. All were to rise and retire at the same time, to hear Mass daily, and to meditate for a quarter of an hour morning and evening. Once a month, for the edification of the English pilgrims, they were to receive Communion together in the Hospice church. Later, when there were a sufficient number of theological students, they were to hold public debates at table after dinner, on topics of theology suggested by the morning's lectures or the refectory reading. At the beginning of each month the custos was to give to each chaplain and each scholar five *scudi di moneta* for their keep ; at the end of each month he must present accounts to the Protector's deputy. The earlier statutes of the Hospice were revoked, and the chaplains forbidden to interfere in the scholars' affairs.[42]

During the summer of 1577,[43] an anonymous memorialist suggested to Cardinal Morone that the nascent seminary should be united with the German College in Rome, and governed by the Jesuits who supervised and tutored the German seminarists. It was pointed out that the Hospice was inconveniently far from the Roman College, and unhealthily overcrowded : the scholars were forced to rub shoulders with sailors, merchants, soldiers, noblemen, paupers and other undesirables. The *Congregatio Nationis Anglicanae*, being a many-headed beast, was unfitted to govern a Seminary ; only the Jesuits, it was suggested, were capable of disinfecting youths who had been corrupted by the schismatic atmosphere of England. The scheme could easily be put into practice : next to S. Apollinare there was a house belonging to the Hospice, whose tenants could be pensioned off. Finally, said the memorialist, there was no danger that English and German scholars might not agree together : they hailed

[42] VL, 133.
[43] No date is given in the memorial ; but it is mentioned that there were only nine scholars in the College, which fixes the period.

from almost the same country, and spoke very nearly the same language.[44]

The writer of this quaint piece, whether he was a naive Italian Jesuit, or a cynical fellow of the Hospice anxious at all costs to get rid of the intruding scholars, must have been disappointed at its reception. On reaching Morone, the memorial was filed and forgotten.

The English exiles had not forgotten their plans for the invasion of England. Dr Allen, on the very day on which he sent Gregory Martin to Rome to assist in the foundation of the seminary, sent also Dr Stapleton as 'a very good man to go with the armada'. At Douai, he pressed on with invasion preparations, hampered only by lack of money. King Philip, however, even after the settlement of the rebellion in Flanders, was unenthusiastic about a full-scale invasion.

Pope Gregory and the cardinal Secretary now turned to a less ambitious project. Stukeley had volunteered, if given a few ships and a handful of troops, to harass Queen Elizabeth in Ireland. The pope created him Marquess of Leinster, and provided the money to charter a galleon, the *San Giovanni Battista*. After a set of misadventures worthy of a musical comedy, Stukeley assembled aboard this galleon some six hundred soldiers, four pieces of artillery, and munitions for six months, at a cost to the pope of 40,000 crowns. He spent January 1578 waiting at Porto d'Ercole for a fair wind.[45]

Stukeley's proceedings were not popular with many of the British colony in Rome. Owen Lewis, indeed, had been at his right hand throughout, and had lent 100 ducats to the expedition, receiving as security a handsome emerald worth 400 ducats. Bishop Leslie of Ross, a Scots exile in Rome, also lent his support. But Sir Richard Shelley, the English Prior of the Knights of Malta, who had always hoped for Queen Elizabeth's conversion, and favoured negotiations with her, bitterly opposed Stukeley's warlike plans. He was supported by William Ely, an auditor of the Hospice, Thomas Clements, a papal pensioner and kinsman of St Thomas More, and one Mynhurst, a nephew of Cardinal Pole.

Before leaving, Stukeley attempted to put his opponents out of action. Clements he terrified with threats of murder,

[44] VL, 141.
[45] C.R.S. 9, 44 ; C.S.P. 2, 270–460.

laying violent hands on him in his own house. Ely, 'for that he would not be brought to tell his tale to the Pope as the said Marquesse would have had him', he threatened to hang at the pope's court gates. Shelley was denounced to the Inquisition as 'a friend or honourable spie for the Queene', and would have been imprisoned but for a warning from Fr Persons, then English penitentiary at St Peter's. Finally, in Persons's words, Stukeley 'obtayned a thing very odious and many wondred that Gregory being a man of much moderation and great iustice, would ever yeld unto : to witt, to take perforce in the night out of their beddes so many men of marke of the Irish nation as remayned at that tyme in Rome, and such Englishmen also as the Marques had a tooth against excepting only the greatest. Which was done and all carried out by night by order of Don Paulo Jordano, head of the house of Ursino, to whome the matter by the Pope was comitted.'[46] Paolo Giordano Orsini was the Roman prince, adulterer and murderer known to students of English literature as the hero of Webster's *The White Devil*.

The victims were dumped aboard the galleon, and Pope Gregory came to see the expedition off. He found the ship barely seaworthy and the troops in mutiny. But at last, on 3rd February, the *San Giovanni* sailed under Stukeley's command, and for three months nothing further was heard of her at Rome.[47]

Owen Lewis, left behind as Stukeley's agent, reverted to the cultivation of the new seminary. His involvement in the invasion schemes affected it in two ways : it gave him great, if temporary, influence at the papal court, which turned to the seminary's advantage ; and it made him numerous enemies among the Englishmen in Rome, a fact which contributed to the troubles which disfigured the early years of the College's history.

At the time of Stukeley's departure the number of scholars had grown to seventeen. In autumn 1577 there had arrived from Douai six Englishmen : Ralph Sherwin, Leonard Hyde, William Harrison, Martin Array, Edward Rishton and Arthur Pitts, all future confessors of the faith. At about the same time, two Welsh students arrived and joined the seminary. Since the Hospice had neither rooms nor immediately available funds for more than the nine students already installed, the new arrivals

---

[46] Person s : C.R.S. 2, 161–2.
[47] C.S.P. 2, 373–410.

were placed in the house adjacent to the Hospice on St Bridget's side, which was joined to the main building by a passage.[48] Each scholar was awarded a monthly pension of 5 crowns by Pope Gregory, at Lewis's request. Lewis himself lived in the house next door to that occupied by the new scholars, paying the Hospice a rent of 50 crowns a year. Clynnog sent to the Vatican a bill for the purchases made necessary by the influx of scholars : 60 scudi for black cloth for 8 soprane, and a further 5 for tailoring ; 36 scudi for 8 cassocks ; twelve mattresses, blankets, *imbottiti* and coverlets, totalling 178 scudi ; twelve shirts, doublets, pairs of shoes, pairs of socks and hats, totalling 64 scudi ; 6 scudi worth of tables, 24 scudi of kitchen utensils, and 30 scudi for books.[49]

The admission of the two Welsh students to the College caused some stir. One of them, Rhosier Smith, of St Asaph, aged thirty-eight, was admitted at the recommendation of Bishop Goldwell : he was later to translate the catechism of St Peter Canisius into Welsh. The other, the forty-year-old Owen Thomas, was a nephew of Gruffyd Robert, a former chaplain of the Hospice. Both were examined by the Jesuits at the Collegio Romano and found to be fit for theology ; both were approved by the Cardinal Protector. But it was remembered by many that a year earlier two younger Englishmen had been rejected on the grounds of age. The admission of the Welshmen was attributed by many to nationalistic partiality on the part of Lewis and Clynnog.[50]

During the winter of 1577–8 there arrived another priest from Douai, the twenty-nine-year-old Jonas Meredith, who had already spent a year on the English mission. On 3rd February Douai despatched three priests (Robert Kent, Richard Haydock and George Birkhead) and four theologians (Brisco, Grately, Owen and one other). Most of these were admitted to the seminary but not Kent, who had to live in the city at his own expense. Caesar Clements, the son of Stukeley's victim Thomas Clements, petitioned to be admitted ; he was refused as being too young, but was offered free meals with the servants, which he refused as an insult to his noble birth. Antony Tyrell, whose brother Robert owed a papal pension of 10 crowns a month to Lewis's good offices, was another who was at first refused

---

[48] Cf. Vatican Library, Bar. Lat. 8624, 1.
[49] VL, 187 and 209.
[50] Cleary, *A Checklist of Welsh Students in the Seminaries*, I, 16 ; VL, 135.

admission to the College. Allen's letters of recommendation, so it was said, had been half-hearted ; and there were rumours that he had lived lewdly in England. But later more enthusiastic letters arrived from Douai, and Tyrell was admitted at Lewis's request. Two other Englishmen were refused admission to the College, one because he was a pirate, the other because he was a runaway apprentice. The pirate had gone off with Stukeley ; the other remained in Rome to grumble. Lewis's enemies kept the score.[51]

Fr Persons, the English penitentiary, grew alarmed at the growing hostility between English and Welsh, and warned Lewis more than once of the unpopularity he was acquiring. He found him 'reasonable in answer and, as he seemed, willing to remedy the same'; but afterwards he could detect no alteration in behaviour, and, as he wrote to a friend, 'to my great griefe I saw the grudgings dayly grow on.'[52]

Another incident, of uncertain date, further alienated the English chaplains from Lewis and Clynnog. Fr Persons is our main authority for the story. He tells us that there came to Rome 'Owen Price, a scholler borne in Wales, countryman to Clenock, custos that year, which Price being very poore, was moved (as he himselfe afterward confessed) by the aforesaid two Doctors to be admitted a Fellowe into the Englishe Hospitall, which the Chaplaines utterly denied, partly (as they pretended) for that he was not a priest, he had not sufficient learning to be a Priest, and partly for that they had suspicion of his dissolute life, which after indeed appeared to be true, and withal perhaps, in like manner for that the said Chaplaines stood not well at that tyme with the aforesaid Doctors, and consequently would be loth to have any more of there countrey men among them. But upon the suddaine, when the Chaplaines thought not of yt, this Prise entred into the Hall of the Hospitall, and sate down at the table with them without being invited by them, showing also for his authority a Breve of the Popes, whereby he was ordayned Fellow with them of that house, wherat they storming extreamly went to Cardinall Morone the Protector of England at that tyme, and to him alledged so many reasons against Price his admittance, as albeit the said Cardinall was a great friend to the forenamed two Doctores and to there parte, yet he caused the

[51] VL, 135 ; C.R.S. 2, 106.
[52] Persons to Goode, C.R.S. 2, 143.

said Breve to be suspended and afterwards annulled, and Price to be sent out of the Towne by the two Doctors persuasion and his commandment.'[53]

By May 1578 there were twenty-six scholars living in the Hospice and the adjacent house. May was the month in which traditionally elections were held for the Hospice offices. Clynnog, elected custos in May 1576, had been due to retire in May 1577, but his term of office had been prolonged for a year by Cardinal Morone, on account of the seminary. Now, in May 1578, the chaplains refused to re-elect him, and elected in his stead Henry Henshaw, the one-time Rector of Lincoln College, Oxford. Morone thereupon separated the government of the College from that of the Hospice, and re-appointed Clynnog Rector of the scholars. This did nothing to assuage the chaplains' jealousy. Dr Allen later rebuked Lewis because he 'did not dehort Mr Maurice from taking upon him that charge in the beginning, for which indeed, no dishonour be it unto him, he was not sufficient.'[54] The appointment of Clynnog was not, however, unnatural. He was, after Lewis himself, the most energetic, and the best known to Morone, of all the British exiles in Rome ; and none of the other chaplains appears to have possessed any greater qualification for the post, save only that of not being a Welshman.[55]

To assist Clynnog, Lewis obtained from the General of the Society of Jesus the services of two Italian Jesuits. Fr John Paul Navarola was made spiritual director, and Fr Ferdinand Capecci became prefect of studies. Clynnog remained in charge of discipline and temporal administration.[56]

Relying on his influence with the pope, Lewis obtained frequent favours for the College. In spring he secured from Gregory a regular monthly subsidy of 100 crowns, equal to that given to the four-times-larger College of Douai. In autumn,

[53] Fr Persons adds that Price, falling sick through his lewd behaviour, returned to Rome from Milan, and died at S. Giacomo degli Incurabili, where he showed great sorrow for his sins, and asked pardon of the chaplains who visited him with alms (C.R.S. 2, 84). The story appears also in the *Brevis Narratio* (A.R.S.I. Rom, 156). It can hardly have been invented, but it raises many puzzles. Persons dates the episode in 1578, and says that it 'occasioned the New Colledge', and that the chaplains regarded the introduction of scholars into the Hospice as Lewis's revenge for the expulsion of Price. But there had been scholars in the Hospice for a year before 1578, and when the decision was first taken to admit them, Clynnog was not even custos.

[54] Allen to Lewis, 12.5.1579. Knox, *Allen*, 79.

[55] Martin to Campion, 21.5.1578, D.D. 316 ; *Lib.* 304. Allen was probably justified when, after the event, he said that it would have been prudent to import as Rector a Douai priest such as Dr Bristowe (loc. cit.).

[56] C.R.S. 2, 93 ; Martin to Campion, 21.5.1578, D.D. 316.

Cardinal Como, through the Spanish nuncio, obtained from King Philip of Spain a licence for the College to import 100 barrels of wine tax-free from Naples.[57]

In May, disturbing news arrived of Stukeley's expedition. Cardinal Pole's nephew, it seemed, had 'Spoken words of discontentment'; he had been taken for a spy and nearly hanged at the topmast. By the time the *San Giovanni* reached Lisbon, she was utterly unseaworthy and her crew were all ready to desert. King Sebastian of Portugal at first refused to let the rotting vessel land, appealing to his alliance with Queen Elizabeth, who in any case was well informed about the project, and well prepared to defend herself. He persuaded Stukeley to drop the Irish venture, and instead to join the crusade which he was himself undertaking against the Moors.

Stukeley at first hid his change of plan from the papal government. He wrote to Rome asking that a commission should be given to Owen Lewis for the invasion of England, and that Dr Allen should be sent to join the expedition. On 24th June he embarked for Africa with the papal troops : the cardinal Secretary reluctantly gave his approval to the *fait accompli*. But during Stukeley's absence his confederates in Spain revealed to the nuncio that he had never had any serious intention of going to Ireland, but had sworn that he would 'sell the Pope's arms and with the Pope's soldiers go anywhere that booty was to be had'.

On the 19th August news reached Madrid that the king of Portugal had been killed and his forces routed in an ambush at Alcazar. Ten days later they learnt that Stukeley had been among the slain. Too late, the cardinal Secretary saw how he had been duped. 'This clumsy dance of Stukeley's', he wrote, 'has cost the Pope 50,000 crowns.'

Owen Lewis, who had shared in Stukeley's favour, was affected also by his disgrace.[58] For the moment, however, he retained his influence over the English College. At Easter the collegians at Douai had been expelled by hostile townsfolk and had migrated to Rheims : Lewis had obtained a papal grant of 500 crowns for the refugees. In early summer, Gregory Martin

[57] Sega to Como, 5.5.1578 and 9.9.1578 (C.S.P. 2, 423). King Philip's autograph granting the licence is in the College archives, *Memb.* 7.10.1578 and *Lib.* 5, 176.

[58] C.R.S. 2, 162 ; C.S.P. 2, 410–561. It was suggested to the cardinal Secretary that the emerald which Lewis held as security for his loan to the expedition should be confiscated by the pope 'for the relief of Stukeley's soul'.

left Rome for Rheims, there to begin his translation of the New Testament. With him travelled John Shert, the first scholar to leave the College in Rome for the English mission. The expulsion from Douai resulted in an unusually large transfer of scholars to Rome.[59]

At midsummer Pope Gregory received the scholars in audience, making a gracious reply to their spokesman's loyal address. He sent his treasurer to inspect the College and provided every scholar with a new cloak.[60]

The Douai Diary for 17th August records the departure of seven for Rome : John Neale, John Knighton, John Smithson, Luke Kirby, John Barton, Oliver Holiwell, and Thomas Wright. Kirby, already a priest, and the three logicians—Wright, Holiwell and Barton—were admitted to the College. Neale (a former Rector of Exeter College, Oxford) and the other two took up residence elsewhere in Rome.[61]

As the number of scholars grew a third Jesuit was added to the two already in the College. In November Persons wrote to Campion : 'Heer in Rome the Englishe Seminarie goethe forthe well for ther be about 40 persons under the government of III of our companye'. In the same month William Holt, one of the first students of the College, and later one of its first Rectors, left the Hospice to join the Society of Jesus ; which, wrote Persons 'hath muche amased them'.[62]

TROUBLED BEGINNINGS

The increase of numbers strained the Hospice resources, and during the winter the scholars were ill-clothed and under-fed. Pope Gregory gave 300 crowns to buy clothes and bed-linen ; but the sum was insufficient, and paltry in comparison with the 50,000 crowns he had thrown away on Stukeley's antics. Clynnog complained that he was forced to borrow

---

[59] D.D. 316 ; Como to Allen 19.5.1578. The reason for Martin's departure is not clear. In one letter Persons suggests that he was recalled by Allen, for fear he might become a Jesuit ; in another he says that he was tired of the English-Welsh factions in Rome. (Contrast C.R.S. 2, 143 with C.R.S. 39, 2).

[60] News of this reached Rheims on 2nd August (D.D. 143).

[61] Neale, Smithson and Knighton appear on a list of the English colony in Rome in 1579 (VL, 130).

[62] Persons to Campion, C.R.S. 39, 1.

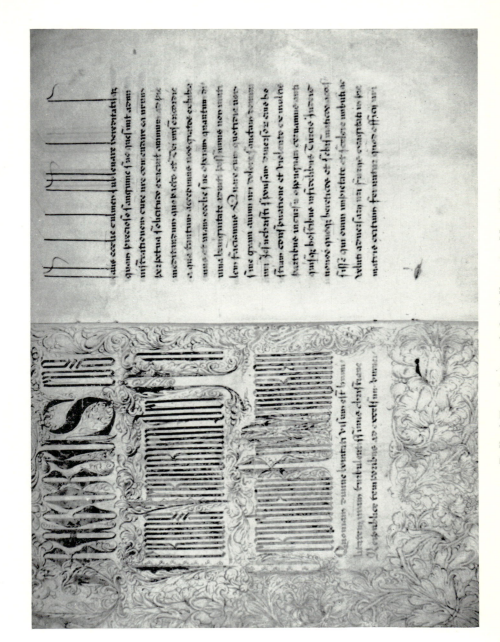

Bull of Foundation of the College, 1st May 1579

Gregorius XIII. Pont. Max. huius Anglorum Collegii fundator, ac parens optimus Alumnos suos Christo commendat: ut, quos in Angliam ad fidei defensionem mittit, adversus hostium insidias, atq. tormenta, divina virtute confirmet: qua freti iam aliquot pro Catholica Romana ecclesia fortiter occubuerunt.

Philippus Boncompagnus S.R.E. presb. Card. tit. S. Sixti eiusdem Pont. Fr. Fil. Collegii Protector, et Benefactor munificentiss. idē a Deo precatu

Gregory XIII and College students

money, and even so had to see the scholars wearing rags and crawling with lice.[63]

To provide room and funds for the new scholars, Lewis persuaded the pope to expel at last the ageing Hospice chaplains. At Christmas time Morone, authorised by a papal *motu proprio*, issued the following decree: 'While the schism lasts in England, and until His Holiness or ourself shall order otherwise, the English Hospital in Rome shall depend in all things on the seminary of scholars established in that place; whosoever shall be for the time being deputed Rector by us shall *ipso facto*, without other election, be custos of the Hospice. The duties of the chaplains shall be carried out by those senior scholars who are priests and who shall be nominated to us by the Rector; so that Rector and scholars shall effect in all things those purposes, both of divine worship and hospitality to pilgrims, for which the Hospice was founded. The chaplains who now reside there shall depart within a time to be fixed by us. We command each and every *confrater* of the Society of the same Hospice to refrain from speaking or acting against this our decree under pain of excommunication to be incurred *ipso facto*.'[64]

Henry Henshaw, the custos, and the other chaplains were allowed fifteen days to depart. Dr Clynnog was made perpetual governor of both Hospice and seminary. The conversion of the old hospital into a College seemed complete. But Clynnog's appointment was unpopular, not least among his expelled fellow-chaplains. The English residents in Rome, who had been annoyed when he was first made Rector, were now doubly incensed that he had been given sole charge of the Hospice too. The scholars in the seminary, hitherto obedient, began to rebel against his government.

Clynnog relates the beginning of the troubles thus: 'On the day on which the old priests left the Hospice, the Jesuit Fr John Paul told me that I ought to remove the Lord Bishop of St Asaph from the two chambers which he had in the Hospice, and use another house, separate from the Hospice, for receiving pilgrims, instead of allowing them to enter the Hospice whenever they wished. I replied that I could not and would not do anything of the kind . . . Immediately afterwards, in less time

[63] Clynnog to Morone, VL, 136; C.R.S. 2, 107; D.D., 12.1.1579.
[64] Persons (C.R.S. 2, 144) and Clynnog (Tierney, II, ccclxii) speak of a Brief expelling the chaplains; this cannot now be traced. Morone's decree is VL, 153.

than it takes to tell, some of the scholars began to tumult, and to say that their conscience would not allow them to suffer me to be Rector any longer. Having started this fire, Fr John Paul went off, and another Jesuit succeeded in his place. Who is the cause of this uproar—whether the Jesuits, or the scholars, or some of the English living outside the Hospice—*Deus scit et ego suspicor.*'[65]

Such was Clynnog's account of the origin of the troubles. There is no reason to believe that he invented the episode he describes ; none the less, he fails to give an adequate impression —or a coherent explanation—of the scholars' hostility. Their opposition to his rectorship had begun long before the expulsion of the chaplains : they had petitioned for his removal in the previous May. The introduction of the Jesuits had quietened them for a time, and the house was peaceful and outwardly happy for several months. But there were muted complaints of partiality shown to the minority of Welsh students, and there was a more important gravamen to which Clynnog alludes when he says that the scholars proclaimed that their conscience would not allow them to suffer him as Rector. What were their grounds for saying this ?[66]

Rector and scholars had quite different concepts of the purpose of the institution. The scholars, brought up under penal laws and fired with missionary ideals by Allen and the Jesuits, saw themselves as training for a dangerous venture into a hostile country, comparable to a mission to convert the heathen Indies.[67] Clynnog and Lewis, belonging to a generation that remembered High Mass in Westminster Abbey, and accustomed to rapid changes of religion, thought of the Elizabethan schism as a temporary setback, and of the College in Rome as a house of studies to secure academic employment for exiles who awaited abroad the inevitable return of England to union with Rome. There can now be no doubt that the views of Clynnog and Lewis were shared by Pope Gregory XIII, the official founder of the College, and by Cardinal Morone, its Protector and effective superior. Events were to show that it was the scholars who had the more realistic view of the situation.

---

[65] From a statement of Clynnog printed by Tierney II, ccclxxii. Tierney wrongly questioned the authenticity of this paper : the passage which he prints is a small portion of Clynnog's apologia of January 1579, which may be found complete among Morone's papers, VL, 135ff.

[66] Compare Clynnog's statement in Tierney, loc. cit., with Persons's letter to Goode (C.R.S. 2, 144 and, less reliably, 2, 84).

[67] This is made clear by their memorials of 1579, printed in C.R.S. 2.

But to Pope Gregory and his cardinals, the seminaries of Douai and Rome were of much less moment for the cause of Catholicism in England than the ducats and galleons of Philip II and the warlike ardour of Geraldine and Stukeley. They would have been astonished to learn that it was the handful of penniless and unruly scholars at Rheims and Rome who would be the instrument of preserving in England that Catholicism which the force of the Spanish Crown was powerless to restore.[68]

Father Persons realised, better than most of Rome at the time, the divergence of spirits between scholars and authorities. He was often consulted by Sherwin, Haydock, Array and other scholars at the Roman College. They told him that some of Clynnog's friends in the seminary had no intention of becoming priests or returning to England; and he suggested that they should petition the pope to offer an oath to all, to test whether they had a genuine missionary purpose. 'These things being so', he wrote to a friend, 'the schollers begane to deale with some of their friends abroad, and I being advised of the tumult like to be, I went to Mr Archdeacon [Lewis] and told him of all the matter . . . requesting him for Gods cause and for the avoydinge of all scandalls, that by his and the schollers falling out might ensue, that he would stay this matter, and somewhat satisfie them . . . He promised me; whereupon I dealt with the schollers to repare unto him . . . Well, after 2 or 3 conferences with Mr Archdeacon they remained less satisfied at his handes than before; the which I saw, and also when I talking with Mr Archdeacon and Mr Morrice [Clynnog] togeather, I perceived the schollers request was, after the removing of Mr Morrice, to have our Society there to governe them; wherof Mr Morrice before me inferred that we had eyther suborned or comforted them in this their request—I retyred myselfe and would meddle no more.'[69]

[68] This misunderstanding was present from the foundation of the College and lasted until the Jesuits assumed its government. In 1577 Allen, telling a friend of the foundation, wrote: 'His Holinesse pleasure is that we should . . . supply as farre as we be able, the great scarsitie of spirituall labourers in our country; hym selfe of his bounteous goodnesse bearing theime . . . partly at Doway and partly att Rome.' (Knox *Allen*, 35.) But in the statutes of Morone founding the house of studies, it was expressly provided that the scholars were to learn Italian, so as to obtain employment in Rome or elsewhere; no words of 'spiritual labourers' for England. Eighteen months later King Philip II prefaces a grant of tax-exemptions to the College with the remark that he has been informed by Pope Gregory that a College has been founded in Rome in which young English exiles are being educated so that *when at last they are restored to their fatherland and property* they may convert other Englishmen and teach them sound doctrine, (Autograph of Philip II, *Memb.* 7.10.1578; *Lib*, 5, 176).

[69] Persons to Goode, C.R.S. 2, 144–5. It is not quite certain that it was at this time that Persons suggested the oath; he says so only in his late and compressed account in C.R.S. 2, 87.

Early in January the English scholars drew up a memorial to Cardinal Morone in which they said that their purpose in coming to the College had been to acquire sufficient learning to return to spread the faith in England. This, they did not doubt, was also His Holiness' intention ; but it was frustrated by the government of Clynnog, who admitted people who had no intention of returning to England, but intended to enjoy the comfort of the seminary at leisure like the old chaplains. English and Welsh, they added, were by nature hostile to each other, and could live in peace only if governed by someone who was a stranger to both parties.[70]

Morone summoned the retiring spiritual director, Fr John Paul Navarola, who was leaving to become Rector at Siena, and inquired about 'the seditious youths' who had given up the memorial. He refused to listen to the Jesuit's defence of the scholars, but told him to pacify them with the promise of a new order. He appointed a commission of three—Lewis, Goldwell, and Mgr Spetiano, a vicar general of St Charles Borromeo—to meet weekly in the College to manage affairs as his deputies and to inspect the accounts.[71]

On 18th January Lewis wrote to Morone apologising for the 'human weakness' of the scholars and trusting that he had been comforted by their quick repentance. He had been intending, he said, to return to Cambrai now that he had finished the archbishop's business in Rome and was running out of funds ; but he feared that if he left before the British seminary were completely established, it would be disrupted by Satan.[72]

The scholars were not easily pacified and continued to press for Clynnog's dismissal. At last Morone agreed to give them audience. Lewis lost patience, and wrote a second, more choleric letter, complaining of the scholars' ingratitude to himself who had worked harder than all for the good of the College. He begged the cardinal to give these 'long-tailed youths' the reproof they deserved, and to threaten them with punishment if they plotted again in their childish conventicles to alter the government or expel the Rector. If discipline broke down in the English college, it would be the ruin of the Germanicum and the other seminaries. So the leaders should be threatened—

[70] C.R.S. 2, 102–03.
[71] C.R.S. 2, 145 ; VL, 120.
[72] VL, 97.

but only in bluff—with expulsion. Most dangerous of all was the discord they fomented between English and Welsh, which was spreading to the British colony in the city.[73]

Indeed Lewis, from being the acknowledged leader of the exiles in Rome, had become in a few years the most unpopular member of the colony. There were about thirty-two English-men in the city at this time, not counting servants and artisans ; and almost half of these had strong personal reasons for dis-liking Lewis or Clynnog or both.[74] All resented the way in which the control of the Hospice had passed from the *congregatio Anglicana* into the hands of two Welshmen ; all were shocked by the treatment which Cardinal Pole's nephew had received from Lewis's crony Stukeley. There were in addition some English Jesuits, notably Robert Persons and Thomas Derby-shire, who had a wholly creditable sympathy with the scholars' ideals, and who were offended by Lewis and Clynnog's insinua-tions that the Society was scheming to gain control of the College. Almost alone, Bishop Goldwell, the English bishop of a Welsh see, seems to have been neutral at the beginning of these sorry quarrels. For the rest, the English exiles lent their support to the scholars.[75]

At the pope's court, too, Lewis had lost influence because of the death and disgrace of Stukeley. For the moment, however, Morone gave him full support. In the presence of Clynnog he rebuked the scholars for their disobedience and threatened them with expulsion unless they approved the government he had appointed. When he dismissed them, one of the scholars—it was Array or Sherwin—protested that they could not with safe conscience remain under Dr Clynnog ; but 'he was of the Lord Cardinall bid hould his peace with some choler'. Father Persons relates what followed.

'But with that stood up on the other side Mr Gore, and with marvelous liberty and protestation that it was Causa Christi spoke three tymes more then the other, and touched

---

[73] VL, 124. Lewis hinted : '*unus fortasse Anglus haec mihi et genti cudit mala omnia*'. Probably Morton is meant.

[74] A list of the thirty-two is given among Morone's papers. Dr Morton had cherished a feud against Clynnog for a dozen years. Prior Shelley had opposed Lewis's invasion schemes and had been brought by Stukeley in danger of the Inquisition. Thomas Clements had been assaulted by Stukeley and narrowly escaped press-ganging ; his son had been refused admission to the College. Six of the exiles were expelled chaplains. Dr Ely had been threatened with hanging by Stukeley. Four former Douai scholars, refused admission to the seminary, were in lodgings in the city. Thus fourteen of the thirty-two are known to have had grudges against Lewis.

[75] According to Lewis, Morton and Ely were in the College every day . . . (VL, 155).

Mr Morrisses government so pithely and vehemently that Mr Morrice stood up and said, *Illme Domine, iste est Gorus ille, qui decipit et seducit bonos hos iuvenes.* Wherwith his Grace was very angry with Mr Gore, but presently all the Company spoke of one voyce, that they were all of the mynd that Mr Gore was, wherat the Cardinall was yet more angry. Then on the other side stood up Mr Haddock, D. Allens nephew, and more at larg spoke and more vehemently than they all, and so answered the threatening of expulsion, and how little they all esteemed that in respect of the least hurt that might be of their conscience, and how ready they were not only to begge but also to dy for the least part of a iust cause, that the Cardinall did never after threaten them more expulsion, but for the space of an hower harkened most patiently to all that they said ; and they so handled their cause in that space, one answering and confirming the others sayings, and giving reason upon reason whie they could never attain unto the end which they pretended under Mr Morrices government . . . that in the end the Cardinall promised them to consider better of their matter, and willed them to give him in wryting both the defects of Mr Morrise in particular, and the maner of government which they desired.'[76]

The scholars presented memorials on these topics the very next day. The first memorial, drawn up probably by Array, repeats the contentions of the earlier manifesto : the scholars seek discipline, not licence ; the seminary must serve the common good of England, not the convenience of private men ; Clynnog's government is alien to the spirit in which the scholars left England. Unlike the earlier paper, the memorial goes on to request that the College should be handed over to the Jesuits who, though reluctant, are the ideal men for its government.

The second memorial is a quite different document. It is a childish rehearsal of trivial grievances designed to convict Clynnog of partiality towards his fellow-Welshmen. Its substance is given with surprising accuracy in a speech which Antony Munday, in his *English Romayne Lyfe*, puts into the mouth of Sherwin. 'When any Englishman commeth to the Hospitall, if hys learning be never so good, or hys behaviour

---

[76] Persons, C.R.S. 2, 146. This interview must have taken place before the middle of February, since there is no mention of the grievances concerning Munday in the memorial which the scholars submitted on the following day. 'Gore' is John Gower, the nephew of Lord Chief Justice Wray.

never so decent : excepte hee [Clynnog] be pleased, hee shall not be enterteyned. But if a Welshman come, yf hee bee never so vylde a Runnagate, never so lewde a person, he can not come so soone as he shall bee welcome to him, whither he have any learning or no, it maketh no matter, hee is a Welshman, and hee must be permitted. Then which of us hath the beste gowne, he must receive one that is all ragged and torne, and the newcome Welshman must have the best, because he is the Custos Countreimen : and many nights hee must have the Welshmen in his chamber, where they must be merry at theyr good cheere, we glad to sitte in our studies, and have an ill supper, because M. Doctor wasteth our Common vpon his owne Countrymen so that we must be content with a snatch and away. If there be one bed better then an other, the Welsh man must have it, if there be any Chamber more handsome then an other, the Welshman must lodge there : in breefe, the things of most account are the Welshmans at command. This maketh many of vs to wishe our selves Welsh men because we would gladly have as good provision as they, and being Countrymen to our Custos, we should be all vsed alike : excepting Maister Doctors Nephew Morganus Clenockus, he must be in his silke, though all the rest goe in a sacke.'[77]

Morone asked Clynnog to reply to these charges. He did so in a detailed screed of 3,000 words, refuting the accusations of favouritism with a pathetic thoroughness. To the last charge he replied : 'The Rector's nephew, an excellent youth, even in the opinion of the opposing party, has no other doublet but the one which he brought from England, and which he had already worn for several years in Flanders before he brought it to Rome. He has not had a single shirt bought for him at the seminary's expense ; he has to wear an old pair of his uncle's cast-off shoes, and has had to buy his own hat. What partiality, I ask you, can this Rector have for the other Englishmen or Welshmen, when he has not better provided out of College funds for his own beloved brother's son ?'

Clynnog was able to show that each of the specific charges made against him was either false or trivial. He admitted that many of the scholars were short of necessary clothing, but maintained that this was due to the poverty of the institution, not to favouritism. Apparently his apologia convinced Morone :

---

[77] The memorials are printed in C.R.S. 2.

a few days later Mgr Spetiano was sent to canvass the scholars to take an oath of obedience to the Rector.[78]

The scholars replied with a memorial to the pope himself, repeating with greater urgency their request for the Jesuits, accusing Lewis of putting private friendship before common good, and threatening to leave the College rather than be oppressed with 'importuning of oaths, and threats of expulsion, and the unbearable favouritism of the man who rules hospice and seminary.'[79]

On the other side, Lewis wrote to Morone. 'It is for the good of this English seminary' he said 'that I, who cultivated it as a tender plant, should continue in its care. This I cannot well do, unless these offended youths trust me ; for no other of our nation in this city can or will do all that I have done and so in this cause, for the love of God and the common cause of church and country.' The scholars should be told that they would obtain the Jesuits as superiors more easily if they did not kick against their present nurse. 'It is I who have so far obtained the Jesuits for them, and I have tried to retain them for the future ; but if I cannot get them for ever, they must bear it with patience.'[80] He concluded : 'It is not true that I am taking the side of Dr Maurice : he is not in my confidence. From the beginning I told your Grace that there would be jealous grumbling if, when the other six chaplains were put out, he alone, a countryman of mine however deserving, were to remain in the Hospice. But certainly he should not be put out now after these delations and accusations, unless his reputation can be safeguarded . . . A Brief should be published, to keep those youths in order by establishing strict discipline, and threatening punishments to all who divide English from Welsh.'[81]

To the pope Lewis wrote more strongly in favour of Clynnog. He asked for a Brief to confirm his Rectorship at the Protector's

[78] C.R.S. 2, 148. Clynnog's paper (*Responsiones D. Mauritii Clenoci Rectoris Collegii Anglicorum in Urbe ad 4 capita*) is VL, 135ff. It abounds in details of the early history of the College. He tells a story to illustrate the scholars' malice. One of his friends, tired after visiting the seven churches, sat by the fire in the Rector's room to eat his own food and drink his own wine. One of the scholars stole out of the Refectory to taste the wine in the guest's flask to see whether it was from the Hospice vineyards.

[79] C.R.S. 2, 108.

[80] Persons too speaks of Lewis's negotiations with the Jesuits (C.R.S. 2, 147–8). Because of the insinuations that the Society was responsible for the troubles, the General wished to withdraw his subjects from the College. Lewis exclaimed that if they went away matters would be much worse, and the seminary not be able to stand for three days. 'Wherein', wrote Persons, 'I think that he was not deceived.'

[81] VL, 120.

pleasure and to give him control of church, hospice, and funds, subject to examination by the commission of three already appointed. To avoid suggestions of favouritism, Lewis suggested that the right to admit scholars be vested in the Protector, and the charge of discipline, studies, and the distribution of food and clothes be confided to the Jesuits.[82]

A Brief was drawn up on the lines suggested by Lewis, threatening excommunication to any scholar who should discuss projects for altering the government of the seminary, and promising a plenary indulgence to all who repented of their present discords. It does not seem, however, that this Brief was ever published.[83]

There now arrived in Rome a young playwright, Antony Munday, who was later to make these stirs the talk of England. The account which he wrote in *The English Romayne Lyfe* long after his return to England is partly fictional, and betrays *parti pris* in places, but it is well informed and vivid. He reached the city, accompanied by John Nowell, on 1st February, and spent the night in an *osteria*. He thus describes his reception at the College on the feast of the Purification:

'On the morrowe by enquiry we founde the English Colledge, where after we were once entered, wee had a number about us quicklye, to knowe what newes in England, and how all matters went there. Not long had we stoode talking with them, but one entered the Colledge, with a great many of wax Candles in hys hande : who gave them to understande, that the Pope had sent to every Scholler in the Colledge a candle, which that day at High Masse he had hallowed, for it was Candlemas day. They receiving them with great account, both of the Pope's favoure, as also the holiness they credited to consist in the candles, went every one to lay them up in their Chambers : in the meane time Maister Doctor Morris the Rector of the house came to vs, to whom we delivered the letter sent to him on our behalfe from Paris, which when he had read, he said we were welcome, allowing vs ye eight days entertainment in the Hospitall which by the Pope was granted to such Englishmen as come thether.'

Munday and Nowell had dinner with Lewis in his house next door but one to the College. Afterwards, they found the

---

[82] According to Clynnog's apologia, this was already the case.
[83] A draft of such a Brief is VL, 215 ; Lewis's letter to the Pope is VL, 114.

scholars walking in the garden. A priest asked Munday why he had come to Rome. 'Only for the desire I had to see it', replied Munday 'that when I come home again, I may say, once in my life I have been at Rome.'

'There ought none to come hither', Munday reports the priest as saying, 'the place being so holy, auncient, and famous, but onely such as with earnest endeavour, seeke and thirst after the Catholique faith . . . They must denounce that damnable heresie, crept in to the Church of England, that proude vsurping Iezabell (meaning our dread and gracious Princesse), whom (quothe he) God reserveth to make her a notable spectacle to the whole world, for keeping ye good Queene of Scots from her lawful rule : but I hope ere long ye Dogs shall teare her flesh, & those that be her props & upholders.'

The priest, Munday tells us, then produced from his pocket a bede-roll of the leading 'props and upholders'. 'First (quoth he) heere is my Lord *Keeper*, the Bacon hogge, the Butchers sonne, the great guts, oh he would fry well with a Faggot, or his head would make a fayre showe vpon London bridge, where I hope shortly it shall stand. Next is eloquent Maister *Cecill*, *Lorde Treasorer*, you shall shortly see if he can save his owne life with all ye wit he hath : had it not been for these two before named, England would have gone to wracke long since. Then heere is the Earle of *Leicester*, the Queenes Ostler, and his brother Ambrose Dudly, a good fat whorson to make Bacon of.'

The conversation reported by Munday is more entertaining than credible, particularly when he represents the priest as insisting that the pope 'is the person of God on earth, and he cannot sinne'. But the story which Munday goes on to tell is vouched for by other sources also. It seems that when his term as a pilgrim was ended, he, with Nowell, applied for admission to the College. As the Hospice was overfull, and the applicants had not been sent from Rheims in the usual manner, their request was refused.[84] But the English scholars took Munday's part, and told him 'If D. Morris would put every Englishman, he thought good on, out, in short time the Colledge would be all Welsh men.' They threatened that if Munday was put out they would all leave with him. So Munday ignored Clynnog, and 'tarried there dinner and supper in spight of his nose'.

[84] Persons says : 'Albeit it was said that D. Allen had recommended them, yet there was answere made, *si Alanus misit, Alanus provideat eis*, which moved much Englishmen' (C.R.S. 2, 155). But from Munday's own account it does not appear that he brought letters from Allen.

Clynnog complained to Morone, who summoned the scholars and reproved them, commanding Munday and Nowell to return to England. However, the Jesuits in the College obtained permission for them to remain for a fortnight, 'to lye in a very sweete chamber, filled with old rusty iron and all the trash of the house'. This room, says Munday, 'was next to the common house of office, which ayred the Chamber with so sweete a perfume : that but for names sake of a Chamber, and feare of catching some disease, I had rather have lyven in the street amongst the beggars.'

The scholars gave the newcomers money to buy food, and repeated their request to Morone to admit them, 'requesting him', as Fr Persons tells us, 'that seeing these youthes were like to perishe in the streets for want, that his Grace would be content to give them leave to devide their portion with them, and so to save them from perishing'. The cardinal was impressed, and promised to discuss the matter with the pope.[85]

While the scholars were striving for the admission of a man who was to be an accessory to the murder of half-a-dozen of them, Pope Gregory performed a surprising *volte-face*. He admitted the discontented scholars to audience, and commanded Morone to accept Clynnog's resignation. The cardinal did so on the following Sunday (probably 17th February) and told the scholars to vote for one of their countrymen as his successor. The scholars were jubilant at Clynnog's downfall, disappointed at not being given Jesuit superiors. In their letter of thanks they told the pope that there was no Englishman fit for the post, and renewed their request for the Society. To the embarrassment of the general, they drew up a long memorial setting out the unique qualifications of the Jesuits to govern them.[86]

[85] Persons, C.R.S. 2, 145. Persons does not give the names of the newcomers ; I have given reasons for believing that Munday and Nowell are the scholars in question in *Recusant History*, 6, 158–162 (Jan. 1962).

[86] The letter is printed by Tierney (II, cclxxiv) from *Liber* 304 in the English College archives. The original is undated : Tierney dates it a month later, after Clynnog's *second* resignation ; but it must be placed after this first resignation, since after the second the scholars submitted the names of Morton and Bavand as possible successors to Clynnog. The memorial about the Jesuits was drawn up in the week following the Sunday audience with Morone, after an interview with the Jesuit General ; it is printed C.R.S. 2, 114 with the covering letter to the cardinal. The scholars' reasons for wanting the Jesuits are as follows. The Fathers are good at training scholars who are destined not for fat benefices but for chains, dungeons and gallows ; they are skilled at governing seminaries, and though overworked are full of charity ; a few will be sufficient, since there are no schoolboys in the Hospice. Only Bristowe among the English is fit for the Rectorship, but he is ill and cannot be spared from Rheims. When England is converted there will no doubt be especial concord between Jesuits and seculars if the two groups are acquainted with each other from the seminary. The Jesuits will be able to reconcile the English and Welsh to each other.

Persons records the Jesuits' embarrassment in C.R.S. 2, 149.

Morone told them that the pope's reluctance to entrust the College to the Jesuits was due to the difficulty which there would be in administering it independently of the Hospice ; he was willing, however, to leave the decision on this point to the English colony. The scholars drew up a circular, addressed to Bishop Goldwell, Prior Shelley, and the other English exiles, asking them to arrange this matter with the Holy Father. They received a favourable reply, supporting their petition for the Jesuits, and suggesting how the seminary and Hospice might be jointly managed.[87]

By the time the scholars had collected all these memorials it was Sunday, 24th February, and the pope was out of Rome. At midday Sherwin, Haydock, Array and Gower set off after him ; they travelled twenty-four miles that day along the sea road. Next morning they found the pope in Cardinal Farnese's castle at Palio ; they were admitted to kiss his feet, but were not allowed to speak to him. They left copies of their petitions with Cardinal Como and were given hopes of an audience after the pope's return to the city. They returned themselves on the same day, 'twenty-two miles after eighteen o'clock, and with great difficulty, and glad to take horse a great pace'. They had been missed in the College the previous day at Vespers. Lewis was annoyed by the news of their journey to Palio : he said (it is reported) that he had three sorts of enemies, boys, Jesuits, and charlatans ; and as for the boys, he would answer them to their beards, if they had any.[88]

When the scholars went to the papal palace on the following Tuesday they were told by Mgr Bianchetti, the *maestro di camera*, that 'his Holiness would send unto their house one who, hearing all reasons, should make an end unto their contention'. Several of the leaders waited also upon Como, but were told that he was too busy, and they must return on the following afternoon. They returned home with high hopes.

The Cardinal Protector was displeased by these appeals over his head to the pope and secretary of state. At the con-

[87] The *Sententia Nationis Anglicanae* (C.R.S. 2, 110) supports the scholars' petition. The memorandum *De modo quo Seminarium et Hospitale Anglorum facillime in unum regimen reduci possint* suggested that the Rector should appoint one of the students custos and others as catechists ; two English externs should be appointed camerarii to manage the Hospice revenues, handing over all net income to the Rector (C.R.S. 2, 111). Prior Shelley, in a minority report (*Sententia Prioris Angliae*, VL, 132), suggested that an English custos should be appointed when the Jesuits were given the seminary. All these papers were submitted at Palio, with the 'reasons that moved to demand the regiment of the fathers'.

[88] R. Haydock to Allen, 9.3.1579 ; Tierney II, cclv ff.

sistory of Wednesday, 27th February, he was on his knees for half an hour to Pope Gregory to revoke his concessions to the discontented scholars. Como and a number of other cardinals were lobbied by Lewis on the same day. When the scholars had audience with Como in the afternoon, they were simply referred back to the Protector. '*Legi rationes vestras singulatim*', said the cardinal Secretary, '*quas probo et valde approbo. Tamen, non expedit ut pontifex concedat vobis petitionem vestram, licet essetis tam sancti atque Sanctus Paulus.*'

Next day the four leaders, with Rishton, Harrison, Pitts and Gifford, saw Morone once again. They were told that they could not have the Jesuits : more, they must accept Clynnog once again as Rector. They asked to be allowed to choose some Englishman in his place : Morone replied that they had already told the pope that there was no one fit for the post. He assembled all the scholars before dinner, and told them that they must obey Clynnog or leave. They said that they had proved their obedience to the pope by leaving England, and were ready to shed their blood for him if God gave them grace ; therefore he might at least suffer them to follow their conscience. The Protector spoke of imprisonment and whipping ; but he gave them a day to decide whether to submit or depart.[89]

Throughout the troubles, about one in four of the scholars had remained loyal to Clynnog. Jonas Meredith, the senior priest among this faction, was commanded by Morone early next morning to collect the names of those who were willing to obey unconditionally the pope, the protector, and all present and future governors by them appointed. He went from room to room, while the scholars 'were in spirituall conferences in congregation', collecting signatures for a supplication in this sense. Only ten signed ; the rest complained that the paper was 'full of deceitful law-terms, to circumvent us with'. Some of the priests 'had some hote wordes against Mr Archdeacon', whom they presumed to be the author of the supplication. Thirty-one put their names to a counter-petition, promising obedience to the pope in more qualified terms.[90]

[89] Haydock, in Tierney, loc. cit.

[90] Both supplications are preserved among Morone's papers (VL, 143–7 v). Meredith's is signed by the Welshmen Thomas, Smith, Bennett, Clynnog, Griffith and Ellis, and by Meredith, Askew, Lovell and Robinson among the English. The counter-petition is signed by Sherwin, Array, Rishton, Birkhead, Kirby, Harrison, the Haydocks, Hide, Wright, Foster, Standish, Bell, Paschall, Mush, Owen, Brisco, Gifford, Hart, Barton, Osborne, Procter, Tyrrell, Halliwell, Woodruff, Hargrave, Gower, Grately, Tedder and Pitts. 'Thomas Lovell', wrote Richard Haydock, 'is spoiled utterly by them, and careth for no man, but only liberty and toys' (Tierney II, cclx).

Gower told Clynnog that the scholars did not acknowledge him as Rector, since he had been deposed. Clynnog forbade him to come to Hall, and told Hugh Griffith, Lewis's nephew, to read at dinner a patent from the Protector proclaiming him Rector. Since Griffith could not read Italian, the patent was read by the reader for the week, Arthur Pitts of the contrary faction. When Pitts had finished reading the letter, he cried '*Falsatum est* !' and refused to return it to Clynnog. The scholars saw that the date of the letter, May 1578, had been altered, so that it looked like a fresh appointment. Pandemonium broke loose ; knives were brought out, and only the Jesuits averted violence.

After Vespers, Haydock and four other priests laid their supplication before Morone and complained of Clynnog's behaviour. The cardinal defended him obstinately : '*Ego nolo audire ; habeo aures surdas, et laterem lavatis*'. He told them that the pope's command was that they should obey their Rector or depart. Haydock replied that they would believe this when they heard the pope say so. '*Abite in malam crucem* !' stormed the Protector, '*Ego profecto te tradam in carcerem, et severissime puniam. Non vultis mihi credere, qui sum cardinalis* ?'

Haydock went home, lucky to avoid arrest. The Welsh faction had audience with Morone after he left ; they were kindly received. Next morning, Lewis, Spetiano and Clynnog were summoned by the incensed Morone ; Lewis refused to reveal the name of the scholar who had insulted the Protector. It was decided that four ringleaders, Mush, Haydock, Array and Gower, should swear unconditional obedience or depart ; if they refused to do either, they must go to prison. The Jesuits were sent for to help in pacifying the other scholars, and one of the cardinal's chaplains was told to carry news of the expulsion to the College.

Clynnog and the chaplain presented the ultimatum after dinner. The four scholars chose to leave, and exhorted their companions to remain and obey, saying 'You may perhaps do with a good conscience and your commodity, but we cannot'. The rest answered, 'No, no : we will go and die with you'. Young Christopher Owen, 'who was lying in his chamber with half an ague', came running down and cried '*Volo potius mergi in Tiberim quam sine istis hic manere*'.

The four leaders went to Morone's palace accompanied by the rest of the English faction. They said that since they could not obey Clynnog with a safe conscience, they would obey His Grace in the other point and depart. Morone told them to go in peace and save their souls. The College Jesuits also waited on him : he told them that he had intended to leave Clynnog as Rector in name only, and place all effective government in the hands of the Society. The scholars, when they learnt of this, were for accepting the compromise ; but the Jesuit General would not agree.

Clynnog was told to provide meals for the scholars only so far as dinner on the following day, Shrove Tuesday. In the event the scholars stayed also to supper. During the afternoon Sherwin, Haydock and four others waited outside St Peter's in the hope of seeing the pope. They caught him as he was entering the basilica to inspect a new altar, and pressed on him a paper containing a statement of their case and a request for an audience. Gregory walked hastily away, cutting off the importunate Sherwin with the words '*Si non potestis obedire, recedatis*'.[91]

On Ash Wednesday morning the thirty scholars shifted their luggage in carts to the house of John Creed, an English friend of Dr Morton, who had promised them beds. Before dawn Lewis had sent to Cardinal Como a memorial, to be given to the pope in his chamber before chapel, begging for a stay of departure. They were only deluded boys, said Lewis, who thought they were living in sin if they obeyed anyone but a Jesuit ; it was heart-breaking to see thirty promising youths leaving Rome penniless at such a time of year. The pope, still angry but a little mollified, wrote a note (on the back of Sherwin's memorial of the previous day) permitting the scholars to come to see him before their departure. When they heard of this the scholars refused to surrender their gowns to Clynnog : they would leave them, they said, at the feet of the pope.

At Creed's they appointed officers among themselves, some to buy meat and others to dress it, some to serve at table and others to read. They cast into a common purse whatever money they had : Paschall gave a chain worth a hundred pounds, and sixty crowns' worth of books, the gift of Bishop Goldwell, were added to the funds. The Jesuit Alfonso Agazzari wrote to Siena, where Navarola was now Rector, to provide

91 The paper is printed in C.R.S. 2, 121.

fifty crowns for them on their way. Other Jesuits, preaching Lenten sermons at S. Lorenzo in Damaso, begged alms from the congregation. Many others gave or begged for them : in all, we are told, they were likely to have a thousand crowns.[92]

At the College, Hugh Griffith gave a leap into the hall, shouting 'Who now but a Welshman ?' Munday, Nowell, and the expelled chaplains were offered places in the room of the departed scholars ; but all refused. The English colony sent to the pope a petition, partly censuring the scholars' actions, but pointing out the scandal their departure would cause. At Persons's instigation the theologian Francisco Toledo pleaded with the pope. Perhaps also at his suggestion, Mgr Bianchetti proposed that the scholars' dispositions should be tested by administering an oath to see which of them were ready to preach against the heretics in England.

On returning from the Lenten station at Santa Sabina, Pope Gregory sent a messenger to the Hospice to summon the scholars. The scholars had already left, and Fr Alfonso came running out of breath to Creed's house. The seventeen who were there hurried to the papal palace ; Gregory 'fell into tears, which trickled down his white beard' and asked why they had left the seminary without telling him. They said that they had been so commanded twice by the Protector. 'Where will you go ?' he asked. Those that were fit would go to England, they told him, for most of them were divines. 'What ?' he asked, pointing to Owen, Pitts and Grately, 'Are these so young divines ?' When they told him that they had refused to leave their gowns, and had intended to place them at his feet, 'the good ould man put his hand to his brest and shooke his head'. He asked them where they had eaten, and how they had dressed their meat ; and was delighted by Grately's reply '*Pater Sancte, his nostris manibus*'. Protesting that he had never meant them to leave Rome, where good manners and learning and religion were to be had, he told them to forget what had passed and give him the names of some other of their countrymen to be Rector in place of Clynnog. Ringing a little bell, he summoned

---

[92] Munday writes : 'everie one tooke an office vpon him, one to fetch milke, another to make ready Rice for the pottage, one to make the fire : so that everie one was imployed till our dinner was despatched. Then they concluded to buie every man an Asse to carrie his Bookes and his cloathes upon.' Hart, Barton, Owen and Gifford asked Lewis for money and were refused ; but Lewis maintained later than he intended to have funds provided for them at Bologna if they had really departed.

one of his camerarii to lead them back to the Hospice and command Clynnog to readmit them.[93]

The scholars were restored amid widespread rejoicing. Next day they sent in the names of Morton and Bavand for the Rectorship. The Welsh party counter-petitioned for Bristowe ; and Lewis sent in a bitter attack on the two English candidates.[94] On 7th March, after Bishop Goldwell had sung St Thomas's Mass at the Minerva, the scholars were told by the cardinal Secretary that they should have a favourable answer from His Holiness within two days, though they should have neither of the Rectors they named. This put them in great hope that they might be given the Jesuits ; and on 9th March Haydock wrote to his uncle Dr Allen in great spirits: 'If the fathers get the government', he said, 'we trust, before it be long, to have here place for a hundred, and thereby the gloriousest College of English in the world.'

For several days no decision came. Lewis and Clynnog were busy daily at the pope's court and in Morone's palace. There were rumours that the seminary and Hospice were to be separated, 700 crowns a year only going to the seminary, while the remaining 1,000 crowns would be Clynnog's for the entertainment of pilgrims. It was said that Lewis had asked for many of the chief scholars to be sent to England to reduce the numbers to thirty. There was truth in these rumours. On the 10th Lewis wrote to Allen that he had persuaded Clynnog to resign, but that the pope had promised to retain him in charge of the Hospice. He said too that he proposed to reduce the numbers, since the pope seemed weary of the expense.

On 16th March, while the scholars were waiting in Como's antechamber, they fell in with one of their supporters among the English exiles.[95] This man told them of a conversation which he had had with the cardinal, who had been very

---

[93] As they were leaving, Lewis arrived hotfoot from an audience with Como. The pope told him what had taken place and told him to carry his instructions to Clynnog and exhort the scholars to obedience. At the Hospice Lewis passed on the message to Clynnog, Sherwin and Array.

The main sources for this often-told story are the letters of Richard Haydock and Owen Lewis to Allen, printed in Tierney's Dodd, the letter of Fr Persons to Fr Goode printed in C.R.S. 39, and Munday's *English Romayne Lyfe*.

[94] Morton, he said, was the true author of the stirs, a man as much at home in trouble as a fish in water. He was a failed Doctor, who could not speak Latin without stumbling, a turbulent and indiscreet fellow, a crony of Gower who ought to be in the galleys. Bavand, said Lewis, though better than Morton, was a troublemaker also. Best to give seminary and Hospice to the Jesuits ; if not, a Douai priest or an Italian should be appointed. But Clynnog was quite capable of governing the Hospice, even though Satan himself should come against him (VL, 155).

[95] Apparently this was Prior Shelley (Persons to Allen, C.R.S. 2, 136).

displeased with the mutiny, and said that 'for his part he would have lett them gone there ways when they were goinge'. He had replied that hostility between Englishmen and Welshmen was very natural ; 'whereto the Cardinall answered that he understood that the diversity betwixt Englishmen and Welch-men was nothing more than might be betwixt two divers provinces as Tuscany and Romagnia'. The Englishman replied 'that his Grace was not informed in the matter, for that the Welchmen and Englishmen were (putting aside Religion) as might be Mores and Spaniards'. 'These words', he reported to the scholars, 'seemed not a little to move the Cardinall, wher-upon after a little pause he brake out and said, I knew not of all this so fully before, but as for the Popes order, it is past to Cardinall Morone 8 dayes past, and yt is that they be governed in all things as the German Colledge is, and I marvell that it is not yet published.'[96]

Hearing this, the scholars rushed home, and sat up the night penning a supplication to the pope. This was a very bitter piece, beginning with an intemperate attack on the Welsh nation, and including the offensive comparison with the Moors. 'It is naturally as impossible', they wrote, 'for a Welshman to treat well Englishmen subjected to him, as it is for a Moor to love a Spaniard ; as we have seen by experience in this government of Dr Maurice and the Archdeacon over us in this our seminary.' Lewis was supporting Clynnog, they said, so that the Welshmen, who were servants of the English at home, should dominate them in Rome ; all with a view to promoting himself and his Welsh friends to ecclesiastical dignities when England should be converted.

This supplication was delivered very early next morning ; some of the scholars' friends, when they heard of it, were afraid that the pope would be offended by its insolence. Persons and others 'were right sorry that they had touched Mr Archdeacon so farre'. But the pope took it in good part and sent it straight on to Cardinal Morone.

Early on the following day, which was the feast of St Joseph, Morone sent for the General of the Jesuits and com-manded him in the pope's name to take the whole charge of the seminary, as he had charge of the Germanicum. Mercurian pleaded that the Jesuits were already overburdened in Rome,

[96] C.R.S. 2, 157.

but Morone replied that 'the Pope was utterly determined to satisfie the schollers request, and to found for the present a Seminary of 50 schollers to be governed in all things as the German Colledg'.

Mercurian had to submit, and at Morone's request sent him the two Jesuits who were in the English College. The Cardinal dilated on his love for the English scholars, and said 'that although the Divell had sought to extinguishe it, or at the least much to hinder it at this beginning, yet God had wone'. The Jesuits, pointing out that there was still to be a custos— Clynnog—made difficulties about the arrangement of rooms between Hospice and seminary, and about the shortage of money. Morone replied that 'this Custoship was but a by thing for the tyme, which his Holiness would have remayne, but the whole consideration must be had of the Seminary, which the Pope meant to be a matter both of perpetuity and of great account'. As for money, the pope's purse would supply all necessities. So the Jesuits were commissioned to take over all the buildings, and displace all others now in the Hospice, providing them with lodgings outside.

Later in the day Fr Agazzari, with Mgr Spetiano, Clynnog and Lewis apportioned the rooms ; 'with great quietnes they divided the house, so that all the body of the Hospitall with divers other rooms annexed are for the seminary'.

Clynnog, Talcarne, and a Welsh chaplain named Sir Robert, were given rooms in a house next door, as also was Bishop Goldwell, who 'like a good man as soone as ever he hard of this resolution came downe in hast, and straightway avoyded his former chambers and resigned them to the Seminary, before he was spoken to, and before he ever asked provision of new'. Munday and Nowell were now admitted among the scholars, and Munday, being ill, was given a 'very fair chamber'. 'And to say generally of all the Nation, there was such generall ioy at the newes of this resolution, as I thinke St Josephes day was never so celebrated of Englishmen before.'[97]

However, the troubles were not even yet at an end. During the next few days Fr Persons appears to have been in charge of the College, and he was asked by the scholars to persuade Dr Allen to come to Rome. Persons wrote to Allen on the 30th, beseeching him to come to Rome, and telling him that they

[97] Persons to Allen, 30.3.1579. C.R.S. 2, 136.

had procured licence for him to come and also travelling expenses from the pope ; he went on to say that there had been faults on both sides in the troubles, and in particular the difference between Welsh and English had been too much urged, so that there were now grudges between the two nations which only Allen could heal. He should also arrange for correspondence between the two Colleges of Rheims and Rome, and for a mission of Jesuits to be sent into England.[98]

Two days before this, on 28th March, Lewis had written to the Protector saying that he had heard that the *confratres*, led by Morton, were in league with Array and Gower, the ringleaders of the lately pacified sedition, to raise a new storm, seeing that they had been rewarded instead of punished for the previous attempts. They were trying to drive the Welsh out of the seminary, by depriving the Protector of the right to admit scholars : they had already introduced two grammar-boys by fraud (Munday and Nowell), and wanted the administration of the Hospice to be given to the Jesuits. This was not a good idea, but if it must be given, let it be given at once, not after tumults. He adds that they want to throw poor calumniated Clynnog out of the Hospice as well as out of the seminary, from sheer hatred for Wales. Clynnog is quite willing to be relieved of the task, but wishes to depart without ignominy, and with some monthly pension from the pope worthy of a bishop-elect such as he is ; he has no desire to go on fighting his impudent enemies. Array and Gower must be checked or removed, and Morton terrified into quiet. Orders should be given that the seventeen-year-old Welsh boy Thomas Williams should be admitted ; he is cleverer than Munday and Nowell and has lived in the Hospice outside of the number of the scholars.[99]

It is not known what result this letter of Lewis's had. Neither Array nor Gower was punished, and Thomas Williams was not admitted as a scholar ; on the other hand Clynnog remained custos for several months after this date. While the government of the College was still uncertain a Scotsman named Seaton, supported by Bishop John Leslie of Ross, a crony of Lewis's, petitioned that Scotsmen, as well as Englishmen and Welshmen, should be admitted as scholars of the College. This petition was regarded as an attempt by Lewis

[98] C.R.S. 2, 135–7.
[99] VL, 201.

to obtain revenge for his defeat ; but Lewis denied this in terms that made it clear that he knew nothing of the request before it was made.[100]

The scholars rejected this suggestion in a vigorous memorial of 25th April,[101] saying that the Scots' petition had been instigated by the Welsh to support their faction, that the English and the Scots could never live peaceably together, and that the Scots had no missionary ardour to reconvert even their own country.[102]

Two days before this, the Missionary oath, which had been suggested early in the troubles by Persons, was exacted. On 23rd April, Mgr Spetiano, acting for Cardinal Morone, the Jesuit provincial and St Robert Bellarmine assembled at the College to ask each of the students, in the name of the pope, whether they were willing to lead an ecclesiastical life and set out for England whenever their superiors saw fit. The first student to be questioned was Ralph Sherwin, who was to be the first to be martyred. He took the oath in words that have become famous : *iuravit se potius hodie quam cras paratum esse ad nutum Superiorum in Angliam ad animas iuvandas proficisci.* Fifty students in all were questioned : all, English and Welsh, took the oath save Owen Thomas and Rhosier Smith, the two middle-aged Welshmen whose admission had been the first cause of murmuring in 1578, Thomas Lovell, an English boy from Douai who had supported the Welsh party in the troubles, and two Englishmen, John Paschall and Robert Middlemore, who wished to be admitted as *convictores* at their own expense. The account of this historic ceremony fills the first page of the *Liber Ruber ;* having reached the beginning of the official annals of the College, this narrative of its foundation may come to an end.

ANTHONY KENNY.

---

[100] Lewis to Allen, 12.5.1579 ; Allen had just learnt of the request, which must therefore have been made about the middle of April. At Douai, among the students, it was reported that Lewis had 'once said to my lord to Rosse, "My lord, let us stick together ; for we are the old and true inhabiters and owners of the isle of Britany. These others be but usurpers and mere possessors." '

[101] C.R.S. 2, 130.

[102] Griffith wrote to Allen at this time that 'the jesuits have no skill nor experience of our country's state, nor of our men's nature ; and that their trade of syllogizing, there, is not fit for the use of our people'; therefore Bristowe should be Rector. Tierney's Dodd, II, cclxx.

APPENDIX 28

THE OFFICIALS OF ST THOMAS'S HOSPICE 1362–1579

This list has been compiled from documents in the College archives. In the three instances where other documents have been used, the names have been put in square brackets.

Date	Custos	Camerarii	Other officials
1362	John Shepherd	John, son of William	William Chandeler
			Robert de Pyne
1365	[John Shepherd, will dated 22 Oct.]		
	[John Palmer, 22 Nov.]		
1371		William Richards	
		Thomas, son of Nicholas	
1373	John, son of Robert	Robert de Pyne	
		William Richards	
1374	John, son of Robert (11 Mar)		
	John Palmer (26 Oct)	William Richards	
		Robert de Pyne	
1375	John Palmer	John Champonese	John Thules
		Thomas, son of Nicholas	
1376	John Palmer		John Thules
			John Picarinibus (?)
			John Champonese
			Thomas de Ponte
			William Mantel
			William Richards
1383	John Palmer (Perhaps until his death, which occurred before 22.12.1387. Cf. *Memb.* of that date.)		
1391		Philip Nelbun, cleric	
		John Cross, lay	
1393	William Richards	John Aclinging	
		William Holderness	
		Symon Barber,	
1395	William Richards	As 1393	
1396	William Richards	Symon Barber	
1397	William Richards	Walter, son of Symon	
		Symon Barber	
1399	William Richards	William Holderness	Walter, son of Symon
			Symon Barber
1400	William Richards	William Holderness	
		Walter, son of Symon	
1401	William Holderness	John Doneys, cleric	
		John Cross, lay	
1402	William Holderness	William Trobriogh	William Richards
1403	William Holderness		

Date	Custos	Camerarii	Other officials
1404	William Holderness	John Haget (Achet), cleric	
		John Cross, lay	
1405	John Boyke	John Haget, cleric	
		John Cross, lay	
1406	John Thomason	William Lovell	
1407	John Thomason	William Lovell	
1408	John Thomason	Philip Newton	Peter de Ragonia
1410		Philip Newton	
1412	John Thomason	Robert Cipeldon	
1418	John Thomason	Philip Newton, cleric	D. Roger, *confrater*
		John Croat, lay	
1425	John Thomason		
1428		John Henrici, cleric	
		John Ely, lay	
1431	John Sparham (232, 1)	Thomas Morden, cleric	
	John Strete (232, 34v)	John Ely, lay	
1432	John Strete	Robert Sutton, cleric	
		John Grymmsby, lay	
1433	John Strete	As 1432	
1435	John Strete	As 1432	
1436	John Strete	Adam Moleyns, cleric	
		John Ely, lay	
1437	John Strete	John Ely, lay	Richard Sylveryn
			(chaplain)
1442	John Ely	Richard Sylveryn (also chaplain)	
		John Grymmsby, lay	
1445	John Browne	John Wellis	
1446	John Browne	Hugh Foster	
		Richard Thwaytes	
1447	John Lacy	Henry Sharpe	
		John Lax	
1449	William Stanley	Walter Sandwich	John Lax
		Thomas Cawudower	
1450	William Fyge (16, 10)		John Wardale
	William Stanley (17, 5)		John Lax
1451	John Kylvyngton	Richard Thwaytes	William Stanley
		William Radclyff	William Astulo
1452[1]	John Kylvyngton	William Radclyff	
	(7 April)	Richard Thwaytes (7 April)	
	William Bynchest	John Lax	
	(17, 7 r)	William Stanley (17, 7 r)	
1453		William Grey	William Radclyff
		Thomas Knight	John Bellholt

[1] *Confratres* for this year : William Grey, Baldwin Fullford, Walter Sandwich, Thomas Cawudower, William Darsett, John Lax, Stephen Close, John Pursell, William Bynchest. *Memb.* 7.4.1452.

Date	Custos	Camerarii	Other officials
1455		Robert Clerk	
1457			John Lax, *confrater*
1458		William Shirwood	
		John Lacy	
1460	Robert Clerk	Robert Marshall (also chaplain)	John Lacy
			William Shirborn
1461		Nicholas Bulwiche	
		William Lax	
1463	Robert Clerk	Thomas Hope (Cal. Pap. Reg. XI, 651)	
		John Lacy	
1466	Robert Clerk	William Clayton, cleric	
		John Lax	
1469	Edmund Connesburgh	John Burton	
		William Bountayn	Auditors
1472	William Coper	John Burton	Richard Belyngham
		William Russell	William Russell
1474	Robert Clerk	John Burton	Thomas Matyn
		Hugh Spaldyng	Hugh Spaldyng
1475	Robert Clerk	Hugh Spaldyng	Robert Wellys
			William Russell
1476	John Wakefield	John Shirwood	John Shirwood
		Hugh Spaldyng	Thomas Caudour (Cawudower)
1477	Hugh Spaldyng	John Shirwood	Robert Walker
		Hugh Spaldyng	William Cheny
1478	Hugh Spaldyng	John Shirwood	John Merbek
		John Merbek	William Maudesley
1479	Hugh Spaldyng	John Shirwood	Robert Fenton
		John Merbek	William Shirwood
1480	Hugh Spaldyng	John Shirwood	Robert Fenton
		Robert Fenton	William Maudesley
1481	Hugh Spaldyng	John Shirwood	William Shirwood
		William Shirwood	William Maudesley
1482	Hugh Spaldyng	John Shirwood	William Maudesley
		William Shirwood	William Lee
1483	Hugh Spaldyng	John Shirwood	William Maudesley
		John Dunmow	William Lee
1484	Hugh Spaldyng	John Shirwood	Thomas Tomyow
		John Dunmow	William Lee
1485	Hugh Spaldyng	John Shirwood	Robert Fenton
		Robert Fenton	William Lee
1486	Hugh Spaldyng	John Dunmow	John Lucas
		John Kendall	William Lee
1487	Hugh Spaldyng	John Dunmow	John Lucas
		John Kendall	William Lee

Year	Custos	Camerarii	Auditors
1488	Hugh Spaldyng	John Dunmow	Robert Fenton
		John Kendall	Thomas Alcok
1489	Hugh Spaldyng	John Kendall	John Cloos
		John Cloos	Richard Trappe
1490	Hugh Spaldyng	John Kendall	John Cloos
		John Cloos	Richard Trappe
1491	Thomas Linacre	David William	Richard Trappe
		John Kendall	William Fell
1492	Hugh Spaldyng	Richard Trappe	Hugh Spaldyng
		John Thornton	John Thornton
1493	Hugh Spaldyng	Ralph Scrope	Thomas Tomyow
		Christopher Bainbridge	William Cosyn
1494	Hugh Spaldyng	Robert Morton	Robert Morton
		John Giglis	Richard Trappe
1495	Hugh Spaldyng	William Robinson (Lib. 232, f. 35 v) William Lovell	
1496 May	Hugh Spaldyng	John Giglis	Thomas Ruthall
		William Robinson	Richard Wyndsone

(Hugh Inge ?)

October : Robert Shirborn replaced Hugh Spaldyng as administrator of the Hospice, and named Edward Scott as his 'substitutum' for the administration of Hospice business. Scott became camerarius.

1497   All officers confirmed

1499 May   All officials confirmed until Shirborn's three-year term of office expired at Michaelmas 1499 when the following officers would take charge

	Hugh Spaldyng	Richard Trappe	John Harrington
		William Barons	

In December 1499 Edward Scott replaced William Barons as camerarius.

1500	Hugh Spaldyng	Sylvester Giglis	Richard Trappe
		Edward Scott	John Tong

At the end of August 1500 Hugh Spaldyng died.

1501 Jan   Edward Scott replaced Spaldyng as custos ; Thomas Cabold replaced Scott as camerarius.

May	Edward Scott	Sylvester Giglis	Thomas Cabold
		Richard Charnoke	Thomas Bowdon

Thomas Cabold replaced Sylvester Giglis when he left Rome in June 1501.

1502	Edward Scott	Sylvester Giglis	Thomas Cabold
		John Taylar	John Tong

Thomas Cabold replaced John Taylor when he left Rome in June 1502.

1503	Edward Scott	Sylvester Giglis	Thomas Cabold
		Thomas Cabold	John Allen

John Allen replaced Thomas Cabold as camerarius when he died on 20th May 1503.

s

Date	Custos	Camerarii	Other officials
1504	There was no election this year, because of the arrival in Rome in May of Henry VII's embassy to Pope Julius II. Edward Scott was ill of a fever until he died on 24th July. John Allen governed the Hospice until 4th November, when Hugh Inge became vice-custos, by royal appointment. The king later confirmed this appointment.		
1505	Hugh Inge		
1506	Hugh Inge		
1507	Hugh Inge		
1508	Christopher Fisher		
1509	Christopher Fisher		
1510 May	William Burbanke (in loco custodis)	John Allen William Styntt	William Fell John Allen Thomas Halsey William Styntt William Burbanke
1511	Richard Pace	William Fell John Wolfe	
1512	Richard Pace	John Clerk Thomas Halsey	
1513	Thomas Halsey (Lib. 13, f. 212—Lib. 232, f. 36)		
1514	John Clifton	John Wolfe John Clerk	
1515	John Bell (January—May)	John Pennande Thomas Halsey	John Pennande Thomas Halsey
1516	Thomas Colman	Thomas Halsey John Blyth	
1517	Edward Bassett	John Pennande Elias Bodley	
1518	Elias Bodley		
1519		Sylvester Giglis Elias Bodley	
1521	Richard Shurley	John Grygg John Huyes	
1522	Richard Shurley		
1523	Richard Shurley (till 1st July 1523)		
	On 1st July, John Clerk took charge of the Hospice by royal command. He appointed Richard Shurley and John Pennande as his commissaries to deal with Hospice business. John Nase and Robert Coket were elected camerarii. Clerk appointed John Pennande and John Borobrigg as auditors of Shurley's computus during his period as custos.		
	Richard Shurley John Pennande	John Nase Robert Coket	John Borobrigg Walter Cretyng
1524	John Pennande	Edmund Grey Robert Coket	Richard Shurley Walter Cretyng

Date	Custos	Camerarii	Auditors
1525 May	John Pennande	Valentine Clerk	Richard Shurley
		John Nase	Walter Cretyng
Nov	Richard Shurley (till his death which occurred between Nov 1526 and June 1527)		
		John Borobrigg	Nicholas Wotton
		John Makyn	William Whyte
1527	Nicholas Wotton (from June 1527 till May 1528)		
		Elias Bodley	William Whyte
		William Whyte	William Tracy
1528 May	William Whyte	Elias Bodley	William Tracy
	(till Nov 1528)	William Tracy	Lewis Evans
1529–38	From March 1529, John Borobrigg was custos of the Hospice. In August 1532 a royal grant made him custos for life. On the 1st March 1538, Cardinal Pole replaced him as custos, and the other officers were elected.		

Liber 22

Date	Custos	Camerarii	Auditors
1538 March–April	[Cardinal Pole]	John Heliar	Robert Buknam
		Thomas Goldwell	George Lily
1538 May		John Heliar	Robert Buknam
		Thomas Goldwell	George Lily
1539 May		John Heliar	John Fisher
		Thomas Goldwell	Michael Throckmorton (Pole's secretary)
1540 May	Thomas Goldwell	John Fisher	George Lily
		Michael Throckmorton	Henry Pyning
1541 May 1st–12th	Thomas Goldwell		Anthony Trovatus
			Michael Throckmorton
1541 May 12th–Dec. 31st	John Fisher (Pole's vice custos)		Anthony Trovatus
			Michael Throckmorton
1543 Jan–Feb.		George Lily	Thomas Goldwell
			Anthony Trovatus
1543 Mar.–Ap.	Thomas Goldwell		Anthony Trovatus
			Vincent Palumbe
1543 May–Dec.	Thomas Goldwell (till 22nd August)		Richard Heliard
	Vincent Palumbe		Michael Throckmorton
	Anthony Trovatus (vice custodes from 22nd Aug.–31st Dec.)		
1544 Jan–April		Richard Heliard	Thomas Goldwell
		William Peto (Pole's commissary)	Michael Throckmorton
1544 May	Richard Heliard (commissary of Peto, now custos)		George Lily
			Henry Pyning
1545 March 'vice custodis'		{ Thomas Goldwell	Richard Heliard
		{ George Lily	Michael Throckmorton
1546 May 'vice custodis'		{ Thomas Goldwell	Richard Heliard
		{ George Lily	Anthony Trovatus

Date	Custos	Camerarii	Auditors
1547 May	Thomas Goldwell (Peto's commissary)	Richard Heliard George Lily	Michael Throckmorton Henry Pyning
1548 May–	Thomas Goldwell (Locum tenens of Pole)	Richard Heliard George Lily	Michael Throckmorton Henry Pyning
Liber 23			
1548 Nov	William Peto	Richard Heliard George Lily	George Lily Henry Pyning
1549 May	Henry Pyning (Pole's deputy, May–August) George Lily (Pole's deputy, Sept–April)		Seth Holland Michael Throckmorton
1550 May		Henry Pyning (Pole's deputy)	Richard Heliard Michael Throckmorton
1551 May	George Lily (Pole's deputy)	Richard Hilliard	Simon Belost Michael Throckmorton
1552 May	Simon Belost (vice custos)		Thomas Riseus Henry Pyning
1553 May– Oct 10th	Simon Belost		
1553 Oct 11th	Robert Talcarn (deputy in absentia confratrum)		
1554 May– 1557 March	Robert Talcarn (vice custodis, Pole)		Henry Pyning (at the end of this period)
1557 April	Robert Talcarn (vice custodis)		George Neville Thomas Freeman
1558 May	Robert Talcarn		George Neville Thomas Freeman
Liber 30			
1559 April	Robert Talcarn		George Neville Thomas Freeman

(Pope Paul IV appointed Sir Edward Carne, Queen Mary's orator to rule the Hospice in 1559, but it is far from clear whether this took effect, and if so in what form. Carne resided in the Hospice till his death in January 1561.)

1560 May	Robert Talcarn		George Neville Thomas Freeman
1561 Jan– April	Robert Talcarn (vice custodis)		Nicholas Sander Thomas Freeman
Liber 33			
1561 Jan	Thomas Goldwell (Bishop of St Asaph)	Robert Talcarn George Neville	Thomas Freeman (sacristan)
1562 May	Thomas Goldwell	Henry Alwaye Robert Talcarn	Henry Alwaye Thomas Freeman
1563 May	Thomas Goldwell	Nicholas Sander Henry Henshaw	Edward Taylor Thomas Kyrton

Year	Custos	Camerarii	Auditors
1564 May	Thomas Goldwell	Charles Parker	
		Thomas Kyrton	
1565 May	Morus Clynnog	Nicholas Morton	Edmund Daniel
		Henry Alwaye	William Knott
1566 May	Henry Henshaw	Nicholas Morton	Edward Taylor
		Thomas Kyrton	William Knott
1567 May	Edward Taylor	Morus Clynnog	George Neville
		Henry Henshaw	William Knott
1568 May	Thomas Kyrton	Nicholas Morton	George Neville
		Edmund Daniel	William Knott
1569 May	Edmund Daniel	Morus Clynnog	Henry Henshaw
		Thomas Kyrton	George Neville
1570 May	Thomas Kyrton	Morus Clynnog	Henry Henshaw
		Edmund Daniel	Thomas Crane
1571 May	Henry Henshaw	Morus Clynnog	William Giblet
		Edmund Daniel	Thomas Crane
1572 May	William Giblet	Henry Henshaw	Thomas Crane
		Richard Bernard	Edward Bromborough
1573 May	Edward Bromborough	Morus Clynnog	Edmund Daniel
		Henry Henshaw	John Bavand
1574 May	Richard Bernard	Henry Henshaw	Thomas Crane
		Edward Bromborough	John Bavand
1575 May	John Bavand	Henry Henshaw	Edmund Daniel
		Richard Bernard	William Giblet
1576 May	Morus Clynnog	William Giblet	Thomas Crane
		John Bavand	Edward Bromborough
1577 Aug	Morus Clynnog	Alan Cope	William Ely
		John Sanderson	William Soonus
1578 May	Henry Henshaw	Alan Cope	William Ely
		John Sanderson	William Soonus

APPENDIX 29

EXTRACTS FROM DOCUMENTS SHOWING THE CONTINUITY BETWEEN HOSPICE AND COLLEGE

(a) Bull of Foundation of the College, 1st May 1579.

. . . si aliquo tempore praedictum Collegium ex quacumque causa dissolvi contingat aedes ecclesia domus census ceteraque omnia praedicta perinde Hospitalis praedicti sunt ac si erectio Collegii et alia praescripta nunquam emanassent prout nos ex nunc in eum eventum Hospitale iterum quoad illa omnia in integrum restituimus.

(b) The College Annals, Liber 303 (the Liber Ruber), pars IIa, f. 12.

Anno Domini M.D.LXXX Mense Decembris die XXIII ad laudem et gloriam Smae Trinitatis, et Sti Thomae martyris, expedita fuit Bulla Fundationis huius Collegii, quae licet in Mense Aprilis Anni superioris a summo Pont. Greg. XIII fuerit concessa, non tamen ad manus nostras ante praedictum diem pervenit, in qua cum praeter multas facultates, et gratiae spirituales et temporales, omnia bona Hospitalis Anglorum sint unita Collegio accepimus illorum possessionem die 29 Decembris, qui Sto Thomae Martyri dicatus est : et licet in Bulla expresse non apparet, declaravit tamen Summus Pont. vivae vocis oraculo, Collegium hoc teneri ad recipiendos, et alendos peregrinos Anglos, secundum statuta praedicti Hospitalis. Quae Bulla posita est in Archivio Collegii.

(c) The Pilgrim Book, Liber 282, f. 3.

Anno Domini MDLXXX Mense Decembris die XXIX qui D. Thomae Martyri sacer est hoc Anglorum Collegium cepit corporalem possessionem Hospitalis Anglorum, eiusque bonorum vigore Bullae Smi D. N. Gregorii XIII cum hoc tamen onere recipiendi et alendi Anglos ad Urbem devotionis causa advenientes, secundum statuta Hospitalis praedicti, quae iubent hospites pauperes octiduo, Nobiles vero et divites triduo retineri.

APPENDIX 30

BULL OF PIUS IV, 24TH APRIL 1560, RESTORING THE CONSTITUTION OF THE HOSPICE TO THAT ESTABLISHED BY PAUL III. CF. APPENDIX 24

. . . Et subsequenter, cum Hospitale prefatum aliquamdiu per eundem Reginaldum Cardinalem aliosque dicte nationis Curiales rectum et gubernatum fuisset, tandem dilectus filius noster Bernardinus tituli sancti Matthei presbyter Cardinalis Trannensis nuncupatus, asserens se hoc ipsum a pie memorie Paulo Papa iiij etiam predecessore nostro tunc in humanis agente vive vocis illius oraculo heic in mandatis die videlicet ultima Martii anni domini MDLIX dilecto filio Edouardo Carne, qui eatenus pro clare memorie Maria Anglorum Regina apud sedem apostolicam egerat Oratorem, in virtute sancte obedientie ac sub maioris excommunicationis omniumque bonorum suorum in Alma Urbe existentium amissionis pena apostolica auctoritate precepit, ut eiusdem hospitalis curam regimen et administrationem susciperet, fructus redditus et proventus ex eo provenientes integre perciperet eosque tam in suos proprios et necessarios usus quam in solita opera dicto Hospitali de iure vel consuetudine incumbentia converteret ; proviso quod librum computorum particularium de redditibus Hospitalis huiusmodi tenere et omnium illius bonorum Inventarium facere infra mensem teneretur. Ut ubicumque (?) quoties ratio de eius administratione ab illo requisita foret, eam fideliter et prompte reddere posset. Subsequenter vero prefatus Edouardus sponte coram

Notario publico et testibus ad id adhibitis dixit et protestatus est se nolle quantum in se erat curam regimen et administrationem Hospitalis huiusmodi in persona sua admittere, seve in illis ullo modo intromittere quinimo id ipsum subire recusavit, omni iuri titulo et interesse sibi in illis vel ad illa competenti renunciando, prout in diversis his et instrumentis aliisque documentis desuper confectis plenius dicitur contineri. Et sicut eadem petitio subiungebat rationi conveniat, et Hospitalis predicti ac dilectorum filiorum modernorum et pro tempore existentium dicte nationis curialium aliarumque personarum praesertim pauperum ad Almam Urbem declinantium plurimum intersit, illud in suum pristinum statum restitui, et ut antiquitus moris erat deinceps gubernari, pro parte Episcopi et Symonis ac se tempore Reginaldi Cardinalis de eius totiusque Confraternitatis consensu hospitalis predictorum administrationem habuisse, et illam per Sex Annos exercuisse, ac de presenti in dicto hospitali commorari, asserentis Roberti Talcarni predictorum nobis fuit humiliter supplicatum, quatenus ipsos dictumque hospitale adversus preceptum et mandatum Pauli iii predecessoris et Bernadini Cardinalis huiusmodi, in pristinum statum restituere ac omnia per ipsum Paulum iij sic ut prefertur statuta confirmare, et alias in premissis opportune providere de benignitate apostolica dignaremur. Nos igitur, qui salubrem hospitalium aliorumque piorum locorum directionem sincero desideramus affectu, Episcopum et Symonem ac Robertum prefatos, qui ut etiam asserunt in ipsa Urbe presentes existunt, et eorum quemlibet a quibusvis excommunicatione suspensione et interdicti aliisque ecclesiasticis sententiis censuris et penis a iure vel ab homine quavis occasione vel causa latis, siquibus quomodolibet innodati existunt, ad effectum presentium duntaxat consequendum harum serie absolventes, et absolutos fore censentes, necnon eidem Edouardo perpetuum super dicto sibi facto precepto silentium imponentes, huiusmodi supplicationis inclinati Episcopum et Symonem ac Robertum necnon Hospitale predicta adversus preceptum et mandatum Pauli iiij predecessoris et Bernadini Cardinalis huiusmodi in pristinum et eum in quo ante illa erant statum auctoritate apostolica tenore presentium restituimus, reponimus, et plenarie reintegramus ; necnon omnia et singula per dictum Paulum iij predecessorem ut prefertur ordinata et statuta et prout illa concernunt alia in dictis litteris desuper confectis contenta et indesecuta quecumque licita tamen et honesta, eisdem auctoritate et tenore ex certa scientia confirmamus et approbamus et illis perpetue inviolabilis firmitatis robur adiicimus ; omnesque et singulos iuris et facti defectus si qui forsan intervenerint in eisdem supplemus, necnon illa valida et efficacia fore, suosque plenarios et integros effectus sortiri et inviolabiliter observari, necnon hospitali ac Confratribus curialibus et pauperibus prefatis suffragari et sic in premissis omnibus et singulis per quoscumque Iudices et Commissarios etiam dicte Romanae ecclesiae Cardinales sublata eis et eorum cuilibet, quavis aliter iudicandi et interpretandi facultate et auctoritate iudicari et definiri debere, ac quicquid secus super his a quoquam quavis auctoritate scienter vel ignoranter attemptari contigerit irritum et inane decernimus . . .

OWEN LEWIS

In an article in THE VENERABILE,[1] I gave the evidence that makes me believe that Fr Persons was responsible for the facts contained in the introductory section of the Sega Report. By allowing these statements to appear over his name Sega obviously made himself responsible for them and they may be referred to as his. We are not here concerned, however, with the propriety of making all these charges without giving a scrap of evidence, but with the value of the report as an historical document, and particularly in so far as it concerns Owen Lewis.

The attack on Lewis, scarce cold in his tomb, is savage even by sixteenth century standards, and it is not rendered less so by the crocodile tears. He is first of all contrasted with a number of distinguished exiles. They strove to bring their country back to Christ : he on the other hand belonged to a class led by a far different spirit, caring nothing for their country and out only for money and personal aggrandisement. Then comes the account of the foundation of the English College. Allen's sole motive was the interests of religion : Lewis had entirely different motives. He had an eye to his private advantage and eagerly canvassed his own rectorship.[2] When the Welsh

---

[1] THE VENERABILE, XX, 208–23 (Nov. 1961). Cf. also *A Hundred Homeless Years* by G. Anstruther O.P., London 1958, p. 28.

[2] The Latin is much stronger than Foley's version (VI, 6). After stating that Allen left the business of founding the College to Lewis, it continues : *Qui quidem hac in re operam suam nec sane invitus dicitur collocasse, sed longe diverso fine ab eo quem sibi proposuerat Alanus. Hic enim, ut iam commemoratum est, nihil aliud praeter commune religionis et Patriae bonum spectabat sperabatve. Ille vero fertur pleraque ad privatam utilitatem revocasse atque iam inde ab eo tempore cum Collegii regimen cupidissime ambiret tantas inter alumnos divisiones concitasse, sic Protectoris Moroni animum ab iis qui in verba sua jurare recusabant abalienasse, ut proprius nihil factum sit ut recens iste partus in cunis elideretur.* (Ottob. Lat. 2473, f. 192 v.).

party lost control of the College Lewis allied himself with spies and traitors in an attempt to wreck what he could not rule. It was he who stirred up all subsequent sedition. Whenever he was absent all went well; whenever he came to Rome there was trouble. Hence the portrait of a grasping, scheming, unscrupulous careerist. I believe this view of him has been so generally accepted because it appears to have the august support of an impartial Italian cardinal. Eighty years ago Gillow regretted that Sega had not confined himself to what he knew and could verify. Modern writers are less critical and accept the report at its face value.[3]

Yet this uncomplimentary report receives no confirmation from strictly contemporaneous documents. Unfortunately most of those that tell in his favour remain unpublished. Allen has his 'Letters and Memorials' and almost everything that Persons wrote against Lewis has been printed, but the abundant material giving the other side has been curiously overlooked. Yet even from what little has been published it is possible to detect the animus and the distortion in the account given by Sega.

One wonders what evidence Sega would have produced as to Lewis's motives for leaving England. His early career[4] follows so closely the pattern of the other exiles that we should require strong evidence to substantiate a charge that his motives were so different from theirs. Like many of them a Wykehamist and graduate of New College, he taught civil law at Oxford till the change in religion made his position impossible. According to his own account he was driven out 'for religion'; according to the college records he left of his own accord.[5] The difference here is more apparent than real and there is no reason to suppose that he resigned a safe and distinguished career at Oxford in the hope of bettering his fortunes abroad. Like so many learned Wykehamists he retired to Louvain, where he matriculated on 5th April 1563, on the same day as his fellow Wykehamist Thomas Hide, headmaster of Winchester College, and less than a month before William Allen.[6]

[3] J. M. Cleary, who calls Sega 'a dispassionate and experienced Papal servant', says 'This document is a devastating exposure of the ambitions and intrigues of Owen Lewis and deserves careful study.' (*Checklist of Welsh Students in the Seminaries, part I* (Cardiff Newman Circle, 1958), p. 5 note).

[4] He was born in Anglesey. If the computation on his monument (F. Ughelli, *Italia Sacra*, IX, 354) is exact he was born on 27th December 1533. He was baptised in the 'ancient and magnificent church' dedicated to St Cadwaladr, presumably the one at Llangadwaladr. (See Appendix 37).

[5] Rait and Rashall, *Hist. of New College, Oxford*, III, 23.

[6] Arch. Gén. du Roy., Brussels; Université de Louvain, no. 24. *Quartus Liber intitulatorum*, f. 391. Allen matriculated 27th May (f. 391 v.).

The poverty of these exiles is evident from many sources. Lewis may have had some private means but he could hardly have been rich. He was moreover burdened with the care and education of his sister's child, Hugh Griffith, who had been left an orphan at an early age and who accompanied his uncle to Flanders.[7] Between them was an affection almost of father and son, and this was to play its part in the sequel. Lewis was more fortunate than many of his colleagues. He was soon appointed to teach civil and canon law in the newly established university at Douai, and was in charge of that faculty for seven years, taking his doctorate there on 15th June 1569. In a list of exiles drawn up by Sir Francis Englefield in January 1570, with a view to obtaining pensions from the king of Spain, he is stated to be '*provisus*'.[8] That he was able to earn his own living rather than depend (like most of them) on the bounty of Spain is hardly to his discredit. His reputation as a canonist must have been considerable, for the archbishop of Cambrai appointed him provost of the Chapter and his archdeacon, though till then he had never set eyes on him.[9] In 1574 he was sent to Rome on legal business concerning the Chapter. For the next six years, besides representing his bishop, he acted as agent of the College at Douai and Rheims. It was he who obtained a pension for it from Gregory XIII,[10] and, of more enduring interest, permission to print the Douai bible.[11] In the appendix will also be found a letter that makes it clear that he was the author of the Welsh translation of the Catechism of Peter Canisius (always attributed to Gruffydd Robert) and other works as well. It is difficult to reconcile his literary activities with Sega's gibe that he cared nothing for his country.

It was also during these years in Rome that he worked assiduously to turn the Hospice into a seminary, and it is this work that has brought such odium on his name. The story has often been told and at great length, but always from the standpoint of the English. Thus all the petitions of the English students have been printed in full but not the dignified little petition of the Welsh.[12] The formidable list of enormities committed by Morus Clynnog has also been printed,[13] but not his

[7] Appendix 39, p. 294.
[8] Simancas, Estado 583 (unpaginated).
[9] Appendix 36, p. 292.
[10] T. F. Knox, *Douai Diaries*, 316, 317.
[11] Appendix 31, p. 287.
[12] C.R.S. 2, 102 sq. ; Appendix 32, p. 289.
[13] Ibid., p. 106.

Cardinal Allen

Owen Lewis, Bishop of Cassano

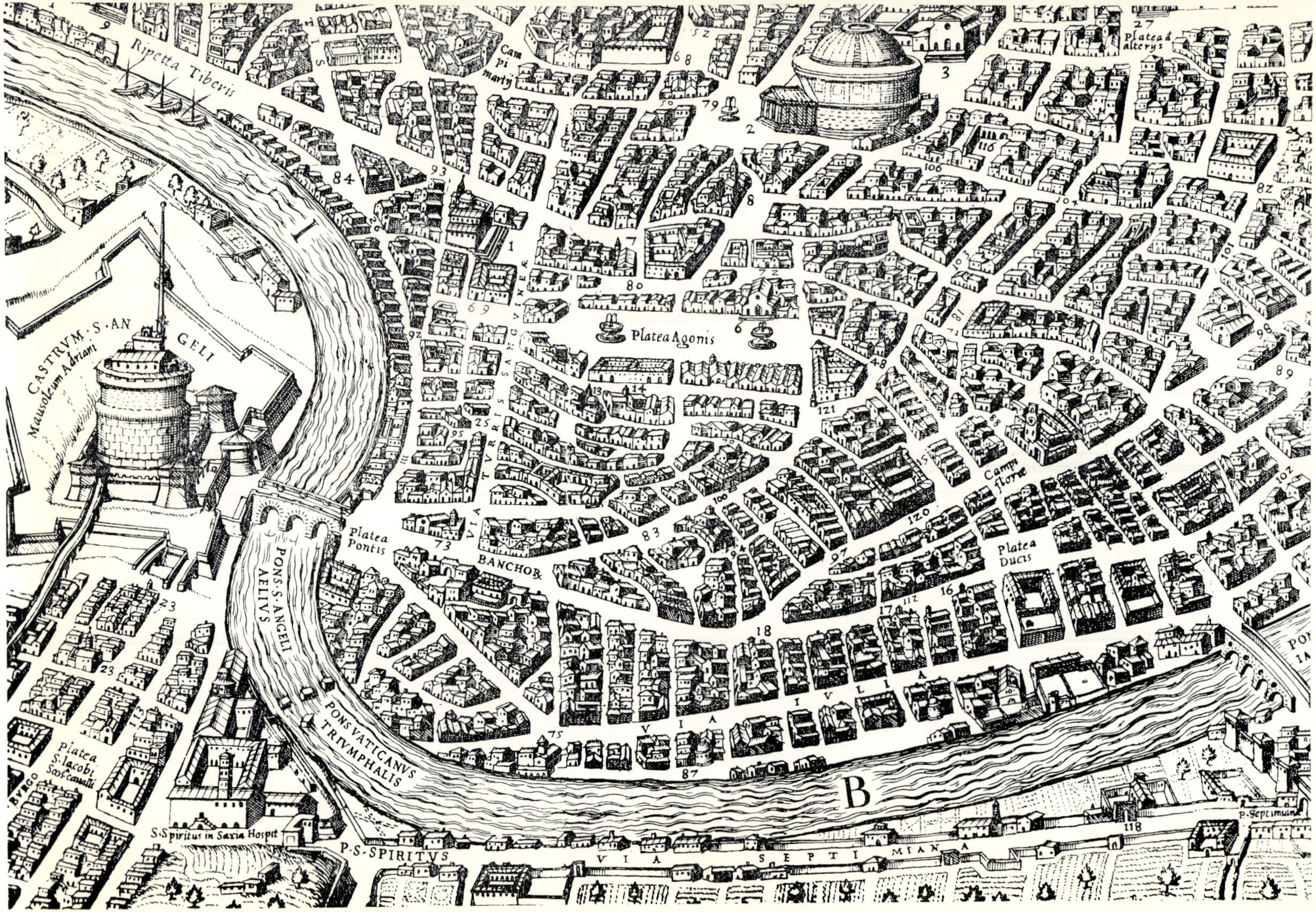

PLAN OF ROME, 1576

16 English Hospice 112 Corte Savella prison 97 Via Pellegrino 100 Via Parione 48 S. Pantaleone 2 Pantheon

detailed reply.[14] The revolt receives much glamour from the presence of three martyrs in the ranks of the rebels. It has been called the Battle of the Martyrs. It could with equal justice be called the Battle of the Apostates, for of the thirty-one who signed the petition no fewer than ten were to deny their faith, at least for a time. This unruly element must be borne in mind if we are to understand the attitude of Owen Lewis.

From his own memorials to Cardinal Morone it is clear that he was not primarily concerned with the candidature of his fellow-countryman, Morus Clynnog. He reminded the cardinal that he had warned him of the difficulties. To turn out all the English chaplains and leave the one Welshman in sole command was to unleash all the bitter jealousy and racial antagonism of the dispossessed. What Lewis fought for was to ensure that this venerable priest and bishop-elect should not be ignominiously hounded out merely because he was a Welshman and at the clamour of a lot of rebellious students. He had no objection to the College being handed over entirely to the Jesuits, and had indeed been responsible for introducing the two Jesuits already there. He warned the students that it was their own unruliness that made the Society chary of accepting so unpleasant a charge. But whatever the final solution he wished to protect Clynnog from the injustice and humiliation that he had done nothing to deserve. Make the students submit to authority and then their grievances can be considered.[15] There was however a want of tact. Both Lewis and Clynnog refer to the new establishment as the '*Seminarium Britannicum*', and '*Britannicus*' at that time had neither the ancient nor the modern meaning of 'British'. In common parlance it was a synonym for 'Welsh', and is so used by Lewis himself. Probably they were looking for a word that was wider than '*Anglicus*' and would embrace both countries, but their choice was not felicitous and gave rise to suspicions that they were planning to oust the English and found an all-Welsh college.

Up to this time there were no serious differences between Lewis and Persons. Both disapproved of the rebellious attitude of the students ; both agreed that the College must not become a country-club where students passed the rest of their lives in idleness. If it was Persons who first thought of the College oath to go to England when commanded, it was Lewis who composed

[14] Vat. Lat. 12159, f. 133 ss. (11 pages).
[15] Appendix 33, and 34, pp. 289, 290.

it.[16] Persons could hardly be expected to feel the same tenderness towards Clynnog as Lewis, but he nowhere attacks him, and although Clynnog was destined to die a sudden death Persons does not include him in his gallery of opponents whom Providence removed from his path.[17]

As everyone knows, the students won. Lewis's petition that they must be brought to heel before the removal of Clynnog went unheeded. The tradition of this famous victory was handed down in the College. They had learnt that they could get their way if only they were sufficiently bold, and the troubles of 1585 and 1595, though due to different causes, were no doubt encouraged by the memory of the day when Sherwin and his twenty-two[18] companions walked out of the College and defied all authority—and won. '*Viam norunt*', said Lewis.

I have not found any contemporary evidence to suggest that Lewis fomented these troubles, though he certainly took an active part. He seems to have done what he could to restore peace. Cardinal Como in a letter to Allen praises the patience, piety and prudence with which he had acted.[19] It is not until the Sega report, seventeen years later, that we meet with the accusation that he had been the cause of all the trouble.

The next accusation brought by Sega is that Lewis had his minions in the College by whose means he could foment perpetual strife, and that when Gregory XIII discovered this he ordered him to depart from Rome. Again there is no contemporary confirmation of this story. The Jesuits took over the College in April 1579 and Lewis remained in Rome more than a year after that. During this year there is no record of any unrest among the scholars. In the autumn of 1579 St Charles Borromeo came to Rome. He was anxious to introduce the Tridentine reforms at his seminary and at the Swiss seminary in Milan. He heard of the reputation that Lewis had won as an authority on these reforms and invited him to become vicar general. That the invitation came from St Charles is borne

[16] Appendix 37, p. 292.

[17] Clynnog was drowned on a voyage from France to Spain, in what Persons, with perhaps unconscious irony, calls *mare Britannicum*. (*Brevis narratio de origine ac progressu Collegii Anglorum in civitate Romana*. There are three copies; Vat. Lat. 3494; A.R.S.I. Rom. 156, I; Bib. Angelica, +8.5 [No. 9]. This last is bound up with a number of *printed* pamphlets, and the reference is to printed books, not MSS. Cf. C.R.S. 2, 89 note).

[18] There were twenty-one signatories to the petition, but since then two more students had arrived and joined the majority.

[19] Knox, *Letters of Allen*, p. 399.

out not only by Lewis's letter of acceptance but by letters of Cardinal Como and of St Charles himself.[20]

For the next four and a half years Lewis was fully occupied with the affairs of the archdiocese of Milan, and particularly with the reform of the seminaries. He would have had little time to brood over past injuries even had he been so inclined. The very considerable correspondence that survives[21] contains little concerning the affairs of England or the English College, but what little there is is devoid of bitterness. There is not the slightest indication that he was anti-Jesuit. He was later to suggest that the Swiss seminary should be handed over to the Jesuits.[22] There is extant a very friendly letter to the Jesuit Rector of the Venerabile dated 21st March 1582, reporting the arrival of eight students from Rheims on their way to Rome, and how he had lodged them in the cardinal's house[23], thus continuing a tradition that began with the hospitality extended to Edmund Campion and his companions in 1580. Two months later we find Persons himself suggesting that Lewis should be recalled to Rome and sent on a delicate diplomatic mission to Madrid which was then the Mecca of all Catholic hopes.

> For though this Dr Owen on account of the differences which have lately arisen between the Welsh and English, he being a Welshman, does not stand very well with the greater part of the English, nevertheless as he is a grave and prudent man, if united to Allen, who possesses the hearts of all, he would be of no small assistance.[24]

Yet according to the Sega report this is the man who had to be expelled from Rome for the peace of the College. There is a further indication that there was still no breach between Persons and Lewis. In October 1583 Lewis writes to Cardinal Como to express his regret that Persons should have passed so close to Milan, going and coming on his visit to Rome, without

---

[20] Appendix 36, p. 292. St Charles's letter (23rd June 1580) is Card. 93, f. 272 ; Cardinal Como's is Card. 92, f. 131.

[21] There are over a hundred of his letters in Bib. Ambrosiana, mostly to St Charles. Only a few (of English interest) are mentioned in the Cal.S.P. Milan. In the Arch. Metropolitano is a volume of letters addressed to the vicar general (mostly to Lewis) but all are on diocesan business. Arch. Spirituale, Carteggio Ufficiale, t. 32 (1579–83). There are many letters scattered in various collections in the Vatican. What little escaped the fire at Cassano (1824) had been printed in *Mr Ludovico Audoeno, Britanno, Vescovo di Cassano e le prime costituzioni del seminario diocesano*, Cosenza 1909. I am indebted to his Lordship Mgr Raffaele Barbieri, the present bishop of Cassano, for the loan of this rare pamphlet.

[22] Nunz. Francia, 25, f. 233 (7th Aug. 1591).

[23] *Douai Diaries*, p. 343.

[24] Ibid., p. 337.

calling on him, but he adds that Persons had written to him from Piacenza.[25]

There was however one cause of bitterness between Lewis and the College, though the bitterness seems to have been mostly on the side of the College. Among the English students his name was not revered. As early as May 1579 Allen wrote to him :

> I see the scholars either will not be persuaded that you did help anything to the mitigation of the matter, or else so far their minds be exasperated that they will accept nothing for benefit that cometh from you, *ut fit in aegris animis.*[26]

Four years later things had not improved. Allen reports that a student at Rheims has smashed a portrait of Lewis, though it hung unobtrusively in the dark little room of a Welsh student.[27] It can be well imagined that the Welsh, now a tiny minority, were not over-welcome either in Rheims or Rome. At Rome there remained Hugh Griffith whose misfortune it was to be not only Welsh but the beloved nephew of Owen Lewis. He was said to be troublesome and fit only to be expelled. We need to know a lot more of the treatment meted out to him before passing judgement. Had he not been Lewis's nephew he would probably have been expelled without ceremony. As it was, the Protector (Buoncompagni) wrote to Lewis early in 1582 asking him to remove his nephew from the College.

> I would willingly do so, wrote Lewis to Allen, were it not that he is needed to conduct some business of mine and of our archbishop of Cambrai. They complain that he talks a great deal against the college. I don't know. But they could have him very friendly if they treated him kindly.[28]

Griffith was however expelled before the end of that year but stayed in Rome. St Charles found him a place in the household of Cardinal Serbelloni whom he served for ten years till that cardinal's death in 1591.[29] This long apprenticeship would seem to imply that Griffith was not by nature a particularly troublesome individual.

[25] Cardinali, 93, f. 383.
[26] *Letters of Allen*, p. 80.
[27] Ibid., p. 217.
[28] Ibid., p. 112.
[29] Bib. Amb. G. 166 inf. f. 162.

More serious is the accusation that Lewis consorted with English spies and informers. It must be confessed that he had a genius for befriending the wrong people. The list is a long one, beginning with the adventurer Thomas Stukeley and the ever-wavering Anthony Tyrell, and including such undoubted spies as Solomon Aldred and Charles Sledd. It should be added that he also befriended a number of deserving exiles. He seems to have had a soft heart and to have been easily taken in. But Sega does not insinuate that he consorted with these scoundrels after they had been exposed ; that has been left to a modern writer who gives no evidence.[30] At most the charge against Lewis was that he lacked discernment in his choice of helpers, and this cannot be denied. Nor was he the only one taken in by plausible rogues. For instance, nobody in Rome seems to have had the slightest inkling that Sir Richard Shelley, Grand-Prior of England, was playing a double game and was in constant correspondence with Burghley. Shelley certainly did not look upon Lewis as an ally. In a letter to Burghley of 24th May 1582 he writes :

> I hear Dr Lewis is at home in good conceit, whom ye must beware of (and you specially, my lord, of all men living). He is the deepest and doublest dissembler that ever I knew since I was born.[31]

Briefly, during these years that Lewis spent at Milan there is not much evidence that he interested himself in the affairs of the English College and what little there is shows that he was on friendly terms with the Rector, that he entertained the students who passed through Milan and that there was no breach with Persons.

Relations between St Charles and Owen Lewis were always most cordial. In his letter accepting the invitation to Milan, Lewis writes : 'I will come, because I wish to experience that sacred pronouncement of the royal prophet: *Cum sancto sanctus eris*'.[32] St Charles calls him '*ottimo personaggio e mio amico carissimo e come fratello*'.[33] It has often been stated (though I can find no contemporary evidence) that the saint died in the arms of his vicar general. With St Charles's death on 4th November 1584 Lewis's appointment came to an end. Certain grandees of Milan petitioned the pope that he might continue

[30] J. M. Cleary, loc. cit.
[31] B. M. Lansd. 38, No. 44.
[32] Appendix 36, p. 292.
[33] *San Carlo Borromeo nel Terzo Centenario della Canonizzazione*, December 1909, p. 242.

there, but it was not to be. He returned to Rome on 9th December and soon after was made secretary of the Congregation of Bishops, a post that often led to a cardinal's hat. Some months after his arrival trouble broke out in the College. It was doubtless this that inspired the statement in the Sega report that Lewis's presence in Rome was always a signal for rebellion. In August 1585 Sega (not yet a cardinal) was ordered to visitate the College. His report has been printed.[34] It is a far more workmanlike document than the Sega report of 1596. It conforms to the reports of canonical visitations of various pontifical colleges that survive in considerable numbers. There is an inventory of the chapel and a financial statement, which are lacking in the later report. When he came to prepare his report of 1596 he would have done well to refresh his memory by reading his report of 1585. He would have found that it contained not the slightest suggestion that Lewis had anything whatever to do with the disturbances. He is mentioned only once, in a tribute to his labours in founding the College. Once again it is not until many years after the event that we get the accusation that he fomented the troubles.

Lewis continued to reside in Rome for some two and a quarter years and they do not appear to have been years of unrest in the College. He was doubtless busy with his new office and he was also agent for Mary Queen of Scots. In 1587 there was a movement to have an English cardinal, and a group of exiles in Flanders favoured Lewis. A long report[35] that has already been quoted was sent to Philip II in August, begging him to use his influence to have Lewis raised to that dignity and to grant him a pension. It states that he is proficient not only in Welsh but in English, Italian, Spanish, Scottish and Flemish, and that he is *gratissimo* with the Welsh and English, and *confidentissimo* with the Scots and Irish. In spite of this the hat was given, in this very month, to Dr Allen.

On 3rd February 1588 Lewis was nominated bishop of Cassano, a see in the kingdom of Naples in the gift of the

---

[34] A. O. Meyer, *England and the Catholic Church under Elizabeth*, pp. 492–519. Meyer left out certain sections of the report as being of little general interest. They are however of considerable interest for the domestic history of the College and give details not to be found elsewhere. Thus there are the saints' names given to the nine cubicula; names of servants; names of singers and the part they sang; College debts to George Gilbert and others; above all an interesting reference to a law-suit then pending over the ownership of the chapel at *Domine Quo Vadis* which the College claimed had been built by the 'Rector' of the Hospice.

[35] Simancas, Estado, K. 1448, f. 156 sq. C.R.S. has published (38, p. 359) only a summary made for the convenience of Philip II. The original is much more detailed.

Spanish king. He was consecrated in Rome on 14th February[36] and left for his diocese on 26th March.[37] On becoming bishop he vacated the office of provost of Cambrai, but he kept it in the family. It went to Hugh Griffith, who however continued to reside in Rome as his uncle's agent. Seventeen letters written from his bishopric survive. They are all addressed to Cardinal Federico Borromeo who had succeeded his uncle as archbishop of Milan. They show that Lewis was, as always, completely absorbed by the job in hand, and there is little of English interest in them. After two busy years in his mountainous diocese he suddenly received (on 1st March 1590) a summons to Rome for his *ad limina*. He wrote indignantly to Cardinal Borromeo complaining that the *ad limina* was triennial and not yet due; that it was the beginning of Lent '*nel quale il vescovo fa qualche frutto nel suo gregge*'; and that he had summoned his first synod to meet after Easter. However he must obey.[38] It would appear that he never returned to Cassano. There are no letters for the next year.[39] Once more there was trouble in Rome, but not this time in the English College, and evidently not the work of the bishop. There was an attempt to sow dissension between Allen and Lewis. The authors were leaders of the anti-Jesuit faction in France and Flanders, especially Thomas Morgan, and Gilbert Gifford. In later years Persons was to accuse them of 'joining themselves with Dr Lewis in Rome and falling out with Dr Allen and F. Persons'.[40] Yet in a letter of January or February 1591 Allen most explicitly denies that they had succeeded in dividing him from Lewis.[41] On 6th May Allen and Lewis signed a joint declaration affirming their mutual affection and esteem and repudiating the suggestion that there was any jealousy or rivalry between them.[42] Which are we to believe, the contemporary and solemn declaration of Allen, or the later statement of Persons?

Like every agitation that shook the Catholic body this one doubtless had its repercussions in the English College.

[36] Garampi Index sub nom. in Arch. Vat. Garampi gives a reference to a consistorial volume that is no longer extant.

[37] C.R.S. V, 187.

[38] Bib. Amb. G. 146 inf. f. 34.

[39] He was at all events in Rome on 10th May 1591 when he addressed a pastoral letter to his clergy and his flock. See pamphlet in note 21, pp. 37–42.

[40] *Letters of Allen*, p. 320.

[41] Ibid., p. 327.

[42] Ibid., p. 334.

But there is no evidence of any unrest and certainly nothing to point to Lewis as a trouble-maker.

On 20th June 1591[43] Lewis was appointed nuncio to Switzerland and set out at once. He reached Bologna on 24th June and Milan on the 29th. Here he met Cardinal Ottavio Paravicini who had been nuncio in Switzerland for the past four years. He gave Lewis a very forbidding account of the trials in store. There was still an unsettled dispute concerning the payment of the Swiss mercenaries by the papal court, and the Swiss refused to receive another nuncio. Rather than risk a rebuff to the Holy See Lewis wrote for advice, and was instructed not to continue his journey till he received further orders.[44] He was not at all sorry. Quite apart from the current tension he had no wish to be in Switzerland, '*dove pur l'aria fredissima, il brusco et barbaro proceder et la conversatione soldalesca di quella natione haveria bisogno di complessione di ferro, d'età manco di 60 anni* (he was fifty-eight), *et di Nuntio che saperia fare il buon compagno et supportare il brindisi di molte hore, et d'esser quasi mezzo-soldato alle volte con loro*'. He also thought that the English government would stir up opposition and possibly have him assassinated. However, he was ready to shed his blood in so good a cause.[45] But he was much relieved when Gregory XIV died (15th October 1591) and his credentials needed renewal. In November he was recalled to Rome and arrived on 22nd December. We should expect to hear of some flutterings in the English College but there were none.

Lewis was destined never to return to Cassano and never to leave Rome again. After Innocent IX's brief pontificate of only two months, Cardinal Aldobrandini became Clement VIII in January 1592. He determined to carry out a thorough visitation of the churches of Rome and on 8th June nominated a body of assistants to accompany him. It included four cardinals; an archbishop; two bishops; and two theologians, a Dominican and a Jesuit. The Jesuit theologian was Francesco Toledo, the future cardinal, and one of the bishops was Owen Lewis.[46] This close association of Lewis and Toledo may account for the

---

[43] H. Biaudet, *Les Nonciatures Apostoliques permanentes jusqu'en* 1648, Helsinki 1910, col. 169.

[44] Bib. Amb. G. 149 inf. f. 285 ; Nunz. Francia, 20, f. 101 ; ibid., 25, ff. 170, 171, 231, 233 ; Principi, 50, f. 424.

[45] Bib. Amb. G. 153, f. 189.

[46] Arch. Vat. Misc. Arm. VII, 3. *Decreta Clem. VIII facta in visitatione ecclesiarum Urbis*, 8th June 1592 (–1596).

latter's contemptuous dismissal of the Sega report recorded in my previous article in THE VENERABILE.

The pope visitated personally, sometimes managing two churches in a single day. He was ruthless in removing scantily dressed statues and anything that savoured of paganism, and was severe in other ways.[47] It fell to Lewis to examine the competence of various ecclesiastics. At St Peter's he found all the Jesuit penitentiaries (including William Baldwin) were worthy, but at the Lateran all the canons were declared 'rudes et ignavos' and were suspended from their functions and benefices for three years while they studied pastoral theology.[48] Hugh Griffith informs us that his uncle had 'molti malevoli' and these visitations would not have increased his popularity. On 8th May 1593 the pope constituted a permanent inquisitorial body 'super visitationem ecclesiarum Urbis' and Lewis was appointed secretary.[49] This work can have left him little time for the affairs of the English College, but there is nothing to suggest that his relations with it were anything but amicable. How otherwise can we account for the fact that he conferred orders on the students, usually in the College chapel?[50] There was surely [no obligation to invite him, and if he had been the enemy that Sega portrays we should expect other arrangements. Only a few months before his death, when poor Walter Marsh was burnt for sacrilege, it was Lewis who sang the Mass of Reparation in the College chapel.[51] As always, we look in vain for evidence of conflict or bitterness.

On 16th October 1594 Cardinal Allen died. For years he had been delegated to grant faculties to all priests going to England and a successor was urgently needed. Persons wanted the granting of these faculties to be vested in the Cardinal Protector. There would then be no particular necessity for an English cardinal. However, this was not everybody's view and there was a good deal of agitation and lobbying on behalf of various candidates. Two stood out : Persons himself and Owen Lewis. Support for Lewis came principally from the anti-

---

[47] For example : *Armarium sacrarum reliquiarum ornatius intus vestiatur et imago S. Mariae Magdalenae extrinsecus in eo depicta densioribus et prolixioribus capillis contegatur. S. Pietro, 3 July 1592. Ibid., f. 28 v.

[48] Ibid., ff. 30 v. and 16 v.

[49] Arch. Vat. Arm. 38, t. 2, f. 79.

[50] From September 1593 till January 1595 practically all the ordinations were by Lewis in the College chapel. His last ordination seems to be that of William Sacheverell O.P. (an old Wykehamist like himself) in the Minerva, 20th May 1595. Arch. di Vicariato di Roma, Lib. Ord. 5.

[51] Bib. Vat. Urb. Lat. 1063, f. 413 (25th June 1595).

Jesuit party in Flanders, led by John Leslie, Bishop of Ross.[52] We all have our moments of history of which we would like to have been eye-witnesses, and one of mine is the day when Persons received a long letter from his confrère Oliverius Manares, dated 24th November 1594. Manares stresses how much more useful Persons is to the Church as a simple Jesuit than he would be as cardinal. That dignity would cramp his secret intelligence with so many people and impede his great work of raising money for the seminaries. He therefore thinks that the bishop of Cassano should be given the preference![53]

Lewis was not above canvassing his own candidature. Joseph Creswell s.j. informs Cardinal Caetani :

> He (Lewis) has written that he is good to the College with his purse and that he helps the Rector, and I have thanked him. He makes the same diligence in the Seminary of Douai to have a letter or common petition subscribed by the scholars, but the Rector does not think it expedient to involve the young men in this affair.[54]

Perhaps he lobbied among the students in Rome though I can find no evidence of this. They were as much divided on the subject as the Catholics generally, and this seems to have been the beginning of the troubles that flared up in the following year and led to the second visitation by Sega. It is not however one of the accusations specifically listed by Sega.

Rome's solution was to create no successor to Allen but to transfer his jurisdiction to the Cardinal Protector. England remained unrepresented in the Sacred College for more than eighty years. Allen's death, far from helping Lewis's candidature, had the opposite effect. He might well have been made a cardinal as a reward for his many responsible offices, but Allen's death revealed once again the divisions among the English Catholics and it was deemed wiser to leave well alone.

Lewis's last extant letter is to Cardinal Borromeo. He sends him a relic of St Thomas of Canterbury and thanks him for his charity to 'our students who recently passed that way'.[55] This is evidence that the archbishop of Milan continued the tradition of lodging the English students on their journeys and it is also evidence of Lewis's abiding interest in the College.

---

[52] Caetani, 124986.
[53] A.R.S.I., Hisp. 139, f. 98. Printed in More's *Hist. Prov. Ang. S.J.*, p. 232.
[54] Caetani, 22591 (16th June 1595). Lewis's letter to Douai is printed in Humphrey Ely's *Certaine Briefe Notes* (1603).
[55] Bib. Amb. G. 170. f. 161. (24th September 1595).

Lewis died on 14th October 1595 and was buried in the College church on the following day. He had appointed his nephew his legatee and left the College 1000 scudi for Masses. He left Cardinal Borromeo a ring and his portraits of SS. John Fisher and Thomas More.[56]

Lewis's letters are full of expressions of somewhat ostentatious piety and naive self-depreciation that were commoner then than they are now, but which always grated on English ears. His vivacious Welsh temperament often annoyed Allen and moved him to hasty phrases that hardly represent his true sentiments. Between them there was a respect and esteem that survived all differences of policy and opinion. Between Lewis and Persons there had been a similar mutual respect though perhaps never the same affection. Persons fell out with most people because of their tepid attachment to, or hostility towards, his Spanish policy, but this was not the case with Lewis, who ever remained a devotee of Spain. Persons appears to have fallen out with Allen, and for reasons that are equally inexplicable.

Be the cause what it may, the Sega report pursues the memory of the dead bishop with a rancour that implies a deep cleavage and some grave friction or, let us hope, misunderstanding. It is strangely out of harmony with the testimony of many who have just as much right to be believed. The confidential servant of four popes and the beloved friend of Charles Borromeo can hardly have been as black as he has been painted.

GODFREY ANSTRUTHER O.P.

APPENDIX 31

OWEN LEWIS TO GREGORY XIII FOR PERMISSION TO PRINT THE ENGLISH BIBLE

undated. *c.* 1579

Vat. Lat. 6416, f. 272

Beatissime Pater

In quarta regula indicis librorum prohibitorum editi per Patres a S. Tridentina synodo delectos de sacris bibliis in vulgari lingua editis prudenter cavetur ne passim permittantur, sed ut episcopi et inquisitoris

---

[56] Appendix, 39, p. 294.

T*

iudicio in hac parte stetur, ut cum consilio parochi aut confessarii bibliorum a catholicis auctoribus versorum lectionem in lingua vulgari eis concedere in scriptis possint quos intellexerint ex huiusmodi lectione non damnum sed fidei et pietatis augmentum capere posse. In regula vero sexta eiusdem indicis idem quoque statuitur de permittenda lectione librorum vulgari idiomate de controversiis inter catholicos et haereticos nostri temporis disserentium catholice.

Sane omnes versiones bibliorum in linguam Anglicam corruptae sunt et mala fide editae nec sine magno animarum periculo permitti cuique potest earundem versionum lectio : et nemo hodie Anglorum catholicorum facultatem habet de huiusmodi versionibus iudicandi aut bibliorum etiam si sane et fideliter verterentur, et aliorum catholicorum librorum de controversiis religionis Anglico idiomate tractantium lectionem secundum regulas praedictas cuiquam permittendi. Unde catholici Angli cum magno detrimento carent fructu et beneficio earundem duarum regularium, et multi interim sine ulla venia cum magno periculo suo edunt et legunt tales libros et biblia quoque in vernaculum idioma male at periculose translata, quae tamen ex manibus hominum Anglorum hodie excuti nullo modo possunt nisi alia versio melior et sanior illis edatur ; cuiusmodi est nunc cum maxima diligentia et cum omnium fere idiomatum, versionum ac textuum collatione in Seminario V. S.tis Anglico apud Remos per D. Gulielmum Alanum et alios Anglos viros doctos facta, purgata et prelo fere matura. Certe vix credi potest quantum hoc tempore sincera et sana bibliorum translatio iuvare et sanare posset Anglos, qui veneno falsarum versionum mirum in modum falluntur, putantes se legere purum Dei verbum cum insanas et falsas interim haereticorum glossas et fraudes haurient.

Dignetur itaque S.V. per suum Breve Apostolicum committere et mandare D. Gulielmo Alano, D. Thomae Stapletono et D. Richardo Bristo Anglis presbiteris et professoribus S. Theologiae in Universitate Duacensi, diocesis Atrebatensis, et eorum cuique, ut primum versionem bibliorum in linguam Anglicam factam diligenter examinent, et eorundem sic versorum ac aliorum quorumcunque librorum catholicorum de controversiis religionis vulgari idiomate quocumque disserentium impressionem permittere possint, ita ut manualis subscriptio unius eorum tutum reddat et securum eorundem bibliorum ac librorum quemcumque impressorem : deinde ut eorum quisque possit secundum regulas praedictas bibliorum sic versorum et librorum praedictorum lectionem permittere in scriptis Anglis et Hibernis catholicis ubicumque terrarum constitutis.

Endorsed S.mo D.N. De bibliis et aliis libris in lingua vulgari edendis et legendis memoriale Archidiaconi Cameracensis.

APPENDIX 32

Vat. Lat. 12159, f. 146 v.

Nos infrascripti alumni S.D.N. Gregorii XIII degentes in eius seminario Anglico in Urbe, cupientes satisfacere voluntati S.S.tis quam intelliximus per os III.mae D.V., patris observantissimi gentis nostrae in senatu Apostolico tutelaris, declaramus cum omni humilitate et reverentia nos tamquam obedientiae filios esse paratos utquamdiu in eodem seminario manebimus prompte et lubenter amplectamur et observemus omnes et singulas eiusdem S.tis S. et III.mae D.V. ordinationes et regulas ad regimen eiusdem Collegii ac personarum mores, disciplinam et letteras ac alia quaecunque pertinentes ; et cum obedientia sit melior quam victima, et nos regi debeamus, non regiminis nostri normam superioribus nostris praescribere, promittimus nobis gratissimum et sacrosanctum esse parere et obedire omnibus et singulis praepositis et gubernatoribus eiusdem collegii praesentibus et futuris nobis S.S.tis vel Ill.mae D.V. decreto constitutis.

Jonas Meredithus sacerdos	Thomas Lovellus
Joannes Ascuus sacerdos	Robertus Benedictus
Audoenus Thomas	Morganus Clenocus
Roger Smyth	Hugo Griffidius
Audoenus Robynsonus	Galfridus Elliceus

(in another hand) die prima Martii exhibitur card. protectori

APPENDIX 33

OWEN LEWIS TO GREGORY XIII.   c. MARCH 1579

Vat. Lat. 12159, f. 114.

(The early part is damaged and in places illegible. The gist is that the English students are offended at being governed by a Welshman ; yet the Welsh have all the rights of Englishmen and differ only in language. He then pays tribute to Morus Clynnog who was confessor to Cardinal Pole both in Rome and in England till the Cardinal's death ; was elected bishop of Bangor by the Chapter but not consecrated 'quia illa Regina tum mortua ille noluit nudum titulum episcopi in exilio suo gestare'.)

Iste, inquam, senex pius, qui duobus iam annis hic in Urbe cum magna invidia et molestia fuit Rector seu procurator Seminarii huius nascentis et multa passus est in ea re propter zelum et obedientiam, dum seminarium una mecum parturiret, non debet ad petitionem iuvenum, qui decepti zelo nescio quo et suorum consilio precipites aguntur, expelli quia est Britannus (nam haec est summa totius coloratae quaerelae, quam niger homo cum suis illi, et implicite mihi quoque qui Britannus sum, cudere iamdiu conatur) nec si esset Anglus idem D. Mauritius eo solum nomine quod Anglus esset removeri deberet. In Anglia enim omnibus muneribus et officiis publicis Angli et Britanni sine discrimine funguntur. Etsi Mauritius est Britannus, fuit per confratres Anglos legitime et saepe electus Custos hospitalis, et illud munus diu gessit annis praeteritis, licet ultimus custos nuper eiectus erat Anglus.

Haec autem controversia iam (salvo meliori iudicio) ita componi poterit si, ad conservandum genti nostrae hospitale perpetuo, per breve S.V. unus sit Rector totius collegii, et is hodie, uti est et quia talis est, maneat iam Britannus, olim vel Anglus vel Britannus futurus uti Ill.mus D. Angliae protector idoniorem suo tempore inveniet, et is supremam habeat curam totius seminarii, et circa ecclesiam et hospitalis peregrinos, ac in dote et redditibus hospitalis et seminarii recipiendis et expendendis, et rationem reddat singulis mensibus deputatis Ill.mi D. Protectoris. Et iam deputati sumus ad eam rem R.mus D. Episcopus Assaphensis, R.D. Spetianus et ego, sed ne partialis sit Rector unquam erga scholares Anglos aut Britannos, solus Ill.mus D. Protector scholares in seminarium admittere possit ; Patres vero Jesuitae, qui nec Angli nec Britanni sint, semper morum, disciplinae et literarum curam habeant ac mensam, vestes, libros et omnia personis scholarium necessaria procurent ac suo iudicio ad partialitatem vitandam distribuant et ministrent ac ad ea comparandum nummos seu res ipsas a Rectore iuxta vires reddituum hospitalis ac dotis seminarii, ut ex rationibus apparebit, competenter recipiant. Si difficultas oriatur in ea quoque re consulatur Ill.mus D. Protector.

(Nine lines on the back of the opening paragraph are also illegible. This document, all in Lewis' hand, is marked 'Copia' and is doubtless the copy sent to Morone and now among his papers.)

APPENDIX 34

OWEN LEWIS TO CARDINAL MORONE. *c.* MARCH 1579

Vat. Lat. 12159, f. 120.

(He begs Morone to appeal to the students and try to restore their confidence in their founder 'qui hoc seminarium cum dolore parturii, et qui D. Mauritii in hac discordia innocentiam dumtaxat defendi, non eum causae communi praetuli'.)

Cupio praeterea illis dici quod poterant petere et forsan obtinuisse facilius Jesuitas sine recalcitratione contra eum suum hactenus charum nutricium, et quod ego semper, sed alio modo et per ipsos etiam Jesuitas illis Jesuitas obtinui hactenus, et porro obtinere conatus sum. Sed si perpetuo obtineri non poterint ferant aequo animo, nam praeter alias causas haec praecipue discordia Jesuitas ab hac cura deterruit.

Ego certe non ago causam D. Mauritii (qui nescit mea consilia) in hoc negotio. Nam et ab initio praedixi Ill.mae D.V. fore ut ex emulatione nascerenti voculae quod, aliis 6 capellanis eiectis, ille meus conterraneus (licet magno suo merito) manebat in Hospitali. Et certe non convenit ut inde iam, post istas delationes et accusationes dimittatur nisi suo honore salvo. Tandem quoque (et quidem cito) illud Breve edendum est, quod certa et stricta disciplina, et poenae ac censuram metu seu comminatione contra dividentes nationem Anglicam et Britannicam, istos iuvenes contineat in officio. Id nisi fiat erunt posteriora peiora prioribus. Iam viam norunt. Quo magis isti juvenes mihi credent eo minus erunt molesti Ill.mae D.V.

APPENDIX 35

OWEN LEWIS TO CARDINAL SIRLETO ASKING FOR HELP TO PRINT BOOKS
IN WELSH. 22 AUG. 1579

Bib. Vat. Reg. Lat. 2020, pt II, f. 431.

1. Ex libro nostro idiomate vernaculo de primatu Romani pontificis scripto latine collegi currente calamo et rudi Minerva summa et nuda quaedam capita ut Ill.a D.V. possit de doctrina iudicare et ad S.S.tem referre. Ea vero capita in eodem libro fuse et eloquenter tractantur et non ita ieiune ponuntur atque ego brevitatis causa notavi.

2. Habemus preterea duos alios tractatus, de venerabili eucharistia et de sacrificio missae et cathechismum P. Canicii quoque in lingua nostra Britannica : quae omnia, cum isto tractatu de primatu, mittemus Mediolanum imprimenda et examinanda per D. Rubertium Grifidium canonicum theologum ecclesiae Mediolanensis et S. illius Cardinalis confessarium, virum linguae Britannicae peritissimum, si S.S.tas ad sumptus impressionis aliquid suppeditabit.

3. Causa vero huius nostri consilii haec est, quod cum xiii provincia in Anglia loquantur linguam Britannicam ab Anglicana lingua prorsus ita diversam atque differt lingua Graeca ab Hebraica, Angli nuper curarunt suos libros haereticos ex Anglico idiomate converti in linguam hanc Britannicam ad inficiendum labe heretica istas xiii provincias quae hactenus magis sanae permanserunt quodnon intelligerent haereses Anglorum Anglice scriptas. Contra hanc fraudem diabolicam ad animas fratrum nostrorum secundum carnem salvandas nos antidotum paramus in istis libris ad illas xiii provincias transmittendis. Nam quamvis multi multa volumina ediderunt Latine et Anglice quoque de istis argumentis hodie contra haereticos, tamen Britannice nihil est hactenus de istis rebus impressum.

Dignetur itaque Ill.ma D.V. pietatis et religionis intuitu hoc meum desiderium S.S.ti commendare et me in favore S.S.tis conservare sua commendatione.

APPENDIX 36

OWEN LEWIS TO ST CHARLES BORROMEO

Rome 30 April 1580.

Milan, Bib. Amb. F. 56 inf. f. 341.

Cum multa mecum anima et cogitatione complector et revolvo non sine singulari Dei providentia factum existimo, quod me hominem peregrinum et vix nomine notum Ill.ma D.V. ad se vocare et ad suam pientissimam familiam invitare voluerit. Ad me vero quod attinet (absit omnis adulationis suspicio) dicam coram Deo qui me videt, dicam quod S.mo Christi Vicario dixi, illud est quod me praecipue invitat ut ad Ill.mam D.V. veniam quod experiri cupio sacrum illud regii prophetae oraculum, *Cum sancto sanctus eris.* Veniam itaque Deo volente Mediolanum quandoquidem me non ambiente, ita vult Ill.ma D.V. et S.Mus quoque Papa Gregorius ita suadet : et veniam tum quando ex R.mo D. Spetiano, viro pientissimo, opportunum fore intellexero : et cum ex Cameraco sim hodie eiectus,[1] incipiam servire celeberrimae ecclesiae Mediolanensi, ut Deum meum cuius est terra et plenitudo eius in omni terra mihi propitium experiar et clementem Dominum qui me ex Anglia ante 18 annos per hereticos fugatum et terra marique iactatum vocari tandem fecit Cameracum ad honestam vitae conditionem per R.mi D. Archiepiscopi, qui me nunquam prius viderat, literas, et iam Cameraco deturbatum vocat Mediolanum simili plane modo.

(There is much more, but of no biographical interest.)

APPENDIX 37

OWEN LEWIS TO CARDINAL SIRLETO

15 December 1580.

Vat. Lat. 6193 (pt II), f. 517.
(Asks his favour at great length)

Commendo quoque prolixe patrocinio et charitati Ill.mae D.V. Hugonem Grifidium meum ex sorore nepotem, iuvenem probum qui in Urbe philosophiae studiis incumbit ut se deinde ad ordinem ecclesiasticum parare possit et eamdem Ill.mam D.V. rogo ut in illis quae ad me pertinebunt rebus omnibus egregium virum D. Laurum Dublium rerum Belgicarum in aula Romana actorem regium tanquam meam vocem clementer

---

[1] He is referring to the recent occupation of Cambrai by the French, when the archbishop was driven out and the cathedral chapter dispersed.

audiat, ne frequentioribus meis epistolis occupatissimo principi sim forte molestus.

S. Cadvalladri ultimi Britannorum regis honorandum corpus in Vaticano repertum esse nuper audio, et multum laetor in Domino. Plane enim mihi persuadeo hoc esse sacrum illud corpus quod ego Romae saepe et diligenter quaesivi, datis etiam ea de re Ill.mae D.V. pluribus scedulis,[1] quibus indicari mihi petebam sepulchrum huius sancti regis, quem Britann omnes summa veneratione colunt, et ego singulariter venerari soleo quod sacro baptismate ablutus fuerim in antiqua et magnifica ecclesia parochiali huic divo tutelari dedicata, quo magis opto Romae me iam esse, huius sancti patroni mei sacra pignora deosculari et ad eius sepulchrum seu memoriam prostratum mihi et genti meae hodie afflictae misericordiam a Deo Opt. Max. per sanctissimam illius intercessionem imprecari.

APPENDIX 38

SIR RICHARD SHELLEY TO BURGHLEY

undated.

B.M. Lansd. 38, no 49.

This mischief that all Christendom now suffereth for be the sending of these Jesuits into England ; after such sort as it is and hath been used, with due and true consideration of the matter, is specially to be imputed (as all other efforts and events ought to be) to the chief cause and to the first original of the same, which I assure you was doctor Lewes, devisor of the oath which the poor scholars, for the relief that they receive by the Seminary, are bound to take, to be ready to go home whensoever they shall be sent, which he invented of a mischievous malice and for a revenge, without any compassion of the English blood, after he saw that neither he himself could become Governor nor keep in for Custos one Sir Morris, a Welsh priest, in the English hospital, which he had devised by a new erection to have made common, or rather wholly given to be inhabited of Welsh, Scottish and Irish men, with a very provident discourse (as he thought it should seem) to show how necessary a thing it was to procure the accomplishing and familiar conversation of those three nations, so shortly like to be united and under the obedience of one prince.
Endorsed Anno 1583. To the L. Treasurer. Giving an account what sort of Catholic he was. The mischief of sending of Jesuits into England.
(Not signed but in Shelley's hand.)

---

[1] These scedulae are in Vat. Lat. 6194 (pt II) f. 324. He quotes the ancient writers who treat of this obscure saint and transcribes 'ex archiviis Academiae Cantab.' a grant of Cadwaladr to Almarius, rector of the scholars at Cambridge, dated 686 !

APPENDIX 39

HUGH GRIFFITH TO CARDINAL FEDERICO BORROMEO

21 October 1595.

Bib. Amb. G. 166 inf. f. 162

Sono sicuro che V.S. Ill. et R.ma haverà havuto grande dispiacere della morte di Mons. Audoeno mio zio, per essere stato a V.S.I. et a tutta l'Ill.ma casa sua tanto anticho et affettionato servitore. Io ho perso assai sendo da trenta anni esiliato dalla mia patria dove ho perso padre et madre et ogni altra cosa ch'havevo al mondo, et il Sig. Iddio me haveva dato questo mio zio in luogo d'essi, et adesso me l'ha tolto : Dio sempre sia lodato. Hora non ho altra speranza si non in Dio benedetto et in V.S.I. la quale spero per l'amore d'Iddio haverà protettione di me (povero orfano et afflitto) come sempre ha havuto di monsignore mio, et non permetterà che la memoria di tanto buono prelato et affet.mo servitore della casa di V.S.I. s'annihili con la sua morte, ma vivrà parte in me suo afflittissimo nipote et affet.mo servitore di V.S.I.

(He goes on to say that Lewis had left the Cardinal a ring and portraits of Thomas More and the bishop of Rochester, and then gives a summary of the late bishop's financial position which he, as legatee, did not consider very satisfactory.)

LIST OF ILLUSTRATIONS

296

LIST OF APPENDICES

298

INDEX

This index includes persons mentioned by name or title in the *articles*. Persons mentioned in the appendices are included here only if they occur in the articles as well.